19 80

EFFECTIVE CORRECTIONAL TREATMENT

compiled and edited by

Robert R. Ross

Department of Criminology
University of Ottawa

and

Paul Gendreau

Ministry of Correctional Services
Province of Ontario

BUTTERWORTHS

Toronto

© 1980 Butterworth and Company (Canada) Limited
            2265 Midland Avenue
            Scarborough, Ontario, Canada M1P 4S1
All Rights Reserved.
Printed and Bound in Canada

The Butterworth Group of Companies:

Canada: Butterworth & Co. (Canada) Ltd., Toronto, Vancouver
United Kingdom: Butterworth & Co. (Publishers) Ltd., London, Borough Green
Australia: Butterworth Pty. Ltd., Sydney, Melbourne, Brisbane
New Zealand: Butterworths of New Zealand, Ltd., Wellington
South Africa: Butterworth & Co. (South Africa) Pty. Ltd., Durban
United States: Butterworth Inc., Boston
                   Butterworth (Legal) Inc., Seattle

Canadian Cataloguing in Publication Data

Main entry under title:

Effective correctional treatment

ISBN 0-409-86310-6

1. Social work with delinquents and criminals —
Addresses, essays, lectures. 2. Corrections —
Addresses, essays, lectures. 3. Juvenile
corrections — Addresses, essays, lectures. I. Ross,
Robert R., 1933-   II. Gendreau, Paul, 1940-

HV7428.E43   364.4'0453   C80-094278-7

Dedicated to those correctional workers who, in spite of the proclamations of purveyors of the "nothing works" doctrine, have persisted in providing effective services to their clients.

Acknowledgements

We wish to express our appreciation to authors, journal editors, and publishers who granted permission to reproduce articles herein.

Many authors responded enthusiastically to our request that they revise earlier materials or provide us with current data. Several prepared original articles for this book: D. Andrews & J. J. Kiessling; L. J. Barkwell; C. H. Blakely, W. S. Davidson, C. A. Saylor, & M. J. Robinson; J. D. Kloss; R. Lee & N. Haynes; J. J. Platt, G. M. Perry, & D. S. Metzger; T. L. Walter & C. M. Mills. We are grateful for their cooperation.

We thank Chi Hoang and Marion Benton who provided stenographic services in their usual competent and industrious manner.

The publication of this book reflects the continuing encouragement of our work by Andy Birkenmayer, Syd Shoom, and superintendents and staff of the Ontario Ministry of Correctional Services.

The preparation of this manuscript was supported by a grant from the Faculty of Social Sciences, University of Ottawa.

BOB ROSS & PAUL GENDREAU

Contributors

JAMES F. ALEXANDER. Department of Psychology, University of Utah.

DONALD A. ANDREWS. Department of Psychology, Carleton University.

LORNE J. BARKWELL. Ministry of Corrective & Rehabilitative Services, Winnipeg, Manitoba.

CRAIG H. BLAKELY. Department of Psychology, Michigan State University.

STEPHEN J. CARMICHAEL. Juvenile Court Services, Kennewick, Washington.

MICHAEL J. CHANDLER. Department of Psychology, University of British Columbia.

THOMAS R. COLLINGWOOD. Division of Continuing Education, The Aerobics Center, Dallas, Texas.

GARY B. COX. Department of Psychiatry and Behavioral Sciences, University of Washington.

WILLIAM S. DAVIDSON II. Department of Psychology, Michigan State University.

CAMERON DIGHTMAN. Law and Justice Planning Division, Olympia, Washington.

ALEX DOUDS. Department of Social and Rehabilitation Services, Montpellier, Vermont.

NEWTON R. FERRIS. National Multiple Sclerosis Society, Honolulu, Hawaii.

DEAN L. FIXSEN. Father Flanagan's Boys' Home, Boys' Town, Omaha, Nebraska.

WALTER S. O. FO. Behavior Therapy Clinic, Honolulu, Hawaii.

VICTOR J. GANZER. Child Study & Treatment Center, Fort Steilacoom, Washington.

PAUL GENDREAU. Ministry of Correctional Services, Province of Ontario.

MICHAEL R. GOTTFREDSON. Criminal Justice Research Center, Albany, New York.

NANCY McGINNIS HAYNES. CREST Services, Inc., Gainesville, Florida.

CARL F. JESNESS. California Youth Authority, Sacramento, California.

JERRY J. KIESSLING. Probation and Parole Services, Ontario Ministry of Correctional Services, Ottawa.

JAMES D. KLOSS. Mendota Mental Health Institute, Madison, Wisconsin.

ROBERT LEE. CREST Services, Inc., Gainesville, Florida.

JUDITH E. LIND. Intensive Intervention Project, Family Court, First Circuit, Honolulu, Hawaii.

CRAIG T. LOVE. Program in Applied Social Sciences, University of Miami.

TONY LYDGATE. Department of Psychology, University of Hawaii.

BRYAN McKAY. Department of Criminology, University of Ottawa.

MICHAEL B. MASKIN. Loma Linda University School of Medicine and Veterans Administration Hospital, Loma Linda, California.

JOSEPH L. MASSIMO. The Newton Public Schools, Newtonville, Massachusetts.

DAVID S. METZGER. Hahnemann Medical College, Philadelphia.

CAROLYN M. MILLS. Mills & Associates, Inc.

HERBERT L. MIRELS. Department of Psychology, Ohio State University.

TERU L. MORTON. Department of Psychology, University of Hawaii.

CLIFFORD R. O'DONNELL. Department of Psychology, University of Hawaii.

THOMAS M. OSTROM. Department of Psychology, Ohio State University.

TED PALMER. California Youth Authority, Sacramento, California.

BRUCE V. PARSONS. Family Therapy Institute, Laguna Beach, California.

GERALD M. PERRY. Hahnemann Medical College, Philadelphia.

ELAINE A. PHILLIPS. Father Flanagan's Boys' Home, Boys' Town, Omaha, Nebraska.

ELERY L. PHILLIPS. Father Flanagan's Boys' Home, Boys' Town, Omaha, Nebraska.

JEROME J. PLATT. Hahnemann Medical College, Philadelphia.

HERBERT C. QUAY. Program in Applied Social Sciences, University of Miami.

JULIAN RAPPAPORT. Department of Psychology, University of Illinois.

MICHAEL J. ROBINSON. Kent Juvenile Court, Grand Rapids, Michigan.

LORNE K. ROSENBLOOD. Department of Psychology, University of Victoria.

ROBERT R. ROSS. Department of Criminology, University of Ottawa.

IRWIN G. SARASON. Department of Psychology, University of Washington.

CHERYL A. SAYLOR. Department of Psychology, Michigan State University.

EDWARD SEIDMAN. Department of Psychology, University of Illinois.

MILTON F. SHORE. Mental Health Study Center, National Institute of Mental Health.

CLAUDE M. STEELE. Department of Psychology, University of Washington.

TERRY C. WADE. Stress Management Systems, Honolulu, Hawaii.

TIMOTHY L. WALTER. Department of Psychology, Rhode Island College.

HADLEY WILLIAMS. Corrections Training, Department of Alberta Solicitor General.

MONTROSE M. WOLF. Department of Human Development, University of Kansas.

Table of Contents

PART IV   COMMUNITY-BASED PROGRAMS FOR JUVENILE OF-
FENDERS

Preface

Over the past decade the criminal justice field has been infected with a pervasive negativism promulgated by academicians who proclaim that, in correctional rehabilitation, "almost nothing works". Practitioners in corrections have been "treated" to many critical reviews of the literature on the rehabilitation of offenders which have concluded with a denunciation of the view that treatment of the offender is an effective or appropriate response to criminal behavior. The conclusion that treatment does not work has been widely endorsed.

We recently drew attention to a body of literature virtually ignored by the cynics which demonstrates that some programs *do* work and have been found to do so in research studies with a methodological rigor which matches the best that applied behavioral science has offered in any area. We reviewed the literature published between 1973 and 1978 and found a substantial number of correctional treatment programs whose effectiveness had been demonstrated through studies which employed at least quasi-experimental designs and statistical analysis of outcome data. They provide convincing evidence that some treatment programs, when they are applied with integrity by competent practitioners to appropriate target populations, can be effective in preventing crime or reducing recidivism.

We were overwhelmed by the enthusiasm which we encountered when we presented this evidence to correctional workers. In retrospect, we think that we struck a responsive chord by providing hope for criminal justice practitioners that their efforts may not be entirely in vain. In spite of the "nothing works" dogma, treatment and counseling continue to be among the mainstays of correctional programming. Some correctional practitioners may be doing something worthwhile.

In this book we present *some* of the best of the effective programs which have been conducted since 1973. In order to be included, a program must have been conducted within an experimental or quasi-experimental design, must have included follow-up assessment of delinquent or criminal behavior, and must have provided a statistical evaluation of outcome data. Accordingly, our collection is by no means exhaustive or even representative of correctional treatment programs which may be judged "successful" by less stringent criteria. Moreover, since the majority of treatment programs in corrections are provided without a scientific evaluation component, we do not claim that the programs included in this book depict the general state of the art of treatment in corrections. We are not blind to the fact that many treatment efforts not only have failed but have had deleterious effects. We acknowledge the criticism of those who will be dismayed by our exclusion of programs that have failed and will decry our presentation of an apparently one-sided picture of correctional treatment. So be it. The failures have had their share of attention. This book represents a plea for equal time for the successes.

The programs we present in this book provide testimony to the conclusion that correctional rehabilitation is possible. But we must emphasize that we do not offer panaceas. No program is touted as the final answer. No program is recommended for *all* offenders. Instead, throughout the book we urge the reader to pay careful attention to interaction effects: the outcome of each and every program will depend on a host of factors including the type of offender, the type of treatment, the nature of the treatment setting, the characteristics of the practitioners, the intensity of their treatment efforts, the program goals, and the nature of the post-treatment environment, among others.

Our review of the correctional treatment literature from 1973 to 1978, "Bibliotherapy for Cynics", is presented in Chapter 1 as an introduction to this book. It describes recent evidence of the effectiveness of correctional treatment, examines some of the fallacies inherent in the "nothing works" doctrine, and suggests five reasons for the apparent failure of some programs: reliance on a single method of treatment; reliance on a single measure of outcome; failure to examine interactions among treatment method, type of offender and type of setting; failure to adhere to the principles of the treatment modality in its application (or to provide *enough* treatment); and failure to integrate community resources with the treatment program.

Some of the program reports referred to in our review appear as chapters herein. In order to provide more recent findings, wherever possible these reports have been updated by the authors or by the editors. Many of the chapters are original articles which have been prepared expressly for this book. Some of the chapters describe new programs which were not discussed in our literature review. These new materials provide important support for the conclusions we reached in that review. They also demonstrate that both the quality of treatment and the quality of research have greatly improved in recent years.

Most of the programs described in this book are based on a social learning approach to the treatment of the offender. None are derived from the much maligned "medical" or "disease" model.

"Requiem for a Panacea", the second chapter in the introductory section, highlights the folly of what has been a long-time preoccupation of correctional treatment practitioners and critics alike: the search for cure-alls. Through a review of behavior modification programs in corrections this article demonstrates the naivete both of the expectation that a particular treatment regimen, which happens to be "in vogue", should be uniformly effective across the correctional spectrum (from community to institution) or for all correctional goals (control vs. rehabilitation). It points out that the principles of many otherwise valuable intervention approaches can readily be compromised by the reality of some correctional settings with the result that programs become treatment in name only: "pacification programs disguised as treatment programs" (Griswold, p. 238). Too often treatment programs have "failed" because their practitioners naively thought they could transform fortress prisons into hospitals and later found to their dismay that "treatment" merely consisted of enlightened professional-scientific appearing masquerades covering up neglect.

Too often efficacious treatment modalities have been rejected because programs in that name have failed in some applications. The search for panaceas has fostered totally unrealistic expectations for correctional programming. The reality of corrections can quickly translate unwarranted optimism into nihilism. As "Requiem for a Panacea" demonstrates, the apparent failure of correctional programs should engender reflection not mere cynicism. Failure can be educational.

In Chapter 3, "Treatment Destruction Techniques", Michael Gottfredson presents an insightful and powerful attack on the logic of the "nothing works" argument. He does so in a laconic, tongue-in-cheek style by providing a training manual complete with script for those who wish to bolster their critism of correctional treatment by pseudoscientific arguments.

The principles, techniques and results of twenty-three effective treatment programs are presented in individual chapters in five sections: (1) diversion programs, (2) intervention with the families of delinquents, (3) community-based programs for juvenile offenders, (4) programs for juveniles in correctional institutions, and (5) programs for adult offenders. Clearly there is considerable overlap among these categories. Rather than providing an introduction for each section we preface each chapter with editorial comments designed to emphasize important findings or implications of each program or to provide additional references.

Effective Correctional Treatment is intended to serve as a text for courses in criminology, corrections, social work, and psychology, and as a sourcebook for personnel and volunteers in correctional agencies who are responsible for counseling offenders.

Part I

Introduction: Nothing Works?

Chapter 1

Effective Correctional Treatment: Bibliotherapy for Cynics*

Paul Gendreau & Robert R. Ross

INTRODUCTION

> As long as personal suffering has a future, so does the search for
> different means of coping with it. (London, 1969, p. 201)

The criminological literature is replete with reports attesting to the view that correctional treatment is a failure (Conrad, 1975; Lipton Martinson & Wilks, 1975; Martinson, 1974; Wilks & Martinson, 1976). Conflicting opinions have been expressed (Chaneles, 1976; Halleck & Witte, 1977; McDougall, 1976; Palmer, 1975; Quay, 1977; Serrill, 1975; Smith & Berlin, 1977) and while the debate still rages, there appears to be a widespread endorsement of the view that in correctional rehabilitation "nothing works".

At the risk of adding more fuel to a debate which may have generated more heat than light, we wish in this paper to appeal the conviction that "nothing works" by presenting some new evidence.

*Portions of this paper have been presented at symposia on correctional treatment programs held at the University of Moncton, New Brunswick, October 1977; Psychological Services Division of the Canadian Penitentiary Service, Ottawa, Ontario, May 1978; National Parole Services, Winnipeg, Manitoba June 1978; and Simon Fraser University, Burnaby, British Columbia, June 1978.

We would like to thank Andy Birkenmayer for providing editorial comments on the manuscript.

The debate about the "impotence of treatment" is bogged down in rhetoric (Adams, 1976). Where one would expect to find reasonable and objective analysis and interpretation of data, one finds hyperbole. The task of testing one's views by seeking and critically evaluating new evidence — what we have naively assumed to be the forte of research — seems to have been studiously avoided by both sides in their struggle to upstage their opponents. The following provides a brief history of some of the highlights of the rhetoric.

Initially, Palmer (1975) reviewed Lipton, et al., (1975) and Martinson's (1974) documentation that "nothing works" and concluded that, in fact, much of the correctional treatment research was successful. Martinson (1976) took exceptional umbrage to Palmer's review. He complained that he had to spend ". . . at least 4 months struggling to decipher the research designs produced by Palmer and his colleagues in California." Furthermore, "the footnotes had to be translated from the original Egyptian . . . reading the California report was like translating a Moscow telephone book into Swahili." According to Martinson "90% of correctional research was pageantry, rumination and rubbish" and any "partly positive results that were reported were akin to a partly pregnant girl friend . . . the answers provided by correctional researchers along with 30¢ could buy a cup of coffee in New York." On the other hand, others have responded to Martinson's work with a measure of personal invective (Chaneles, 1975; Klockars, 1975). Robison (1976) brought the rhetoric full circle by stating that any significant conclusions either Palmer or Martinson came to were simply due to "the discovery of probable random events through sheer diligence." So much for the application of mathematical rules and decision making in correctional research.

The arguments are persuasive, the rhetoric often brilliant, the metaphors appealing, and the objectivity sadly lacking. The antagonists seem to be more intent on winning arguments than on seeking truth. They represent a mixture of different disciplines (sociology, economics, political science, psychology) and professions (academicians, administrators, clinicians) who appear to be "strangers trying to communicate in different languages by raising their voices" (Stuart, 1970).

We determined some time ago that we would resist the temptation to enter into the fray until we were able to add to the debate with some reasonable evidence. Rather then standing on platforms presenting our particular re-interpretation of the history of correctional treatment, we have left "history" to our more articulate and persuasive brethren and instead spent some time conducting prosaic library research to determine whether history should be revised in the light of recent events. We did so because the arguments for and against correctional treatment have been based almost without exception on consideration of treatment evaluation studies published before 1967. More recent (and scientifically more respectable) studies appear to have been virtually ignored. In addition, there were some underlying issues and personal concerns that motivated our examination of the literature. The following perspectives provide the framework for our review.

SOME ISSUES IN CORRECTIONAL EVALUATION

THE DISCOVERY OF ABSOLUTE TRUTH

The eagerness with which researchers have accepted the null hypothesis that correctional treatment has no beneficial effect goes against the grain of all we have learned about research methodology. The study of human behavior and the modification of that behavior is barely in its infancy. It is perhaps the least advanced and the most imprecise of the sciences and yet we talk with such certainty. It is a puzzle to us to understand how social scientists think they have obtained a completely satisfactory and final answer to an extremely complex question. Our colleagues in other disciplines, e.g., physics, biology, acknowledge that they have obtained very few such firm conclusions in their areas of interest even though their scientific techniques are at a much more sophisticated level of analysis. We are frankly perplexed by the degree to which some scientists have been *adamant* in their conclusion that treatment is ineffective. They seem to have found some absolute knowledge which permits them to be blind to new data.

At another level of analysis the issue concerns what we know about how individuals learn. While there have been some who have argued that the majority of North American varieties of delinquents are the political prisoners of a corrupt state (Platt, 1974) or the victims of biochemical accidents (Hippchen, 1976), most behavioral scientists have agreed, with varying emphasis on the sociological and the psychological, that delinquent behavior is learned in some manner (cf. Nettler, 1978). The "nothing works" belief reduced to its most elementary level suggests that delinquents are *incapable* of re-learning or acquiring new behaviors. We wonder why this strange learning immutability is peculiar only to the delinquent species of humans. Presumably we must know almost all there is to know about how individuals learn and how their behavior can be changed. Behavioral scientists who, for decades, have studied human learning in well controlled laboratory settings are still very much divided as to whether different kinds of learning actually exist, and whether there is a distinction between learning and performance. We do not yet have an adequate theory that can explain how individuals learn even in very well defined controlled situations. There does not even appear to be an exact, comprehensive learning theory for simpler organisms, let alone the human species (cf. Mackintosh, 1974). The empirical investigation of how human behavior can be modified in real life settings has only just begun. It is perhaps a trifle premature to declare that delinquents' behavior cannot be modified.

Finally, we would affirm that the discovery of absolute truth regarding the efficacy of social programs assumes that we have rigourously and thoroughly evaluated our attempts at ameliorating social skills. While these claims have often been made it has become increasingly clear that North America, despite what is said, has failed miserably in attaining the goals of an experimenting society (Campbell, 1969; Fairweather, 1977; Tavris, 1975; Waldo & Chiricos, 1977). This fact applies alarmingly to the field of delinquency.

Yaryan (1973), in a review of delinquency and youth development prevention programs in the United States, reported that of 11.5 billion dollars spent on programs less than 1% was spent on research and of the few studies that were conducted only 18% had any statistical evaluation of the program. Bernstein (1975) examined 236 evaluation studies of correctional programs and found that 75% did not use an experimental or quasi-experimental design, 41% selected the subjects on a non-random basis, 50% used non-representative samples, and 65% did not employ statistics to analyze their data. Logan (1972) stated that most prevention programs have not even approximated the minimal requirements for adequate experimental design. Indeed, Gendreau & Andrews (1969) and Roesch (1978) have commented that often correctional systems appear to disavow the use of research.

In addition, we should note some other problems in the treatment literature: intervention programs have often been based on (a) incomplete theory and woeful lack of descriptive data (Lundeman, McFarlane & Scarpitti, 1976), (b) poor integration of theory with treatment modules (Slaikeu, 1973), (c) atheoretical approaches that led to no feasible treatment program (Glaser, 1974), and (d) techniques that were adopted wholeheartedly and foolishly with little question as to their applicability to the individuals being treated (Ross & McKay, 1978).

THERAPEUTIC INTEGRITY

> In Chicago our parole officers go to their daily appointed rounds
> with Freud in one hand and a .38 in the other. It is still not clear
> that they do not need another .38. Being a cop and a counselor is a
> tough business. (Fogel, 1975)

Recently, some pertinent questions have been asked about the *integrity* of correctional treatment programs (Austin 1977; Quay 1977; Ross & McKay 1978; Wright & Dixon 1977). To what extent do treatment personnel actually adhere to the principles and employ the techniques of the therapeutic modality they purport to provide? To what extent are the treatment staff competent in providing the therapy they claim to offer? What is the intensity of their effort? To what degree is treatment diluted or bastardized in the correctional environment so that it becomes treatment in name only? Quay (1977) has provided an illuminating answer in this regard by focusing on one of the classic correctional treatment studies that is frequently cited as an example of "nothing works": the program of Kassebaum, Ward & Wilner (1971). In his critique of correctional treatment, Martinson (1974) claimed the Kassebaum et al. counseling program was an "exceptionally extensive and experimentally rigorous transformation of the institutional environment." Quay seems to have actually read the method and procedure sections of the project report and brought to light some interesting facts regarding what actually happened. He found the project did not conceptualize the treatment and define it in operational terms. In addition he pointed out the following:

a) Only one-third of the practicing group counselors felt the treatment would affect recidivism.
b) The counselors were primarily lay people with no particular expertise in the area.
c) The training provided by the researchers focused on the personality of the *counselors*.
d) Training meetings were poorly attended.
e) Once the program began, training of the counselors was not in operation.
f) The counseling co-ordinator for the project was seldom consulted by the counselors.
g) Kassebaum et al. listed 5 other major problems with the functioning of the group counseling sessions and noted that counseling groups were notably unstable.
h) Inmate participation was involuntary, the groups were mixtures of extreme types of inmates, and inmate ratings of the content and structure of the counseling sessions were poor.

To Kassebaum's et al. credit they clearly outlined these major deficiencies. One can only guess what the results of further analyses of program integrity would uncover if applied to other prevention programs less honest than theirs.

Emory and Marholin (1977) examined 27 empirical investigations conducted by applied behavior analysts. They found that in only 9% of the studies were target behaviors individually selected for clients, and in just 30% of the studies were the referral behaviors and target behaviors clearly related (e.g., one client was referred for stealing cars and treated for promptness). In only 8% of the studies was there a follow-up of one year. The reviewers noted that in most cases a comprehensive functional analysis had not been carried out: behavior modifiers have demonstrated that numerous target behaviors can be modified but they have typically failed to show that these modifications necessarily lead to a decrease in delinquency itself (Ross, 1977).

THE RECENT LITERATURE

One of the anomalies of the debate is that the reviews of the literature which led to the conclusion of the failure of rehabilitation were concentrated on a research literature before 1967.* Given the importance of the debate it would seem appropriate that there would be comprehensive literature reviews of intervention programs since 1967. This has not been the case. In fact, post-1967 literature reviews are rather curious. Wright & Dickson (1977) researched the delinquency prevention literature up to the end of 1973. For some reason, their literature search abstracted only those reports which had the words "delinquency prevention" or their equivalent. Obviously, as they admit, there could be many studies relevant to the question that they omitted. Halleck & Witte (1977) argued for the rehabilitation model but quoted just three studies produced in recent years. Gold (1978) argued that educational programs can reduce delinquency but relied only on evidence produced at least 10 years ago. Thus, while there have been some good reviews focussing on specific intervention strategies (Braukman, Fixsen, Phillips & Wolf, 1975; Gibbons & Blake, 1976; Johnson, 1977) there has not been a recent comprehensive survey of intervention programs. In reading the correctional literature one gets the impression that the "nothing works" doctrine has had a pervasive effect in stamping out treatment.

RECENT RESEARCH

Given the fact that the "nothing works" debate has focussed on an outdated literature of questionable scientific merit, a search of the recent literature was undertaken to determine if there exists recent research which indicates that intervention does reduce recidivism. If so, do these studies overcome some of the conceptual and methodological objections made earlier? Do they involve theoretically relevant treatments? Do they employ adequate experimental designs? Finally, do the types of studies and the results they provide pattern themselves so as to relate meaningfully to substantive issues underlying the "nothing works" debate?

The present review picks up where Wright & Dixon (1977) left off and examines the published literature (edited journals, published texts) from late 1973 to early 1978, a span of five years. The requirement for including a study was that at the minimum a quasi-experimental design was employed and statistical analysis of the data was reported.

It can be reported that "something exists"; in fact, 95 studies were reported on in the literature that focused on treating anti-social behaviors. Since many of the studies used a multi-method approach, categorization was difficult in some cases. For purposes of discussion we have grouped them as follows:

---

*To give Martinson credit, he recognized this fact when he stated, "Our studies ended in December 1967. How do I know the next 200 studies won't show tremendous success." See Serrill (1975).

family intervention, contingency management, counseling, diversion, biomedical, miscellaneous, and related problems.

FAMILY INTERVENTION

The family intervention literature gives testimony to one of the most impressive and significant gains made in the treatment of delinquent behavior. It is based on two simple notions: (1) the sooner the problem behavior is treated the better, and (2) intervention should be community-based involving the family and the school. Ten studies have been reported recently with eight reporting successful intervention.

One of the best examples of these types of studies comes from Alexander & Parsons (1973). Their approach to family therapy with delinquents has three components: (a) assessing family interactions which maintain delinquent behavior, (b) modifying family communication to achieve greater clarity, precision, and reciprocity, and, (c) proposing alternatives to delinquent behavior within the home. The treatment program assumes that the modification of family interactions is the key. The therapists model appropriate roles to the family. The family is taught how to negotiate, communicate, develop alternatives to maladaptive behavior, differentiate rules from requests, how to use interruptions in disciplining behavior, and how to reinforce behavior using such techniques as token economies and contingency contracting. Data has been reported for a 6 to 18 month follow-up. The experimental group was compared to client-centered family therapy groups, eclectic psycho-dynamic treatment, no-treatment controls, post-hoc controls, and county wide recidivism rates. The treatment group produced recidivism rates ranging from 21% to 47% less than the other control groups.

Alexander, Barton, Schiaro & Parsons (1976) replicated the Alexander-Parsons' program and added valuable information by focusing on important individual characteristics which were related to treatment success. They found that treatment success was heightened in the families which had less defensive process measures and were more supportive. They also found that therapists' characteristics were related to success. In fact, this variable accounted for 56% of the variance in outcome. The crucial therapist characteristics included directiveness and self-confidence in structuring the counseling sessions, as well as humour, warmth and affect behavior integration in the relationship developed with the client and family. Maskin (1976) used a procedure similar to Alexander's in a correctional setting for boys. After 10 months, the group had a 2% recidivism rate, while the controls had a rate of 20%.

Patterson (1974) and his colleagues have produced a series of excellent studies on intervention programs for boys with conduct problems. Both the parents and teachers are trained in a social-learning based child management technique and in recording and observing behavior in the home and classroom (Patterson, Cobb & Ray, 1972; Patterson & Reid, 1973). A noteworthy aspect of the Patterson programs is the extensive training given the family. Approximately 60 hours in training is given in family and classroom intervention. Training "booster shots" are also administered. Patterson (1974) reported that after twelve months, compared to baseline data and matched controls, there was a 43% decrease in deviant behaviors in the home. Appropriate school behavior increased by 29%. Patterson also found that individual differences (e.g., socio-economic status of the family) were related to treatment success.

The Patterson approach has been extended to children as young as 6 – 8 years of age with successful results (Karoly & Rosenthal, 1977; Wiltz & Patterson, 1975). Also of interest is the generalization study conducted by Arnold, Levine & Patterson (1975). Following the Patterson model, they treated 27 pre-delinquents and then examined the program's effects on 55 siblings of their clients. Over a 12 month follow-up period it was found that deviant behavior was reduced in the siblings!

Particularly noteworthy in these family intervention programs is that the less actual contact time spent with the family, the weaker the results. This has been demonstrated both by Eyeberg & Johnson (1974) and Kent & O'Leary (1976).

It is worth commenting that family intervention techniques have been limited to the extent that they do not seem to work with the families that show severe disintegration and may well fail with families whose childrens' behavior is exceptionally disruptive. The failure of the Weathers & Liberman (1975) program was attributed, in part, to the fact that the disruptive behaviors of their clients were too severe.

This body of intervention research provides ample testimony to the importance in evaluation of including an analysis of treatment integrity and of therapist and client characteristics. It also underlines the futility (and naivete) of a search for a cure-all that works for all clients all of the time in all situations and with all therapists. "Panaceaphilia" is a deviance which has long characterized treatment in corrections (Halleck & Witte, 1977; Ross & McKay 1978).

Fo & O'Donnell (1974) developed a community intervention program that employed paraprofessional "buddies" as therapists. Methods employed were counseling with a Truax & Carkhuff (1967) orientation, modeling, role playing and the use of contingencies. The target group was 11 – 17 years old. In comparison to controls, the treatment groups increased school attendance, decreased fighting and improved behaviors at home. After a 2 year follow-up the program showed little effect on those children who had had no major previous offenses prior to treatment (Fo & O'Donnell, 1975). The difference in recidivism rates between these children and controls was only 9%. However, the program was effective with children with previous histories of major offenses. Some programs appear most effective with the most severe cases! The experimental group's recidivism rate was 38% vs. 64% for the controls. Not all therapists were equally effective. O'Donnell & Fo (1976) reported that treatment was not effective with therapists who tended to perceive situations non-contingently (externals on a locus of control dimension).

CONTINGENCY MANAGEMENT

Behavior modification programs have frequently been used in corrections. The most common type of behavior modification programs have been contingency management programs with token systems as one of their main features. Contingencies have been aimed at changing discrete social behaviors in the home, school, and on the job. Many of these programs have attempted to change behavior in institutional settings. Braukmann, Fixsen, Phillips & Wolf (1975) have provided a detailed summary of the early studies dating from 1967 to 1975. They report 27 studies which have demonstrated positive results. Presently, behavior modifiers have developed programs geared to facilitating community adjustment. We found 25 studies that provided community follow-up of varying duration. Highlighting this approach have been the series of studies conducted at Achievement Place by Phillips and his colleagues. Achievement Place serves as a model for community-based programs for adolescents in trouble with the law. Basic to the program is a combined token economy/levels system. Individuals at the lowest level are reinforced on a token system. Tokens are earned for target behaviors which include appropriate verbal interactions, chore completion, and promptness in school work. A participant's advance is a function of his behavioral improvement. The highest level is a "homeward bound" program where the emphasis is upon reintegration into the family and community. The Achievement Place studies serve not only as a model for treatment but as a model for evaluation research. A series of studies has been conducted, each logically following each other and building up a strong base of program knowledge and there have been detailed, constructive critiques of the programs (Burchard & Harig, 1976; Hoefler & Bornstein, 1975). The generality and usefulness of this intervention strategy has also been demonstrated in several variations of the Achievement Place model (Braukman et al., 1975; Durlack, 1977; Marholin II, Plienis, Harris & Marholin, 1975; Wagner & Breitmeyer, 1975).

Phillips, Phillips, Fixsen & Wolf (1973) have provided community follow-up data. Students in Achievement Place were compared to controls committed to the Kansas Boys' School, and to controls on probation. After a one year follow-up the Achievement Place students had 35% lower recidivism rates. Ninety percent of the Achievement Place students were attending school while only 9% of the Boys' School and 37% of those on probation were doing so.

Phillips and his colleagues also carefully documented the failures they experienced in establishing Achievement Place programs in other settings. They found that these instances were due to a lack of social teaching components in the training system, lack of communication between the teaching parents and the home's board of directors and community agencies, failure of the teaching parents to give adequate instructions regarding social skills, and failure to teach the clients how to negotiate and criticize constructively.

Davidson and Robinson (1975) have also set up a similar community based program for hard-core male offenders. They used a time series analysis for a year prior and an average of 18 months after completing their program. The program increased school attendance rates by 59%, decreased arrest rates from 3 offences per year to .46 per year and increased achievement test grade ratings by a full year. They also compared graduates of the program versus non-graduates and found that those who completed the program were more often employed (27%), or attending school (31%), and had lower (38%) recidivism rates.

McCombs, Filipczak, Friedman & Wodarski (1978) followed up, five years later, 15 of 24 adolescents who participated in a school-based, social learning program. Their results were mixed at best but in the absence of any control group no conclusive statements were made.

Three behavior modification programs are of interest in that they were done within correctional settings and demonstrated significant long term treatment results. In an impressive large scale study Jessness (1975) randomly assigned 983 delinquents to two institutions, one of which emphasized behavior modification (token economy), the other transactional analysis. The token program is discussed in this section. Each year of the three year project, approximately 80 to 100 hours of training was given to the staff. A two year follow-up was provided. In comparison to two companion institutions, which had no particular program in operation, the behavior modification recidivism rates were 10% lower. Baseline data on the behavior modification institution indicated that, two years after the program was instituted, the program produced recidivism rates 15% lower than the two years prior to the program. Individual differences were also related to program success. Recidivism rates were 20 – 25% lower for those offenders diagnosed as situational emotional reaction types and manipulators. Higher recidivism rates were found for those diagnosed as unsocialized passive. Jessness' data is also germane in that the type of treatment program interacts most meaningfully with individual differences. It would be expected both on the basis of clinical knowledge and experimental evidence (Hare, 1970) that contingency management programs would be most successful with individuals exhibiting sociopathic traits and just the opposite with individuals who are passive and present substantial neurotic symptoms.

Jenkins, Witherspoon, DeVine, DeZalera Muller, Barton & McKee (1974) reported on an 18 month follow-up of the Draper Prison token economy program. The token economy group was compared to three control groups. Recidivism rates ranged from 4 to 19% lower for the behavior modification groups.

Not all types of behavior modification programs, however, have enjoyed success (Ross & McKay, 1978). In one study using matched no-treatment controls three different token economy programs were found to have led to an increase in recidivism (Ross & McKay, 1976). These programs involved severely disordered female adolescent offenders in an institutional setting. Again we are reminded of the futility of searching for all-inclusive remedies. The Ross & McKay study highlighted the importance of involving offenders in planning and conducting treatment programs which are designed to help them rather than merely imposing them on the offenders without ensuring their genuine participation. In the final stages of the Ross & McKay study their offender clients were persuaded to conduct their own treatment program. They were trained in the principles of behavior modification and encouraged to act as "therapists" for each other. After a 9 month follow-up the peer reinforcement therapist group had recidivism rates ranging from 26 to 53% lower than for a matched, no treatment control group and three other matched groups who were involved in token economies.

Five studies focused on the use of behavioral contracts in alleviating delinquent behavior (Doctor & Palikow, 1973; Douds, Englesgjord & Collingwood, 1977; Jessness, Allison, McCormick, Wedge & Young, 1978; Stuart, Jayaratne & Camburn, 1976). These studies were characterized by rigorous design and thorough process evaluation. The focus of the Stuart studies was to change the behavior of teachers and parents through education. The parents became mediators of the behavior of the youth and the desired outcome was the interaction between the adolescent and the important adult in his environment. Significant differences were found in teacher evaluations, counselor evaluations, and mothers' evaluations of their children and of their marital adjustment. Behavioral contracts were most effective with at risk populations, i.e., those who were black, were older, had less well educated parents, larger families, and lower incomes. Much of the success of the program was determined by the quality of the contract negotiated (Stuart & Lott, 1974). Also, Stuart et al., commented that their studies were very conservative as they utilized only one method whereas most of the contingency management studies have used several methods in combination. Contracts, per se, do not change the pattern of communication or offer the clients a chance to explore personal goals.

Jessness et al., used behavioral contracts with probationers. They found that the behavioral contracts reduced the incidents of problem behaviors by 16%. After 6 months, recidivism was reduced by 6%. Like Stuart et al., they found that the quality of the contract was important. Individual differences were also important in that those clients who held a probation officer in high positive regard, and vice versa, achieved lower recidivism rates.

Dramatic results were reported by Doctor & Palikow (1973) in a study which utilized an extremely powerful reinforcer with their contracts. They negotiated behavioral contacts for reductions in probation time in return for development of new behaviors, e.g., employment. On the behavioral contract program the time employed increased from 45% to 77%, probation violations decreased from 1.7 to .15 per year and new arrests decreased from 2.0 to .15 per year. In another impressive program, Douds et al. used contracts to teach parents and youth skills in improving home, school and neighbourhood behavior. The study was noteworthy in the number of clients handled (N = 1200) and extensive therapist contact hours. Compared to controls, the contract group had 31% lower rearrest rates and large increases in home, school and neighbourhood activities (45 – 72%).

There have been instances where short term goals have been met by contingency management programs. School settings were examined in six studies (Alexander, Corbett & Smigel, 1976; Brown, Frankel, Birkimer & Gamboa, 1976; Camp, Blom, Herbert & Van Doornick, 1977; Csapo & Agg, 1976; Grala & McCauley, 1976; Greenwood, Hops, Delquadri & Guild, 1974). Their studies collectively reported marked changes in increasing school attendance and appropriate classroom behavior, reducing curfew violations and stealing, and increasing basic skills. Interestingly, in keeping with the findings of Ross & McKay (1976), the combination of group contingencies and peer reinforcement seemed to be powerful techniques in some of these studies.

Finally, there have been four small subject (N = 1 − 4) studies that have demonstrated successful modification of specific behaviors (Emshoff, Redd & Davidson, 1976; Fedoravicius, 1973; Guidry, 1975; Lysaght & Burchard, 1975).

COUNSELING

Eight studies were included in this section. Their main characteristic was the use of varied counseling-oriented techniques ranging from modeling to I-level theory.

The Chandler (1973) and Sarason & Ganzer (1973) studies were good examples of a modeling, social-learning approach to behavior change. Chandler argued that social deviancy was associated with persistent egocentric thought. His role-playing sessions aimed at breaking down this type of thinking with young (11 – 13 year old) delinquents with lengthy records coming from high crime areas. The intervention program lasted 10 weeks. Follow-up was for 18 months. The experimental group decreased their egocentric levels, improved significantly in their role-playing ability and produced recidivism rates 50% lower than the following: a comparable control group that came from the same geographic area, a control group from a middle class environment, a placebo-attention control, and a no-treatment group. Sarason & Ganzer randomly assigned first offenders to modeling, or group discussion, or a control group that received the normal institutional program. Training consisted of 14 one hour sessions and subjects learned to imitate roles regarding how to apply for a job, delay gratification, resist peer pressures, etc. The subjects in the modeling program rated the program content highly, were more satisfied with their treatment and applied more of the content of their program to their home life. Recidivism rates three years after release were 18% and 14% for the modeling and discussion groups and 34% for the controls. Subjects classified as neurotic and passive dependent were most influenced by modeling. Sarason (1978) recently reported on a 5 year follow-up and found recidivism rates of 23% for each of the two treatment groups and 48% for the controls.

Barkwell (1975) used probation officers trained in I-Level theory with 12 – 17 year old juveniles in probation. Control groups were a random alternate treatment group and a "surveillance" group that met with the client as often as the I-Level treatment group (four times per month). Assignment of subjects was double-blind. Caseload size and experience of the probation officers was controlled. After one year Barkwell's I-Level groups had more positive changes in self-concept, higher rates of school attendance and recidivism rates 19 – 31% lower than the two controls. Consistent with a study to be reviewed later (Andrews, Kiessling, Russell & Grant, 1977) Barkwell emphasized that the best results are obtained where client and probation officer characteristics were matched to produce the most beneficial counseling relationship.

Similarly, Palmer (1974) found that it was important to match client characteristics with the treatment setting. For example, he reported that one type of client ("status 1" offenders) produced offence rates 110% higher after a 18 month follow-up if they were placed inappropriately. Austin (1977) re-analyzed the Preston study (Jessness, 1971) and found support for the use of I-Level theory to reduce parole violation. Not only did he replicate much of the previous California work (e.g. Palmer, 1974) he also found that the quality of the treatment environment was related to individual differences.

Vorrath & Brendtro (1974) employed a peer program that also had elements of "modeling and guided group interaction treatment philosophy." The recidivism rates of the training school for which they developed the program were compared for the two years prior to program initiation and for two years later. A 32% reduction in recidivism was found.

Platt, Labate & Wicks (1977) described a comprehensive, well evaluated treatment program for incarcerated heroin abusers that included guided group interaction, life skills and interpersonal problem solving therapies. The program included four phases: a 30 day orientation, a 60 day work program, individual therapy and then work release. Compared to the no-treatment control group the experimental group (2 year follow-up) had significantly higher ratings of good adjustment by parole officers, lower reconviction rates (12%), and fewer arrests (17%). The treatment group also took more days to receive their first arrest. Several variables interacted with success. These were traits of conformity, alienation, locus of control, self-esteem, interpersonal skills, age, previous record and employment record after release.

Jessness (1975) randomly assigned subjects to an institution that was run on a transactional analysis model. He found that this method produced reduced recidivism rates as successfully as the behavior modification program which we described previously. Transactional analysis was found to be most successful with neurotic/anxious and unsocialized/passive individuals. It was a failure with manipulators.

DIVERSION

One of the popular sentiments in the criminal justice system has been that far too many individuals in North America come in contact with the system thus overloading the courts and correctional agencies. The push for "decriminalization" has been operationalized in the plethora of diversion programs that have been recently established. The initial promise of diversion programs has now been counterbalanced by a more sober view. Nejelski (1976) has concluded that diversion programs may be prone to more bureaucracy, less accountability and more restrictions of freedom for the diverted client. From an evaluative perspective, Gibbons and Blake (1976) and Roesch (1978) reviewed some of the early diversion projects and found very few that involved an objective evaluation. These earlier projects had several shortcomings and Gibbons and Blake argued for large scale sophisticated evaluation of new diversion programs.

There are, nevertheless, reasons to remain optimistic about the potential of diversion programs. While they contain dangers, useful recommendations have been made to resolve these problems (Maron, 1976). In addition, the recent literature indicates that diversion programs have had a beneficial effect. Those diversion programs that provided a variety of intervention strategies, and were the most intensive in terms of contact hours with the client and his family reported the strongest results (e.g., the Oxnard & Stockton projects, Bohnstedt, 1978; Quay & Love, 1977; Wade, Morton, Lind & Ferris, 1977).

The Wade et al. (1977) program concentrated on family communication, modeling procedures, training family members to act as intervention agents, and behavioral contracts. Paraprofessionals and probation staff acted as the therapists and they were trained to provide an immediate response to a family crisis, focus on the family as a system that needs change, match therapists with clients on the basis of sex and ethnicity and rely on adjunct agencies to maintain behavior change. In comparison to a baseline control group, Wade et al. reported that recidivism rates over a one and two year period were 25 – 53% lower depending on whether the client was a first or second offender. They also reported on a variety of program goals such as improving family communication, increasing school attendance, improving involvement with peers, acceptance of responsibility in the family, eliminating runaways, and decreasing curfew violations. They found 71 – 100% success rates in these categories. Of the diversion studies the Quay & Love (1977) study had the most rigorous experimental design and was the most thoroughly analyzed. Their follow-up was for approximately one year and they reported that various groups in the diversion program produced re-arrest rates ranging from 8 – 40% less than randomly assigned controls. They found that success rates and the prediction of successes were enhanced by considering individual differences and the type of program referral. Bohnstedt reviewed 11 California diversion projects and found 3 that reduced recidivism (16 – 35%) over a 6 month period. Two of the projects (Oxnard, Stockton) had lower recidivism rates after 12 months. These two projects demonstrated that just service brokerage was not enough. The projects required well-trained staff and additional services to the family. Bohnstedt also found that diversion appeared to work best with high risk offenders.

Other diversion programs that concentrated on a single method or had relatively limited contact with the client and his family reported effects of less magnitude (Baron & Feeney, 1973; cf. Gibbons & Blake, 1976; Stratton, 1975). Nevertheless, they did find that diversion produced significantly lower re-arrest rates (10 – 15%) than their respective control samples.

Two diversion studies were of interest conceptually. Clements (1975) set up a school relations bureau to prevent the escalation of potentially dangerous situations in and around schools. Their therapy teams were composed of police, consultants, and psychologists. The techniques employed were Truax and Carkhuff counseling methods, role playing, problem solving and contingency contracts. Students' grades were improved, and there was a reduction in truancy and law violations. Unfortunately, Clements provided an inadequate description of the actual data.

The pre-arrest diversion project of Palmer (1975) was also innovative and the data is impressive. Instead of following the usual arrest — jail — court procedure, criminal complaints involving interpersonal disputes were diverted to a night prosecutor's "office trial" one week after the reported crime was committed. The victim, the accused and neighbours met in hearings based on victim confrontation. Of 3,626 complaints only 2% of the complaints led to a formal charge. In only 3% of the cases did the complainant return to make a new charge. The program cost $80,000 in contrast to the $725,000 it would have cost if the complaints had been handled in the usual way. How many of the 3,626 complaints would have led to a conviction in the absence of Palmer's program is not noted but it would be unlikely to be anywhere as low as 5%.

Fishman's (1977) negative evaluation was very difficult to categorize. He produced a post-hoc analysis of 18 programs carried out in New York but it was not clear how many of the programs he reviewed would actually qualify as diversion. Moreover, for control comparisons Fishman relied on post-hoc data and one control sample where it was unclear how equivalent the sample was in comparison to the others being evaluated. But most important, Fishman noted that the goals and priorities of the evaluation made it impossible to directly assess project characteristics or projects themselves in terms of how recidivism is influenced by type of services, types of staff, or staff-client ratios. None of the projects used intensive individualized therapy programs, operant conditioning or medical treatment. Each of these procedures has been found to be successful in some of the other studies reviewed in this paper. Roesch (1978) has remarked that no definite conclusions can be made from Fishman's study because of inadequate analysis and description.

BIOMEDICAL

The notion that at the basis of delinquent behavior there exists some sort of biological defect has its roots in the early history of the study of criminal behavior. Claims that a biomedical approach is applicable to the treatment of delinquents have re-surfaced.

Hippchen (1976) has examined this literature. He presented hypotheses of those such as Hoffer that behavioral deficits in criminals with serious crimes are caused by chemical deficiencies in the body or by brain toxicity. Hippchen then reviewed claims that hyperactivity was common in inmates and was due to nutritional deficiencies and low blood sugar. To support his views Hippchen referred to the unpublished studies of Smith, Pawlik and Hawkins which have claimed 70% to 80% success rates with drug users and alcoholics using vitamin therapy.

Von Hilsheimer, Philpott, Buckley and Klets (1977) have actually reported some empirical evidence. They stated that over an 11 year period their program had a 86% success rate with unco-operative adolescent delinquents with long histories of failure in special correctional programs. These authors based their treatment on biological stress theories, e.g., Selye's general adaptation syndrome. Their treatment methods employed the restoration of ACTH balance, support for the adrenals and nutritional rehabilitation. While writing persuasively and providing some physiological data on their sample they unfortunately reported their recidivism outcome data and control comparisons in a rather cavalier fashion. Until they provide much more careful documentation in this area their claims have to be treated, at best, as an intriguing curiosity.

MISCELLANEOUS

There were ten studies that were difficult to classify and are included in this section. These studies ranged from probation to work furlough programs. Some reports relied on weak correlational analyses (Martinson & Wilks, 1977) others had thorough statistical analyses (Andrews, et al., 1977).

Peck & Klugman (1973) organized a pre-release program for drug offenders. Counseling regarding jobs, education, and personal problems was initiated in the prison and when the offender reached the street he was given access to group therapy, medication and assistance from government agencies. After 3 years (N = 145) the re-arrest rate was 25% (13% for drug offenses).

Hayes (1973) gave alcoholics the option of a jail sentence or one year probation with antabuse. Failure to appear at the probation office resulted in reinstatement of the jail sentence. The year prior to the program the sample averaged 3.8 arrests per year, the year afterwards it was 0.3.

Oldroyd & Stapley (1976-77) did a time series analysis of the effects of probation on individuals convicted for misdemeanours and felonies. Recidivism was lower for misdemeanours.

Baunach (1977) reported on the "Baltimore life study" which compared the effects of financial assistance, job finding services, job and financial service combined, and no assistance upon release. After two years the combined service produced the lower recidivism rates.

Work furlough as an alternative to incarceration has been attempted. Two studies (Jeffrey & Woopert, 1974; Rudoff & Esslstyn, 1973) reported successful results. Jeffrey & Woopert provided an impressive 4 year follow-up and found 20% lower reconviction rates for work furlough vs. control group subjects. Several individual differences were related to program success. In contrast, Waldo & Chiricos (1977) found no effect of work furlough on recidivism compared to randomly assigned controls. Also, length of time on work furlough and individual differences were not related to recidivism.

Andrews et al. (1977) related recidivism rates over a two year period with kinds of probation supervision and individual differences among supervisors and probationers. They found substantial decreases in recidivism rates (up to 70%) depending on the particular interaction of these factors.

Martinson & Wilks (1977) compared parole supervision with release from prison in 80 studies and found in 74 instances that recidivism rates were lower for parole supervision. The rates ranged from 0.2 – 43.6%. Most were in the 10% range.

Kitchener, Schmidt & Glaser (1977) provided an 18 year follow-up of 1956 Federal prison releases and compared their recidivism with 1970 releases. They contended that since the 1970 rates were similar to those in 1956, correctional services (e.g., work release, parole, financial aid, community resources) have been effective since the type of person convicted in recent years (drug offenders, assaulters, etc.) were greater risks than those incarcerated 20 years ago. Kitchener et al. also note several demographic characteristics that differentially relate to recidivism rates.

RELATED PROGRAMS

For some obscure reason the criminal justice community seems to have remained isolationist in its perception of what programs might be fruitfully employed to deal with the offender. A typical example of this perceptual set came from Martinson (1976) who stated that success or failure in related fields had little generalizeability to corrections. On the other hand, others (Milan & McKee, 1976; Ross & McKay, 1978) have commented that the programs employed in corrections are not an adequate reflection of the variety and quality of treatments available in, for example, the mental health field. Moreover, they have also questioned why there has been a refusal to recognize that programs derived from conceptual models that have proved effective with school children, mental patients and other clinical groups might be effective with adult felons. Even if one were a convinced radical criminologist believing firmly in the "facts of human diversity whether personal . . . are not subject to the power to criminalize" (Taylor, Turk, Walton & Young, 1973), there still remains the reality that there are individuals, currently incarcerated for breaking society's laws, who have personal problems of a severe nature. It is these personal problems i.e., alcoholism, drug abuse, sexual misbehaviors, which directly account for their incarceration. A brief survey of some of the more notable research programs in these three areas is provided.

ALCOHOLISM

Much of the recent research in this area indicates that alcoholism can be treated successfully (Armor, Polich & Stambul, 1978). The studies on alcohol treatment are characterized by sophisticated design, theoretically relevant treatment procedures, careful evaluation and lengthy follow-up. Two of the most commendable series of investigations have been carried out by Azrin (1974), Hunt & Azrin (1976), and Sobell and Sobell (1974, 1976).

The Sobells developed individualized behavior therapy programs for each client focusing on assertiveness training, role playing and modeling, and aversive conditioning procedures. The dependent variables were daily drinking disposition, emotional adjustment, vocational satisfaction, occupational status, and residential status. Subjects were randomly assigned to the treatment paradigm or conventional state hospital treatment. Comparisons were for controlled drinking and abstinence. Follow-up data at both one and two years indicated the alcoholics on a controlled drinking program or abstinence were functioning at drinking rates 43 – 60% less than the control group.

The Azrin (1974) and Hunt & Azrin (1976) studies employed a community reinforcement approach to alcoholism. They employed a variety of techniques such as vocational counseling and job placement, marriage and family counseling, placing alcoholics in self-governing social clubs, employing a buddy system for counseling help, and antabuse therapy. In comparison to controls who were housed in the same units but received only counseling and advice to take antabuse or to go to AA programs, the control group spent six times more time drinking, were institutionalized fifteen times as much, spent twice the amount of time away from home and were employed twelve times less than the experimentals.

The alcohol literature is also instructive in that it demonstrates that type of problem (Lloyd & Salzberg, 1975; Orford, Oppenheimer & Edwards, 1976), individual differences (Bromet, Moos, Bliss & Wuthmann, 1977; Glover, McCue, 1977; Orford et al., 1976), and type of treatment paradigm (Bromet et al., 1977; Miller, 1978), are all meaningfully related to outcome. Furthermore, they demonstrate that controlled drinking can be a desirable goal for offenders with alcohol problems. On the other hand, for many, abstinence is an unrealistic goal as their home environments ridicule such behavior.

DRUG ABUSE

While drug addiction has long been considered to be a most difficult problem to treat there is some recent evidence indicating promise. Two of these studies which dealt with incarcerated heroin abusers have already been reviewed (Platt et al., 1977; Peck & Klugman, 1973). There have also been successful attempts to treat heroin addicts in the community. While the methadone and maintenance programs have been criticized, it is interesting to note that the initial successful methadone maintenance programs were limited in size allowing for the therapist to provide individual attention, gain a knowledge of the strength and weaknesses of each addict, and plan for ancillary programs to help community adjustment (Dole, 1971). As Platt and Labate (1976) commented, once the methadone maintenance programs became popularized they were decentralized, and had poorer management control with the result that the programs were applied to many patients who were not suitable. The drug was also diverted to the black market and became the primary drug of choice. It is not surprising that with these developments methadone programs became limited in value.

There have been seven other studies that have reported success in treating drug addicts. Four of these were with heroin addicts (Cheek & Mendelson, 1973; Grizzle, 1975; O'Brien, Raynes & Patch, 1972; Reeder & Kunce, 1976). Three of these studies developed an extensive and pragmatic theoretical approach towards their clients' problems. O'Brien et al. (1972) originated a program for two heroin addicts which was comprised of treatment sessions consisting of aversive therapy to cut down the appetitive drive for heroin, progressive relaxation to overcome tension and develop alternative behaviors as a substitute for drug induced relaxation, and systematic desensitization to treat the anxiety cueing the consummatory response of heroin. The two subjects received 19 and 27 treatment sessions respectively. Follow-up at 6 and 14 months indicated the subjects had abstained from heroin use. Grizzle (1975) compared an education, methadone, therapeutic community, and two law enforcement programs on the prevention of drug abuse with adolescents in high school. The results of the treatment package were compared after two years with the students attending similar schools in the community which did not receive the program. Grizzle, in a not entirely satisfactory report of the data, extrapolating into the future, found that her results indicated the programs saved 685 years of alcoholism and 240 years of heroin addiction. Reeder & Kunce (1976) founded a residential vocational program for heroin addicts which was noteworthy in that it focussed on role playing techniques and utilized components that emphasized the existing "street" skills of her sample. Subjects were randomly assigned to treatment and placebo attention groups. Vocational outcome at 30, 90 and 180 days afterwards were superior for the treatment group.

There has been an increased incidence in other forms of drug abuse (e.g., amphetamines). Three studies (Frederikson, Jenkins & Cann, 1976; Gotestam & Melin, 1974; Melin & Gotestam, 1973) claimed success in treating these types of addicts for up to a year's duration. The techniques employed in these studies were similar to those reviewed in the behavior modification section.

SEXUAL DEVIATION

The assessment and treatment of sexual behaviors such as child molestation, pedophilia and various types of fetish behaviors is still in its infancy. Nevertheless some preliminary data has now been reported indicating that programs can be successful with these individuals. One of the pioneering studies in the area was by Marshall (1973). He studied 13 individuals, 5 of whom were from a penitentiary. There was a follow-up of 3 to 16 months on 10 subjects, 8 of whom reported complete success. Wolf and Marino (1975) reported 18 of 19 child molesters had gone an average of 10 months after treatment without incident. Three very thorough single subject designs have reported success in treating pedophilia (Levin, Barry, Gambaro, Wolfinsohn & Smith; Marshall, 1978) and sexually assaultive (Marshall & Lippens, 1977) behavior. Follow-up periods ranged from several months to one year. These studies were impressive in that they provided comprehensive, intensive treatment programs emphasizing covert sensitization, orgasmic conditioning, satiation therapy and aversive conditioning.

THEORETICAL & PROGRAMMING IMPLICATIONS

We have limited our review of the literature to articles published in periodicals and texts which are available to anybody interested in the issue. We have not touched upon unpublished government reports nor do we claim that our existing review is entirely comprehensive. We also wish to avoid a "box score" analysis and debate but certainly 95 intervention studies reported since late 1973, of which 86% reported success, should and cannot be ignored. The range of situations within which these studies were carried out i.e., community settings, institutions, and the variety of services attempted, is also noteworthy. But these facts in themselves are not the only important facts that can be generated from this review. Rather, another salient inference is that the present literature review can be categorized in such a way as to shed considerable light on the fallacy of the "nothing works" doctrine. That is, these studies collectively address themselves to five major issues which provide satisfactory answers as to why much of what has been done in the name of delinquency prevention in the past has been an abject failure. Indeed, if certain segments of the criminal justice system continue to argue themselves out of a meaningful operational role then the present literature points to several easy remedies with which to hasten the demise of treatment.

RELIANCE ON A SINGLE METHOD

Glaser (1975) remarked that correctional researchers in the past have strongly resembled the early medical adventurers forlornly seeking the single cure for a complex problem. Fortunately, the majority of studies carried out in the last few years have applied a multi-method approach to delinquency problems. This is consistent throughout the recent literature no matter what type of intervention was examined.

There is not one study in this review which produced meaningful treatment results by relying on a single method. A good example of this came from some of the behavioral contract studies (Stuart, et al., 1976) and diversion studies (Stratton, 1975). These studies did produce significant results but the magnitude of these, particularly in the area of recidivism, was considerably less than those other behavior modification studies reviewed which employed behavioral contracts and other complementary behavioral techniques.

RELIANCE ON A SINGLE OUTCOME

This literature review nicely illustrates the fact that treatment studies can enhance interpersonal, familial, educational and vocational goals as well as reduce recidivism. Recidivism will remain an important variable in further tests of program effectiveness but a slavish adherence to it in the past has obscured other meaningful gains that can be achieved by programs. In fact, recidivism as it is commonly measured, can be an arbitrary and imprecise measure (Gendreau & Leipciger, 1978; Sarri & Selo, 1974).

INTERACTIONS AND INDIVIDUAL DIFFERENCES

The rationale behind a single method type of program has serious implications in that there has been neglect of a differential treatment approach. This mentality denies that individual differences, kinds of treatment and settings may not interact.

The reluctance to recognize the fact that individual differences are crucial to any treatment program belies a fundamental lack of knowledge of basic learning principles. One of the basic tenets of the experimental learning literature is that individual differences are important. This has been demonstrated time and again in experimental research on learning (cf. Spence, 1956). There is also ample proof with delinquent samples that individual differences are strikingly related to how well an individual learns even in what would be labelled (by non-behaviorists) as trivial conditioning paradigms (e.g. Gendreau & Suboski, 1971; Hare, 1970). To deny that individual differences would not be important in dealing with complex, rich human behaviors in naturalistic settings is an incredible assertion. This denial has a second aspect to it: it is to deny that individual differences can interact with different types of settings. Indeed, there are over a couple of dozen experimental publications on this topic all of which indicate (cf. Bowers, 1973; Endler & Magnusson, 1976) that our ability to predict behavior is enhanced considerably when we take into account how traits and settings interact. It is reasonable to assume that when treatment studies include these type of interactions in their analysis program success will be enhanced.

This review bears out these facts and further confirms what Adamo (1977), Glaser (1975), Palmer (1975), and Warren (1977) have been tirelessly repeating. That is, there is a literature that indicates that a differential treatment approach is valuable in corrections and will become more so. Consider the following evidence outlined in this paper. Individual differences, types of treatment and settings were predictive of success in diversion, behavioral contracts, family intervention studies, contingency management, probation, and counseling approaches. In addition, those studies in delinquency related areas reported the same fact of life. Is all of this a coincidence? Is it a coincidence that there is a consistency across content areas as to what individual differences are important e.g., age, race, employment history, family stability, neuroticism, anxiety, sociopathic traits, self-esteem? Is it a coincidence that specific types of individual differences interact with types of treatment to produce substantially higher treatment success rates?

NOT ENOUGH TREATMENT

It is truly remarkable that the issue of amount of treatment has been apparently dismissed as a minor problem in the criminal justice field. Two general points should first be made. In terms of services provided for offenders it has been estimated that the U.S. spends less than $100 per year, per inmate, on social services and extends rehabilitation services to only 5% of the inmate population (Chaneles, 1976). It has been said time and again that some correctional environments are some of the worst within which to change behaviors applicable to community adjustment (Ross & McKay, 1978; Slaikeu, 1973).

More specifically, Berleman & Steinburn (1969) pointed out that some of the early classic prevention studies supposedly failed to allow for more than one treatment contact per month with the client. The recent literature empirically and emphatically proves the point. As an example, Wade et al. (1977) and Stratton (1975) both used diversion; the former applied a greater diversity of techniques and more intense service and reported greater success rates. The same finding held true in the family intervention literature (Eyeberg & Johnson, 1974; Patterson, 1974). DeLeon, Hollands & Rosenthal (1972) found that inmates who spent 3 months in a program had 90% recidivism compared to those who spent 11 months who had a 30% recidivism rate.

There is a corollary to this issue. It has been expressed by Martinson (1974) and Wilks & Martinson (1976). They were understandably upset as to what was going to be done with the crime problem in the 20th precinct where they lived. They characterized the precinct as a place where citizens had to dodge bullets, avoid hoodlums, stay off the street at nights, have bars on their windows, etc. They made both a very good and a very poor point. First, it is a peculiar tunnel vision to assume that the type of crime problem existing in the 20th precinct in New York is typical of that which exists elsewhere in North America. They are likely correct in asserting that with many of the individuals involved in crime in New York city most of the routinely employed counseling and behavior modification treatment is not powerful enough. This is nothing new. The treatment literature attests to the fact that there are some situations where the behavior is so disruptive that the usual methods were not effective (Weathers & Liberman, 1975).

There are, in fact, programs that can cope with the serious problems Martinson talks about. Where behavioral anarchy exists then only the most direct and harsh punitive measures may have an effect, albeit a transitory one (Gendreau & Surridge, 1978). This is not to say that there are no treatments that can be developed for severe problems. Some of the most powerful interventions lie in the behavior modification area but these types of programs can be bastardized and misused to the point where they can contribute to the problem they initially set out to alleviate (e.g. Ross & McKay, 1976; Bassett & Blanchard, 1977). Thus there will likely be a limit as to how far treatment programs will be extended to reach severe problem behaviors in North American society. These limits are fairly clearly defined by the cultural and professional ethics under which we operate. Such limits are not logically an indictment of the failure of treatment.

LACK OF RELATION BETWEEN AGENCIES

In corrections in North America separate systems operate with different goals and organizational principles and all too often political expediency prevents cooperation and encourages programs that are too conservative and limited to succeed in the first place (Berk & Ross, 1976; McDougall, 1976). Birkenmayer, Polonoski, Backett and Ardron (1976) put it more bluntly. In their review of community services in Canada and the U.S. they noted that, if anything, the present system appears to be counterproductive, with services provided on a fragmentary, disjointed basis with little rhyme or reason as to who provides services and when. There are two apt examples supporting the above point. The first comes from the Harvard recidivism study on correctional reform in Massachusetts (Ohlin, 1975; Ohlin, Miller & Coates, 1976). They found that in regions of Massachusetts with high rates of recidivism there was a lack of program diversity with most youth being placed in secure or group home programs with little utilization of other community alternatives. Moreover, they concluded that type of program does make a difference. Where lower recidivism rates were found there was evidence that staff were building community linkages for youth. Specifically, in one of the Massachusetts regions where there were relatively well developed stable community programs, court appearances were 11% lower and probation commitment was reduced by 25%.

In support of their findings, the present literature review also attested to the fact that where programs have established meaningful links between the institution and community resources, successful results can be obtained (Clements, 1975; Davidson II & Robinson, 1975; Grizzle, 1975; Markolin II et al., 1975; Phillips et al., 1973; Wagner & Breitmeyer, 1975). The second example comes from research carried out in Ontario (Gendreau, Madden & Leipciger, 1978), a province with supposedly one of the most expensive and comprehensive social service systems to be found anywhere. It was discovered that very few of the delinquents (and their families) that were incarcerated in the Ontario system ever received help for their problems while in the community. What little aid that was received came from police and correctional agencies (e.g., parole) rather than from other social agencies that might more appropriately have provided personal and family assistance.

In the future this kind of problem may be compounded in the following way. Recently, it has been very fashionable among government agencies to de-institutionalize. This has definitely occurred in the mental health field. But, in fact, this de-institutionalization has not been backed up by community programs, rather, the "enlightened revolution" may well be viewed as an abdication of responsibility by government agencies (Bassuk & Gerson, 1978). Where might some of the overflow be going? Likely to the correctional system. For example, Gendreau, Leipciger, Grant & Collins (1978) have found that samples of young offenders, compared to previous norms, now present psychological symptoms markedly similar to those currently found in out-patient psychiatric hospital samples.

In conclusion, it is our view that the substantive amount of recent successful treatment programs recently reported squarely places the onus on those involved in planning for the criminal justice system. Unfortunately, the irony is that while we have often heard the clinical observation that many offenders today seem to avoid responsibility for their behaviors, the fact is that if we persist in the verdict that treatment is unsuccessful then the "nothing works" doctrine also encourages the correctional system to avoid responsibility. By labelling the offender as untreatable we make it apparent to one and all that we cannot be held responsible for his improvement *or* his deterioration.

REFERENCES

Adams, S., "Evaluation: A way out of rhetoric." In *Rehabilitation, Recidivism, & Research* (Hackensack, New Jersey: National Council on Crime & Delinquency, 1976).

Adams, S., "Evaluating correctional treatments: Toward a new perspective," *Criminal Justice & Behavior*, 1977, 4, 323–329.

Alexander, J.F., Barton, C., Schiavo, R.S., & Parsons, B.V., "Systems-behavioral intervention with families of delinquents: Therapist characteristics & family behaviour & outcome," *Journal of Consulting & Clinical Psychology*, 1976, 44, 656–664.

Alexander, R.N., Corbett, T.F., & Smigel, J., "The effects of individual & group consequences on school attendance & curfew violations with pre-delinquent adolescents," *Journal of Applied Behavioral Analysis*, 1976, 9, 221–226.

Alexander, J.F., & Parsons, R.J., "Short-term behavioral intervention with delinquent families: Impact on family process & recidivism," *Journal Abnormal Psychology*, 1973, *81*, 219–225.

Andrews, D.A., Kiessling, J.J., Russell, R.J. & Grant, B.A., *Volunteers & the 1- to -1 supervision of adult probationers: An experimental comparison with professionals and a field-discipline of process & outcome*, (Ottawa: Canadian Volunteers in Corrections, 1977).

Armor, D.J., Polich, J.M., & Stambul, M.B., *Alcoholism & treatment*, (New York: Wiley, 1978).

Arnold, J.E., Levine, A.G., & Patterson, G.R., "Changes in sibling behavior following family intervention," *Journal of Consulting & Clinical Psychology*, 1975, *5*, 683–688.

Austin, R.L., Differential treatment in an institution: Re-examining the Preston study," *Journal of Research in Crime & Delinquency*, 1977, *14*, 177–194.

Azrin, N.H., "Improvements in the community-reinforcement approach to alcoholism," *Behavior Research & Therapy*, 1976, *14*, 339–348.

Barkwell, L.J., "Differential treatment of juveniles on probation: An evaluative study," *Canadian Journal of Criminology & Corrections*, 1975, *18*, 1–16.

Baron, R., Feeney, F., & Thornton, W., "Preventing delinquency through diversion: The Sacramento County 601 Division project," *Federal Probation*, 1973, *37*, 13–18.

Bassett, J.E., & Blanchard, E.B., "The effect of the absence of close supervision of the use of response cost in a prison token economy," *Journal of Applied Behavior Analysis*, 1977, *10*, 375–379.

Bassuk, E.L., & Gerson, S., "Deinstitutionalization & mental health Services," *Scientific American*, 1978, *238*, 46–53.

Baunach, P.J., "Framing the questions in criminal justice evaluation: Maybe you can get these from here if you ask the "right" question," *The Prison Journal*, 1977, *57*, 19–27.

Berk, R.A., & Rossi, P.H., "Doing good or worse: Evaluation research politically re-examined," *Social Problems*, 1976, *23*, 337–349.

Berleman, W.C., & Steinburn, T.W., "The value & validity of delinquency prevention experiments," *Crime & Delinquency*, 1969, *15*, 471–477.

Bernstein, I.N., "Evaluations research in corrections: status & prospects revisited," *Federal Probation* 1975, *39*, 56–57.

Birkenmayer, A.C., Polonski, M., Beckett, D., & Ardron, D., *A Review of Alternatives to the Incarceration of the Youthful Offender*, (Toronto: Ontario Ministry of Correctional Services, 1976).

Bohnstedt, M., "Answers to three questions about juvenile division," *Journal of Research in Crime & Delinquency*, 1978, *15*, 109–123.

Bowers, K., Situationism in psychology: An analysis & critique," *Psychological Review*, 1973, *80*, 307–336.

Braukman, C.J., Fixsen, D.L., Phillips, E.L., & Wolf, M.W., "Behavioral approaches to treatment in the crime & delinquency field," *Criminology*, 1975, *13*, 299–331.

Bromet, G., Moos, R., Bliss, F., & Wuthmann, C., "Post treatment functioning of alcoholic patients: Its relation to programm participation," *Journal of Consulting & Clinical Psychology*, 1977, *45*, 829–842.

Brown, J.H., Frankel, A., Birkimer, J.C., & Gamboa, A.M., "The effects of a classroom management workshop on the reduction of children's problematic behavior," *Corrective & Social Psychiatry*, 1976, *22*, 39–41.

Burchard, J.D., & Harig, P.T., "Behavior modification & juvenile delinquency." In H. Leitenberg (Ed.), *Handbook of Behavior Modification & Behavior Therapy*, (Englewood Cliffs, New Jersey: Prentice-Hall, 1976).

Camp, B.W., Blom, G.E., Herbert, F., & Doorninck, W.J., "Think aloud": A program for developing self-control in young aggressive boys," *Journal of Abnormal Child Psychology*, 1977, *5*, 157–169.

Campbell, D.T., "Reforms as experiments," *American Psychologist*, 1969, *24*, 409–428.

Chandler, M.J., "Egocentrism & antisocial behavior: The assessment & training of social perspective-taking skills," *Developmental Psychology*, 1973, *9*, 326–333.

Chaneles, S., "Prisoners can be rehabilitated now," *Psychology Today*, 1976, *10*, 129–133.

Chaneles, S., "A look at Martinson's report," *Fortune Society News*, 1975, *3*.

Cheek, F.E., & Mendelson, M., "Developing behavior modification programs with emphasis on self-control," *Hospital & Community Psychiatry*, 1973, *24*, 410–415.

Clements, C.B., "The school relations bureau: A program of police intervention," *Criminal Justice & Behavior*, 1975, *2*, 358–371.

Conrad, J.P., "We should never have promised a hospital," *Federal Probation*, 1975, *39*, 3–9.

Csapo, M., & Agg, B., "Educational rehabilitation of delinquents in a community setting," *Canadian Journal & Criminology & Corrections*, 1976, *18*, 42–48.

Davidson, W.D., & Robinson, M.J., "Community psychology & behavior modification: A community based program for the prevention of delinquency," *Corrective & Social Psychiatry*, 1975, *21*, 1–12.

DeLeon, G., Hollands, S., & Rosenthal, M.S., "Phoenix House: Criminal activities of dropouts," *Journal of American Medical Association*, 1972, *222*, 686–689.

Doctor, R.M., & Polakow, R.L., "A behavior modification program for adult probationers," *American Psychological Association* (Los Angeles: Department of Psychology, UCLA, 1973).

Dole, V.P., "Methodone maintenance: Treatment for 25,000 heroin addicts," *Journal American Medical Association*, 1971, *215*, 1131–1134.

Douds, A.F., Engelesgjord, M., & Collingwood, T.B., "Behavior contracting with youthful offenders & their parents," *Child Welfare*, 1977, *51*, 409–417.

Durlack, J.A., "Description & evaluation of a behaviorally oriented school-based preventive mental health program," *Journal of Consulting & Clinical Psychology*, 1977, *45*, 27–33.

Emshoff, J.G., Redd, W.H., Davidson, W.S., "Generalization training and the transfer of prosocial behavior in delinquent adolescents," *Journal of Behaviour Therapy & Experimental Psychiatry*, 1976, *7*, 141–144.

Emery, R.E., & Marholin II, D., "An applied behavior analysis of delinquency: The irrelevancy of relevant behavior," *American Psychologist*, 1977, *32*, 860–873.

Endler, N.S., & Magnusson, D., "Toward an interactional psychology of personality," *Psychological Bulletin*, 1976, *83*, 956–974.

Eyeberg, S., & Johnson, S.M., "Multiple assessment of behavior modification with families: Effects of contingency contracting & order of treated persons," *Journal of Consulting & Clinical Psychology*, 1974, *42*, 594–606.

Fairweather, G.W., *Social Change: The Challenge To Survival* (Morristown, N.J.: General Learning Press, 1977).

Fedoravicius, A.S., "The patient as shaper of required parental behavior: A case study," *Journal of Behavior Therapy & Experimental Psychiatry*, 1973, *4*, 395–396.

Fishmen, R., "An evaluation of criminal recidivism in projects providing rehabilitation & diversion services in New York City," *Journal of Criminal Law & Criminology*, 1977, *68*, 283–305.

Fo, W.S.O., & O'Donnell, C.R., "The buddy system: Relationship & contingency conditions in a community intervention program for youth with non-professionals as behavior change agents," *Journal of Consulting & Clinical Psychology*, 1974, *42*, 163–169.

Fo, W.S.O., & O'Donnell, C.R., "The buddy system: Effect of community intervention on delinquent offences," *Behaviour Therapy*, 1975, *6*, 522–524.

Fogel, D., "The politics of Corrections," *Federal Probation*, 1977, *41*, 27.

Frederikson, L.W., Jenkins, J.O., & Carr, C.R., "Indirect modification of adolescent drug abuse using contingency contracting," *Journal of Behavioral Therapy & Experimental Psychiatry*, 1976, *7*, 377–378.

Gendreau, P., & Andrews, D.A., "Psychological consultation in correctional agencies: Case studies & general issues." In J.J. Platt & R.W. Wicks (Eds.), *The Psychological Consultant* (New York: Grune & Stratton, 1979).

Gendreau, P., Grant, B., Leipciger, M., & Collins, S., "Norms & recidivism rates for the MMPI & selected experimental scales in a Canadian delinquent sample," *Canadian Journal of Behavioural Science*, 1979, *11*, 21–31.

Gendreau, P., & Leipciger, M., "The development of a recidivism measure & its application in Ontario," *Canadian Journal of Criminology & Corrections*, 1978, *20*, 3–17.

Gendreau, P., Madden, P., & Leipciger, M., "Norms & recidivism rates for social history & institutional experience of first incarcerated: Implications for programming," *Canadian Journal of Criminology*, 1979, *21*, 416–441.

Gendreau, P., & Suboski, M.D., "Classical discrimination eyelid conditioning in primary psychopaths," *Journal of Abnormal Psychology*, 1971, *77*, 282–286.

Gendreau, P., & Surridge, C.T., "Controlling gun crimes: The Jamaican experience," *International Journal of Criminology & Penology*, 1978, *6*, 43–60.

Gibbons, D.C., & Blake, G.F., "Evaluating the impact of juvenile diversion programs," *Crime & Delinquency*, 1976, *22*, 411–420.

Glaser, D., "Remedies for the key deficiency in criminal justice evaluation research," *Journal of Research in Crime & Delinquency*, 1974, *11*, 144–154.

Glaser, D., "Achieving better questions: A half-century's progression in correctional research," *Federal Probation*, 1975, *39*, 3–9.

Glover, J.H., & McCue, P.A., "Electrical aversion therapy with alcoholics: A comparative follow-up," *British Journal of Psychiatry*, 1977, *130*, 279–286.

Gold, M., "Scholastic experiences, self-esteem & delinquent behavior: A theory for alternative schools," *Crime & Delinquency*, 1978, *24*, 290–308.

Gotestam, K.G., & Melin, L., "Covert extinction of amphetamine addiction," *Behavior Therapy*, 1974, *5*, 90–92.

Grala, C., & McCauley, C., "Counseling truants back to school: Motivation combined with a program for action," *Journal of Counseling Psychology*, 1976, *23*, 166–169.

Greenwood, C.R., Hops, H., Delquadri, J., & Guild, J., "Group contingencies for group consequences in classroom management: A further analysis," *Journal of Applied Behavior Analysis*, 1974, *7*, 413–425.

Grizzle, G.B., "Preventing drug abuse: A comparison of education treatment & law enforcement approaches," *Criminal Justice & Behavior*, 1975, *2*, 372–382.

Guidry, L.S., "Use of covert punishing contingency in compulsive stealing," *Journal of Behavioral Therapy & Experimental Psychology*, 1975, *6*, 169.

Halleck S.L., & Witte, A.D., "Is rehabilitation dead?" *Crime & Delinquency*, 1977, *23*, 372–382.

Hare, R.D., *Psychopathy: Theory & Research*, (New York: Wiley, 1970).

Hayes, S.N., "Contingency management in a municipally-administered antabuse program for alcoholics," *Journal of Behavior Therapy & Experimental Psychiatry*, 1973, *4*, 31–32.

Hippchen, L.J., "Biomedical approaches to offender rehabilitation," *Offender Rehabilitation*, 1976, *1*, 115–123.

Hoefler, S.A., & Bornstein, P.H., "Achievement Place: An evaluative review," *Criminal Justice & Behavior*, 1975, *2*, 146–168.

Hunt, G.M., & Azrin, N.H., "A community-reinforcement approach to alcoholism," *Behavior Research & Therapy*, 1973, *11*, 91–104.

Jeffery, R., & Woolpert, S., "Work furlough as an alternative to incarceration: An assessment of its effects on recidivism & social cost," *Journal of Criminal Law & Criminology*, 1974, *65*, 405–415.

Jenkins, W.O., Witherspoon, A.D., DeVine, M.D., DeZalera, S.K., Muller, J.B., Barton, M.C., & McKee, J.M., *The Post-Prison Analysis of Criminal Behavior and Longitudinal Follow-Up Evaluation of Institutional Treatment* (Montgomery, Alabama: Rehabilitation Research Foundation, 1974).

Jessness, C., "The Preston Typology study: An experiment with differential treatment in an institution," *Journal of Research in Crime & Delinquency*, 1971, *8*, 38–52.

Jessness, C.F., "Comparative effectiveness of behavior modification & transactional analysis programs for delinquents," *Journal of Consulting & Clinical Psychology*, 1975, *43*, 758–779.

Jessness, C.F., Allison, T.S., McCormick, P.M., Wedge, R.F., & Young, M.L., "An evaluation of the effectiveness of contingency contracting with delinquents," *Journal of Research, Crime & Delinquency*, 1978, in press.

Johnson, V.S., "Behavior modification in the correctional setting," *Criminal Justice & Behavior*, 1977, *4*, 397–428.

Karoly, P., & Rosenthal, M., "Training parents in behavior modification: Effects on perceptions of family interaction & deviant child behavior," *Behavior Therapy*, 1977, *8*, 406–410.

Kassebaum, G., Ward, D., & Wilner, D., *Prison Treatment & Parole Survival: An Empirical Assessment* (New York: Wiley, 1971).

Kent, R.N., & O'Leary, K.D., "A controlled evaluation of behavior modification with conduct problem children," *Journal of Consulting & Clinical Psychology*, 1976, *44*, 586–596.

Kitchner, H., Schmidt, A.K., & Glaser, D., "How persistant is post-prison success?" *Federal Probation*, 1977, *41*, 9–15.

Klockars, C.B., "The true limits of the effectiveness of correctional treatment," *The Prison Journal*, 1975, *55*, 53–64.

Levin, S.M., Barry, S.M., Gambaro, S., Wolfinsohn, L., & Smith, A., "Variations of covert sensitivity in the treatment of pedophilia behavior: A case study," *Journal of Consulting & Clinical Psychology*, 1977, *45*, 896–907.

Lipton, D., Martinson, R., & Wilks, J., *The Effectiveness of Correctional Treatment* (New York: Praeger, 1975).

Lloyd, R.W., & Salzberg, H.C., "Controlled social drinking: An alternative to abstinence as a treatment goal for alcoholic abusers," *Psychological Bulletin*, 1975, *82*, 815–842.

Logan, C.H., "Evaluation research in crime & delinquency: An appraisal," *Journal of Criminal Law, Criminology & Police Science*, 1972, *63*, 378–388.

London, P., *Behavior Control* (New York: Harper & Row, 1969).

Lysaght, T.V., & Burchard, J.D., "The analysis & modification of a deviant parent-youth communication pattern," *Journal of Behavior Therapy & Experimental Psychiatry*, 1975, *6*, 339–342.

Lundeman, R.J., McFarlane, P.T., & Scarpitti, F.R., "Delinquency prevention: A description & assessment of project reported in the professional literature," *Crime & Delinquency*, 1976, *22*, 297–308.

Mackintosh, N.J., *Psychology of Animal Learning*, (New York: Academic Press, 1974).

Marholin II, D., Plienis, A.J., Harris, S.D., & Marholin, B.L., "Mobilization of the community through a behavioral approach: A school program for adjudicated females," *Criminal Justice Behavior*, 1975, *2*, 130–145.

Maron, A.W., "The juvenile diversion system in action: Some recommendations for change," *Crime & Delinquency*, 1976, *22*, 461–489.

Marshall, W.L., "The modification of sexual fantasies: A combined treatment approach to the reduction of deviant behavior," *Behavior Research & Therapy*, 1973, *11*, 1–8.

Marshall, W.L., "Satiation therapy with a multiple sexual deviant," *Journal of Applied Behavior Analysis*, 1978, in press.

Marshall, W.L., & Lippens, K., "The clinical value of boredom: A procedure for reducing inappropriate sexual interest," *Journal of Nervous & Mental Disease*, 1977, *165*, 283–287.

Martinson, R., "What works? Questions & answers about prison reform," *The Public Interest*, 1974, *35*, 22–54.

Martinson, R., "Evaluation in crisis — a postscript." In *Rehabilitation, recidivism, & research* (Hackensack, N.J.: National Council on Crime & Delinquency, 1976).

Martinson, R., California research at the crossroads," *Crime & Delinquency*, 1976, *22*, 180–191.

Martinson, R., & Wilks, J., "Save parole supervision," *Federal Probation*, 1977, *41*, 23–27.

Maskin, M.B., "The differential impact of work oriented vs. communication-oriented juvenile correction programs upon recidivism rates in delinquent males," *Journal of Clinical Psychology*, 1976, *32*, 432–433.

McCombs, D., Filipczak, J., Friedman, R.M., Wodarski, J.S., "Long-term follow-up of behavior modification with high-risk adolescents," *Criminal Justice & Behavior*, 1978, *5*, 21–34.

McDougall, E.C., "Corrections has not been tried," *Criminal Justice Review*, 1976, *1*, 63–76.

Melin, G.L., & Gotestam, K.G., "A contingency management program on a drug free unit for intravenous amphetamine addicts," *Journal of Behavioral Therapy & Experimental Psychiatry*, 1973, *4*, 333–337.

Milan, M.A., & McKee, J.M., "The cell-block token economy: Token reinforcement procedures in a maximum security correctional institution for adult felons," *Journal of Applied Behavior Analysis*, 1976, *9*, 253–275.

Miller, W.R., "Behavioral treatment of problem drinkers: A comparative outcome study of three controlled drinking therapies," *Journal of Consulting & Clinical Psychology*, 1978, *46*, 74–86.

Nejelski, P., "Diversion: The promise & the danger," *Crime & Delinquency*, 1976, *22*, 393–410.

Nettler, G., *Explaining Crime*, (New York: McGraw-Hill, 1977).

O'Brien, J.S., Raynes, A.E., & Patch, V.D., "Treatment of heroin addiction with aversion therapy, relaxation training & systematic desensitization," *Behavioral Research and Therapy*, 1972, *10*, 77–80.

O'Donnell, C.R., & Fo, W.S.O., "The buddy system: Mediator — target locus of control & behavioral outcome," *American Journal of Community Psychology*, 1976, *4*, 161–166.

Ohlin, L., "Harvard recidivism study," *Corrections Magazine*, 1975, *11*, 21–23.

Ohlin, L.E., Miller, A.D., & Coates, R.B., *Juvenile reform in Massachusetts*, (Washington, United States Department of Justice, 1975).

Oldroyd, R.J., & Stapley M., "Some correctional programs do reduce recidivism," *Offender Rehabilitation*, 1976–77, *1*, 132–141.

Orford, J., Oppenheimer, E., & Edwards, G., "Abstinence or control: The outcome for excessive drinkers two years after consultation," *Behavior Research & Therapy*, 1976, *14*, 409–418.

Palmer, J.W., "Pre-arrest diversion: The night prosecutors' program in Columbus, Ohio," *Crime & Delinquency*, 1975, *21*, 100–108.

Palmer, T., "The youth authorities community treatment project," *Federal Probation*, 1974, *38*, 3–13.

Palmer, T., "Martinson revisited," *Journal of Research in Crime & Delinquency*, 1975, *12*, 133–152.

Patterson, G.R., "Interventions for boys with conduct problems: Multiple settings, treatments & criteria," *Journal of Consulting & Clinical Psychology*, 1974, *42*, 471–481.

Patterson, G.R., Cobb, J.A., & Ray, R.S., "Direct intervention in the classroom: A set of procedures for the aggressive child." In F. Clark, D. Evans & L. Hamerlynck (Eds.), *Implementing Behavioral Programs for Schools & Clinics* (Champaign, Illinois: Research Press, 1972).

Patterson, G.R., & Reid, J.B., "Intervention for families of aggressive boys: A replication study," *Behavior Research & Therapy*, 1973, *11*, 383–394.

Peck, M.L., & Klugmen, D.J., "Rehabilitation of drug dependent offenders: An alternative approach," *Federal Probation*, 1973, *37*, 18–23.

Phillips, E.L., Phillips, R.A., Fixsen, D.L., & Wolf, M.W., "Behavior shaping works for delinquents," *Psychology Today*, 1973, *6*, 75–79.

Platt, T., "Prospects for a radical criminology in the United States," *Crime & Social Justice*, 1974, *1*, 2–10.

Platt, J.J., & Labate, C.I., *Heroin Addiction: Theory, Research & Treatment*, (New York: Wiley, 1976).

Platt, J.J., Jabate, C., & Wicks, R.J., *Evaluative Research in Correctional Drug Abuse Treatment* (Lexington, Mass.: Heath, 1977).

Quay, H.C., "The three faces of evaluation: What can be expected to work," *Criminal Justice & Behavior*, 1977, *4*, 341–354.

Quay, H.C., & Love, C.T., "The effect of a juvenile diversion program on rearrests," *Criminal Justice & Behavior*, 1977, *4*, 377–396.

Reeder, C.W., & Kunce, J.T., "Modeling techniques, drug-abstinence behavior, & heroin addicts: A pilot study," *Journal of Counseling Psychology*, 1976, *23*, 560–562.

Robison, J.O., "Book review; The effectiveness of correctional treatment — A survey of treatment evaluation studies by R. Martinson, D. Lipton, & J. Wilks," *Crime & Delinquency*, 1976, *22*, 483–486.

Roesch, R., "Does adult diversion work? The failure of research in criminal justice," *Crime & Delinquency*, 1978, *24*, 72–80.

Ross, R.R., *Behavioural management in the contrast & treatment of the offender*, (Ottawa: Criminology, University of Ottawa, 1977).

Ross, R.R., & McKay, H.B., "A study of institutional treatment programs." *International Journal of Offender Therapy & Comparative Criminology*, 1976, *20*, 165–173.

Ross, R.R., & McKay, B., "Treatment in corrections: Requiem for a panacea," *Canadian Journal of Criminology*, 1978, *20*, 279–295.

Rudoff, A., & Esslstyn, P.C., "Evaluation work furlough: A follow-up," *Federal Probation*, 1973, *37*, 48–53.

Sarason, I.G., "A cognitive social learning approach to juvenile delinquency." In R.D. Hare & D. Schalling, (Eds.) *Psychopathic Behavior: Approaches to Research*, (New York: Wiley, 1978).

Sarason, I.G., & Ganzer, U.J., "Modeling & group discussion in the rehabilitation of juvenile delinquents," *Journal of Counseling Psychology*, 1973, *20*, 442–449.

Sarri, R.G., & Selo, E., "Evaluation process & outcome in juvenile corrections: Musings on a grim tale." In P.O. Davidson, F.W. Clark, & L.A. Hamerlynck (Eds.), *Evaluation of Behavioral Programs in Community, Residential & School Settings* (Champaign, Illinois: Research Press, 1974).

Serrill, M.S., "Is rehabilitation dead?" *Corrections Magazine*, 1975, *11*, 3–12, 21–26.

Slaikeu, K.A., "Evaluation studies on group treatment of juvenile adult offenders in correctional institutions: A review of the literature," *Journal of Research in Crime & Delinquency*, 1973, *10*, 87–100.

Smith, A.B., & Berlin, L., "Can criminals be treated?" *New England Journal on Prison Law*, 1977, *3*, 487–502.

Sobell, M.B., & Sobell, L.C., "Alcoholics treated by individualized behavior therapy: one year treatment outcome," *Behavior Research & Therapy*, 1973, *11*, 599–618.

Sobell, M.B., & Sobell, L.C., "Second year treatment outcome of alcoholics treated by individualized behavior therapy: Results," *Behavior Research & Therapy*, 1976, *14*, 195–215.

Spence, K.W., *Bheavior Theory & Conditioning*, (New Haven: Yale University Press, 1956).

Stratton, J.G., "Effect of crisis intervention counseling on predelinquent & misdemeanour juvenile offences," *Juvenile Justice Journal*, 1975, *26*, 7–18.

Stuart, R.B., *Trick or Treatment* (Champaign, Illinois: Research Press, 1970).

Stuart, R.B., Jayaratne, S., & Tripodi, T., "Changing adolescent deviant behaviour through reprogramming the behaviour of parents & teachers: An experimental evaluation," *Canadian Journal of Behavioural Science*, 1976, *8*, 132–143.

Stuart, R.B., Tripodi, T., Jayaratne, S., & Camburn, D., "An experiment in social engineering in serving the families of predelinquents," *Journal of Abnormal Child Psychology*, 1976, *4*, 243–261.

Stuart, R.B. & Lott, Jr., L.A., "Behavioral contracting with delinquents: A cautionary note." In C.H. Franks & G.I. Wilson (Eds.), *Annual Review of Behavior Therapy & Practice* (New York: Brenner/Manel, 1973).

Tavris, C., "The experimenting society: To find programs that work, government must measure its failures, *Psychology Today*, 1975, *9*, 47–56.

Taylor, I., Turk, T., Walton, P., & Young, J., *The New Criminology: For a Social Theory of Deviance* (London: Routledge, 1973).

Truax, C.B., & Carkhuff, R.R., *Toward Effective Counseling & Psychotherapy* (Chicago: Aldine, 1967).

Von Hilsheimer, G., Philpott, W., Buckley, W., & Klotz, S.D., "Correcting the incorrigible: A report on 229 incorrigible adolescents," *American Laboratory*, 1977, *101*, 107–118.

Vorrath, H.H., & Brendtro, L.K., *Positive Peer Culture* (Chicago, Ill.: Aldine, 1974).

Wade, T.C., Morton, T.L., Lind, J.E., & Ferris, N.B., "A family crisis intervention approach to diversion from the juvenile justice system," *Juvenile Justice Journal*, 1977, *28*, 43–51.

Wagner, B.R., & Breitmeyer, R.G., "PACE: A residential, community oriented behavior modification program for adolescents," *Adolesence*, 1975, *38*, 277–286.

Waldo, G.P., & Chiricos, T.G., "Work release & recidivism: An empirical evaluation of a social policy," *Evaluation Quarterly*, 1977, *1*, 87–108.

Warren, M.Q., "Correctional treatment & coercion: The differential effectiveness perspective," *Criminal Justice & Behavior*, 1977, *4*, 355–376.

Weathers, L., & Liberman, R.P., "Contingency contracting with families of delinquent adolescents," *Behavior Therapy*, 1975, *6*, 356–366.

Wilks, J. & Martinson, R., "Is the treatment of criminal offenders really necessary?" *Federal Probation*, 1976, March, 3–8.

Wiltz, N.A., & Patterson, G.R., "An evaluation of parent training procedures designed to alter inappropriate aggressive behavior of boys," *Behavior Therapy*, 1975, *5*, 215–221.

Wolfe, R.W., & Marino, D., "A program of behavior treatment for incarcerated pedophiles," *The American Criminal Law Review*, 1975, *1*, 69–83.

Wright, W.E., & Dixon, M.C., "Community prevention & treatment of juvenile delinquency: A review of the literature," *Journal of Research in Crime & Delinquency*, 1977, *14*, 35–67.

Yaryan, R.B., "Federal efforts to coordinate juvenile delinquency & related youth development programs," *Journal of Abnormal & Child Psychology*, 1973, *1*, 308–316.

Chapter 2

Behavioral Approaches to Treatment in Corrections: Requiem for a Panacea*

Robert R. Ross and Bryan McKay

> Every person who has reason to believe that a deceased person
> died, . . . as a result of, . . . misadventure, negligence,
> misconduct or malpractice; by unfair means; . . . under such
> circumstances as may require investigation, shall immediately
> notify a coroner of the facts and circumstances relating to the death
> (Coroners Act, R.S.O. 1970, ch. 87, s. 7.).

It has become fashionable to adopt the position that treatment in corrections
is dead. Martinson, the funeral director, may have signed the death certificate
for treatment through his critical review of the published research on treatment
in corrections (Lipton et al., 1975; Wilks and Martinson, 1976). In spite of
opposing opinions (Palmer, 1975) there seems to be a widespread acceptance
of the view that treatment has been tried and found wanting. The rush to
"bury the remains" is reminiscent of an Agatha Christie novel. The apparent
tacit agreement to leave stones unturned, the collective sigh of relief at the
funeral director's words of reassurance, the haste to inter the remains are
familiar grist for the mystery writer's scenarios.

---

*We are grateful to the Research Services Division of the Ontario Ministry of
Correctional Services for the support and encouragement which they provided
throughout our research programs. We are particularly appreciative of the helpful
suggestions of A.C. Birkenmayer and R.E. Smith.

Ross, R.R. and McKay, B., "Behavioral approaches to treatment in corrections:
Requiem for a panacea," *Canadian Journal of Criminology*, 1978, *20* (2), 279–295.
Copyright © 1978, Canadian Journal of Criminology. Reprinted by permission.

> A coroner may at any time during an investigation or inquest issue his warrant for a *post-mortem* examination of the body . . . or such other examination or analysis as the circumstances warrant (R.S.O. 1970, ch. 87, s. 24(1)).

After a death it is sometimes profitable to conduct an autopsy before the funeral. Our failure to do a careful autopsy on treatment in corrections will, we contend, lead to four erroneous conclusions:

1. The quality of correctional research is sufficiently good to make possible an adequate assessment of the efficacy of correctional treatment. It is not.
2. The treatment employed in corrections is an adequate reflection of the variety and quality of treatment more broadly available in the mental health field. It is not.
3. There are no treatment programs which have been shown through adequate research to be efficacious. There are.
4. The "failure" of treatment reflects simply the inadequacy of the treatment and not the inadequacy of the environment in which the treatment is applied. It does not.

> . . . he shall issue his warrant to take possession of the body and shall view the body and make such further investigation as is required to enable him to determine whether or not an inquest is necessary (R.S.O. 1970, ch. 87, s. 12(1)).

Clearly, there is not a plethora of evidence that the programs in corrections which were engendered by the mental health movement lead to improved rehabilitation or a reduction in the rate of crime.

One might argue that the "treatment approach" has done little more than modify our language, aid in the documentation of the failure of corrections, engender major role conflict for criminal justice personnel and increase the cost of preparing the offender to recidivate to his correctional home. In fact, a case could be made to the effect that some treatment approaches have made our "patient" worse (Stuart, 1970; Ross and McKay, 1976). However, the failure needs to be brought into perspective before we complete the funeral arrangements. We ought to identify what we are burying. Often in corrections new treatment techniques are adopted both wholeheartedly and foolhardily; at times exclusively, and often with little question as to their applicability to the population in the field. Often, too, once they are accepted they are modified so much by the pressures of the correctional environment that their similarity to the actual techniques is apparent but hardly real. More regrettable, perhaps, is the characteristic acceptance by correctional staff of new techniques *in name only*. Whereas psychology has often been characterized by radicalism, corrections too frequently suffers from euphemism (McKay, 1976). Offenders are often remarkably (albeit negatively) affected by their entry into the criminal justice system. So are treatment programs.

Where a person dies while in the custody of an officer of a correctional institution or lock-up or while a ward of a training school, the officer in charge thereof shall immediately give notice of the death to a coroner and the coroner shall issue his warrant and hold an inquest upon the body (R.S.O. 1970, ch. 87, s. 23).

In the present paper we will provide an autopsy of behavioural approaches to the treatment of the offender.

The advent of behaviour modification in corrections was heralded with considerable excitement, enthusiasm, and optimism. Tremendous sums of money were poured into the new strategy. It quickly pervaded the field of corrections and often completely replaced established and apparently progressive programs in institutions. For example, we discovered through a survey conducted in 1968 (Ross, 1968; Ross and McKay, 1974; Ross and McConkey, 1975) that sixty-three correctional settings in the United States and Canada had been involved in projects which were labelled as "behaviour modification programs", and that in at least sixty per cent of these cases behaviour modification programs were viewed by the officials of the correctional jurisdiction as core elements in their criminal justice system. When one considers that operant was first introduced to corrections in other than short-term experimental projects not before the early 1960's one can see how rapidly this "new" technique was adopted in corrections.

Yet operant was a relatively untried treatment modality. Correctional settings were adopting this technique more on promise than accomplishment. Lavish praise had been heaped on the efficacy of the method in other areas, particularly in mental hospitals and institutions for retarded children. However, seldom could one find any solid evidence that the technique brought improvement to the success of these institutions in discharging or rehabilitating their patients.

OPERANT; TREATMENT OF CHOICE

The men who rush into undertakings of vast change usually feel they are in possession of some irresistible power (Hoffer, 1951, p. 17).

The reasons for corrections' adoption of operant with such enthusiasm and alacrity deserves some scrutiny. One of the reasons for the ready acceptance of operant was that it was relatively new. In corrections novelty frequently serves as a substitute for efficacy. It was not new in the sense that it departed in a major way from the goals of the traditional correctional program it was to supplant. Its intended accomplishment was almost isomorphic with the goal of many correctional programs: behavioural control. There are, in fact, many apparent similarities between what is standard fare in a correctional institution and the characteristics of an operant program. The emphasis on consequences for behaviour has a key position in both, although the type of consequence and the type of behaviour in question might differ. The treatment intervention is in the form of environmental manipulation — clearly characteristic of penological approaches for decades. In many ways the new operant could be perceived by the administrators as just fancy, socially acceptable, professional, "treatment appearing" versions of what generations of wardens had been providing for ages — incentive programs. The new operant did much to bolster the ego strength of many correctional administrators by showing that there was an empirical base for what they viewed as their creations. It would be comforting, in a sense, to feel that one of the reasons that operant was adopted so eagerly was that it was founded on laboratory evidence and appealed to the wardens as a logical common-sense system. In truth, it was a reinforcer for their efforts; a way for them to rapidly elevate their status through making them equal to the professionals who often before had stolen their glory. Science had finally discovered what they had known all along. No wonder it was adopted; it made their common-sense into scientific enterprise. The administrators immediately became experts in the field that so long had bothered them — treatment.

Few correctional administrators would venture into a new field unless they were prepared to withstand the criticism they might expect to receive as they usually do when they break with tradition. Operant posed little threat in this regard — they could bring innumerable "experts" to testify with clear statements as to the success of these programs elsewhere. One of the characteristics of reinforcement therapists may be that they become so versed in dispensing reinforcement that they develop strong habits of making highly reinforcing statements about their own efforts. Praise for the success of operant abounds. It is a little more difficult to find the justification for such praise.

The mental health movement is very prone to fads. Often treatment of choice is determined not by what is therapeutic but by what is fashionable (Ross, 1976). The behaviour modification movement, once it got rolling, very quickly achieved the peak of fashion. New journals for this "discipline" sprang up; "behaviour mod." clubs became active; a large number of new books were published; training centres, workshops, internships and whole departments were established in a phenomenally short time. One cannot be sure, of course, to what extent the popularity and social acceptance of the movement determined its rapid adoption by corrections but it seems, in retrospect, that it was more than just the promise of success that appealed to corrections officials. It is customary for new movements to be acclaimed through statements of their underlying principles which, too often, are simple generalizations, trite verbiage, or emotionally laden truisms whose basis is frequently evangelical zeal rather than objectivity. The chants of the behaviour modifiers, however, had great appeal; theirs was the song of science.

> Proselytizing is more a passionate search for something not yet found than a desire to bestow upon the world something we already have. . . The creed whose

legitimacy is most easily challenged is likely to develop the strongest proselytizing impulse (Hoffer, 1951, p. 102).

The proponents of behaviour modification programs generally made three claims in selling their product:

1. The treatment strategy was rigorously derived from laboratory based empirical research with animal and human subjects. The claim of scientific respectability had considerable appeal to corrections officials and not just because it provided a strong defence against political critics. Corrections in the sixties was being taken to task for basing its programs on tradition, administrative expediency and rationalism rather than on scientific enquiry. The introduction of operant coincided with the introduction of many correctional research departments, increased correctional research grant support, and heightened criminological research activity in the universities. The time was ripe, then, for the advent of an empirically based treatment program.

2. The time was particularly ripe for a treatment strategy that, its adherents claimed, was not only based on research but was itself eminently researchable. In a field where almost no adequate data were available regarding program efficacy (a source of considerable embarrassment) here was a new form of intervention which purported to make the assessment of success not only simple, possible and desirable, but essential. No program based so solidly on science could do otherwise. Now that they had the behaviourists they could find out how well "we" (the officials) were doing or how badly "they" (the offenders) were doing. Moreover, they got two birds with one stone — a "window-dressing" psychologist and a researcher who could do what they should have been doing for years. Finally, their critics would not only be reluctant, but would have serious difficulty arguing down scientific objectivity.

3. A major feature of operant programs is their apparent simplicity. The principles are few in number; easy to understand and recall; and simple to express and explain. Operant principles are not shrouded in a mystique of intellectual loftiness; they are stated in common, everyday language easily grasped by academician or layman; the jargon which characterizes so many treatment methods is almost nonexistent in operant; one does not need to have a bachelor's degree as a prerequisite to understanding the approach and, more important, one does not need years of graduate training to be an effective practitioner. Correctional administrators could readily become competent in this approach — the administrator who had a couple of undergraduate credits in psychology through extension courses could view himself as an authority on the subject. Correctional officers and "even" inmates could thoroughly understand the major principles after several courses of instruction and implement a program after some twelve weeks of training. Or so it

appeared. Operant was decidedly not "professional" as that term is misunderstood in the correctional field, and was common-sensical rather than mystical. It dealt with things one could see (behaviour) rather than with things one had to be a member of the cult to understand.

Administrators accepted operant because they were sure they understood it and, thus, could control it and the people who used it. They accepted it because it was something their own people could do — in fact, they *were* doing it only not as intensively as they ought, or as systematically. They "bought it" because their "professionals" would now be busy intensifying, systematizing, and researching what the corrections people had been doing instead of rocking the boat.

The new breed of "professional", the behaviour modifier, seemed a delightful contrast to many others of their ilk whom corrections officials had encountered. Too often the "professionals" had engendered improvements in the standard of care in the correctional setting but at considerable cost and for questionable goals.

(As The Riot progresses a newly acquired psychologist begins the role as liaison between the few hard core prisoners responsible for it and the outside authorities.)

Wiping a hairy forearm across his face, Kelley sat back on his heels. "What's goin' on out there? Fletcher still runnin' the show?"

"Yeah, him and the headshrinker. The headshrinker got into the act."

"How'd that happen?"

"Remember when you saw him leavin' the kitchen? Well, he was goin' out front. Skinny Burns drew up a petition, and Fletcher wouldn't take it out there. So Skinny saddled up the headshrinker."

"Whose side is he on?"

"The headshrinker?"

"Yeah."

"Ours, man. He's more on our side than we are. I guess you'd hav'ta call him a ring-leader. Been out front three, four times already. Acts like he's really getting his kicks. Got on the radio and said he agrees with what we're askin' for"

"What we askin' for?" (Elli, 1968, p. 111)

With this new treatment modality the institution did not have to become a hospital. One did not have to view the inmate as a poor sick patient who needed treatment and tender love and care and warmth and empathy. The administrators did not have to transfer their authority to the part-time medical staff; they just gave it to the psychologist who actually behaved more like an administrator than the administrators. The psychologist promised to make the institution more efficient and the staff's work easier. They even seemed to relish making out forms! No more would the administrator have to live with the excessive molly-coddling or the explaining away of the inmate's behaviour as a result of some mysterious inner compulsions — notions which were thought to characterize "traditional" professional programs — nor would he have to revert to rigid and regimented discipline and aversive controls. Operant was a happy medium in the treatment of offenders; it promised equity — clear-cut predictable consequences for one's behaviour delivered neither sympathetically nor harshly, just matter-of-factly, objectively, unemotionally but fairly, and on the basis of clear-cut criteria: more just than the system of justice that sent them.

Another reason for the willing acceptance of operant by corrections officials was the eagerness of the practitioners to work with the most difficult patients. Psychotherapists are often accused of working most with those who need treatment the least. They often work with only a highly selected type of patient; often those who evidence the YAVIS syndrome (young, attractive, verbal, intelligent, successful) (Schoffield, 1964). Frequently the poorly motivated, behaviourally disordered, inarticulate, negativistic inmate is seen as "unlikely to benefit from treatment". Many superintendents report the experience of having most of their "problem" inmates referred back to them as "not amenable to therapy at this time" while many of their "good" inmates were being saturated with treatment. A pleasant contrast it was, indeed, when, with the advent of operant they were invited to send their worst inmates for treatment. Many behaviour modifiers extended this invitation as their initial step in convincing the administration to adopt the behaviour modification approach. Nor were these merely extravagant claims for the power of the method; the claims were backed up by action; frequently with very dramatic effects. Here, the administrators thought, is a treatment that not only will satisfy our needs for window-dressing, but may also help us — and, as an afterthought, it might even work. These practitioners also appeared to be interested not just in altering the "psyche" of the offenders (not of much interest to an administrator if the behaviour problems didn't change, as was usually the case); they were interested in changing his *behaviour* — in ameliorating his antisocial acts and fostering his prosocial behaviour. It appeared, in short, that they seemed intent on reducing management problems, and on helping the offenders conform. Surely, this is a new breed of professionals — they speak our language, copy our methods, and even share our goals.

Finally, operant promised to be an economically feasible treatment endeavour which would be administratively efficient, cheap and quick. It would be efficient both because the approach is highly systematic and because almost all matters requiring decisions and action would be handled according to clear principles in the form of contingencies that were easily and clearly communicated, automatically enacted and relatively fixed. Discussions were required for very few decisions; logistical matters and problems would be minimal in comparison with other treatment endeavours. In most instances rather lavish grants could be obtained by the treatment staff through outside agencies to finance the project — for professional salaries, technical help, bookkeeping, and equipment and materials. The beauty of it, of course, was that the warden would not have to obtain monies for salaries for a large number of ''professionals'' — they would not be needed. These programs would utilize the facilities and the staff already available. Although the program fitted to some extent the educational rehabilitation model (in contrast to the treatment model) one did not have to wait for long periods of time until the inmate's scholastic level or internal dynamics had improved sufficiently before he might be expected to behave better. Operant promised to deliver behaviour change very quickly; attitude change and educational achievement would come about later, fostered by the inmate's new behaviour.

In sum: the psychologist with operant could do things other than those that didn't seem to work; could do so without blowing up the established system; could be expected to bring great success with major problems, and do so economically, justly, efficiently, and quickly. The new professional supported the administrator's goals and elevated his status; emphasized control of behaviour and was admirably scientific and easy to understand, and, perhaps, just perhaps, he might rehabilitate a few offenders.

The behaviour modifiers who dubbed themselves ''environmental engineers'' prided themselves on their ability to modify people's behaviour — including administrators. After all that is what their techniques purported to do. They used all of their techniques, as well as most of the foregoing arguments to sell their method. It was bought very quickly; it was easy to sell and its acceptance probably reflects not at all on the special skills of the psychologists who sold it. Yet the wardens who ''bought it'' felt that they were the ones who sold their program to the psychologists! Surely a reflection of the genuine skills of the psychologists. Or was it?

> The coroner shall summon such persons to attend an inquest as he considers advisable (R.S.O. 1970, ch. 87, s. 26(1)).

Our survey of the use of behaviour modification in corrections both impressed and dismayed us. We learned of a considerable number of ''operant conditioning'' programs being conducted not just by psychologists but by a variety of practitioners from probation officers to prison wardens. Operant was being employed throughout the range of correctional settings — from community programs for pre-delinquents to maximum security hospital programs for the criminally insane. We learned of an operant program which was designed to increase the yield of milk in a prison dairy farm* and a complex token economy designed and administered by a prison inmate. We

---

*Correctional Industries, Department of Public Institutions, State of Nebraska.

received an impressive quantity of information on correctional operant programs in the form of letters, pamphlets, brochures, manuals, journal articles, technical notes and the like. Much of the material was unpublished, and some was classified as "confidential". Many of the "operant" programs were operant in name only — they were a masquerade.

> When a youth it assigned to CHAPS, he is counseled in reference to the rules and regulations of the Arizona State Industrial School and the CHAPS Project. The student is played a tape that explains the CHAPS project and our Behavior Modification Program. . . Our Behavior Modification Program is a system that places more emphasis in rewarding adaptive behavior rather than punishing maladaptive behavior. It was, however, felt that for this program to succeed some forms of sanctions are needed (Cochise Hall Accelerated Services Project: CHAPS, cited in: Ross and McKay, 1974).
>
> Some CHAPS "sanctions": march 1–5 hours. Cochise meditation 1–15 days, transfer to Miles meditation (Ross and McKay, 1974).

Beginning with the early 1960s and up until 1974 it became almost customary to affix the label "behaviour modification" to corrections programs, particularly incentive programs, which had been in existence for decades before the beginning of laboratory investigations of operant conditioning. Unfortunately, the label was also applied to many programs which were exclusively punitive. The label was used at times as an euphemism for tyranny (Ross and McKay, 1974; Ross, 1975; Ross and Price, 1976). In one correctional jurisdiction the reduced diet which is used as a punishment for inmates already being punished by segregation was re-labelled "behaviour mod. meat loaf".

Bastardizing therapy techniques, we would argue, is characteristic of correctional treatment. The adverse effect in the case of behaviour modification was seen in 1974 when two significant events occurred.

1. The United States Bureau of Prisons halted all behaviour modification programs under way in their institutions; and
2. The L.E.A.A. withdrew funding for behaviour modification programs in corrections (Bailey, 1975a).

Interestingly one year after the United States Bureau of Prisons halted those programs, the G.A.O. (the auditing agency for Congress) condemned behaviour modification programs in three prisons: Leavenworth, El Reno, and Marion (Bailey, 1975b). The institutions' spokesman, in response, declared they were not using behaviour modification programs — what they were doing was the same but the label was dropped.

Our review of the published literature made it quite clear that as a rehabilitative tool the kind of behaviour modification programs used in correctional institutions (typically token economy, programmed learning, contingency management) was singularly unimpressive. There were twenty-four programs described in the literature which had been conducted in

TABLE 1
Institutional Programs

Senior Author	Subjects	Target Behaviours	Control Group	Follow-up
Staats (1965)	Case study	Reading problem	Case study	No
Tyler (1967)	Case study	School grades	Case study	No
Tyler and Brown (1968)	Juvenile males n = 15	Knowledge of current events	Yes	No
Meichenbaum (1968)	Juvenile females n = 10	Classroom behaviour	Yes	No
Bednar (1970)	Juvenile males n = 32	Academic achievement and behaviour	Yes	No
Clements (1968)	Adult males n = 16	School work	Yes	No
Jesness and DeRisi (1973)	Juvenile males n = 15	Classroom behaviour	Yes	No
Fineman (1968)	Juvenile males n = 20	Rule compliance	No	No
Rice (1970)	Juvenile males n = 20	Rule compliance	No	No
Burchard (1972)	Juvenile males n = 11	Aggressive behaviour	No	No
Pavlott (1971)	Juvenile females n = 60	Rule compliance	Yes	No
Krueger (1971)	Juvenile males n = 18	Positive comments	Yes	No
Burchard (1965)	Juvenile males n = 12	School behaviours	Yes	No
Tyler (1967)	Juvenile males n = 15	Institutional behaviours	Yes	No
Burchard (1972)	Case study	Aggressive behaviour	Case study	No
Wetzel (1966)	Case study	Stealing	Case study	Yes
Brown (1968)	Case study	Aggressive behaviour	Case study	No
Horton (1970)	Juvenile males n = 6	Aggressive behaviour in card-playing	No	No
Fodor (1972)	Juvenile females n = 8	A.W.O.L.	No	No
Cohen (1971)	Juvenile males n = 41	Academic and social behaviour	Yes	Yes
Jesness (1972)	Several hundred	Token economy various behaviours	Yes	Yes
McKee (1971)	Adult males n = 29	Cellblock token economy and staff training	Yes	Yes
Ross (1976)	Juvenile females n = 200	Various behaviours	Yes	Yes
Petrock (1971)	Adult males n = ?	Token economy various behaviours	No	No

TABLE 2

Institutional Programs with Follow-up

Senior Author	Subjects	Program	Control group	Major results
Cohen (1971)	Juvenile males n = 27	Programmed Learning Token economy	Questionable Control Group	Less recidivism at 1 and 2 year follow-up but = at 3 years
McKee (1975)	Adult males n = 29	Cellblock Token economy	3 control groups (n = 113) 1. Occupational training 2. Trade School 3. Regular institutional program Not matched Not randomly assigned	18 month follow-up 28% convicted of criminal offence vs 1. 47% 2. 32% 3. 37%
Jesness (1972)	Several hundred	Token economy contingency management	3 control groups: 1. Former inmates 2. Other institutions 3. T.A.	12 month follow-up Parole violations less than controls
Ross (1976)	Juvenile females n = 25	Token economy contingency management	Matched controls	12 month follow-up increased recidivism increased negative reports

institutional settings which adequately qualify as behaviour modification programs.

As can be seen from Table 1 only a small number of these programs present any outcome data related to rehabilitation. Of those that do provide outcome data (see Table 2) the adequacy of the research is, in most cases, questionable.

Our review leads us to essential agreement with that of Braukman et al. (1975) which concluded:

> In general, when program comparison between these behaviorally oriented programs and comparison programs have been possible, little or no differences in outcome have been reported (p. 311).

In fact, there is evidence that with female adolescent offenders increased recidivism has been fostered by "behaviour modification" (Ross, 1968; McKay and Ross, 1973; Ross and McKay, 1974; Ross, 1974; Ross, 1975; Ross and McKay, 1976). Perhaps too much was promised. In spite of the limitations of the research both in quality and quantity, we can conclude with confidence that behaviour modification is not the panacea it was touted as when it was introduced to corrections.

Rehabilitation of the offender, however, is only one goal of corrections (perhaps an unrealistic one); institutional management is another. In this regard there is rather impressive evidence that behaviour modification is worthwhile. In each of the programs presented in Table 1 a behavioural approach was found to be successful in either reducing anti-social behaviour in the institution or in enhancing the offenders' academic achievement or industrial productivity. Again, unfortunately, the adequacy of the available research is often poor, but there is sufficient evidence to support the conclusion that behaviour modification can be effective in institutional management and in the academic and vocational training of the offender. We should note that there now are established standards to safeguard the right of offenders in behaviour modification programs (A.P.A., 1974).

The efficacy of behaviour modification programs in community-based programs has been quite clearly demonstrated, particularly through the

TABLE 3

Community-based Programs

Senior Author	Setting	Subjects	Target Behaviour	Control Group	Follow-up
Bailey (1970)	Group home	Pre-delinquents n = 5	Classroom behaviour	No	No
Miller (1971)	School	Pre-delinquents n = 40	English classwork	No	No
Phillips (1968)	Group home	Pre-delinquents n = 3	Aggressive statements	No	No
Phillips (1971)	Group home	Pre-delinquents n = 4	Punctuality	No	No
Schwitzgebel (1964)	Street-corner	17 years 8 previous arrests n = 2	Talking to a tape recorder	Yes	Yes
Schwitzgebel (1964)	Street-corner	17 years n = 20	Interview attendance	Yes	Yes
Tharp and Wetzel (1969)	Probation	Delinquents n = 89	Various	No	Yes
Ross (1970)	Probation	Delinquents n = ?	Various	No	No
Alvord (1971)	Family behaviour management	Delinquents n = 28	Child management	No	No
Stuart (1971)	Home	Pre-delinquent n = 1	Curfew, chores	No	No
Alexander (1973)	Home	Families n = 46	Family training management	Yes	Yes
Kirigin (1975)	Group home	Pre-delinquent n = ?	Homework	No	No
Jeffrey and Jeffrey (1970)	Slum project	16-21 years n = 50	Social and academic behaviours	No	Yes
Doctor (1973)	Probation	Adults n = 24	Attending meetings; positive behaviours	No	Yes
Braukman (1974)	Group home	Pre-delinquents n = 6	Job interview skills	No	No
Weathers and Liberman (1975)	Probation	Delinquents n = 6	Family management	Yes	Yes
Werner et al. (1975)	Group home	Pre-delinquents n = 6	Interaction with police	No	No

TABLE 4

Community Programs with Follow-up

Senior Author	Subjects	Target Behaviours	Control Group	Major Results
Schwitzgebel (1964)	Males 17 years X = 8 arrests n = 20	Interview attendance and performance	Matched controls (street-corner B. Mod.)	(3 years follow-up) — fewer arrests — less "time"
Tharp and Wetzel (1969)	Males probationers n = 89	Various social and academic behaviours	Own control: A-B-A (behavioural consulting to parents, teachers)	(18 month follow-up) 1. decline in offences 2. increase in grades 3. improved behaviour ratings
Jeffrey and Jeffrey (1970)	Males delinquents n = 50	Appropriate social and academic behaviours	No controls (Slums of Washington)	Increased anti-social behaviour
Doctor and Palakow (1973)	Adults probationers n = 26	Meeting attendance: contingency management re: new positive behaviour	No control group "Baseline"	Employed time 45%→77% X prob. viol. 1.7→1.5 yr. X new arrests 2.0→0.15 yr.
Phillips (1971)	Males Pre-delinquents n = 16	Group home behaviour program	Achievement Place 2 control groups	(1 year follow-up) 19% committed to instit. vs 53%-54% controls
Kirigin et al (1975)	Males pre-delinquents n = 18	Group home behaviour program	Achievement Place Institution controls matched (matched by PO as "comparable")	(2 year follow-up) — 22% vs 47% controls committed to instit. — 56% vs 33% in school
Alexander and Parsons (1973)	Families court-referred n = 46	Behavioural family management	Controls: 1. Rogerian group 2. Psychodynamic group therapy 3. No intervention	(6.8 month follow-up) — less referral to juvenile court
Weathers and Liberman (1975)	Juvenile males probationers n = 6	Behavioural family management	Untreated control	(3 month follow-up) No effect on: curfew viol., school attendance; number of anti-social incidents or grades

pioneering street-corner work of Schwitzgebel, (1964) the Achievement Place group home programs of Hoefler, (1975) family management programs of Alexander and Parsons, (1974) and the behavioural consulting work of Tharp and Wetzel (1969) in probation.

Table 3 presents an overview of the published programs in community-based behaviour modification in corrections. Table 4 presents those programs which do provide follow-up data within an adequate research framework. Clearly, there is evidence of success.

However, not all programs either in institutions or community are successful in offender management or rehabilitation. When we examined the parameters in these behaviour modification programs we found three factors which seem to differentiate the successful programs from the failures:

1. The successful programs were not *imposed* on the offenders in authoritarian fashion but *involved* the offenders in program planning.

2. In successful programs the target behaviours were not anti-social behaviour. They sought to strengthen prosocial behaviours rather than attempting directly to reduce the frequency of inappropriate or anti-social acts. They thus avoided the pitfall of strengthening anti-social behaviour by giving it undue attention and avoided generating expectancies for anti-social behaviour.*

3. They neutralized or mobilized the offender's peer group.

Clearly behaviour modification has considerable potential for corrections, but it is no panacea. If one looks only at recidivism data one gets a gloomy picture. It is only by a close examination that one can obtain an adequate understanding of the limitations and the value of behaviour modification. If we adopt the position that treatment should be buried because nothing works across the board we are indeed throwing the baby out with the bath-water.

On the other hand there are those who would blame not the treatment but the environment — the correctional institution — and would have us discard not only the baby and the bath-water but the entire plumbing system!

We should never have promised panaceas.

REFERENCES

Alexander, J.F. and Parsons, B.V., "Short-term behavioral intervention with delinquent families: Impact on family process and recidivism," *Journal of Abnormal Psychology*, 1973, *81*, 219–225.

Alvord, J.R., "The home token economy: A motivational system for the home," *Corrective Psychiatry and Journal of Social Therapy*, 1971, *17*, 6–13.

A.P.A. Monitor, "Psychology briefs . . . START . . . unconstitutional," 1974, *12*, 5 (November).

Bailey, J.S., Wolf, M.A. and Phillips, E.L., "Home-based reinforcement and the modification of pre-delinquents' classroom behavior," *Journal of Applied Behavior Analysis*, 1970, 3, 223–233.

Bailey, C.A. (Ed.), *Corrections Digest*, 1975(a), July, *6*, 3.

Bailey, C.A. (Ed.), *Corrections Digest*, 1975(b), August, *6*, No. 17, 1.

Bednar, R.I., Zelhart, P.F., Greathouse, L. and Weinberg, S., "Operant conditioning principles in the treatment of learning and behavior problems with delinquent boys," *Journal of Counseling Psychology*, 1970, *17*, 492–497.

Braukman, C.J., Maloney, D.M., Fixsen, D.L., Phillips, E.L. and Wolf, M.M., "Analysis of a selection interview training package for pre-delinquents at achievement place," *Criminal Justice and Behavior*, 1974, *1*, 30–42.

Braukman, C.J., Fixsen, D.L., Phillips, E.L. and Wolf, M.M., "Behavioral approaches to treatment in the crime and delinquency field," *Criminology*, 1975, *13*, 299–331.

---

*For elaboration of these pitfalls, see Ross and Price (1976).

Brown, G.D. and Tyler, V.O., "Time out from reinforcement: A technique for dethroning the 'duke' of an institutionalized delinquent group," *Journal of Child Psychology and Psychiatry*, 1968, *9*, 203–211.

Burchard, J.D. and Barrera, F., "An analysis of time out and response cost in a programmed environment," *Journal of Applied Behavior Analysis*, 1972, *5*, 271–282.

Burchard, J.D. and Tyler, V., "The modification of delinquent behavior through operant conditioning," *Behavior Research and Therapy*, 1965, *2*, 245–250.

Clements, C.B. and McKee, J.M., "Programmed instruction for institutionalized offenders: Contingency management and performance contracts," *Psychological Reports*, 1968, *22*, 957–964.

Cohen, H.L. and Philipczak, J., *A New Learning Environment* (San Francisco: Jossey-Bass, 1971).

Coroners Act, R.S.O. 1970.

Doctor, R.M. and Polakow, R.L. *A Behavior Modification Program for Adult Probationers*. Presented at American Psychological Association Convention, 1973.

Elli, F., *The Riot*. (New York: Avon, 1966).

Fineman, K.R., "An operant conditioning program in a juvenile detention facility," *Psychological Reports*, 1968, *22*, 1119–1120.

Fodor, I.E., "The use of behavior modification techniques with female delinquents," *Child Welfare*, 1972, *51*, 93–101.

Griswold, H.J., Misenheimer, M., Powers, A., and Tromanhauser, E., *An Eye for An Eye* (New York: Holt, Rinehart and Winston, 1970).

Hoefler, S.A., "Achievement place: An evaluative review," *Criminal Justice and Behavior*, 1975, *2*(2), 146–168.

Hoffer, E., *The True Believer* (New York: Harper and Row, 1951).

Horton, L.E., "Generalization of aggressive behavior in adolescent delinquent boys," *Journal of Applied Behavior Analysis*, 1970, *3*, 205–211.

Jeffrey, C.R. and Jeffrey, I.A., "Delinquents and drop-outs: An experimental program in behaviour change," *Canadian Journal of Corrections*, 1970, *12*, 1–12.

Jesness, C.F. and DeRisi, W.J., "Some variations in techniques of contingency management in a school for delinquents." In J. Stumphauser (Ed.), *Behavior Therapy With Delinquents* (Springfield, Ill.: Thomas, 1973).

Jesness, C.F., DeRisi, W.J., McCormick, P.M. and Wedge, R.F., *The Youth Center Research Project* (Sacramento: California Youth Authority, July 1972).

Kirigin, K.A., Phillips, E.L., Timbers, G.A., Fixsen, D.L. and Wolf, M.M., "Achievement place." In Etzel, B., LeBlanc, J.M. and Baer, D.M. (Eds.) *New Developments in Behavioral Research: Theory, Method, and Application* (Trenton, N.J.: Lawrence Erlbaum Associates, 1975).

Krueger, D.E., *Operant Group Therapy with Deinquent Boys Using Therapist's Versus Peer's Reinforcement*, Doctoral dissertation, University of Miami, 1971.

Lipton, D., Martinson, R. and Wilks, J., *The Effectiveness of Correctional Treatment Evaluation Studies* (New York: Praeger, 1975).

McKay, H.B. and Ross, R.R., *Token Gestures for Offenders*, Presented at Canadian Psychological Association Meeting, Victoria, B.C., 1973.

McKay, H.B. "Desperate diseases require desperate remedies," *Crime and/et Justice*, 4(1), 1976.

McKee, J-M. and Clements, C.B., "A behavioral approach to learning: The Draper model." In H.C. Rickard (ed.) *Behavioral Intervention in Human Problems* (New York: Pergamon Press, 1971).

Meichenbaum, D., Bowers, K. and Ross, R.R., "Modification of classroom behavior of institutionalized female adolescent offenders," *Journal of Behavior Therapy and Research*, 1968, 6, 343–353.

Miller, L.J., *Effects of tokens and tokens with backup reinforcers on the academic performance of juvenile delinquents*, Unpublished doctoral dissertation, University of Kansas, 1971.

Palmer, T., "Martinson revisited, "*Journal of Research in Crime and Delinquency*, 1975, 12(2), 133–152.

Pavlott, J., *Effects of reinforcement procedures on negative behaviors in delinquent girls*. Unpublished doctoral dissertation, University of Pittsburgh, 1971.

Petrock, F. and Yeargan, C. *Readjustment Unit Project: A Behavior Modification/Therapeutic Community in a Maximum Security Correctional Setting.* Unpublished manuscript, Youth Reception Centre, Yardsville, New Jersey, 1971.

Phillips, E.L., "Achievement place: Token economy reinforcement procedures in a home-style rehabilitation setting for 'pre-delinquent' boys," *Journal of Applied Behavior Analysis*, 1968, 1, 213–223.

Phillips, E.L., "Achievement place: Token economy reinforcement procedures in a home style rehabilitation setting for pre-delinquent boys," *Journal of Applied Behavior Analysis*, 1971, 4, 45–49.

Rice, P.R., "Educo-therapy: A new approach to delinquent behavior," *Journal of Learning Disabilities*, 1970, 3, 16–23.

Rose, D.S., Sundel, M., DeLange, J., Corwin, L. and Palumbo, A., "The hartwig project: A behavioral approach to the treatment of juvenile offenders." In R. Ulrich, R. Stachnik and J. Mabry (Eds.), *Control of Human Behavior*, 2 (New York: Scott, Foreman, 1970).

Ross, R.R., *Problems in Applying the Operant Model to Treating Delinquency*. Paper presented at Clarke Institute of Psychiatry, Toronto, July 1968.

Ross, R.R. and McKay, H.B., *Token Gestures for Offenders*. Paper presented at Annual meeting of Canadian Psychological Association, Victoria, 1973.

Ross, R.R. and McKay, H.B., *Rewards for Offenders: Modifying the Correctional Environment*. Unpublished manuscript, University of Waterloo, 1974.

Ross, R.R., *Treatment of Adolescent Offenders: Some New Findings*. Presentation at Conference on Research in Corrections, Parliament Buildings, Toronto, 1974.

Ross, R.R., *The Effectiveness of Behavioral Treatment Programs for Female Delinquents in a Correctional Institution*. Paper presented at Symposium: "New trends in Criminology," Simon Fraser University, Vancouver, B.C., April 1975.

Ross, R.R. and McKay, H.B. *Behavior Modification and the Offender Therapist: Are They Compatible?* Paper presented at annual meeting of the Canadian Psychological Association, Quebec City, June 1975.

Ross, R.R. and McConkey, N., "Behavior modification with the offender: An annotated bibliography," *Canadian Journal of Criminology and Corrections*, 1975 (Special Supplement).

Ross, R.R. and Price, M.J., "Behavior modification in corrections: Autopsy before mortification," *International Journal of Criminology and Penology*, 1976, *4*, 305–315.

Ross, R.R. and McKay, H.B., "A study of institutional treatment programs," *International Journal of Offender Therapy and Comparative Criminology*, 1976, *20*, 165–173.

Ross, R.R., *Behavior Modification in the Control and Treatment of the Offender*. Presented at Criminology Colloquium, University of Ottawa, 1976.

Schoffield, W., *Psychotherapy: The Purchase of Friendship* (Englewood Cliffs, New Jersey: Prentice-Hall, 1964).

Schwitzgebel, R.L. and Kolb, D.A., "Inducing behavior change in adolescent delinquents," *Behavior Research and Therapy*, 1964, *1*, 297–304.

Schwitzgebel, R.L., *Street Corner Research: An Experimental Approach to the Juvenile Delinquent* (Cambridge: Harvard University Press, 1964).

Staats, A.W. and Butterfield, W.H., "Treatment of nonreading in a culturally deprived delinquent: An application of reinforcement principles," *Child development*, 1965, *36*, 925–942.

Stuart, R.B., "Behavioral Contracting within the families of delinquents," *Journal of Behavior Therapy and Experimental Psychiatry*, 1971, 2, 1–11.

Stuart, R.B., *Trick or Treatment: How and When Psychotherapy Fails* (Champaign, Illinois: Research Press, 1970).

Tharp, R.G. and Wetzel, R.J., *Behavior Modification in the Natural Environment* (New York: Academic Press, 1969).

Tyler, V.O., "Application of operant token reinforcement to academic performance of an institutionalized delinquent," *Psychological Reports*, 1967, *21*, 249–260.

Tyler, V.O. and Brown, G.D., "The use of swift, brief isolation as a group control device for institutionalized delinquents," *Behavior Research and Therapy*, 1967, *5*, 1–9.

Weathers, L. and Liberman, R.P., "Contingency contracting with families of delinquent adolescents, "Behavior Therapy, 1975.

Werner, J.S., Minkin, N., Minkin, B.L., Fixsen, D.L., Phillips, E.L. and Wolf, M.M., " 'Intervention package': An analysis to prepare juvenile delinquents for encounters with police officers," *Criminal Justice and Behavior*, 1975, 2: 55–83.

Wetzel, R., "Use of behavioral techniques in a case of compulsive stealing," *Journal of Consulting Psychology*, 1966, *30*, 367–374.

Wilks, J. and Martinson, R., "Is the treatment of criminal offenders really necessary?" *Federal Probation*, 1976, March, 3–9.

Chapter 3

Treatment Destruction Techniques*

Michael R. Gottfredson

The conventional wisdom in criminology is that rehabilitation has been found to be ineffective. In fact, the lack of demonstrated effectiveness is agreed upon by criminologists of nearly every persuasion and theoretical orientation:

> True successes in rehabilitation have been virtually nonexistent (Doleschal and Klapmuts, 1973:610).

> Rehabilitative treatment has not been shown to be effective in reducing recidivism: the recidivism rates of those treated in different programs by different methods do not differ from the rates of those not treated at all, whether in the U.S. or elsewhere (van den Haag, 1975:188).

> In the last few years . . . the weight of informed opinion in the United States about correctional rehabilitation has shifted to the negative. Rehabilitation, while still recognized as a meritorious goal, is no longer seen as a practical possibility within our correctional structure by the empirical observer (Conrad, 1973:208).

Even a panel from the National Research Council of the National Academy of Sciences, in a report on deterrence and incapacitation, argues that rehabilitation is ineffective:

> The available research on the impact of various treatment strategies both in and out of prison seems to indicate that, after controlling for initial selection

---

*Gottfredson, M.R., "Treatment destruction techniques," *Journal of Research in Crime and Delinquency*, 1979, January, 39–54. Copyright © 1979, Journal of Research in Crime and Delinquency. Reprinted by permission.

differences, there are generally *no statistically significant* differences between the subsequent recidivism of offenders, regardless of the form of "treatment" (National Research Council, 1978:66; emphasis added).

Confronted with this unanimity, there are still those who persist in their attempts to reopen the case for treatment and to argue the facts with claims of a scientific point of view (see, e.g., Palmer, 1975, and Adams, 1977). These revisionists suggest that if traditional standards of scientific proof are applied to much of the treatment research literature — for example, standards relating to the control of extraneous variance, sampling, and the reliability and validity of instrumentation — many of the better studies in the field provide us with knowledge about effective treatment. Some defenders of conventional wisdom dismiss this revisionism simply by questioning the motives and objectivity of those who suggest that there are convincing indications that some treatment programs are effective and that further research is desirable. But motives can only be inferred, making them inherently disputable and, hence, inconclusive evidence in rebuttals. Fortunately, there is a variety of general principles (or, more accurately, pseudoscientific criteria) that may be invoked to fend off any attack on our conventional wisdom regarding the effectiveness of treatment.

In fact, there are at least five distinguishable methods that may be used to demonstrate the ineffectiveness of any and all treatment modalities in the criminal justice system. Individually (but, most effectively, in combination), these methods are capable of destroying any positive results that might appear in the literature. Perhaps more important, each can be used to show that continuing research in the area would be a mistake. Because of the power inherent in these methods, it may well be useful to describe and catalog them carefully; many of them are already an integral part of the working vocabulary of many criminologists. Because no study or research proposal can withstand an assault from a carefully chosen arsenal of these destruction techniques, their value is obvious; they will be defined briefly below and examples of their use will be provided.[1]

CONTAMINATE THE TREATMENT

To contaminate the treatment, simply raise plausible alternative interpretations for the reported effect. Not plausible interpretations that suggest there

---

[1]These methods should not be confused with standard methodological criteria that have been established for the conduct of behavioral research (such as sampling principles, reliability of instrumentation, and principles of experimental design). The distinction is that, to be applicable, standard methodological critiques depend on what the treatment researchers have done, whereas the destruction techniques discussed here do not. The methods described here can always be invoked (for instance, regardless of the rigor of the sampling design) and therefore are probably more useful.

was *no* effect; on the contrary, suggest that the effect reported in the study was due to some treatment *other than that suggested by the authors of the study*. Obviously, if there is ambiguity about precisely *what* caused an effect, it is absurd to claim effectiveness. The method is universally applicable, and capable of use against the best studies, the most rigorous designs.

As with all the treatment destruction techniques discussed here, the style with which this method is invoked is critical. Rarely is the concern in evaluations of treatment studies with the specific study per se. We are interested in a bigger issue — the effectiveness of rehabilitation in the criminal justice system. To that end, the critique of individual studies should have a psychological impact that is lasting and generalizable. And that is a matter of *style*.

Clues to effective style for contaminating the treatment are available in the literature. Timing appears to be essential. For maximum impact, the technique should be invoked only after a review of the study has appeared to show a substantial treatment effect. Let the reader grasp this ray of light in an otherwise darkened room of negative findings. Suddenly, snap the windowshade shut by contaminating the treatment. When properly done, the method has such power that the reader is likely to generalize, if only to avoid the appearance of seeing light. Some examples will demonstrate the power of the technique:

> There is a third study that does report an overall positive finding as opposed to a partial one. Truax (1966) found that girls subjected to group psychotherapy and then released were likely to spend less time reincarcerated in the future. But what is most interesting about this improvement is the very special and important circumstance under which it occurred. The therapists chosen for this program did not merely have to have the proper analytic training; they were specially chosen for their "empathy" and "non-possessive warmth." In other words, it may well have been the therapists' special personal gifts rather than the fact of treatment itself which produced the favorable result. (Martinson, 1974:32)

Note how adroitly the glimmer of hope is first raised, and then is followed by a rapid shot of contamination. (When applying this method, it is of utmost importance that the critic not spawn further treatment research by attempting to resolve the rival hypotheses.)

Multiple contamination is usually more effective than a single rival hypothesis:

> Five of these studies have dealt with youthful probationers from 13 to 18 who were assigned to probation officers with small caseloads or provided with other ways of receiving more intensive supervision. . . . These studies report that, by and large, intensive supervision does work — that the specially treated youngsters do better according to some measure of recidivism. Yet these studies left some important questions unanswered. For instance, was this improved performance a function merely of the number of contacts a youngster had with his probation officer? Did it also depend on the length of time in treatment? Or was it the quality of supervision that was making the difference rather than the quantity? (Martinson, 1974:42)

Some scientific-minded observers will note that contaminating the treatment is pure scientific method; when applied to experimental research generally, it sets the stage for future research because a significant effect, even if there is uncertainty about what caused it, can be studied further by designing another experiment to separate out various competing factors. Such reasoning, however, should not deter those employing the contaminate-the-treatment destruction technique. To accept this general approach would require an admission that research in treatment, as in all science, is a cumulative process. Acceptance of such principles implies that treatment research should continue, a conclusion that is inconsistent with the demands of conventional wisdom, as will be shown below. In any event, when embedded in a review of what is known about treatment, this technique can always prove that nothing is known with *certainty*.

STRESS THE CRITERION PROBLEM

Many treatment strategies in criminal justice have as their aim the reduction of the probability of future law violations on the part of those treated. They therefore require as a criterion measure some indicator of illegal behavior. But because, as everyone knows, it is impossible to measure illegal conduct accurately, every study is vulnerable to attack on the basis of the criterion problem. Not all parole violators are criminal; not all those engaged in illegal conduct are caught (or better yet, discovered); not all those arrested are guilty; not all those arrested are convicted. So, regardless of the care given to refinement of outcome measures, the criterion is vulnerable. If the investigators use arrest, point out it was not conviction. If they use conviction, ask about those not caught. If they use self-reported measures, wonder aloud about the veracity of criminals.[2] It is a perfectly general technique — no study is immune. Simply raising the aura of the criterion problem is usually sufficient to question the effectiveness of treatment.[3]

Stressing the criterion problem has two applications. First, it can be used to destroy an individual study, by questioning the specific criterion chosen by the authors. Second, it can be used to show generally that every study ever undertaken — or, more important, that ever will be undertaken — is suspect.

---

[2]Disregard the generally high consistency among these measures for serious illegal behavior. If the investigators are presumptuous enough to use criteria other than measures of illegal conduct (e.g., changes in attitudes, work habits, or self-concept), simply point out that the main concern of the criminal justice system is crime and not self-actualization. Either way you've got them.

[3]There is absolutely no obligation to attempt to ferret out the potential impact of the criterion problem on the size of the effect reported or even to be specific about how the experimental/control differences could result from a particular criterion problem.

Some crusty philosophers of science will undoubtedly argue that the criterion problem is universal in science. Accuracy in measurement, they will point out, is always a matter of degree, and progress in science is largely attributed to refining the tools by which we observe nature. Thus, there are no perfectly reliable and valid criteria, only goals toward which we strive. What is important, they will argue, is that the criterion used have *some* validity (the more the better, admittedly) and that the association between the treatment and the criterion rest on this true variance.

Treatment researchers are likely to argue that major improvements have been made in recent years regarding measurement of the criterion. Thus, they will argue, multiple-outcome measures are now fairly common, and some research even attempts to scale the criterion along a seriousness dimension. Some might even note that many effectiveness claims are supported regardless of the criterion used. The main points they are likely to make is that the criterion problem should be recognized, serious efforts should be made to deal with it in research, and results should be interpreted in light of the potential bias associated with the criterion.

Those familiar with recent advances in criminology will perceive the fatal defect in these arguments. Rehabilitation in criminal justice is concerned with changing the behavior of those treated, but the "behavior" of those treated is dependent on the behavior of agents of social control. Criminals are those whom agents of social control choose to define as criminal; thus, any criterion of criminality may be as much a measure of the behavior of social control agents as a measure of the behavior of the persons in the sample. The first hypothesis that must be advanced upon the discovery of an "effective" treatment, therefore, is that it was the behavior of the agents of social control that was altered, not the behavior of the sample.[4] In its extreme, this technique effectively negates the claim that the criterion in treatment research has *any* true variance, thus refuting the notion that rehabilitation ever could work since it attempts to change something that does not exist.

Perhaps the most effective example of the use of "stressing the criterion problem" is provided in a recent critique of the California Community Treatment Program (CTP) (Lerman, 1975). Using parole revocation rates as a measure of recidivism, the treatment researchers claimed effectiveness (Palmer, 1971). However, Lerman shows that the rate of parole *suspensions* for alleged violations — which he terms "youth behavior" — is greater for the experimental group than for the control group. But, because the experimental group had lower rates of *revocation* than the controls, Lerman concludes:

---

[4]Only the cynic will argue that it doesn't matter and that if criminality is largely socially constructed, then effecting treatment by altering the definitional propensity of agents of social control is a successful treatment.

> In actuality, CTP can only demonstrate that rates of official decision making changed. The program influenced the labeling and social control process, and not the rates of behavioral input that presumably triggers the discretionary reactions to youth. (Lerman, 1975:61)

His argument is that the farther into the criminal justice process one penetrates (in this case from parole suspensions to parole revocations), the less likely one is to obtain criteria that are valid.

Of course it would be possible to make the argument the other way around (i.e., to argue that these criteria demonstrate effectiveness). The experimental group was much more closely supervised and therefore at greater risk of being *suspended* by parole agents, and the treatment program for some experimentals included brief suspensions for acts probably not *typically* resulting in a suspension.[5] Therefore, it might be preferable to use as a criterion some measure that involves a relatively independent assessment of the legitimacy of the charges (e.g., by a parole board at a *revocation* hearing) and the seriousness of the infractions. Some might argue that this would be reimprisonment, the criterion used by CTP.[6] But Lerman (1975:50) rebuts this logic: "The further we proceed in the discretionary labeling process in order to obtain violational data, the greater is the likelihood that we shall be measuring *official* behavior rather than youth behavior." Thus, according to Lerman, investigations are more valid than arrests, arrests more valid than charges, and charges more valid than convictions as criteria for treatment studies. The fact that others may suggest, and frequently have suggested, exactly the opposite is the outstanding feature of this destruction technique.

Although there are numerous ways that the criterion problem may be stressed, the general argument always should be that because no criminality criterion is *completely* valid, it is impossible to know anything. One particularly destructive technique is to point out that the *absence* of recidivism might be more indicative of the failure of treatment than is the presence of recidivism:

---

[5] It is fairly easy to cull from the data support for the "differential at-risk" hypothesis. The suspension rate for the experimental group for status offenses and technical violations was three times as great as was the suspension rate for the control group for these offenses. It would seem logical that at least part of this difference can be attributed to the much closer supervision by parole officers in the experimental group because the treatment plan called for intensive supervision. By extension, the closer supervision probably also accounts for some of the suspensions for more serious charges in the experimental group as well.

[6] Considerable support for the use of this criterion is provided in additional follow-up data reported by Palmer (1974). It should be noted that revocation was not the sole criterion reported by the CTP staff, but rather they reported a large array of criterion measures (see, e.g., Palmer, 1974).

Recidivism should not be confused with social maladjustment, nor should the absence of recidivism be equated with rehabilitation. Because an offender does not again become involved with the criminal justice system, one cannot assume that he is socially adjusted or rehabilitated. He may, in fact, be a more effective criminal, or he may not engage in criminal activity but may be deviant in a variety of other ways — for example, he may be unemployed or he may be mentally ill. (Lipton, Martinson, and Wilks, 1975:608)

Stressing the criterion problem essentially involves demonstrating the lack of a one-to-one relationship between the study's measure of recidivism and actual illegal conduct. Since this technique invokes a standard that is unattainable in behavioral research, and despite the fact that such a standard is unnecessary for scientific confidence, it is extremely effective and totally general. It might be noted that this destruction technique could be used in reverse (i.e., to point out that a claim of ineffectiveness cannot be made with certainty). But this use of the method is of limited interest and will not be discussed here in detail.

SHOW THAT MASSIVE EFFORTS HAVE FAILED (APPEAL TO COMMON SENSE)

The treatment ideology has dominated our thinking about crime for decades. On the basis of this ideology, massive investments have been made in programs and personnel. After all this effort, it is time we learned to recognize failure when we see it. If this plethora of resources has failed to produce unambiguous demonstrations of effectiveness, why continue the search?

The choice of the unit of analysis for demonstrating that massive efforts have failed is critical. It can be either money or time; it should not be the number of rigorous, independent experimental studies that have been undertaken. Nor should the focus be placed on the extent of careful program development with sound implementation of theoretically useful treatments. That is, if the number of scientifically acceptable studies in conjunction with quality treatment programs are used to judge the amount of effort expended thus far, the treatment proponents' cry that "it has never been tried" might appear credible.

Bailey's oft-cited survey of the literature published during the twenty-year period between 1940 and 1960 uncovered only 22 studies with "some form of control group design." Seventeen of these (77 percent) were reported to have positive results. Robison and Smith (1971), another frequently cited review, discussed only 10 studies, clearly not chosen to be representative of the literature, most of which did not involve experimental designs. Wright and Dixon (1977) searched the juvenile delinquency literature for studies conducted between 1965 and 1974, finding only 9 that used "random assignment of subjects, inferential analyses of their data, an outcome measure of delinquent behavior (self-reported, police records, court records), and at least six months' follow-up after the subjects had left the project." Of these, 6 (67 percent) reported positive results. Logan (1967) reviewed 100 studies, published between about 1940 and 1970, 18 of which had both some form of control group (loosely defined) and some follow-up in the community. Ten of these (56 percent) were evaluated by Logan to have positive results.

If these reviews of the treatment literature do not appear to rebut the treatment researcher's harp that "it hasn't been tried yet," the massive review of Lipton, Martinson, and Wilks (1975) must. These authors reviewed 231 treatment studies in corrections, published between 1945 and 1967. However, those researchers claiming that "it hasn't been tried" are not likely to be satisfied with this 231 figure. They are likely to point out that, of these 231, only 138 used some measure of recidivism as a criterion. Of these, only 65 used a design that met the minimum standards for scientific confidence; that is, a design in which (1) "the researcher can effectively control the selection of subjects, the administration of treatment, the measurement of variables and physically control or restrict the interference of unwanted outside factors" (Lipton et al., 1975:16); and (2) there is either a matched or a random allocation control group. Of these 65, the treatment advocates are likely to stress that 32 (49 percent) reported positive results. If the field of studies is further restricted according to the quality ratings given by Lipton et al. (1975) to only "A" studies ("acceptable for the survey with no more than minimal research shortcomings")[7] then the number falls to 40. Of these, 19 (48 percent) reported positive results.[8] Those who claim that "it hasn't been tried" will undoubtedly argue that the large number of *potential* studies, given the vast array of types of offenses, types of offenders, and types of treatment — when coupled with the strong indicators of success reported to date — suggests that 40 studies hardly scratch the surface. These studies might best be viewed, they may argue, as the foundation for further research.

Therefore, when invoking the critique that massive efforts have failed to uncover substantial treatment effects, it is clear that it is the efforts of the reviewers rather than the efforts of the researchers that should be alluded to. The *reviewers* have searched through decades of literature and scrutinized hundreds of studies to reach the conclusion of ineffectiveness, whereas the *researchers* have undertaken only about three dozen control group studies with random allocation. Clearly, it is preferable to stress that the ideology of

---

[7]"B" studies were "acceptable for the survey with research shortcomings that place reservations on interpretation of findings" (Lipton et al., 1974:6). The authors do not specify the criteria used to classify the studies into "A" or "B".

[8]The restrictions used to arrive at the 40 studies are those required for a study to receive a "1A" or "2A" rating by Lipton et al. All of the "1A" studies (five) reported statistically significant results in the direction favorable to the treatment hypothesis.

the criminal justice system has been geared toward rehabilitation for *decades*, rather than to note that the average number of scientifically acceptable studies during 1940–65 *soared* to one per year.[9]

DEMONSTRATE THAT TREATMENT STRATEGIES ARE PREMISED ON FAULTY THEORY

If it can be demonstrated that the assumptions upon which rehabilitative programs are built are false, then, as a consequence, the empirical claims of all treatment programs must also be false. This method is not only a useful mechanism by which entire classes of studies can be destroyed, but it can also effectively deny the utility of further research into the question. Obviously, there is little need to ascertain the empirical validity of theoretically impossible relationships.

There are several routes that may be taken in disproving the theory of rehabilitation, but since they all ultimately arrive at the same point, there is little practical benefit in choosing one over the other. They all destroy the need for future research. The most common method is what may be referred to as the "medical delusion." Because it is the most widely agreed-upon means of showing that all rehabilitation is premised upon faulty theory, a brief discussion of how it works is warranted.

That all rehabilitative programs rest on the "medical delusion" and, as a consequence, are doomed to empirical failure is easy to prove. This probably accounts for the technique's widespread adoption:

> Our present treatment programs are based on a theory of crime as a "disease" — that is to say, as something foreign and abnormal in the individual which can presumably be cured. (Martinson, 1974:49)

> Only diseases can be cured by treatment. Few offenders are sick. (van den Haag, 1975:188)

> The treatment approach assumes that the causes of crime, which inhere somewhere in the person of the offender or in his social situation and must be remedied, are *pathological*. By this is meant that offenders are *abnormal* in a way which makes them socially *unhealthy*. (Weiler, 1974:124)

The "rehabilitationists" must necessarily view delinquency or criminality as symptomatic of pathology. In order to eradicate the symptom, the theory

---

[9]See, for example, Lerman's statement that "Robison and Smith (1971), reviewing over a decade of innovative correctional research, reached a similar conclusion regarding ineffectiveness" (1975:95). This is more compatible with the "massive efforts" technique than a report that "Robison and Smith (1971), reviewing ten studies, some of which were capable of providing evidence on the question, reached a similar conclusion regarding ineffectiveness."

goes, it is necessary to cure the pathology. To support this idea, the "rehabilitationists" must construct a faulty world view, consisting of the dichotomous classification of the criminal (sick) on the one hand and the law abider (healthy) on the other. The destruction technique, therefore, simply consists of noting the theoretical implausibility of this medical delusion. Obviously, we are all capable of committing crimes. If necessary it is even possible to point to data showing that everyone does bad things sometimes.

Some treatment researchers are likely to resent this portrait of their theories as being a naive caricature. When pressed, they are likely to agree with Schur (1973:29) that "the treatment reaction is grounded in the *assumption of basic differentness*," but they would typically refer to these as individual differences. Many of them would disagree, however, that they ever said, or meant to imply, that criminality is an all-or-nothing affair. Rather, what most behavioral scientists mean by the phrase "individual differences" is a *continuum* of behavioral differences (see Hirschi, 1975). There are a few saints, a few sinners, and a lot of folks somewhere in between. Such a notion is consistent with, and usually demanded by, every positivistic theory of etiology, be it psychological, sociological, or economic. It is even consistent with the data showing that everyone does bad things sometimes — and the same data that show that a few people do bad things much more than others (see Hirschi, 1975). Depending on the theory, most "rehabilitationists" would argue that these differences (variations) arise from differences (variations) in the ways that parents, siblings, friends, teachers, school systems, and the economic order are experienced by people as they move through life. Some say what is important is the way these factors produce criminality: others, the way that they inhibit it. Few would claim that these factors produce two altogether different kinds of people. The treatment task is to identify which of these producing or inhibiting factors are capable of being decreased or enhanced. They would argue that emphasizing the statement of *some* rehabilitationists, who clearly do ascribe to the medical model (e.g., Menninger, 1968), as being a logically required premise for *all* rehabilitation programs is unfair. Thus, they might argue that whether or not some forms of vocational education programs reduce recidivism for some offenders is a question that can be answered apart from an assumption that job skills cure the disease of unemployment.

These arguments are no impediment to the use of the "medical delusion" technique. "Correction," "diagnostic center," and "treatment" — the very terms used by rehabilitationists — demand a medical analogy. The theory of crime as pathology, which is the least common denominator of all rehabilitation programs, confuses a moral judgment with a medical judgment.

Continuing their rebuttal, many who cling to the rehabilitative ideal will argue that not only is it false to claim that all rehabilitation programs are based on the single faulty theory of pathology, but also that most programs have never been based on *any* theory. At that point they should be attacked for engaging in atheoretical research.

SEEK UNIVERSALS

This is perhaps the most widely known of the various destruction techniques (see, e.g., Palmer, 1975). In seeking universals, it is only necessary to show either (1) that although the treatment method has been found to work with some offenders, it is ineffective with others, or, more simply, (2) that it has not even been tried on everyone.

Palmer (1975:140), although clearly critical of the method, demonstrates its utility and generality. Using the example of group counseling, he points out:

> if, out of ten studies, three or four were associated with negative outcomes, then the findings for *group counseling as a whole* would be considered conflicting or contradictory, even though all remaining studies may have produced clear positive results. Whether or not any specific patterns of success had been observed — e.g., in connection with older adolescent girls (say that every study of this offender group, four in all, yielded positive results) — it would still be the case that the method of group counseling, when viewed as a totality, would have failed to satisfy the criterion in question. . . . (Palmer, 1975:140)

Martinson (1974) demonstrates application of the method to community treatment. He asks whether "the way to rehabilitate offenders is to deal with them outside an institutional setting" (Martinson, 1974:38), and then proceeds to review studies of community treatment ranging from Outward Bound programs, individual psychotherapy in the community, and group psychotherapy in the community, to intensive supervision and parole. Some dealt with adolescents, others with adults; some with individuals, others with gangs. Despite the fact that at some levels of disaggregation (e.g., individual counseling with adolescents)[10] there are notable and consistent positive results, *taken as a whole*, the results of community treatment are mixed. Thus, invoking the technique of "seeking universals," Martinson (1974:47) concludes the review of the section by saying, "In sum, even in the case of treatment programs administered outside penal institutions, we simply cannot say that this treatment in itself has an appreciable effect on offender behavior."

As Palmer (1975) has noted, the relative size of the offender subgroup for which the treatment is shown to be effective does not appear to be an impediment to the use of this destruction technique. Something either works for everyone or it does not.

---

[10]For example, in Lipton, Martinson, and Wilks (1975:213), the parent study serving as a basis for Martinson's review, the authors conclude, "While clearly definitive information is not yet available, it appears that individual psychotherapy administered to young offenders in the community can be effective in reducing recidivism when it is focused on immediate, day-to-day problems rather than being psychodynamically oriented."

In case the generality inherent in the method is not apparent, it should be stressed that the only thing required to make it work is to increase the level of aggregation. Thus, of some types of individual psychotherapy work with young institutionalized males, as apparently they do (Lipton, Martinson, and Wilks, 1975:211), but not with institutionalized young females, aggregate the two subgroups and conclude that individual counseling fails (see, e.g., Martinson, 1974:31).

SOME SELECTED SUMMARY TECHNIQUES

A truly effective treatment destruction effort does not cease with the demonstration that the results of a particular study, or group of studies, cannot be interpreted unambiguously. Embedded within every treatment study worthy of destruction are the seeds of policy analysis, waiting only for the critic to bring them to fruition.

Perhaps the most powerful argument against rehabilitation (and, by extension, against research in the area) is that it offends our sense of moral decency. The ultimate criterion for a rehabilitative strategy is that it works to prevent crime. There is nothing *inherent* in the theory that places any limit on the amount of punishment that can be invoked in the name of treatment:

> These treatments have on occasion become, and have the potential for becoming, so draconian as to offend the moral order of a democratic society. (Martinson, 1974:46)

Rehabilitationists will be hard pressed to dispute the fact that things have been done in the past in the name of rehabilitation that are offensive, regardless of whether or not they "worked." And, on a purely philosophical basis, there are no restraints on the severity of punishment permissible under the treatment rationale. Thus, the treatment philosophy has permitted the castration of sex offenders and lobotomies of the "incurably" violent.

Those who cling to the rehabilitative ideal will undoubtedly argue that every punishment philosophy — whether based on utilitarian aims or not — has trouble with the notion of limits. Thus, there is nothing *inherent* in the general deterrence doctrine that prohibits whipping parking violators, provided that it would effectively deter. Similarly with incapacitation: hanging pickpockets (or, less severely, cutting off their hands) is a sure method of precluding their opportunity to offend. As for retribution, the rehabilitationists might argue that getting even is seldom regarded as enough.

Those who cling to rehabilitation might even argue that, as with rehabilitation, the alternative punishment rationales have in fact gotten out of hand in the past. Pickpockets actually have been hanged to prevent the picking of pockets by others, and blood feuds inspired by retribution have tended to get bloody. They might even point to modern incapacitation-based preventive detention laws that allow punishment even in the absence of a finding of guilt.[11] They are likely to argue that setting limits on punishments is a complex issue, usually contingent on several punishment rationales as well as the offense under consideration (see O'Leary, Gottfredson, and Gelman, 1975).

Of course, these arguments need not be addressed. The task is to destroy treatment, not to defend the alternatives.

A derivative postulate of the notion that immorality is inherent in treatment is the now firmly established truth that benevolence is actually tyranny in disguise. In criminal justice, the overwhelming evidence indicates that well-intentioned reforms have evil consequences.[12] The link that needs to be established is that rehabilitation researchers essentially are trying to do good for the offender. Most researchers in the area would probably not dispute this (although most might argue that they also are seeking programs that do good for society as well). They probably believe that being hanged, incarcerated, or otherwise penalized is typically not in the best interests of most people. Thus, these researchers are likely to suggest that if they can somehow get people to stop doing things that have the potential of getting them hanged, incarcerated, or otherwise penalized, this might be beneficial for the offender. Most would argue, however, that there are some things that could be done to offenders to keep them out of jail that would not, ultimately, be in the offenders' best interests; that is, treatment researchers would probably claim that they could distinguish between vocational education and prefrontal lobotomies.

The destruction technique requires noting only that the *motives* underlying treatment research have led to evil consequences. Because all treatment strategies are ultimately motivated by the "best interests of the client" and because it can be shown that such motives in the past have produced results contrary to the best interests of the client, every program is suspect. Hence, the issue of effectiveness need not be raised.

Occasionally, a treatment research program comes along that, on its face, appears to be an exception to the law that beneficient motives produce tyrannical results. Ignoring the lessons of the past, the researchers might claim boldly that it is possible both to reduce recidivism effectively and to do so within the boundaries of common decency. Initially, this appeared to be the case with the famous Community Treatment Project (CTP). However, behind the facade of the "community treatment" perspective lay a punitive result, as Lerman (1975) has shown. Because the methods of proof used by Lerman appear capable of generalization, a discussion of them might be useful in the event that similar research programs are proposed in the future.

---

[11]Rehabilitationists might also point out that many of the most onerous punishments — such as castration and lobotomies — that have been attributed to a rehabilitative rationale actually were based on an incapacitative intent.

[12]Curiously, most contemporary reformers use this fact as a basis for urging that their reforms would be beneficial.

Briefly, the CTP research initially set out to accomplish three goals[13]: (1) to test the feasibility of releasing some California Youth Authority (CYA) wards directly to a treatment program in the community, (2) to determine the effectiveness of this community-based treatment, and (3) to develop hypotheses about differential treatment plans. The design appeared straightforward. Eligible cases were to be assigned randomly to experimental and control groups. The control cases went the traditional CYA route and experimentals into a three-staged program: Stage A was an intensive period of treatment lasting about eight months; Stage B was a transition period; and Stage C was a minimum supervision period. The differential treatment strategy was to be based on the theory of interpersonal maturity.

The tyranny latent in the program eventually was uncovered by Lerman. He demonstrated that the experimental group was, in fact, subject to more social control than treatment; the average amount of time in detention for the experimentals was about ten times the average amount of time spent in "treatment," according to Lerman's calculations. Thus, he concludes, the program for the experimentals was far more punitive than it was beneficial.

Lerman was being generous by his calculations. He only defined *detentions* as "social control." After all, the experimentals were under some form of state control *twenty-four hours a day*, either in detention or under parole supervision. Using this broader concept of social control, the ratio of social control to treatment increases from 10 to 1 to about 60 to 1.

The genius of the method, of course, rests on the selection of the basis for comparison. The treatment researchers might argue that the proper comparison should be between the ratio of treatment to social control in the experimental group and the same ratio in the control group. A comparison of these ratios, they might argue, would indicate that the experimentals received a greater dose of treatment relative to social control than did the persons in the traditional CYA program. That is, they might argue that the basis for comparison should be the cases regularly processed, rather than a standard of no social control at all. Pointing to Lerman's (1975:53) figures for noncriminal violators, they might argue that the experimental group averaged 18 days in detention compared to the average of 240 days experienced by the control group during the first 8 months of the social control period (a ratio of about 13 to 1 in favor of the experimentals). Or, being fair, they might include the detention periods for the entire project, since the data subsequent to the initial phase are somewhat more supportive of the benevolence-turned-tyranny doctrine. This would produce an average of 258 detention days for the controls and 24 for the experimentals (and the ratio plummets to about 11 to 1). Thus, they might argue that, when compared to the control group, the experimental group experienced far less social control.

---

[13]This description is adapted from Lerman (1975:20–22).

The destruction technique can withstand this logic. The program staff promised *treatment*, and even using Lerman's conservative figures, they delivered more social control than treatment. Because anything compared with nothing will always be greater than nothing, it will always be possible to prove that all treatment programs in criminal justice involve more social control than does absolute freedom.

CONCLUSION

Although implausible, in the event that a combination of these destruction techniques does not convincingly destroy a positive research report, it is possible to borrow the ultimate destruction technique from Bailey (1966:156):

> When one recalls that these results, in terms of success or failure of the treatment used, *are based upon the conclusions of the authors of the reports, themselves*, then the implications . . . regarding the effectiveness of correctional treatment become rather discouraging. (Emphasis added)

Because it is inconceivable that anyone other than the author of the research will be the one to report the findings, and because such self-reports are inherently suspect, our conventional wisdom is unlikely to be upset.

REFERENCES

Adams, S., "Evaluating correctional treatments," *Criminal Justice and Behavior*, 1977, 4 (4), 323–339.

Bailey, W., "Correctional outcome: An evaluation of 100 reports," *Journal of Criminal Law, Criminology and Police Science*, 1966, 57(2), 153–160.

Conrad, J., "Corrections and simple justice," *Journal of Criminal Law, Criminology and Police Science*, 1973, 64(2), 208–217.

Doleschal, E., and Klapmuts, N., "Towards a new criminology," *Crime and Delinquency Literature*, 1973, 5 (4):607–627.

Hirschi, T., "Labelling theory and juvenile delinquency: An assessment of the evidence." In W. Gore (ed.), *The Labelling of Deviance* (Beverly Hills: Sage, 1973).

Lerman, P., *Community Treatment and Social Control* (Chicago: University of Chicago Press, 1975).

Lipton, D., Martinson, R., and Wilks, J., *The Effectiveness of Correctional Treatment* (New York: Praeger, 1975).

Logan, C., "Evaluation research in crime and delinquency: A reappraisal," *Journal of Criminal Law, Criminology and Police Science*, 1967, 63 (3): 378–387.

Martinson, R., "What works? — Questions and answers about prison reform," *The Public Interest*, 1974, Spring, 22–54.

Menninger, K., *The Crime of Punishment* (New York: Viking, 1968).

National Research Council, *Deterrence and Incapacitation: Estimating the Effects of Criminal Sanctions on the Crime Rate* (Washington, D.C.: National Academy of Sciences, 1978).

O'Leary, V., Gottfredson, M., and Gelman, A., "Contemporary sentencing proposals," *Criminal Law Bulletin*, 1975, 11 (5): 555–586.

Palmer, T., "California's community treatment program for delinquent adolescents," *Journal of Research in Crime and Delinquency*, 1971, 8 (1): 74–92.

Palmer, T., "The youth authority's community treatment project," *Federal Probation*, 1974, March, 3–14.

Palmer, T., "Martinson revisited," *Journal of Research in Crime and Delinquency*, 1975, 12 (2): 133–152.

Robison, J., and Smith, G., "The effectiveness of correctional programs," *Crime and Delinquency*, 1971, 17 (1): 67–80.

Schur, E., *Radical Non-Intervention: Rethinking the Delinquency Problem* (Englewood Cliffs, N.J.: Prentice-Hall, 1973).

Van Den Haag, E., *Punishing Criminals* (New York: Basic Books, 1975).

Weiler, P., "The reform of punishment." In *Studies on Sentencing* (Ottawa: Law Reform Commission of Canada, Information Canada, 1974).

Wright, W., and Dixon, M., "Community treatment of juvenile delinquency: A review of evaluation studies," *Journal of Research in Crime and Delinquency*, 1977, 14 (1): 35–67.

Part II

Diversion Programs

Chapter 4

Editors' Remarks

Major doubts have recently been voiced (e.g., Gibbons & Blake, 1976) about the success of the ever-increasing number of diversion programs and about the quality of research by which investigators have attempted to assess such programs. In the following article Herbert Quay and Craig Love describe the results of a large-scale pre-trial diversion program for 436 delinquent children who were provided with a variety of services including personal and vocational counseling, academic and vocational training, and job placement.

The Quay and Love project is an excellent example of the value of combining, in diversion programs, competent and thorough research with appropriate and adequate treatment.

REFERENCE

Gibbons, D.C. & Blake, G.F., "Evaluating the impact of juvenile diversion programs," *Crime & Delinquency*, 1976, *22*, 411–420.

The Effect of a Juvenile Diversion Program on Rearrests*

Herbert C. Quay and Craig T. Love

Various approaches to the diversion of juveniles from the criminal justice system have been advocated and a variety of these have been implemented. While evaluation of these efforts has also been advocated, the criteria for success and the evaluative designs have differed widely. This paper reports on the effects of a diversion program on rearrest experience of participants and of an equivalent control group.

The Juvenile Services Program (JSP) for Pinellas County, Florida, was operated by Learning Systems, Inc., under a contract from the U.S. Department of Labor. The program received referrals of two types from the juvenile court: children, aged 12 to 16, legally adjudicated as delinquent (DEL); and children designated as being in need of supervision (CINS). Informal referrals (INF) of children not in formal contact with the court system were received from police, schools, and various other community agencies.

The JSP provided services to its clients in three major areas: vocational counseling, training and job placement; academic education on a tutorial and small-group basis; and personal and social counseling, both individual and group. Considerable use was made of volunteers from the community in the academic program in particular.

*The authors are indebted to Jonathan Peck, president, and Michael Cahn, director of operations, of Learning Systems, Inc., as well as to David Vinikoor and Peter Parrado, directors of JSP during the period covered by this evaluation.

Quay, H.C. and Love, C.T., "The effect of a Juvenile diversion program on rearrests," *Criminal Justice and Behavior*, 1977, *4*(4), 377–396. Copyright © 1977, Sage Publications, Inc. Reprinted by permission.

METHOD

SUBJECTS

Since there were many more potential clients than could be served, it was possible to construct a classical experimental-control group research design to test the effectiveness of the JSP in reducing client rearrests. From a pool of juveniles deemed eligible according to the established criteria, cases were assigned, after an intake interview, on a random basis to one of the two groups. This evaluation was based on 436 program participants and on 132 control cases. The participants had a minimum of 30 days post-program community exposure and an average of 89 days in-program exposure, while the controls had a minimum of 90 days exposure.[1]

At the decision point, data were available on the number of variables potentially relevant to outcome. In addition to age, race, sex, socioeconomic status, and school grade completed, information was obtained on the number of prior offenses subdivided into the categories of status offense, offense against the person, property offense I, property offense II, and victimless offense.

Ratings were also obtained, with few exceptions, from the parents or parent surrogates on the Behavior Problem Checklist. This extensively validated checklist contained a list of 57 deviant behaviors which broke down into three major-factor, analytically derived dimensions of deviant behavior: Conduct Disorder, Personality Disorder, and Inadequacy-Immaturity (Peterson, 1961; Quay, 1964; Quay & Peterson, 1975).

In addition, the intake interviewers completed a checklist with respect to behavior characterizing the client's life history. This checklist (see Quay, 1964a; 1966) yields scores on dimensions of deviant behavior labeled Conduct Disorder, Personality Disorder, Inadequacy-Immaturity, and Subcultural Delinquency.

Subsequent to selection, participants (but not controls) were administered the Beta Nonverbal Intelligence Test, the Slosson Oral Reading Test, and the Personal Opinion Study. The latter is a factor analytically derived questionnaire measuring three dimensions of personality associated with delinquency: Anti-social Aggressiveness; Neurotic Acting-Out; and Socialized Delinquency (see Peterson et al., 1961; Quay & Peterson, 1964).

The average Beta IQ was 98.74 ($SD = 13.94$); the Slosson Oral Reading Test mean was 150.44 ($SD = 42.22$), which translates into a school-grade equivalent of about 7.4.

The scores on the Personal Opinion Study were very similar to those

---

[1] In fact, program participants had an average of 311 days post-program exposure and 89 days in-program time. Controls averaged 450 days exposure from the time of their designation as such.

obtained from other delinquent samples (Quay & Peterson, 1975) except that the antisocial-aggressive scale was somewhat more elevated.

Table 1 provides descriptive data on all these variables for both experimental and control groups. As can be seen, the means are all very much the same for the two groups. Testing the observed differences between the means of the two groups for statistical significance reveals that only in the case of the intake interviewer's rating of a history of Conduct Disorder ($t = 2.93$, $p = .004$) were the groups significantly different. Although the obtained difference is quite small, this finding suggests that the participants had a history of somewhat more acting-out, aggressive behavior than did the controls.

Clearly, the two groups do not differ on any of those variables on which they were compared with the one exception noted. Therefore, any differences obtained between the two groups in outcome cannot be due to preexisting differences between the groups with respect to the variables on which they have been compared.

TABLE 1

Characteristics of Participants and Controls

Characteristic	Participants Mean	S.D.	Controls Mean	S.D.
Age	15.83	1.26	15.82	1.35
Highest School Grade Completed	8.62	1.18	8.76	1.20
Socio-Economic Status	34.56	22.25	35.97	23.03
Prior Status Offenses	.43	.92	.58	1.33
Prior Offenses Against the Person	.09	.34	.11	.32
Prior Property I Offenses	.22	.65	.30	.66
Prior Property II Offenses	.27	.74	.33	.78
Prior Victimless Offenses	.13	.42	.18	.46
Behavior Rating: Conduct Disorder	7.48	4.74	7.23	4.98
Behavior Rating: Personality Problem	4.84	3.44	4.20	3.68
Behavior Rating: Inadequacy-Immaturity	3.05	2.18	2.83	2.28
History Rating: Conduct Disorder	1.50	1.96	.98	1.69
History Rating: Personality Disorder	1.54	1.58	1.69	1.64
History Rating: Inadequacy-Immaturity	.70	.87	.79	.69
History Rating: Socialized Delinquency	1.58	1.77	1.79	1.74
Race	303 white (70%) 133 black (30%)		99 white (75%) 33 black (25%)	
Sex	316 males (72%) 120 females (28%)		96 males (73%) 36 females (27%)	

RESULTS

ANALYSIS OF REARRESTS

Rearrest data for the two groups were obtained from the files of the Florida Division of Youth Services and reflect rearrests from the date of acceptance (experimentals) or the date of referral (controls) to April 7, 1976.[2]

These data have been enumerated and analyzed in a number of ways: (1) individuals rearrested and number of rearrests, both total and by offense catagory for the experimentals overall, during their time of participation and subsequent to their termination; (2) individuals rearrested and number of rearrests, both total and by offense category, for the controls from date of designation as a control; (3) rearrests of both groups by referral type; and (4) rearrests for participants rated as successful or unsuccessful terminators.

Table 2 provides data on the rearrest experience of the two groups over all three time segments. In Table 3 may be found the post-program rearrest data of the experimentals compared to the overall rearrest experience of the controls, subdivided by referral type.

The effects of the JSP are best evaluated by a comparison of the performance of the participants in the post-program period as compared to the controls. In-program rearrests frequently occurred shortly after entry and before any effects on the program could have reasonably been expected to occur.

With respect to the percent of each group rearrested, the participant versus control difference of 32% as compared to 45% was statistically significant ($z = 3.78$; $p = .0004$).

The average number of arrests for each group, subdivided by referral type, was analyzed by analysis of variance.[3] The participant versus control comparison yielded an F of 9.007 ($p = .003$; $df = 1,558$); the effect for referral type yielded an F of 5.243 ($p = .006$; $df = 2,558$), while the

---

[2]It should be noted that the data are actually in terms of counts, rather than rearrests. For example, if a rearrest resulted in two separate charges each was tallied as a "rearrest." "Recorded offenses" might be a more appropriate term for the data. Had multiple counts been tallied as a single rearrest, the number of rearrests would have decreased by 26 for the experimentals and by 6 for the controls, although the number of individuals arrested would obviously remain the same. Such a reduction in rearrests, would, although favoring the experimental group, have had very little effect on comparisons between the two groups.

[3]Our expectation was that rearrests would vary as a function of exposure time. However, the obtained correlations between number of rearrests and days exposure time were .25 for the participants and .20 for controls. Since the need for, and effectiveness of, covariance is a function of the degree of relationship between the covariate and the dependent variable (see Kerlinger, 1973, p. 371) these small correlations between exposure time and offense were not thought to justify covariance analysis even if the rather stringent assumptions for covariance could have been met.

TABLE 2

Rearrest Experience of Participants and Controls

	Participants	*Controls*
Sample size	436	132
Number of individuals re-arrested either in or post-program	173	59
Percent of group rearrested	40%	45%
Total number of rearrests in and post-program	377	132
Average number of rearrests per individual	.86	1.00
Number of individuals arrested in-program	72	59
Percent of group rearrested in-program	16%	45%
Total number of rearrests in-program	107	132
Average number of arrests in-program per individual	.24	1.00
Number of individuals arrested post-program	136	59
Percent of group rearrested post-program	32%	45%
Total number of arrests post-program	270	132
Average number of arrests per individual post-program	.62	1.00

TABLE 3

Post-Program Rearrest Experience of Participants and Controls by Referral Type

	Participants			*Controls*		
	CINS	*DEL*	*Informal*	*CINS*	*DEL*	*Informal*
Sample size	71	268	93	18	92	22
Number of individuals rearrested	36	76	23	12	33	14
Percent rearrested	50%	28%	24%	66%	36%	64%
Total number of rearrests	77	155	35	22	74	36
Average number of rearrests per individual	1.09	.58	.38	1.22	.80	1.64

interaction of group by referral type produced an F of 4.621 ($p = 0.10$; $df = 2,558$).

Subsequent analyses for simple main effects revealed that the CINS cases in the two groups did not differ significantly ($F = .154$), nor did the difference between the delinquent referrals ($F = 1.99$; $p > .10$). With the informal referrals the difference was highly significant ($F = 16.09$; $p < .001$).

Within the participant group, the informal cases did significantly better than the CINS cases ($F = 11.536$; $p < .001$). No other pairwise comparisons within either group were significant.

The foregoing analyses indicate that the effects of the JSP were to reduce both the number of individuals rearrested following termination from the programs and to reduce the mean number of arrests experienced by the participants. While the greatest success came with the informal referrals, for the other two groups the average number of arrests was lower among the participants, although the differences did not reach statistical significance.

Rearrests subdivided by offense category may be found in Table 4. There is really very little difference in the pattern of offenses between the two groups. Twenty-five percent of all offenses committed by participants were status

TABLE 4

Rearrest Experience of Participants and Controls by Offense Category

	Participants	*Controls*
Sample Size	474	132
Total number of offenses	377	132
Status offenses		
Total	96 (25%)*	39 (30%)*
In-program	31 (29%)	
Post-program	65 (24%)	
Total number cases offending	57 (12%)**	24 (18%)**
In-program cases offending	40 (8%)	
Post-program cases offending	26 (5%)	
Offenses against the Person		
Total	32 (8%)	14 (11%)
In-program	6 (6%)	
Post-program	26 (10%)	
Total	29 (6%)	12 (9%)
In-program	4 (1%)	
Post-program	26 (5%)	

TABLE 4 (Continued)

	Participants	Controls
Property I Offenses		
Total	100 (27%)	35 (27%)
In-program	32 (30%)	
Post-program	68 (25%)	
Total	68 (14%)	23 (17%)
In-Program	24 (5%)	
Post-program	50 (11%)	
Property II Offenses		
Total	78 (21%)	23 (17%)
In-program	24 (22%)	
Post-program	54 (20%)	
Total	65 (13%)	19 (14%)
In-program	22 (5%)	
Post-program	49 (10%)	
Victimless Offenses		
Total	71 (19%)	21 (16%)
In-program	16 (15%)	
Post-program	55 (20%)	
Total	52 (11%)	17 (13%)
In-program	16 (3%)	
Post-program	42 (9%)	

*percent of total offenses for that time period
**percent of total sample offending in that time period

offenses while this category accounted for 30% of all offenses committed by the controls. Only 8% of all the participants' offenses were against the person; a similarly low percentage (11%) of all the controls' offenses were in this category. The more serious property offenses accounted for 27% of all offenses in both groups. The less serious property offenses were also similar in pattern (21% and 17%), as were the victimless offenses (19% and 16%).

It is of interest that status and victimless offenses account for 44% of all rearrests for participants and 46% of all rearrests for the controls; thus almost half of all rearrests for both groups is for these mostly minor transgressions.

TABLE 5

Post-Program Rearrest Experience of Successful and Unsuccessful Terminations versus Controls

	Successful	*Unsuccessful*	*Controls*
Sample Size	344	92	132
Percent of total sample	79%	21%	100%
Number of cases rearrested	96	40	59
Percent of group rearrested	28%	44%	45%
Total number of rearrests	177	93	132
Average number rearrests per individual	.51	1.01	1.00

TABLE 6

Frequency of Post-Program Rearrests for Participants Rearrested

Number of Rearrests	*Frequency*	*Cumulative frequency and percentage*	*Cumulative number of rearrests and percentage*
10	1	1	10 (4%)
9	0	1	10 (4%)
8	1	2 (1%)	18 (7%)
7	0	2 (1%)	18 (7%)
6	3	5 (4%)	36 (13%)
5	3	8 (6%)	51 (19%)
4	7	15 (11%)	79 (29%)
3	19	34 (25%)	136 (50%)
2	32	66 (49%)	200 (74%)
1	70	136 (100%)	270 (100%)

REARREST EXPERIENCE OF THOSE COMPLETING THE PROGRAM SUCCESSFULLY VERSUS UNSUCCESSFUL CASES

Each of the participants was terminated from the JSP, according to staff judgment, as either having successfully completed the program or not. Of the total of 476 participants, 344 (72%) were considered successful terminators. Those cases averaged 89 days in the program. The 92 unsuccessful cases also averaged 89 days in the program so that the "unsuccessful" label was apparently not applied to quickly rid the program of nonresponders.

The rearrest experience of these two groups is set forth in Table 5. During the post-program period only 28% of the successful cases were rearrested as compared to 44% of the unsuccessful cases. The 21% unsuccessful cases also accounted for 34% of the total rearrests among participants.

Obviously, were the JSP to be evaluated solely on the rearrest performance of only those cases (still 79% of the total) who were judged program successes at termination, it would show an even greater advantage over the controls. The difference percentage of cases rearrested (28% versus 45%) is large, and the average number of rearrests is one-half (.51 versus 1.00).

MULTIPLE REARRESTS

Among those participants who were rearrested, there was not an equal contribution of each participant to the rearrest total; far from it. As can be seen from Table 6, only 51% of the rearrested group experienced a single post-program rearrest, while 49% were rearrested more than once. Thirty-four of those rearrested were rearrested more than twice; these 25% of the rearrested participants accounted for 50% of all post-program rearrests.

A somewhat similar finding emerged with respect to in-program arrests (see Table 7) as 71% of this group were arrested only once. Twenty-nine percent were arrested more than once with this group, accounting for 52% of the rearrests.

TABLE 7

Frequency of In-Program Rearrests for Participants Rearrested

Number of Rearrests	Frequency	Cumulative Frequency	Cumulative number of Rearrests
6	1	1	6 (6%)
5	1	2 (3%)	11 (10%)
4	1	3 (4%)	15 (14%)
3	5	8 (11%)	30 (28%)
2	13	21 (29%)	56 (52%)
1	51	72 (100%)	107 (100%)

TABLE 8

Frequency of Rearrests for Controls Rearrested

Number of Rearrests	Frequency	Cumulative Frequency	Cumulative number of Rearrests
8	2	2 (3%)	16 (12%)
7	2	4 (7%)	30 (23%)
6	0	4 (7%)	30 (23%)
5	3	7 (12%)	45 (34%)
4	4	11 (19%)	61 (47%)
3	4	15 (25%)	73 (55%)
2	15	30 (50%)	103 (78%)
1	29	59 (50%)	132 (22%)

A similar pattern emerged for rearrests among the controls (Table 8), in that only 50% experienced a single rearrest. Twenty-five percent were rearrested three or more times, accounting for 55% of all rearrests.

When one looks at this data in light of the total number of cases in each group, it is clear that only a small proportion of both participants and controls were subsequently in repeated contact with police (as indexed by arrests). Of the entire 436 participants, only 34 (8%) were responsible for 136 (50%) out of a total of 270 post-program rearrests. Of the smaller group of 132 controls, 15 cases, only 11%, accounted for 75 (55%) of the total of 132 rearrests.

Combining the participant and control groups (total of 568) revealed that some 49 cases (9%) accounted for 209, or 52%, of the total of 402 participant post-program and total control rearrests. This small group of persistent offenders, deterred from offending by neither the JSP nor whatever other services might have been provided to the controls, are an obvious target for some more intensive form of intervention.

THE RELATIONSHIP BETWEEN IN-PROGRAM AND POST-PROGRAM REARRESTS

Of the 136 participants rearrested post-program, 35 (26%) had also been arrested during the program. Conversely, of the 72 cases arrested during the program, 35 (49%) were rearrested post-program as well. These 35 participants rearrested during both time periods experienced a total of 132 arrests and accounted for 48% of all in-program rearrests, 30% of all post-program rearrests, and 35% of *all* rearrests. To reiterate, these 35 cases, representing only 8% of the 436 participants, accounted for a third of *all* rearrests charged against the participant group.

Can we predict the likelihood of a post-program rearrest from knowledge about in-program rearrests? With the knowledge that 35 cases were arrested during both time periods, 38 were arrested during but not after, 100 were arrested after but not during, and 263 were arrested not at all, a four-fold table was constructed which yielded a phi-coefficient of .15, indicating little predictability for the entire participant group.

Of course, the major interest is in those participants who are in-program rearrests. There are a total of 73 of these, of whom 35 go on to be post-program rearrests as well. Thus, 48% of participants arrested during the program go on to suffer post-program rearrest within the limits of the post-program follow-up period (average of 311 days) of this report. Thus, there was about a 50:50 chance that a participant who has had an in-program arrest will go on to a post-program rearrest.

As noted, there were 100 participants who were not arrested while in the program, but who were subsequently rearrested. Since 72 of the total group of 436 were arrested in-program, there remain 364 who were not. The 101 post-program-only arrests represent 28% of this group. Participants not arrested in-program have only a 28% chance of being arrested after termination. Thus, those arrested in-program are at greater risk to be arrested post-program (although still only 50:50), and might well have been the target of a more intensive effort.

PREDICTION OF SUCCESS AND FAILURE AS DEFINED BY IN-PROGRAM PLUS POST-PROGRAM REARRESTS

The collection of demographic, academic, and behavioral data on the participants permitted the use of this preprogram information to be used in the prediction of outcome. The application of the multiple discriminant function technique revealed that weighted combinations of certain variables could be used to predict success and failure.

These variables and their weight in the prediction of either success or failure are presented in Table 9. To obtain either prediction requires that the raw score value be multiplied by the indicated value, the resultant values summed, and the constant added. The highest score obtained by using both the sets of multipliers determines the prediction, i.e., if the application of the "predict success" multiplier plus the constant results in a higher total than the use of the "predict failure" multiplier plus the constant, the prediction would be for success. If the reverse were the case, the prediction would be for failure.

The application of this formula to those 406 cases (of the 436 total) on whom all the data were available produced some interesting findings. Of those cases who would have been predicted to succeed (305), 217 (71%) did so. Of those cases who would have been predicted to fail (101), 66 (65%) actually failed.

TABLE 9

Prediction of Success or Failure by Results of Multiple Discriminant Function

Variable	Multiplier to predict success	Multiplier to predict failure
Age	1.089	1.059
Sex*	7.494	6.706
Prior status offenses	− 0.775	− 0.546
Prior Property II offenses	0.793	1.030
Behavior Rating: Conduct Disorder	0.315	0.363
Behavior Rating: Personality Problem	0.383	0.334
Questionnaire aggression scale	0.477	0.498
Questionnaire anxiety-withdrawal scale	0.612	0.635
Key Math pretest score	1.297	1.178
Constant	− 119.122	− 113.337

*where male = 0 and female = 1

Had the JSP taken only those cases predicted to succeed, its failure rate (defined here as a rearrest either in-*or* post-program) for these 406 cases would have dropped to 29% as opposed to the obtained 38%. To have done so would have resulted in rejecting 35 cases who would have succeeded (8.6% of the total sample).[4]

What is perhaps more appropriate is that the JSP might have identified the potential failures as targets for a more intensive intervention than could have been provided for the entire group of participants.

CHARACTERISTICS OF THE MULTIPLE OFFENDERS

As was noted previously, 35 cases were rearrested both in- and post-program. The small sample size precluded the use of predictive equations or statistical comparisons of this group with the total sample of participants. The best that could be done was a hypothesis-finding look at those of this group as they compared with the total participant sample on the variables

---

[4]It should be noted that formulas obtained by these types of procedures tend to "shrink," i.e., they do not generally predict so well when applied to new samples. However, extreme cases do not generally shift to the opposite group so that making decisions about extremes can be done safely without cross-validation in a new sample.

TABLE 10

Comparison of Cases Rearrested both In- and Post-Program and Cases Rearrested Three or More Times Post-Program with the Total Participant Group

Characteristic	Total Participants		In-and post-program rearrested		Three or more post-program rearrested	
	Mean	S.D.	Mean	S.D.	Mean	S.D.
Age	15.83	1.26	15.60	1.28	15.31	1.21
Highest School Grade Completed	8.62	1.18	8.00	1.14	7.94	1.06
Socio-Economic Status	34.56	22.25	33.02	22.44	32.80	23.42
Prior Status Offenses	.43	.92	.83	1.29	.71	1.20
Prior Offenses Against the Person	.09	.34	.14	.43	.00	.00
Prior Property I Offenses	.22	.65	.51	.82	.31	.63
Prior Property II Offenses	.27	.74	.71	1.43	.57	1.17
Prior Victimless Offenses	.13	.42	.14	.36	.14	.35
Behavior Rating: Conduct Disorder	7.48	4.74	8.62	4.48	8.47	4.65
Behavior Rating: Personality Problem	4.84	3.44	4.53	2.94	4.47	3.51
Behavior Rating: Inadequacy-Immaturity	3.05	2.18	3.23	2.05	3.20	2.12
History Rating: Conduct Disorder	1.50	1.96	2.47	1.95	2.03	2.01
History Rating: Personality Disorder	1.54	1.58	1.71	1.73	1.20	1.32
History Rating: Inadequacy-Immaturity	.70	.87	.97	.76	.86	.94
History Rating: Socialized Delinquency	1.58	1.77	2.03	2.28	2.46	2.06

TABLE 10 (Continued)

Characteristic	Total Participants		In- and post-program rearrested		Three or more post-program rearrested	
	Mean	S.D.	Mean	S.D.	Mean	S.D.
Questionnaire — Aggression	12.28	6.94	14.77	7.75	14.64	6.80
Questionnaire — Anxiety-Withdrawal	12.38	5.63	15.23	4.70	15.52	4.72
Questionnaire — Socialized Delinquency	13.72	3.64	14.85	2.80	15.56	3.01
Beta IQ	98.76	13.83	93.63	17.02	96.94	17.74
SORT	148.67	50.19	131.06	58.58	139.96	57.68
Key Math	6.91	2.06	5.88	1.78	6.07	2.01
Race: white	303 (70%)		21 (60%)		25 (71%)	
black	133 (30%)		14 (40%)		10 (29%)	
Sex: male	316 (72%)		24 (69%)		27 (77%)	
female	120 (28%)		11 (31%)		8 (23%)	

listed in Table 1 and their score on the Personal Opinion Study. Beta, SORT, and Key Math Test. These comparisons are presented in Table 10. It should be noted that these contrasts are minimized slightly by the fact that the 35 special cases are also represented in the total sample.

The major differences suggested were that the in- and post-program offenders are slightly younger, had a higher incidence of prior status and property offenses, were rated by parents or their surrogates as more aggressive, saw themselves as both more aggressive and more neurotic, were somewhat less bright, and had lower academic achievement. None of these differences were striking, but in combination they might well have been predictive. In fact, the variables that were predictive of overall failure (see Table 9) are those which, by inspection, seem to set this group apart from the total sample. Of course, these 35 cases were represented in the sample of rearrests on which the predictive equations are based. What this really adds up to, however, is that this subgroup of multiple rearrestees was very much like the failure cases in general.

Table 10 also presents the same data on the 35 cases who were arrested three or more times during the post-program period. By inspection, these cases are very much like the both in- and post-program rearrestees and similar to the failure cases as a whole.

CONCLUSIONS

Since the participants and their controls were selected randomly from the same pool of eligible juveniles and did not differ in any significant way, it is reasonable to conclude that the total efforts of the JSP had a significant effect on the post-program rearrest experience of its clients.

The greatest degree of success was obtained with the informally referred participants as contrasted to those informally referred who were designated as controls. The highly significant difference here could be interpreted as suggesting that intervention for these adolescents is very important at the time they have come to the attention of some social service or educational agency.

Only 23 (25%) of the 93 treated informals were rearrested post-program as compared to 14 (64%) of the 22 control informals. It seems likely that intervention by a noncriminal justice agency (The JSP) successfully diverts a group, two-thirds of whom would otherwise have become involved in the criminal justice system. The successful diversion of these juveniles should not be overlooked; in a sense this represents delinquency prevention.

In the initiation of a new program of a similar nature, the data with respect to the prediction of success versus failure can be used to good advantage in either selection or program design.

REFERENCES

Fitts, W.H., & Hamner, W.T., *The Self-concept and Delinquency*. Nashville Mental Health Center Monograph I. Nashville, T.N.: Counselor Recordings and Tests, July, 1969.

Kerlinger, F.N., *Foundations of Behavioral Research* (New York: Holt, Rinehart & Winston, 1973).

Peterson, D.R., Behavior problems of middle childhood,'' *Journal of Consulting Psychology*, 1961, 25, 205–209.

Peterson, D.R., Quay, H.C., & Tiffany, T.C., "Personality factors related to juvenile delinquency. *Child Development*, 1961, 32, 355–372.

Quay, H.C., "Personality dimensions in delinquent males as inferred from factor analysis of behavior ratings," *Journal of Research in Crime and Delinquency*, 1964(a), 1, 33–37.

Quay, H.C., "Dimensions of personality in delinquent males as inferred from the factor analysis of case history data," *Child Development*, 1964(b), 35, 479–484.

Quay, H.C., "Personality patterns in preadolescent delinquent boys," *Educational and Psychological Measurement*, 1966, 26, 99–110.

Quay, H.C., & Peterson, D.R., The questionnaire measurement of personality dimensions associated with juvenile delinquency. Mimeographed, 1964.

Quay, H.C., & Peterson, D.R., Manual for the behavior problem checklist. Unpublished manuscript, 1975.

Chapter 5

Editors' Remarks

As the authors note in their article, police diversion is becoming very prevalent. In our view, among the programs reported in the diversion literature, Dallas Police Department's Youth Services Program is exemplary for its programming structure, comprehensiveness and follow-up. In particular we draw attention to their three-stage six-month process assessment, treatment, and follow-up, their multi-facetted treatment approach and their involvement of the family and school. Their staff training component is noteworthy also.

Besides the impressive results reported by the authors in the following article, Dr. Collingwood kindly provided us with further follow-up data which we have appended. These data attest to the program's viability and success.

Juvenile Diversion: The Dallas Police Department Youth Services Program*

Thomas R. Collingwood, Alex Douds,
and Hadley Williams

Police diversion is a current trend in law enforcement to divert and correct youthful offenders within the community and outside the traditional court and correctional system. Traditional methods of handling juveniles from release with a warning through referral to the juvenile court are not alleviating the problem of delinquency. The scope of the problem has facilitated the development of alternatives to the over-burdened juvenile justice system and police diversion is one unique approach.

The President's Commission on Crime (1967) made specific recommendations toward the development of alternatives to the traditional juvenile justice programs especially in terms of community-based diversion and treatment programs. Most recently the International Association of Chiefs of Police (1973) and the National Advisory Commission on Criminal Justice Standards and Goals (1973) have strongly recommended the development and implementation of police juvenile diversion programs.

The police officer is, in many respects, the single most significant decisionmaker within the juvenile justice system. While different types of alternatives are being developed to the juvenile justice process, law enforcement agencies are uniquely suited to provide effective diversion. At the police level, an immediate impact can be made to ensure maximum cooperation while early identification and intervention can be functionally delivered. The concept of police diversion is so new, however, that there has been little assessment of the tangible effects of such approaches upon juvenile crime.

---

*Collingwood, T.R. et al., "Juvenile diversion: The Dallas Police Department Youth Services Program," *Federal Probation*, 1976, *40*(3), 23–27. Copyright © 1976, Federal Probation. Reprinted by permission.

The Youth Section of the Dallas Police Department has developed a unique voluntary police diversion program to meet the needs of juvenile offenders. The Dallas Police Department received a Federal grant (through the Law Enforcement Assistance Administration) to implement the Youth Services Program. There are two major goals of the program: (1) to divert juveniles from the juvenile justice system and (2) to reduce recidivism. It involves using policemen and civilian counselors both within a helping role.

Prior to the advent of the Department's Youth Services Program, the only alternatives for disposition of arrested youths were either release to parents or referral to the juvenile court. The overburdened court system was not able to provide a program for the majority of referrals and as a consequence, 75 to 80% of all arrested youths did not receive any tangible program to prevent further criminal acts. A juvenile rearrest rate of over 50% reflected the lack of alternatives to prevent juvenile crime and recidivism.

THE YOUTH SERVICES PROGRAM

The Youth Services Program (YSP) is an operational unit of the Dallas Police Department's Youth Section. It is staffed by sworn officers and civilian personnel with a lieutenant of police as director. Fourteen counselors supervised by a counseling psychologist have been added to the Youth Section as a counseling unit to provide direct programs to arrested youths.

The type of youth served by the YSP consists of arrested youths between the ages of 10 and 16. Both felons and misdemeanants, first offenders, and repeat offenders are referred to the unit. Since the YSP is a diversion program, it is, by law, voluntary. As such, a voluntary agreement by a youth and his parent is required and a signed statement of participation is obtained.

There are two subprograms to the YSP: (1) the First Offender Program (FOP) and (2) the Counseling Unit. The FOP consists of a 3-hour lecture awareness program conducted by sworn officers for minor first offender youths covering such topic areas as the law, implications of future illegal acts, and drug abuse. The Counseling Unit program is developed for more serious offenders, such as repeaters, impact offenders (stranger to stranger felonies such as burglary, robbery, assault), and other felons as well as misdemeanants and runaways.

YSP PROGRAM OPERATIONS

The Youth Services Program began handling cases in December of 1973. The process is a co-operative effort between the police investigator and a counselor. When an arrested youth is brought to the Youth Section, an investigator initiates an interview to determine the needs of the child and the most functional disposition of the case. The police officer has a choice of either: (1) sending a youth home, (2) referring him or her to the juvenile court, (3) referring him or her to a First Offender lecture program, or (4) the counseling unit. Established criteria are utilized by the police investigator in making his disposition. First time minor offenders are usually referred to the First Offender lecture program, while the most serious repeat offenders are referred to the juvenile court. The middle range youth who may have committed a moderate to severe offense (theft or burglary) or may have a less serious prior record (one to six previous arrests) is enrolled in the YSP. A key determination that the investigator makes in his disposition judgment is whether a youth and the parents could benefit from the relatively short-term YSP alternative. Time is allocated for the investigator to get a more personal view of the youth. The entire Youth Section (sworn and civilian staff) have been given training on Carkhuff's (1971) Human Resource Development skills such as inter-personal-counseling and problem-solving skills enabling the police officer to function more effectively as a helper to a youth. If the youth is referred to the FOP, he or she will receive the 3-hour awareness lecture by police officers on two successive nights within 1 month of arrest. If a youth is assigned to a counselor, the referring investigator maintains contact with the case throughout the course of the program.

A youth assigned to the Counseling Unit undergoes a systematic three-stage process lasting approximately 6 months. The first stage is the intake stage, whereby the counselor assesses the youth's physical, intellectual, and emotional functioning. The youth next enters a direct treatment phase whereby they receive 16 hours of skills training within a group. This training is provided over a 4-week period. The parents also receive training during this period on how to monitor their child's activities and implement behavioral contracts to help their child reach the program goals. After the direct phase, a youth enters followup and is given "homework" assignments or behavioral contracts to apply the skills learned to critical outcome areas that relate to avoiding trouble. These include following limits at home, school attendance and grades, and constructive activity participation. Throughout the three-stage process, individual programs, family counseling, and community agency referral programs are also implemented as needed.

The basic direct treatment given to referred youths is the skills training group lasting 16 hours over a 1-month period. The program systematically teaches the youths three basic skills with important implications for avoiding trouble. *Physical fitness* is taught as a physical skill to give youths energy, self-respect, and awareness of self. It is also geared toward getting them involved in constructive recreation activity. *Inter-personal skill* is taught as an emotional skill to increase the youth's ability to deal decently with others and obey parents. *Study/learning skills* are taught as intellectual skills to increase the youth's ability to get more out of a learning situation and attend school. For those youths requiring remedial reading a 24-hour reading program provided over a 2-month period is provided. The skills are taught within the framework of a youth learning the skills as a vehicle to avoid trouble and be more successful in home, school, and neighborhood problem areas.

STAFF TRAINING

The initial training of both police and counseling personnel was based upon Carkhuff's HRD training methodology. The emphasis was on helping skills. Sixty-six police officers from the Youth Section received 40 hours of training on interpersonal skills and problem-solving skills to better enable them to interview youths and their parents and make a more functional disposition. Counseling personnel underwent an additional 40 hours for a total of 80 hours on those skills, plus 24 hours on physical fitness training and 24 hours on program development skills as the initial training. Training once a week has been given counseling staff on a continuing basis. Content of the training covers such areas as (1) review and retraining of basic skills. (2) training on new skills such as behavioral contracting, (3) program review and revision, (4) community referral utilization, and (5) case reviews. The emphasis in the ongoing training is on staff development via skills training and program development via group input, problem solving, and program planning assignments.

RESULTS

During the first full year of operation 2,282 youths were referred to the First Offender Program with 69 percent participating. The youths were primarily first offender misdemeanants. Referrals to the Counseling Unit were 1,084 with 75% participating. Nonparticipating youths did not receive services nor did they receive any additional police or court action. In terms of prior record, 59% were first offenders and 41 percent were repeat offenders. Of youth referred to the counseling unit, 47% were felons and 53% misdemeanants. Average age was 14. By providing its own diversion program, the Youth Section reduced referrals to the County Juvenile Department by 7.2%. One year prior to the YSP 69.6% of all arrested youths were referred to the County Juvenile Department while only 62.4% were referred since the inception of the YSP. This reduced the burden on probation staff and, in turn, provided needed services to youths.

In terms of rearrest both YSP programs have some success to date. The repeat rate for FOP youths was 9.6% as opposed to a comparison group (n = 445) of 15.5%. The repeat rate for Counseling Unit youths was 10.7% contrasted to a comparison group (n = 196) rate of 50.5% during the same time period. The recidivism rate for those youths who had completed the Counseling Unit (n = 264) program was even significantly lower at 2.7%.

The comparison sample for both FOP and Counseling Unit consisted of youths with similar offense records (FOP — first offender misdemeanant. CU — 53% first offender, 47% repeat offender, 65% misdemeanant, 35% felon). These youths met the selecting criteria, were referred to the YSP by the police investigator and agreed to participate but did not receive treatment for various reasons such as (1) inability to contact, (2) refusal to participate, (3) seeking out other treatment alternatives. While not perfect comparison samples they do represent similar samples of the same offender population as the YSP youths.

Assessment of physical, intellectual and emotional skill level was done on a pre-post basis for Counseling Unit juveniles. Physical functioning involved around level of physical fitness as rated by a 5 point scale whereby level 1 represents 0%, level 3 equals 50%, and level 5 equals 100% on national norms for fitness tests on flexibility, dynamic strength and cardiovascular endurance. A 5 point scale was also employed to assess the youth's emotional-interpersonal skills in which level 1 equals least effective, level 3 equals minimally effective and level 5 equals most effective interpersonal skills. The measure of intellectual functioning revolved around the youth's ability to study and learn within a classroom setting. A 5 point scale was utilized whereby at level 1 the youth does not know any strategy for learning and studying to level 5 whereby he or she knows a systematic and full learning studying process. In terms of skill level, the Counseling Unit program increased the physical functioning of participating youths from 2.89 to 3.25, the emotional functioning from 2.38 to 2.94, and intellectual functioning from 1.97 to 2.40. Those youths receiving the reading program (n = 28) increased their reading level on the average of 1.1 years. The gains represent skill increases over a 1- to 2-month period that the youth received the 16 hour skills training or 24 hour reading program and represent gains not attributable to that from normal maturation.

A follow-up parent evaluation questionnaire was administered to assess the impact of the Counseling Unit program upon certain outcome factors affecting recidivism. The factors were (1) communication with parents, (2) obedience to parents, (3) responsibility at home, (4) school attendance, (5) study time, (6) grades, (7) trouble in schools, (8) part-time job, (9) career planning, (10) recreation participation, and (11) hobby participation. The questionnaires were subjective in nature recording whether there was positive change, negative change or no change on a variable. In terms of juvenile functioning in home, school, and neighborhood outcome factors, the following was noted: 72% improved communication with parents, 74% improved their obedience to parents, 54% accepted more responsibility at home, 63% improved their school attendance, 54% studied more, 52% made better grades, 60% got into less trouble in school, 29% got a part-time job, 20% got involved in career planning and between 43% and 49% were more actively participating in recreation and hobby programs. It was also found that participating youths increased their self-concept and positive attitude toward police.

CONCLUSION

The need for effective diversion programs to help the juvenile offender has led to many innovative approaches to reduce juvenile recidivism. Effective alternatives are sorely needed within the field. The Dallas Police Department is implementing its unique approach with some significant effects.

A longer time span is needed to fully assess the long-term effect of the program on rearrest recidivism. However, the current results of the YSP's effect — in relation to a similar comparison sample for the same time period — are significant. At present, the positive results can only be generalized for the type of juveniles served (the middle-range offender) with the applicability for more serious offenders yet to be tested.

When looking at the sources of variance for the program's effect, three major factors appear to emerge: (1) the police-based nature of the program, (2) the employment of counselors within a law enforcement setting, and (3) the skills approach to training and treatment.

With the YSP as an operational unit of the Police Department, immediate impact can be made upon a youth to insure his cooperation and participation voluntarily at the point of arrest. The employment and utilization of counselors within a law enforcement setting such as the Youth Section has brought an emphasis upon helping youths instead of just the legal processing of a juvenile. Besides the direct service the counselors provide, they also serve as valuable resources for police investigators in terms of handling and working with juveniles. The HRD skills approach has facilitated the development of skilled helpers (police and counselors) and systematic programs to help the youth. It appears that by undergoing skills training the youths learned tangible responses they could translate and utilize in their lives. In turn, the various outcome programs they were placed on focused the use of those skills in certain areas, such as school attendance, which relate directly to avoiding trouble. As a consequence the rearrest probability appears reduced.

The need for effective diversion programs to prevent the juvenile offender from committing further law violations is critical. Diversion at the police level is the most immediate moment to have impact on a juvenile. Police diversion programs can have an impact upon preventing further juvenile crime and the Youth Services Program offers one promising approach toward dealing with this problem.

REFERENCES

Carkhuff, R.R., *The Development of Human Resources*, (New York: Holt, Rinehart and Winston, 1971).

Kobetz, R.W. and Bosarge, B.B., *Juvenile Justice Administration*, (Gaithersburg, Md.: 1.A.C.P., 1973).

Peterson, R.W. (Ed.), *Report on Police* (Washington: National Advisory Commission on Criminal Justice Standards and Goals, 1973).

President's Commission on Law Enforcement and Administration of Justice, *The Challenge of Crime in a Free Society* (Washington: U.S. Government Printing Office, 1967).

Addendum

We have abstracted the following data from Collingwood et al (1978) to further demonstrate the success of their program. The magnitude of their program has been impressive: 2,645 adolescents have been referred, 2,011 participated, 1,383 completed the program, 320 dropped out before completing and 584 served as controls. Some of the recidivism data are as follows (Collingwood et al., 1978, p. 10–11).

TABLE 1

Percentage Who Recidivate

24.3%	YSP Total
13.7%	YSP Process (recidivate while participating)
10.6%	YSP Closed (recidivate after completion)
42.7%	Control
53.3%	Total Arrested Youths (1975)

The control sample had a statistically significant higher percentage recidivism than the YSP group. Both samples had satistically significantly lower rates than the total arrest population. (For both samples, the figures are slightly different than the total figures previously reported. The YSP is a little higher and the control is lower.)

TABLE 2

Number of Repeat Offenses by Recidivists

	Average (X)
YSP	1.6
Control	2.3

The control recidivists committed a significantly higher average number of repeat offenses.

TABLE 3

Type of Repeat Offenses by Recidivists

	Misdemeanors	Felony Total	Felony Impact	Felony Non-Impact
YSP	67.3%	32.7%	26.9%	5.8%
Control	44%	56%	40.9%	15.1%

The YSP recidivists committed significantly less felony offenses and significantly more misdemeanors than the control recidivists.

TABLE 4

Petitions Filed in Juvenile Court (limited data)

	Percent Of Recidivists	Percent Of Total
YSP (N = 28)	14%	1.5%
Control (N = 81)	55%	23.5%

Significantly more of the control recidivists had cases filed on them.

REFERENCE

Collingwood, T.R., Douds, A., Williams, H., & Wilson, R.D. *The Effects of a Police-based Diversion Program upon Youth Resource Development*. Carkhuff Institute of Human Technology Research Reports, 1978, II, #3.
(Available from T.R. Collingwood, The Aerobics Centre, Division of Continuing Education, 12202 Preston Rd., Dallas, Texas, 75230.)

Chapter 6

Editors' Remarks

In the following article, Seidman, Rappaport and Davidson describe the development, operation and results of a multi-facetted juvenile diversion program which has been demonstrated within a carefully controlled and thoroughly analyzed study to be effective in two mid-western American cities in diverting delinquents from deeper penetration into the juvenile justice system.

This program and many of the other effective programs in this book could serve as models for replication in other jurisdictions. However, if in the replication the program is implemented for inappropriate clients or by inappropriate practitioners or without adequately dealing with those system variables which impact on the program, it would be folly to expect success and might, in fact, be a disservice to the clients (cf. Ross & McKay, Chapter 2).

In a sequel to the project description provided in the present chapter, the authors re-examined the program some three years after the formal research project was completed and they had retired from actual direction and control of the program. They found that the program, which was ostensibly the same program, had been allowed to deviate from the original not in terms of technique but in terms of ideology. Rappaport, Seidman and Davidson (in press) have discussed the potential adverse consequences of the failure to maintain the "essence" of their program in a paper which we recommend to those who consider adopting this or any other of the programs presented in *Effective Correctional Treatment*.

One of their findings is particularly noteworthy. While they were directing the program they took pains to ensure that only youths for whom the police were about to file a court petition could be referred to the project. After the director's supervision was withdrawn, "problem children", "pre-delinquent children", "mental health-adjustment problem children" and "school problem children" were referred — children who would ordinarily be "left alone" by the juvenile justice system; children for whom the program was never designed; children who may not be helped and, in fact, may be harmed by their involvement in the juvenile justice system. Such a "widening the net" phenomenon is an everpresent danger in diversion projects. As Rappaport et al. point out, an adequate replication must not compromise either the technique or the "spirit" of the model program. Effective correctional treatment projects are not "supermarket style cellophane packages of supposedly transportable programs."

REFERENCE

Rappaport, J., Seidman, E., & Davidson, II, W.S. "Demonstration research and manifest versus true adoption: the natural history of a research project." In R.F. Munoz, L.R. Snowden, J.G. Kelly (Eds.) *Social and Psychological Research in Community Settings: Designing and Conducting Programs for Social and Personal Well-being* (San Francisco: Jossey-Bass, in press).

Adolescents in Legal Jeopardy: Initial Success and Replication of an Alternative to the Criminal Justice System*

Edward Seidman, Julian Rappaport,
and William S. Davidson, II

Before I begin to explicate the details of our efforts to divert adolescents in legal jeopardy from further involvement in the criminal justice system, I would like to place this research in its larger context. For the past several years we have been examining the systematic use of college student nonprofessionals as human service deliverers in several social systems. The larger program included four sub-projects aimed at developmentally representative target groups, i.e., school children, emotionally disturbed adults, and senior citizens residing in a nursing home, in addition to adolescents in legal jeopardy. Each sub-project involved college student change agents as the mode of service delivery. The college students are paired with target individuals on a one-to-one basis. The total set of four projects has been directed at questions such as who works best with whom, using what training techniques (Kiesler, 1966, 1971; Paul, 1969). In line with this overall goal, more specific project endeavors addressed the questions of volunteer selection, volunteer training, supervision strategies, resultant changes in the volunteers per se, resultant changes in the respective target populations, and

---

*Invited presentation on receipt of first prize in the 1976 National Psychological Consultants to Management Watson-Wilson Consulting Psychology Research Award competition. Presented at the American Psychological Association Convention, Washington, D.C., September, 1976. A more detailed version of this research is now in preparation.

This work was supported for the most part by Grant No. MH 22336 from the National Institute of Mental Health, and to a lesser extent by a grant from the University of Illinois Research Board and Law Enforcement Assistance Administration administered through the Law and Society Program at the University of Illinois (title LEAA 75NI-99-0077 FIR).

Reprinted by permission.

the impact of the projects on the social service systems in which they were embedded.

We have recently described the specific method of operation used in the program as a whole in a paper entitled "The Educational Pyramid: A Paradigm For Research, Training and Manpower Utilization in Community Psychology" (Seidman & Rappaport, 1974). In brief, each sub-project operated according to a triadic organizational model. Each was "staffed" by two principal investigators who supervised two graduate students, who shared or split responsibility for training/supervision of the nonprofessional change agents and the project specific research. Each year the two graduate student co-directors were responsible for direct supervision of undergraduate student change agents. The research reported here is based on one of the four sub-projects which was aimed at diversion of alleged adolescent offenders from the criminal justice system.

Our work is predicated on several specific values and related objectives (Fairweather, 1972; Rappaport, 1977). First of all, a major concern is intervening as early as possible to thwart an individual's envelopment by "rehabilitation" systems that are often detrimental to human welfare. We are committed to avoiding, or at least minimizing, the effects of "disculturation" (Goffman, 1961), isolation, pushouts, etc. Similarly, we endeavor to avoid "blaming the victim" (Ryan, 1971; Shur, 1973) or focusing on his/her deficits, but instead we attempt to identify and build upon an individual's assets and strengths (Rappaport et. al., 1975; Rappaport, 1977). We try to avoid placing the individual in a client or patient role. Instead, we try to foster self sufficiency by enabling the person to become his/her own advocate (Davidson & Rapp, 1976; Sarason, 1976) and/or to learn critical negotiation skills in dealing with significant individuals and/or agencies in their particular social support networks. Finally, we are concerned that we have an impact on the relevant social system, in this case, the juvenile justice system, so that the system itself may be more likely to prevent or minimize the exacerbation of difficulties for future entrants. In short, our efforts are directed at experimental social model building rather than exclusively the individual level of assessment or change.

As most of you know, the field of juvenile delinquency prevention has been and is experiencing an unparalleled search for alternative intervention strategies. Although enthusiastic adherents for various approaches can be found, there is little basis for strong belief in the relative efficacy of contemporary approaches when compared to each other or when compared to more traditional strategies. While some community based programs have indicated promising results (Palmer, 1971; 1975; Shore & Massimo, 1973), most of these programs are poorly evaluated and the majority continue to be operated out of highly traditional corrections facilities (Griggs & McCume, 1972).

From our prior experiences in the local juvenile justice system as well as the relevant research literature it was apparent to us that the point at which a youngster reaches the probation stage is not the most ideal point in the system at which to intervene, since at that time the child is already deeply entangled in the system. Consequently, we attempted to gain the cooperation and participation of the police officers responsible for alleged juvenile offenders in two adjacent midwestern American cities (joint population — 90,000), as well as the county police department.

Over the course of a pilot semester and summer we worked in close collaboration with the relevant police officers in an attempt to develop an alternative that was sensible and potentially beneficial to the youth with whom we would be involved. In developing these relationships, a good deal of "sizing up" of each other occurred. It became apparent that we did share a common concern with the juvenile officers of the two city police departments centering on the apparent ineffectiveness of the typical juvenile court and probation intervention methods.

After an initial role negotiation phase, more attention was paid to specific plans for actual project initiation. The plans for referral procedures, pre and post assessment, random assignment, insuring volunteer involvement on the part of referred youth, protection of the constitutional rights of the youth, specification of our intervention methods, and detailing of our plans for community continuation of the project following cessation of the NIMH funds were all discussed. This phase was critical in order to adequately work out the "bugs" in both the measurement and referral procedures and to get to know each other.* After a period of negotiation, we decided that the decision to refer a given youth would be left to the discretion of the juvenile officer, with the following agreed upon guideline:

> Since the project does not want to become involved with youth who have been involved in only a single minor offense and are not likely to find themselves in further legal difficulty, only refer youth for whom court referral is being seriously considered.

This agreement is crucial to our thinking. Unlike the youth service bureau approach, we did not wish to be involved with children who were not likely to be recidivists. They could much more reasonably be dealt with by the policeman's "warn and release procedures". We are also aware that such children, if they are overidentified, might even have problems created rather than alleviated (e.g., Fo & O'Donnell, 1975). On the other hand, we did want

---

*An interesting example of a "bug" occurred during the pilot semester. The police opened an envelope to determine the youths' random assignment to the experimental or control condition. We discovered that with certain youth the officers would continue to unseal envelopes until they found what they considered to be the appropriate assignment. Obviously, we altered the procedure to protect against such bias prior to our first full academic year of operation.

to identify the child for whom the police officer was ready to file a petition for court referral, and thus to divert him from the system.

FIRST YEAR OF RESEARCH

Following formal referral of 37 youths by the juvenile officers of the two metropolitan police departments, an interview was held with the youth and one of his or her parents. At that time a staff member explained the program to them, reviewing their constitutional rights and their rights as voluntary subjects; participation agreements and confidentiality agreements were signed at this time. There were no refusals. Following the introduction, the interviewer separately administered four assessment instruments to the youth and the parent. These instruments were the Marlow-Crowne Social Desirability Scale (1963), utilized to assess the positive description of one's behavior, a 16-item version of Rotter's Internal-External Locus of Control Scale (1966), revised specifically for the project to more adequately accommodate the reading level of the youth, a social labeling scale developed specifically for this project to assess the degree to which a youth identified himself as having been labeled delinquent or deviant by significant others in his life, and a 15-item behavioral checklist of commonly committed offenses designed to assess self-reported illegal activities in the prior three months. In addition, at the end of the interview, the youth was asked to nominate a close friend who would also be asked to complete the same assessment procedures, all of which asked questions about the referred youth. Nominated peers were interviewed within 48 hours of initial referral and paid $5 for their time. Following pre-assessment, the youth and his or her parents were informed as to whether they would be assigned to the program or whether they would be asked only to complete the post assessment approximately four months later. In other words, the pre-assessment was completed with the interviewer blind to eventual experimental condition.

In summary, pre-assessment consisted of youth, parent and youth-nominated peer verbal reports on analogous forms of four assessment instruments, all pertaining to the youth's behaviors and perceptions. At the time of termination, the four interview-based measures were re-administered to all three sources. Both the youth and the nominated peers were paid, by prior agreement, $5 for completing the post assessment instruments. In addition, police, court, and school records were searched, covering the time periods one year prior to, and throughout the duration of the program; police and court records were also gathered for a two-year follow up period.

In each case, referral to the program was accomplished as an alternative to a juvenile court petition being filed. The youths referred to the program had the following characteristics: 28 were males, 9 were females; 28 were white and 9 were black; the age range was 11 to 17 years with the mean age being 14.1

years; an average youth was in the eighth grade; the mean number of police contacts in the year prior to referral was 2.16. The 37 youths were randomly assigned to the experimental program or a control group. More specifically, randomization followed a procedure resulting in two-thirds of the youths being assigned to the experimental condition with stratification for sex, race, police department, and order of referral. Since goals for a given youth might be accomplished at any time during the program, it was expected that date of termination of contact between the college students and their referred youth would vary on an individual basis. In order to insure a consistent pre to post interval for experimental and control groups, control youths were randomly yoked with experimental youths, and each member of the experimental-control pair was evaluated over the same time interval.

The college students were assigned to youths following the completion of pre-assessment. Every effort was made to match student and youth on the basis of mutual interests, race and sex. The student initiated the contact by phone and thereafter was involved working with and for the youth six to eight hours per week for an average of four and one-half months (range three to five months). Intervention duration was determined by a goal attainment procedure (Kiersuk & Sherman, 1968) whereby behaviorally specific goals were established for each case one month after assignment and termination was completed when the specified goals were accomplished or closely approximated.

Strategies used by students can best be described as a combined effort involving the ingredients of relationship skills, behavioral contracting and child advocacy. The contracting component involved the assessment and modification of the interpersonal contingencies in the life of the youths, (e.g., with parents, teachers). The specific methods employed involved the establishment of written interpersonal agreements between the youth and significant others, as mediated by the students, according to the procedures outlined by Stuart (Stuart, 1971; Stuart & Lott, 1972; Stuart & Tripodi, 1973). In addition to the enhancement of specific behavioral changes on the part of the youth and significant others in his or her life, it was necessary in most cases to mobilize needed community resources for the youth in order to insure durability of desired change, and to provide legitimate avenues for attainment of the youth's goals. The strategies employed have recently been labeled child advocacy and involve the targeting of community resources such as educational, vocational, or recreational programs for change. The specifics of these procedures have been reviewed by Kahn, et. al. (1973) and further detailed in a recent paper by Davidson & Rapp (1976).

RESULTS

There were no statistically significant changes on any of the verbal report measures either from the adolescent's, his parents' or his peers' perspectives. An apparently dramatic program impact on the youths involved was evidenced primarily by police and court records and an isolated trend in school records.

Police and Court Records

Figure one depicts the differences between experimental and control subjects during the year prior to referral, during the intervention interval, and during the first and second year follow-up intervals since termination. During the one year period prior to referral, there were no significant differences in the number of police contacts, seriousness of police contacts (accomplished by a scheme developed by Sellin & Wolfgang (1964) modified to accommodate uniquely juvenile offenses), or the number of petitions filed with the court. As can be seen from Figure 1, all of the differences during the intervention, first year and second year follow-up intervals favor the experimental group, in that they have fewer contacts of lesser severity and fewer petitions filed than the control subjects. Most of these differences are significant at conventional levels, although a few only exhibit a trend. When we collapse across the approximately 27-month interval from time of referral through a two year follow-up period, the number of police contacts, severity of police contacts, and the number of petitions filed strongly corroborate the efficacy of the experimental program (see Figure 2). Controlling for prior level of "difficulty" of the youths by employing the severity of police contacts during the year prior to referral as a covariate leaves the results unaffected.

If we stringently define a success as no further contact with the police and a failure as one or more contacts (no matter how trivial) with the police, we again find the results to be quite powerful, despite the time interval (see Table 1). While an increasing number of experimental subjects have further contact with the police, you will recall that there was no substantial increase in the average number of contacts, severity of contacts or petitions filed with the passage of time.

School Records

Grade-point averages achieved by youths for the pre-period (one year prior to referral) were not detectably different. There were no differences in grade-point averages calculated for the period spanning the program's operation for youths in the experimental and control groups. Attendance records were similarly lacking in positive results.

An encouraging trend in the school data involves the percentage of youths still enrolled in school at termination. All youths were enrolled at the time of

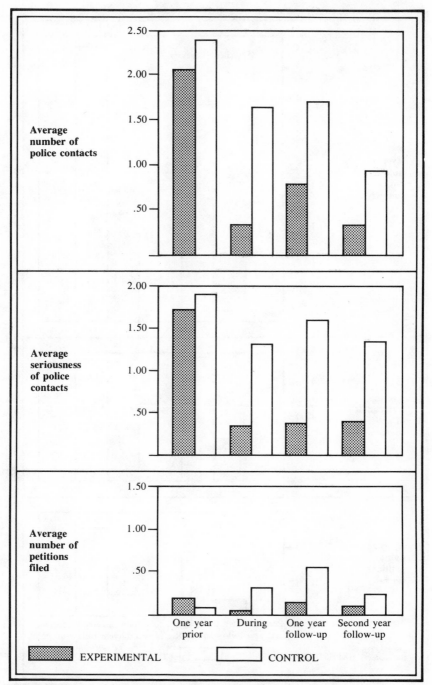

Figure 1   *Police and Court Record Data for First Year of Research*

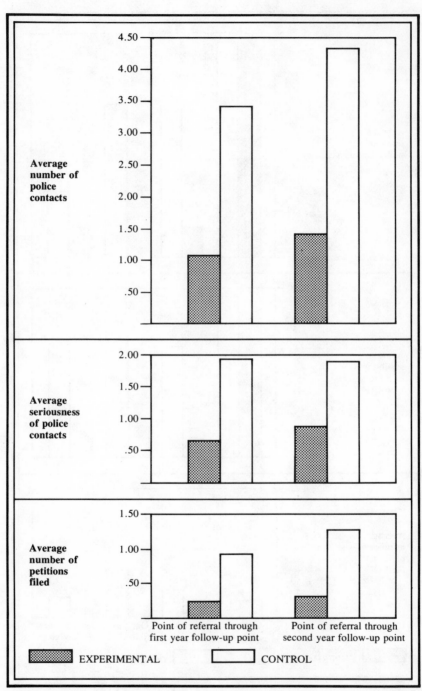

Figure 2   *Police and Court Record Date for First Year of Research from Referral*
Through First and Second Year Follow-up Points

TABLE 1

Success[a] and Failure[b] of Experimental and Control Subjects During Several Time Periods Subsequent to Referral (First Year of Research)

	During Intervention Interval		*Point of Referral to First Year Follow-Up Point*		*Point of Referral to Second Year Follow-Up Point*	
	Success	Failure	Success	Failure	Success	Failure
Experimental	20	5	16	9	13	12
Control	4	8	0	12	0	12
	$\chi^2_{cor.} = 5.79, p < .025$		$\chi^2_{cor.} = 11.05, p < .001$		$\chi^2_{cor.} = 7.47, p < .01$	

[a]Success = no further police contacts
[b]Failure = one or more additional police contacts

referral; 71% of youths in the experimental group were still enrolled at termination while only 50% of the control group remained in school. The remainder of both groups had either voluntarily dropped out or were extruded through suspension procedures. This trend, however, did not achieve conventional levels of statistical significance.

Juvenile Justice System

The total number of cases in which court petitions were filed by the police on any juvenile (regardless of program referral) were recorded on a month-by-month basis for the year prior to program implementation and during the months of program operation. The mean proportion of cases in which petitions were filed during the program operation was less than that of a corresponding period the previous year.

During program operation, from September, 1973, to March, 1974, only 11% of all juvenile cases investigated involved the filing of petitions. This is in contrast to the parallel period during the year (September, 1972, to March, 1973), when 16% of all cases investigated resulted in petitions filed. This occurs at a time when yearly averages were on a steady rise. An analysis of variance for time series designs (Gentile, et. al., 1972) was performed utilizing the two successive years of September to March monthly means as data points. The results were significant ($F = 8.41$, $df = 1/10$, $p < .01$).

SECOND YEAR OF RESEARCH

When we began our second academic year of operation, we were only aware of the reduced recidivism rates and the failure to achieve internal attitudinal changes during the intervention interval in the prior year. With the hope that we would replicate our efficacy on the so-called "hard" recidivism data, we made one major change and one major addition in an effort to more clearly understand some of the processes related to this success. These issues are presented in detail in Davidson's dissertation (1976). First, we separated the training and supervisory orientations of behavioral contracting and advocacy. We went from three small training/supervisory groups with a conglomerate orientation to two sets of two small groups with each set exclusively receiving either a behavioral contracting orientation or child advocacy orientation. While all groups had the same pair of co-supervisors, the college students were exposed to distinctively different training manuals, mastery evaluations, and content of supervision. Supervisory behavior was monitored weekly. Obviously, this separation was intended to feret out differential effects of behavioral contracting, child advocacy, and "treatment as usual" conditions. The pre/post interval for all groups was 18 weeks. A second major foci was to gain a detailed monitoring and understanding of the critical components of events in the lives of the youth, the components of the intervention approaches, and the salient features of the training and supervision sessions. Given the previously uncharted nature of this particular endeavor, it was also necessary to assess the outcroppings of these processes in a very exploratory fashion. The goal of this component of the research design was to both provide behaviorally specific data about these domains *and* to allow sufficient breadth in scope of the events assessed to provide ecological validity for the results.

Process interviews were conducted at four, ten, and sixteen weeks after referral with the target youth, their parents, the volunteer student (experimentals only), and the student's supervisor (experimentals only). A rational empirical strategy was employed to construct 33 process scales reflective of critical life events, perceptions of change, characteristics of the interventions, and performance in training and supervision.

Several changes in the pre-post measures were made. First, the Gough-Peterson (1952) Socialization scale was used as an indicant of socialization. Second, the recently developed Nowicki-Strickland (1973) Locus of Control Scale was used as a measure of Rotter's notions of internal-external locus of control. Third, the card sort procedures developed by Gold (1970) were used as a measure of self-reported delinquency. Fourth, the social labeling scale described earlier was maintained. All questionnaire based measures were administered to the target youth, one of his/her parents, and a peer nominated as a close friend in the second interview following the referral.

Thirty-six youths were referred to the project (33 males and 3 females). The mean age was 14.5. Twenty-one of the youth were white and 15 were black. In terms of the social characteristics of the youth's families, all youth came from lower to lower-middle class families. On the average, the group had 2.22 police contacts in the year prior to program referral. The type of offenses for which they had been arrested literally ranged from curfew violations to attempted murder. Following the completion of pre-assessment the youth were randomly assigned (according to similar procedures outlined for the 1973-74 project) to one of three conditions: behavioral contracting, child advocacy or "treatment as usual" control.

RESULTS

In brief, the results of the pre-post experimental component of the design provide a pattern very similar to the data from the 1973-74 project. Namely, the verbal report data regardless of instrument or source failed to yield any significant findings for condition, time, or the interaction term.

Police and Court Records

As you will note in Figures 3 and 4, the results of the 1973-74 project are strongly replicated at each time interval (i.e., through a first year follow-up point, to date) and on all recidivism and severity of recidivism variables. Furthermore, there do not appear to be any significant differences between the two experimental conditions — behavioral contracting and advocacy. Again, controlling for prior level of "difficulty" of the youths by employing the severity of police contacts during the year prior to referral as a covariate leaves the results essentially unaffected.

Again, stringently defining failure as one or more further contacts with the police following referral as a failure, we find the results quite powerful during the intervention interval. As can be seen from Table 2, there does appear to be some deterioration at the first year follow-up point, but the experimental conditions taken together still exhibit significantly less recidivism than the controls ($X^2_{cor.} = 6.30$, $p < .05$). However, advocacy subjects compared with controls manifested only a trend toward less recidivism ($X^2_{cor.} = 3.23$, $p < .10$).

School Records

Turning to school records, while analysis of grade point average failed to yield any significant results, analysis of attendance rates indicated a maintenance of school attendance among both experimental groups across time and a highly significant decrement at a two month follow-up point in the control group. (See Figure 5.)

Process Analyses

The basic design used to analyze the process dimension data was a three by two by three analysis of variance with repeated measures. The three factors included were condition, success versus failure, and the three process time periods. A success-failure criteria was determined for all youth by categorizing any youth who had one or more further police contacts *and/or* attended school less than an average of two days per week as a failure. Youth who remained out of trouble and stayed involved in school to some extent were categorized successful.

Table 3 presents a summary of the findings of the process and outcome data. These results lead to the beginning formulations of multiple contingency model of program operation and impact. First, for all conditions it was apparent that the success-failure criteria was closely related to what has been described as socially acceptable or sanctioned role involvement. The youth who end up in further trouble with the police and completely uninvolved in school are characterized by low levels of involvement at home, with the

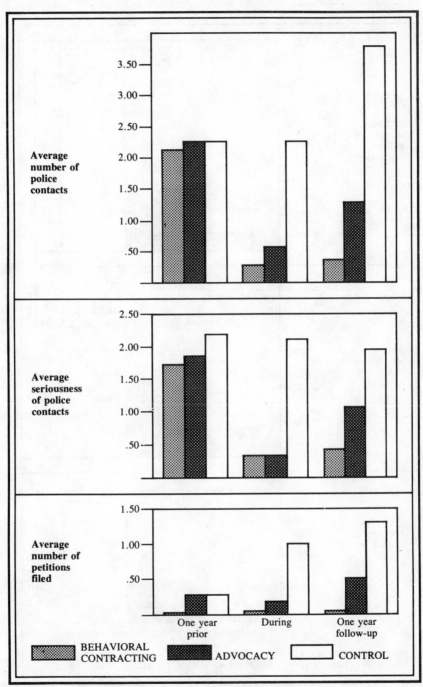

Figure 3 *Police and Court Record Data for Second Year of Research.*

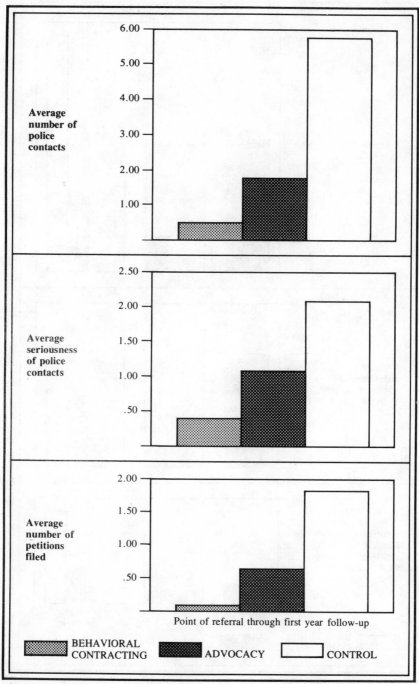

Figure 4 *Police and Court Record Data for Second Year of Research from Referral through a One Year Follow-up Point.*

TABLE 2

Success[a] and Failure[b] of Behavioral Contracting, Advocacy and Control Subjects During Two Intervals Subsequent to Referral
(Second Year of Research)

	During Intervention Interval		Point of Referral to First Year Follow-Up Point	
	Success	Success	Success	Failure
Behavioral Contracting (B.C.)	9	3	8	4
Advocacy (Adv.)	10	2	6	6
Controls (Cont.)	3	9	1	11

$\chi^2_{E \text{ vs Cont. cor}} = 7.73, p < .01$

$\chi^2_{E \text{ vs Cont. cor}} = 6.30, p < .025$
$\chi^2_{B.C. \text{ vs Cont. cor}} = 6.40, p < .025$
$\chi^2_{Adv. \text{ vs Cont. cor}} = 3.23, p < .10$

[a]Success = no further police contacts
[b]Failure = one or more additional police contacts
[c]Combined experimentals = behavioral contracting and advocacy youths

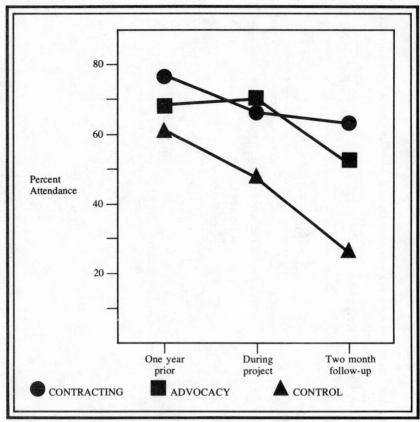

Figure 5 *Percentage of School Attendance — Second Year of Research*

school system, and with the employment market. Second, two of the intervention scales were specifically constructed as checklists of the model intervention conditions to assess the compliance of the volunteers in carrying out the prescribed intervention. Both experimental groups were assessed on the advocacy *and* contracting scales. The results strongly indicate that the two interventions were distinct. In other words, those in the contracting condition carried out their interventions according to the contracting model and not the advocacy strategy and vice versa.

Most striking, however, was the differential pattern of interventions displayed by different success and failure groups in both conditions related to the events in the youth's life. Youth who were more involved in socially approved roles received interventions focusing on multiple life domains. In addition for successful youth the intervention more closely followed the prescribed model. The interventions of those groups were characterized by higher levels of various intervention dimensions following from their intervention models. The contracting success group was observed to focus on

TABLE 3

Relationships of the Multiple Contingency Model (Second Year of Research)

	Behavioral Contracting	Child Advocacy	Control
Success	1. Involved in socially approved roles. 2. Stability on Change Dimensions. 3. Initiating contracting model. 4. Working on changes in the family area. 5. Working on changes in the youth's school performance.	1. Involved in socially approved roles. 2. Stability on Change Dimensions. 3. Initiation of advocacy model. 4. Working with the youth's friends. 5. Working on changes in the school system.	1. Involved in family and school. 2. Stability on Change Dimensions.
Failure	1. Uninvolved in socially approved roles. 2. Deterioration on Change Dimensions. 3. Initial trouble initiating contracting model. 4. Responding to juvenile justice system. 5. Attempting to get youth employed. 6. Family intervention focused on youth per se and minimal school intervention.	1. Uninvolved in socially approved roles. 2. Deterioration on Change Dimensions. 3. Initial trouble initiating contracting model. 4. Responding to juvenile justice system. 5. Attempting to get youth employed. 6. No family and minimal school intervention.	1. Involved in job seeking. 2. Deterioration on Change Dimensions.

the family and on the youth's behavior in school. On the other hand, the successful advocacy group focused on employment, the youth's friends, and changes in the school per se.

The contracting group which failed to meet with success, tended to focus on changing the youth within the family across time. In the school area, the intervention of the contracting group started with an intense effort which quickly desists. Since they showed increases over time in employment interventions and legal interventions, it is most likely that they began reacting to the demands of the justice system directly. These events coincided with the time the youth get into further official trouble with the police. In addition, they further responded to the quick failure on school area indirectly through attempts at employment. In other words, they remained relatively focussed on the youth in the family throughout. Their attempts at school intervention were replaced by an unproductive search for employment. In addition, they began responding to the juvenile justice system's need for information, reports, etc., when the youth becomes reinvolved in the justice system.

The advocacy failure interventions showed a somewhat different pattern in response to similar patterns of life events. Namely, the target youth in this group were reinvolved in trouble almost immediately (by Wave I process assessment) and consequently the intervention was characterized by responses to these legal problems. This took the direct form of engaging in interventions in the justice system as well as intensifying efforts towards obtaining a job for the youth. Essentially, the advocacy failure group included no intervention in the family domain and only minimal school intervention. In other words, the advocacy failure interventions focused from the beginning, both by actual life events and the prescriptions of the advocacy model, on responding to the justice system.

It is apparent then that the outcomes observed in the experimental and control youth were related not only to group assignment but to an apparent set of critical events. Given that the relationship of the youth to important social systems showed some deterioration following referral to the project, successful outcomes are unlikely to result. These patterns of interaction were observed much more frequently in the case of controls. When the interventions of the experimental youth met with initial success both in terms of their impact on the youth and the degree to which they can get things going in multiple areas of the youth's life, the program provides a stabilizing influence.

CONCLUSIONS AND FUTURE DIRECTIONS

Our alternative to the traditional juvenile justice system has demonstrated efficacy in reducing the rates and severity of official delinquency in two successive years with two independent groups of youngsters. Presently, these changes have endured through a two and a one year follow-up point for the first and second set of participants, respectively. In the most recent phases of this intervention we have been concerned with dissemination of the project to local agencies, and have involved local professionals who we have trained in the supervision of the college students. As this program continues, cooperation has developed between police and the new program professionals such that the local community now has a viable alternative to court actions on youthful offenders.

Providing alternatives which avoid the entanglement of youth in the legal system, it will be recalled, was a major motivation for this work from its onset. Although we can no longer justify randomly assigning some adolescents to a "treatment as usual" control group, we have arranged with the local agency now responsible for program administration for a continual monitoring of the results of the intervention for youth who participate. This should provide on-going feedback about success and failure, and enable continual readjustment of procedures, rather than program stagnation.

Before the program can be disseminated to other locations, it is necessary for other interventionists to compare experimental and control groups in their own locale; in order to test its efficacy in communities different than our own (e.g., those of varying size, differential police procedures, and community resources).

There remain a number of unanswered questions. Prime among them is "Why does it work?" What are the necessary ingredients for an effective intervention of this nature? For example, are college students (or college age people) necessary, or can similar programs operate by using older community volunteers? How crucial are the various contingencies contracted for in such a program? How salient is the intensity and format of training and supervision? What occurs in the lives of the youth and their social support networks one or two years following referral that maintains their continued non-involvement with the juvenile justice system? While we have a variety of hunches about these and other questions, we are continuing our attempts to explore and unravel the answers to these questions as systematically as possible. We hope many others will join in the quest to develop, implement and systematically evaluate similar innovative social programs designed to reduce the negative impact of the criminal justice system on young people. In this regard, we might add, not incidentally, that while programs such as the one described here may be of value for some youth, at least part of the answer to problems of delinquency will need to consider proposals for the elimination of uniquely juvenile status offenses from the realm of crime (c.f. Schur, 1973). It is only through multi-level interventions which combine such institutional changes with the kind of treatment alternatives suggested here that we can hope to have a significant impact on the problem of delinquency.

REFERENCES

Davidson, W.S., *The Diversion of Juvenile Delinquents: An Examination of the Processes and Relative Efficacy of Child Advocacy and Behavioral Contracting.* Unpublished dissertation, University of Illinois at Urbana-Champaign, 1976.

Davidson, W.S. & Rapp, C.A., "Child advocacy in the justice system," *Social Work*, 1976, 225–232.

Fairweather, G.W., *Social Change: The Challenge to Survival* (Morristown, N.J.: General Learning Press, 1972).

Fo, W.S.O. & O'Donnell, C.R., "The buddy system: The effect of community intervention on delinquent offenses," *Behavior Therapy*, 1975, *6*, 522–524.

Gentile, J.R., Roden, H. & Klein, R.B., "An analysis of variance model for intrasubject replication design," *Journal of Applied Behavioral Analysis*, 1972, *5*, 193–198.

Griggs, B.S. & McCune, G.R., "Community-based correctional programs: A survey and analysis," *Federal Probation*, 1972, *36*, 7–13.

Goffman, E., *Asylums* (New York: Anchor Books, 1961).

Gold, M., *Delinquent Behavior in an American City* (Belmont, CA: Brooks-Cole, 1970).

Gough, H.G. & Peterson, D.R., "The identification and assessment of predispositional factors in crime and delinquency," *Journal of Consulting Psychology*, 1952, *16*, 207–212.

Kahn, A.J., Kamerman, S.B. & McGowan, B.G., *Child Advocacy: Report on a National Baseline Study* (Washington, D.C.: U.S. Department of Health, Education and Welfare, 1973).

Kiersuk, T.J. & Sherman, R.E., "Goal attainment scaling: A general method for evaluating comprehensive community mental health programs," *Community Mental Health Journal*, 1968, *4*, 443–453.

Kiesler, D.J., "Some myths of psychotherapy research and the search for a paradigm" *Psychological Bulletin*, 1966, *65*, 110–136.

Kiesler, D.J., "Experimental designs in psychotherapy research." In A.E. Bergin & S.L. Garfield (Eds.), *Handbook of Psychotherapy and Behavior Change: An Empirical Analysis* (New York: Wiley, 1971).

Marlowe, D. & Crowne, D., *The Approval Motive* (New York: Wiley, 1964).

Nowicki, S. & Strickland, B., "A locus of control scale for children," *Journal of Consulting and Clinical Psychology*, 1973, *40*, 148–154.

Palmer, T.B., "California's community treatment program for delinquent adolescents," *Journal of Research in Crime and Delinquency*, 1971, *9*, 74–92.

Palmer, T.B., "The youth authority's community treatment project," *Federal Probation*, 1974, *38*, 3–13.

Paul, G., "Behavior modification research: Design and tactics." In C.M. Franks (Ed.), *Behavior Therapy: Appraisal and Status* (New York: McGraw-Hill, 1969).

Rappaport, J., *Community Psychology: Values, Research and Action* (New York: Holt, Rinehart & Winston, 1977).

Rappaport, J., Davidson, W.S., Wilson, M. & Mitchell, A., "Alternatives to blaming the victim or the environment: Our places to stand have not moved the earth," *American Psychologist*, 1975, *30*, 525–528.

Rotter, J.B., "Generalized Expectations for Internal vs. External Control of Reinforcement," *Psychological Monograph*, 1966, *80*, (1, Whole No. 609).

Ryan, W., *Blaming the Victim* (New York: Vintage, 1971).

Sarason, S.B., "Community psychology, networks, and Mr. Everyman," *American Psychologist*, 1976, *31*, 317–328.

Seidman, E. & Rappaport, J., "The educational pyramid: A paradigm for training, research, and manpower utilization in community psychology," *American Journal of Community Psychology*, 1974, *2*, 119–130.

Sellin, T. & Wolfgang, M.E., *The Measurement of Delinquency* (New York: Wiley, 1964).

Shore, M.F. & Massimo, J.L., "After ten years: A follow-up study of comprehensive vocationally oriented psychotherapy," *American Journal of Orthopsychiatry*, 1973, *43*, 128–132.

Schur, E.M., *Radical Non-Intervention: Rethinking the Delinquency Problem* (Englewood-Cliffs: Prentice-Hall, 1973).

Stuart, R.B., "Behavioral contracting within the families of delinquents," *Journal of Behavior Therapy and Experimental Psychiatry*, 1971, *2*, 1–11.

Stuart, R.B. & Lott, L.A., "Behavioral contracting with delinquents: A cautionary note," *Journal of Behavior Therapy and Experimental Psychiatry*, 1972, *3*, 161–169.

Stuart, R.B. & Tripodi, T., "Experimental evaluation of three time-constrained behavioral treatments for pre-delinquents and delinquents." In Rubin, et. al., *Advances in Behavior Therapy*, 1973, *4*, 1–12.

Part III

Intervention with the Families of Delinquents

Chapter 7

Editors' Remarks

The following study is a classic example of the value of involving the family in the treatment of delinquent behavior. This article presents well researched evidence of the efficacy of Alexander and Parsons's behavioral approach to family intervention and describes each component of their multi-modal technique which clearly differentiates this successful program from the often superficial "family counseling" programs which are more typical of correctional treatment services. Further research on this family therapy approach has demonstrated that the outcome of therapy very much depends on both the characteristics of the family and the skills of the therapists (Alexander et al., 1976).

REFERENCE

Alexander, J.F., Barton, C., Schiavo, R.S., & Parsons, B.V., "Systems-behavioral intervention with families of delinquents: therapist characteristics, family behavior, and outcome," *Journal of Consulting & Clinical Psychology*, 1976, *44*, 656–664.

Short-Term Behavioral Intervention with Delinquent Families: Impact on Family Process and Recidivism*

James F. Alexander and Bruce V. Parsons

Throughout the history of psychotherapy, evaluation of the effects of intervention have been notoriously absent. When evaluation has been attempted, most studies have failed to utilize control groups that really controlled for such major alternative hypotheses as attention placebo, maturation, and other intervening experiences. Other studies have used dependent measures of questionable relationship to overt behavior, such as projective devices, self and therapist reports, personality inventories, and Q sorts (Bergin, 1971). The field of family therapy also suffers from these deficiencies, with most reports characterized by enthusiastic program description and little or no data (Parsons & Alexander, 1972).

In response to this problem, the present investigation adopted the philosophy that family therapy research should involve four main goals. These goals, pursued in this project, are: (a) to provide a clear description of the intervention techniques; (b) to describe and evaluate the behavioral changes in family process expected from intervention (process measures); (c) to use clearly defined and essentially nonreactive behavioral criteria to evaluate the effects of intervention (outcome measures); (d) and, of course, incorporate adequate controls for maturation and professional attention.

The intervention program (designated short-term behavioral family

*Portions of this paper were presented to the meeting of the Rocky Mountain Psychological Association, Albuquerque, New Mexico, May 1972. This study was supported by a grant from the United States Department of Health, Education, and Welfare (#72-P-40061/8-01) entitled Intake Services for Detained Children.

intervention) involved a set of clearly defined therapist inverventions with delinquent families designed to: (a) assess the family behaviors that maintain delinquent behavior; (b) modify the family communication patterns in the direction of greater clarity and precision, increased reciprocity, and presentation of alternative solutions; (c) all in order to institute a pattern of contingency contracting in the family designed to modify the maladaptive patterns and institute more adaptive behaviors.

To evaluate the impact of these interventions and control for the effects of maturation and professional attention, families receiving the program (described below) were compared to families receiving alternative forms of family intervention and families receiving no formal intervention. It was hypothesized that families in the short-term behavioral family program, in contrast to these comparison groups, would demonstrate changes in family interaction (process measures) in the direction of less silence, more equality of speech, and greater frequency of positive interruptions. Further, reflecting these adaptive changes in family process, it was hypothesized that families receiving the program would demonstrate significantly lower recidivism rates than comparison groups on follow-up.

METHOD

SELECTION OF SUBJECTS

During the project, a total of 99 families were referred by the Salt Lake County Juvenile Court to the Family Clinic at the University of Utah from October 1970 to January 1972. Subsequent to the program, follow-up records were available only on 86 families of 38 males and 48 female delinquents, ranging in age from 13 to 16 years, who had been arrested or detained at the Juvenile Court for a behavioral offense. Such offenses included adolescents who had: (a) run away; (b) been declared ungovernable; (c) been habitually truant; (d) been arrested for shop-lifting; (e) been arrested for possession of alochol, soft drugs, or tobacco. With minor exceptions caused by program availability, families were randomly assigned upon detention to either the treatment program, comparison groups, or a no-treatment control condition.

TREATMENT CONDITION

Forty-six families were randomly assigned to the short-term behavioral family intervention program. Systems theory (Coles & Alexander, 1971; Haley, 1971; Waltzlawick, Beavin, & Jackson, 1967) provided the theoretical underpinning for the program, with the general proposition that families of delinquent teenagers represent maladaptive, disintegrating systems (Alexander, 1973). In this model, deviant behavior is seen as a function of the entire system in which the individual is embedded. The fact is, however, that systems theory represents more of a model, or point of view, than a specific theory, and does not include a set of clearly derived specific techniques for changing maladaptive patterns of family interaction. Thus, the specific treatment techniques, as well as the goals of intervention, were based on prior family interaction studies which have found that deviant families, as compared to normals, are more silent, talk less equally, have fewer positive interruptions, and in general are less active (Alexander, 1970; Duncan, 1968; Mischler & Waxler, 1968; Stuart, 1968; Winter & Ferreira, 1969). These manifestations of maladaptive interactions may be subsumed under the general concept identified by Patterson and Reid (1970) as lack of reciprocity in family interaction. Specifically, Patterson and Reid have demonstrated that when the amount and balance of mutual positive reinforcement have been altered (i.e., made more equitable by therapeutic intervention), families have moved from "bedlam" to relatively low rates of disruptive behavior.

Utilizing this concept, the present investigation was aimed at systematically extinguishing maladaptive interaction patterns and instituting reciprocity instead. Based on a matching to sample philosophy (Parsons & Alexander, 1972), the goal was to modify the interactions of deviant families so that they would approximate those patterns (described above) characteristic of "normal," or "adjusted" families. To meet this goal, therapists emphasized the removal of the circumstances (interactions) that elicited the behavioral offense, and replacing them instead with a process of contingency contracting (Stuart, 1968). In this process, therapists actively modeled, prompted, and reinforced in all family members: (a) clear communication of substance as well as feelings; and (b) clear presentation of "demands" and alternative solutions; all leading to (c) negotiation, with each family member receiving some privilege for each responsibility assumed, to the point of compromise.

In most cases, one or more family members were initially unwilling to negotiate about the major issue(s) that led to the delinquent offense (e.g., curfew times, choice of friends, etc.). Thus, in general, therapists chose a less crucial issue to use in training family members in contingency contracting (e.g., staying away after school until dinner in return for washing dishes). Generally, success in resolving such "minor" issues led to a willingness to deal with the major issues. To assist therapists in identifying the major issues, a training manual describing major "themes" in delinquent families was developed, together with a series of specific "do's" and "don'ts."

To facilitate training in reciprocity of communication behavior management skills, several specific manipulations were applied to all treatment families. First, therapists differentiated rules from requests. Rules were defined as limits designed to regulate and control the action and conduct of the family. Requests, on the other hand, were defined as "asking behavior" designed to prevent response constriction, that is, the person being requested to perform an act could reply in the affirmative or the negative without fear of negative sanction. By differentiating rules from requests, an unambiguous structure was placed upon the family system. Research in the area of delinquency development indicates that parents often set too many rules and are inconsistent with their use of punishment when these rules are broken. In doing this, a general lack of structure is built into the home and an environment for adolescent acting out is fostered. The aim of this treatment manipulation, then, was to make rules explicit, thus aiding in the development of an understandable environment in which the family could deal with one another.

A second major manipulation involved the systematic application of social reinforcement. In order to increase the family's ability to be variable in their communication patterns (negotiate for change constructively), it was necessary to train the family members in labile, solution-oriented communication patterns while they negotiated the specific content of the rule-request/token economy features of the program. Specifically, these communication patterns were categorized as: (a) interruption for clarification; (b) interruptions designed to increase information about the topic or about one's self in relationship to the topic; and (c) interruptions designed to offer informative feedback to other family members. This training consisted of having the therapist explicitly state the meaning and purposes of interruptions and the manner in which he would reinforce those behaviors. This was done because prior research (e.g., Mischel, 1958; Mischel & Grusec, 1967; Rotter, 1964) indicates that informational feedback about the situation and contingencies that will confront the subject in the future critically affect his behavior. Additionally, most experiments fail to obtain performance gains in the absence of accurate or at least partially correct hypotheses regarding the reinforcement contingencies (Adams, 1957; Dulany, 1962; Speilberger & DeNike, 1966). This explanation was followed with the subsequent dispensing of social reinforcement (e.g., verbal and non-verbal praise) by the therapist for the elicitation of the above types of communication variability.

Two additional manipulations were applied to some but not all families. A family training manual was designed for the project, basically consisting of a behavior modification primer aimed at the acceleration and extinction of behaviors on a systems level. This manual was a modification of a manual developed by Patterson and Gullion (1968) entitled *Living With Children*. It was felt that by alerting the family to the treatment rationale, they would be better able to incorporate and utilize the basic tenets of the treatment program. Unfortunately, few families read the entire manual, and experience demonstrated that the therapist time taken to insure reading could be more efficiently spent directly modifying the family's interaction patterns.

Token economy programs were also occasionally used, particularly with younger teenagers displaying home-specific behaviors in a context of high family contact. In designing the token system, each family member was asked to specify exactly what responses he would like to see accelerated in the other members. In addition to specifying three such responses, each family member identified the way in which he would like to be rewarded by the other. When a means was developed for the exchange of these responses, the family members were assisted in achieving reciprocity in their interactions.

SELECTION AND TRAINING OF THERAPISTS

Therapists consisted of 18 first- and second-year graduate students in clinical psychology participating in a clinical practicum series emphasizing family treatment, each of whom (with a few exceptions) saw two families. These students had little previous training and thus were more or less unbiased as to theoretical treatment regarding family therapy. Later, two selected undergraduate paraprofessionals were also assigned families after serving an "internship" as cotherapists with more experienced therapists.

Training included: (a) an initial four weeks of group training including role playing, discussions of therapist training manuals, and live observation (one-way mirrors) of each of the authors seeing a family; (b) subsequent live supervision (one-way mirrors) and group observation of therapists as they saw families; (c) biweekly group supervision of therapists to discuss and role-play interventions with families. In general, therapists received 6 hours of training and supervision each week. In addition, a session by session description of a "model" treatment program was developed (Parsons & Alexander, 1972), though therapists were allowed to spend more or less time on each phase of training as needed (e.g., some families were initially reasonably clear and precise concerning demands, while other families required several sessions of training in this preliminary skill).

COMPARISON CONDITIONS

To provide comparison groups to control for the effects of maturation and professional attention, an additional 30 families were randomly assigned (with minor exceptions due to program availability) to one of three comparison groups:

Client-Centered Family Groups Program   Nineteen of the families were assigned to a program representative of treatment in many juvenile centers; a basically didactic group discussion context focusing on attitudes and feelings about family relationships and adolescent problems based on the client-centered model. These families met for the same total time as families in the short-term behavioral treatment program. The two therapists, hired by the court to see families, were, of course, unaware that they represented a "comparison" condition. These therapists, one a fifth-year graduate student, one a recent Ph.D., did differ from therapists in the treatment condition in terms of having more clinical experience. However, it was assumed that any resulting bias would operate in favor of the comparison group.

Psychodynamic Family Program An additional 11 families were referred to a (Mormon) church sponsored family counseling program, which represents exactly the form of treatment a significant proportion of teenagers in Salt Lake County receive upon referral to the court. Because these referrals were made through local clergy to a separate agency, specific information on treatment parameters in this condition was impossible to obtain. However, one master's of social work (MSW) staff member (personal communication, April 1971) described the program as placing emphasis on insight as a vehicle for therapeutic change based on an eclectic psychodynamic model. Average treatment duration was estimated at 12–15 sessions, with considerable variation from family to family. The therapy staff, consisting of M.S.W.s and Ph.D.s generally represented a more experienced group than in the experimental treatment condition.

No-treatment Control An additional 10 randomly selected families were released from the court with no formal treatment but were contacted for testing on process measures (described below) 5–6 weeks after intake (comparable to posttesting interval for treatment families).

PROCEDURE: PROCESS MEASURES

As described in greater detail elsewhere (Parsons & Alexander, 1973), the first 20 treatment families completing the program, 10 client-centered family program families completing their program, and the 10 no-treatment controls were tested on family interaction tasks upon completion of their programs. Families were met in the waiting room of the Counseling Center by an experimenter naive as to their group designation and escorted into the interviewing room. After being seated in a prearranged order (father, child, mother), the family was given a series of three tasks: (a) behavior specificity phase; (b) vignette phase; and (c) interaction phase.

Accuracy of Perception (Behavior Specificity Phase) Each family member was given a pencil and a clipboard with two mimeographed sheets attached. The family was then instructed by the experimenter to list, in an independent fashion, the three behaviors each would like to see changed in each of the other members. Each family member was also asked to list the three behaviors each other member might want him to change.

Accuracy of Perception (Vignette Phase) Each family member was then asked by the experimenter to record, independently, in writing, his responses to each of three situations calling for parental action in relation to the child's behavior (e.g., the child's coming home long after curfew time). Both parents and child defined the type of action he would expect each of the other members to take.

Interaction Phase   Upon completion of these tasks the family was instructed to discuss, for a period of 20 minutes, their responses made during the behavior specificity phase and vignette phase. Families were told that they need not reach an agreement on the task. The experimenter then left the room after informing the family that during this time their interactions would be observed and recorded on an audiotape.

Dependent Measures: Changes in Family Process   The three interaction measures were based on the 20-minute audiotape sample of families discussing the accuracy of perception tasks. To obviate problems of reliability, all data were automatically recorded on event recorders by means of voice actuated microphones worn by each family member.

As decided above, the treatment manipulations, designed to increase reciprocity and clarity of communication, were hypothesized to produce changes in three dependent measures found in prior research to differentiate adaptive from nonadaptive family systems. Specifically, it was hypothesized that families receiving the program, as opposed to the comparison groups, would demonstrate: (a) more equality of interaction as measured by lower average within family variance of talk time across groups; (b) less silence, reflecting greater family activity; and (c) a greater frequency of interruptions, measured by overlapping event recorder deflectors. This measure was derived from recent work by Duncan (1968) and Mischler and Waxler (1968), who found (contrary to early findings in family research) that high rates of interruptions were characteristic of normal families, while deviant families demonstrated low interruption rates. An increase in such interruptions, as a function of therapy, was expected as a reflection of increases in both general activity level and attempts at clarity of communication.

OUTCOME MEASURES

As discussed above, even if changes in family process could be demonstrated as a function of intervention, such changes by themselves may not relate to the ultimate goal of intervention, reducing problematic (i.e., delinquent) behavior. Thus for the present report, juvenile court records were examined following termination of treatment for recidivism, that is, referral for behavioral offense. It was hypothesized that, congruent with the positive changes in family interaction, treated families would demonstrate a significant reduction in recidivism, while controls who were not expected to show changes in family interaction patterns would also demonstrate no reduction in recidivism.

RESULTS

To insure that random assignment of families resulted in comparability of groups, subjects were compared on demographic variables (i.e., age, socioeconomic status, and distribution of sex), prior recidivism rates, and pretest scores on the three interaction measures. As described elsewhere (Alexander & Parsons, 1972; Parsons & Alexander, 1973), no differences for any of these variables were found.

PROCESS MEASURES

Table 1 contains the group means for each of the three process variables. As can be seen, statistically significant differences were found on each dimension, with families receiving short-term behavioral family intervention, as hypothesized, demonstrating significantly lower variance (i.e., more equality) in talk time, less silence, and more interruptions.

Note that one-way analyses of variance were run and found to be significant. However, severe heterogeneity of variance, skew, and sample sizes raised serious doubts about the appropriateness of F tests. Thus significance values are presented for the rank-sum test for several samples (Dixon & Massey, 1957).

TABLE 1

Process Measurers: Posttest Means on Three Interactions Variables

Group	Variance of talk time[b] (in seconds)	Silence (seconds)	Fre- quency of inter- ruptions
Short-term family be- havioral treatment ($N = 20$)	1194.8	154.4	65.9
Client-centered family groups ($N = 10$)	1494.6	220.1	18.5
No-treatment controls ($N = 6$)[b]	2099.5	237.0	20.2
II value[c] ($df = 2$) of differences	11.19*	11.70*	13.75*

[a]Four families were unavailable for testing.
[b]Lower score indicates more equality of speech.
[c]Rank sum test for several samples.
* $p < .05$.

OUTCOME MEASURES: RECIDIVISM

At a 6- to 18-month interval following termination of the various treatment programs and control condition, juvenile court records of 86 families were examined for recidivism. (Note that the follow-up period for individual families varied widely, but across groups the period was comparable.) Table 2 presents recidivism rates for the four groups, plus data on two additional comparison groups.

Specifically, 46 cases were randomly selected from several hundred court cases referred during the project period but not assigned treatment due to program availability. These families were randomly selected during the same periods as the referrals on the treated families, in a yoked control fashion. Demographic and prior recidivism variables were comparable to treated families. The second additional "comparison group" represents recidivism rates for 2,800 cases seen county-wide during 1971, some of whom received various treatments (i.e., community mental health, church-sponsored counseling, private therapy, etc.) while many did not. Because these two

TABLE 2

Outcome Measures: Recidivism Rates for Treatment and Comparison Groups

Condition	N	No. of cases of recidivism	No. of non-recidivism cases	% recidivism
Groups compared statistically				
Short-term family behavioral treatment	46[a]	12[c]	34[c]	26
Client-centered family groups, treatment	19[b]	9[c]	10[c]	47
Eclectic psycho-dynamic family treatment	11	8[c]	3[c]	73
No treatment controls	10	5[c]	5[c]	50
Groups not included in statistical comparison				
Post-hoc selected no-treatment controls	46	22	24	48
County-wide recidivism rates, 1971	2800			51

[a] Includes 12 cases who dropped the program before completion.
[b] Includes 9 cases who dropped the program.
[c] Differences between samples: $X^2 = 10.25$, $df = 3$, $p < .025$.

latter groups were examined only on a *post hoc* basis, they were not included in the statistical analysis.

As can be seen in Table 2, the randomly assigned no-treatment controls demonstrated a 50% recidivism rate and the (comparison) family groups program a 47% rate, comparable to the county-wide 51% rate and the 48% rate demonstrated by the *post hoc* selected no-treatment controls. Further, the eclectic psychodynamic family program demonstrated a 73% rate, while the short-term behavioral family program demonstrated a significant (tested by chi-square) reduction in recidivism to 26%.

In addition to recidivism in behavioral offense, subsequent criminal offenses (i.e., felony, hit and run, etc.) were also evaluated. In a comparable direction to the behavioral data, though not significant, the treatment group demonstrated the lowest rate (17%) of subsequent criminal referral. The other groups ranged from 21% to 27%.

Two additional comparisons are of interest. First, although the treatment group had the lowest recidivism rates and the "best" scores on process measures, the hypothesized relationship between the two had still not been directly and statistically demonstrated. To do this, cases were divided into recidivism versus nonrecidivism groups, independent of treatment category. As expected, the nonrecidivism cases compared to recidivism cases, demonstrated significantly lower variance ($\bar{x}$s = 801.9 and 2143.8, respectively, $t = 3.97$, $df = 34$, $p < .01$), significantly less silence ($\bar{x}$s = 171.5 and 203.3, respectively, $t = 2.94$, $df = 34$, $p < .01$) and significantly more interruptions $\times$s = 58.7 and 28.5, respectively, $t = 4.17$, $df = 34$, $p < .01$).

Finally, time to recidivism was evaluated for the treatment group, the two comparison treatment groups, and the no-treatment controls. For families in which recidivism did occur, these average times were equivalent (2.4, 2.4, 2.8, and 2.7 months, respectively). Thus the program seemed to be effective in reducing the rate of recidivism but not in delaying its onset given its occurrence.

DISCUSSION

The results clearly demonstrate the efficacy of a short-term, specific, behavioral family treatment program for delinquent teenagers. Although the program was not completely successful in eliminating recidivism, a significant (both statistically and economically) reduction was demonstrated. Further, the inclusion of the control and comparison groups suggests that the beneficial effects of this form of treatment cannot be attributed to the effects of attention placebo or maturation. Finally, the fact that the comparison groups received forms of therapy representative of existing treatment procedures suggests that the treatment program utilized in the present project provides an efficient and economical alternative to existing practices.

The results also support the philosophy of therapy evaluation adopted in the project. Specific therapist interventions were found to significantly modify family interaction patterns, while nonspecific interventions did not. More importantly, however, these changes in interaction were related to decreased recidivism rates, while families that demonstrated no changes in interaction also demonstrated no reduction in recidivism. These results, of course, have important implications not only for implementing family treatment programs, but they also suggest directions for prevention.

Concerning the issue of outcome evaluation, it should be noted that the recidivism rates reported above included families who had dropped out of the program. All too often, psychotherapy outcome research involves only clients who have completed the program or have met some criterion such as attending four or five sessions. The inclusion of all referrals in outcome data, in contrast, provides a more meaningful, and honest, evaluation of the particular therapy program in question. For example, dropout information was available for the treatment group, the client-centered family groups program, and the no-treatment controls. With dropouts exlcuded, the recidivism rates for these groups were 22%, 50% and 50%, respectively, suggesting (somewhat unfairly) an even greater positive impact of the treatment program.

One final point must be emphasized. The fact that treatment and two comparison conditions involved some form of "family therapy" emphasizes that a focus on families *per se* is not sufficient to modify family interaction patterns or reduce rates of delinquency. Instead, it appears that family intervention programs may profitably be focused on changing family interaction patterns in the direction of increased clarity and precision of communication, increased reciprocity of communication and social reinforcement, and contingency contracting emphasizing equivalence of rights and responsibilities for all family members. This, of course, does not mean that other forms of therapy, not evaluated here, might not be as effective. Nor do the results imply the forms of family therapy used for comparison might not be considerably more effective in different contexts (i.e., different client populations, problem natures, therapists, etc.). However, at this stage of development in family therapy techniques, the burden of proof rests with the adherents of these alternative models.

REFERENCES

Adams, J.K., "Laboratory studies of behavior without awareness," *Psychological Bulletin*, 1957, *54*, 393–405.

Alexander, J.F., *A Systems Approach to Family Interaction*. Paper presented at the meeting of the Rocky Mountain Psychological Association, Salt Lake City, May 1970.

Alexander, J.F., "Defensive and supportive communications in normal and deviant families," *Journal of Consulting and Clinical Psychology*, 1973, *40*, 223–231.

Alexander, J.F. & Parsons, B.V., *Short Term Behavioral Intervention with Delinquent Families: Impact on Family Process and Recidivism*. Paper presented at the meeting of the Rocky Mountain Psychological Association, Albuquerque, May 1972.

Bergin, A.E., "The evaluation of therapeutic outcomes." In A.E. Bergin & S.L. Garfield (Eds.), *Handbook of Psychotherapy and Behavior Change* (New York: Wiley, 1971).

Coles, J.L. & Alexander, J.F. *Systems Theory and Family Behavior: Principles and Implications*. Paper presented at the meeting of the Rocky Mountain Psychological Association, Denver, May 1971.

Dixon, W.J. & Massey, F.J., *Introduction to Statistical Analysis* (New York: McGraw-Hill, 1957).

Delany, D.E., "The place of hypotheses and intentions: An analysis of verbal control in verbal conditioning. In C.W. Eriksen (Ed.), *Behavior and Awareness — A Symposium of Research and Interpretation* (Durham, North Carolina: Duke University Press, 1962).

Duncan, P., *Family Interaction in Parents of Neurotic and Social Delinquent Girls*. Unpublished doctoral dissertation, University of Wisconsin, 1968.

Haley, J., *Changing Families: A Family Therapy Reader* (New York: Grune & Stratton, 1971).

Mischel, W., "The effect of the commitment situation on the generalization of expectancies," *Journal of Personality*, 1958, *26*, 508–516.

Mischel, W. & Grusec, J., "Waiting for rewards and punishments: Effects of time and probability on choice," *Journal of Personality and Social Psychology*, 1967, *5*, 24–31.

Mischeer, E. & Waxler, N. *Interaction in Families* (New York: Wiley, 1968).

Parsons, B.V. & Alexander, J.F., "Short-term family intervention: A therapy outcome study," *Journal of Consulting and Clinical Psychology*, 1973, *41*, 195–201.

Patterson, G.R. & Gullion, M.E., *Living with Children: New Methods for Parents and Teachers* (Champaign, Ill.: Research Press, 1968).

Patterson, G.R. & Reid, J.B., "Reciprocity and coercion: Two faces of social systems." In C. Neuringer & J. Michael (Eds.), *Behavior Modification in Clinical Psychology* (New York: Appleton-Century-Crofts, 1970).

Patterson, G.R., Reid, J.B., & Shaw, D.A., "Direct intervention in families of deviant children," *Oregon Research Institute Bulletin*, 1968, Whole No. 8.

Rotter, J.B., *Clinical Psychology* (Englewood Cliffs, N.J.: Prentice-Hall, 1964).

Spielberger, C.D. & DeNike, L.D., "Descriptive behaviorism versus cognitive theory in verbal operant conditioning," *Psychological Review*, 1966, *73*, 306–326.

Stuart, R.B., "Token reinforcement in marital treatment." In R. Rubin & C.M. Franks (Eds.), *Advances in Behavior Therapy* (New York: Academic Press, 1968).

Watzlawick, P., Beavin, J. II, & Jackson, D.D., *Pragmatics of Human Communication* (New York: Norton, 1967).

Winter, W.D. & Ferreira, A.J., "Talking time as an index of intrafamilial similarity in normal and abnormal families," *Journal of Abnormal Psychology*, 1969, *74*, 574–575.

Chapter 8

Editors' Remarks

That point in a delinquent's life when his contact with the police creates a crisis situation within his or her family may create the ideal motivational conditions and optimal timing for treatment intervention. A demonstration of the value of responding immediately to such family crises with an intensive and comprehensive counseling service is provided in the following report. The report demonstrates how such a crisis-service can be provided efficiently and economically with a large number of delinquents through the use of volunteer counselors, and it demonstrates the effectiveness of such an approach as assessed by a variety of measures.

This project is also noteworthy because of its use of teams of male and female counselors, and its programmatic assessment of treatment outcome. Like several other projects presented in this book, it is a good demonstration of the gains, in terms of goal achievement at minimal costs, that can accrue to the juvenile justice system by systematically and efficiently tapping the human resources of a local university.

A Family Crisis Intervention Approach to Diversion from the Juvenile Justice System*

Terry C. Wade, Teru L. Morton,
Judith E. Lind and Newton R. Ferris

INTRODUCTION

The juvenile justice system has enjoyed the relatively rare distinction of an emphasis on prevention. However, continued increases in adolescent offenses underscores the need for expanded efforts in this area. In response to this need a variety of programs have been implemented which focus on diverting adolescents from court involvement. Although many of these programs report effective diversion, evaluation of their usefulness is limited by insufficient information concerning such factors as characteristics of the counselors and the populations served, types of intervention procedures used, how outcome criteria were obtained and measured, and the program costs. Further, without experimental control comparisons, suggested relationships between intervention components and attainment of treatment goals cannot be accepted with confidence.[1]

In defense of attempts to evaluate public service programs, and especially those intended to divert adolescents from court involvement, it should be noted that a host of factors mitigate against mounting research which

*Wade, T.C. et al., "A family crisis intervention approach to diversion from the juvenile justice system," *Juvenile Justice Journal*, 1977, *28*(3), 43–51. Copyright © 1977, National Council of Juvenile and Family Court Judges. Reprinted by permission.

[1]Lundman, R.J., McFarlane, P.T., and Scarpitti, F.R., "Delinquency prevention: A description and assessment of projects reported in the professional literature," *Crime and Delinquency*, 1976, *22*, 297–308.

successfully avoids all threats to validity.[2] Indeed, demands for service delivery typically preclude using powerful experimental designs. Moreover, proposals to provide identical treatment to all clients, as required by experimental group research, often ignore the individual needs of clients and are therefore unacceptable to program administrators.

Faced with such pressures, evaluation is perhaps best approached in a programmatic fashion, where research questions are answered only through a succession of investigations, each of which attempts to control for a subset of validity issues. Thereby, evaluation research can be implemented while programs continue to provide services in accord with administrative and treatment demands. For example, data may be gathered to provide a demographic profile of the populations served. Recidivism may then be correlated with family characteristics and treatment procedures used. Finally, successful treatment procedures may be systematically varied to determine which are the most effective for which types of families. What is essential in this approach is that treatment efforts are individually tailored to the needs of clients, that evaluation methodology is useful in evaluation efforts, and that data collected at an individual level are translatable into evaluation at a program level.

Evaluation measures which focus on improving services and serve a useful function for counselors can be expected to increase staff cooperation and the probability that implementation of the measures will be successful.[3] If the measures used in evaluation are also useful in treatment, their use will not contribute substantially to program costs. In this regard, moreover, time allocated to training in the use of the measures could be largely attributed to training in service delivery.

The present paper concerns a demonstration program which was designed to divert first-time adolescent offenders from further penetration into the juvenile justice system in Honolulu, Hawaii. The program has not only proven highly effective, but has demonstrated the use of procedures which lend themselves to answering evaluation questions in a programmatic fashion. The purpose of this paper is to describe the functions of the program and a combined evaluation and training procedure in sufficient detail that other agencies might initiate similar programs, incorporate relevant aspects to increase their effectiveness, or implement the evaluation procedures to provide data for accountability or refining treatment procedures.

---

[2]Campbell, D.T., and Stanley, J.C., *Experimental and Quasi-Experimental Designs for Research*, (Chicago: Rand-McNally, 1963).

[3]Reinke, W.A., "Methods and measurements evaluations." In W.A. Reinke (Ed.), *Health Planning: Qualitative Aspects and Quantitative Techniques* (Baltimore, Md.: Waverly, 1972).

PROGRAM DESCRIPTION

The Intensive Intervention Project (IIP) is a demonstration program funded by the State Law Enforcement Planning Agency under the sponsorship of the Family Court of the First Circuit in Honolulu. Conceptually, it is similar to the Sacramento Diversion Project.[4] The purpose of the project is to provide effective diversion of those adolescents from the court system who are referred for the first time for behaviors, such as runaway, incorrigibility, need for supervision, and first time minor law violations.

PROJECT AND COUNSELING STAFF

The permanent (paid) staff of the IIP consists of a coordinator, one full-time counselor, and one half-time secretary. The remaining counseling staff are comprised primarily of graduate student volunteers recruited from the University of Hawaii from the disciplines of clinical psychology, educational psychology, human development, psychiatric nursing, public health, and social work. Student volunteers typically receive practicum or internship credit which is arranged through their graduate departments. Other volunteers occasionally include probation officers, staff from other agencies, and qualified interested citizens.

Although an average of twenty-one volunteers is trained in a given year, only about twelve are active at any time (many participate for only six or nine months). Nevertheless, the reliance on volunteers enables the project to provide services to many more families than could the permanent staff alone. Because of periodic turnover of students, counseling teams are used. More experienced counselors are coupled with less experienced counselors so that ongoing training and client continuity are provided as counselors enter and leave the project.

POPULATION

During its four years in operation, the IIP has provided services to 321 families. Because of its focus on family systems, counseling includes parents and siblings, as well as adolescent offenders, and also includes other relatives or unrelated persons who are involved in the problem, such as school counselors and friends of the adolescent. As a result, over 1,350 persons have received counseling through the IIP in four years.

---

[4]Baron, R., Feeney, F. and Thorton, W., "Preventing delinquency through diversion: The Sacramento County diversion project," *Federal Probation*, 1973, 13–19.

The adolescents have included 36.2% males and 63.8% females. Their ages varied predominantly from thirteen to seventeen, with a mode of sixteen. Ethnic backgrounds have varied widely, including 36.2% Caucasians, 21.7% part-Hawaiians, 11.6% Filipino, 11.6% Japanese, 4.3% Portuguese, and a remainder of families of other less frequently occurring ethnic composition. Approximately fifty percent of the families served had experienced some degree of family disorganization, such as divorce, separation, remarriage, adoption, or death of a natural parent.

REFERRAL AND THE COURT

The predominant reasons for referral to the IIP are runaway (49.3%) and incorrigibility (36.2%). Other referrals include theft (2.9%), need for supervision (2.9%), and a variety of infrequent offenses, such as burglary and curfew violations. The great majority of cases (approximately 80%) are referred from a juvenile detention center. Other referrals are sometimes made by various public and private agencies and probation officers, and occasionally parents request services directly. Cases referred from the detention center are considered on an intake status with the family court. This helps insure family participation. In addition, a ninety-day restriction for counseling serves as an incentive for both families and counselors to work actively at resolving problems.

INTERVENTION STRATEGIES AND TECHNIQUES

The training for the IIP counselors is a composite of the family systems and crisis intervention approaches of Ackerman, Langsley and Kaplan, and Satir.[5] The core of intervention *strategies* used by the IIP includes five components: (1) immediate response to referrals, which is intended to capitalize on the motivation because of a family crisis situation with respect to contact with the juvenile justice system (police and the court); (2) intensive but time-limited outreach services, where the time and place of counseling meetings, their duration, and their frequency are accommodated to the family situation to reduce client resistance; (3) a focus on the family as a system which is functioning maladaptively and which requires change as a unit for long-term remediation to be effected; (4) use of counseling teams consisting of a male and female, typically of similar ethnic extraction to act as role models and to

---

[5]Ackerman, N.W., *Treating the Troubled Family* (New York: Basic Books, 1966). Langsley, D.G., and Kaplan, D.M., *The Treatment of Families in Crisis* (New York: Grune and Stratton, 1968). Satir, V., *Conjoint Family Therapy* (Palo Alto, Calif.: Science and Behavior Books, 1967).

increase the probability that all family members will be able to relate to the counselors; and (5) frequent reliance on adjunct agencies for accepting referrals to maintain changes initiated by intensive counseling.

During the first year of the project, out of the total of sixty-nine families served, only forty-seven adolescents were actually first-time offenders with no prior court contact. Of the total of sixty-nine families, fifty-two siblings (75% of siblings seen) were already known to the court. Of the first-time offenders, thirty-six (76.6%) were diverted and had not recidivated at a one-year follow-up. However, of the twenty-two repeated offenders, only twelve (54.5%) were diverted, while the remainder required continued court services. Thus, while the rate of recidivism was reduced for repeated offenders, as well as first-time offenders, the greater recidivism rate for repeated offenders recommends early intervention.

During the second year, seventy out of the eighty-four families served (83.3%) did not require adjudication during treatment. Of these only ten percent had recidivated at a one-year follow-up. Of the fourteen who were adjudicated, seven were law violators and seven were placed outside their homes. During these two years, no additional siblings became known to the court. Thus, the project has been successful in diverting adolescents from court involvement. In addition, a further benefit of the family focus of treatment is apparent in the reduction in rates of court contacts by siblings. Therefore, the prevention function of the project has been extended one step further.

It should also be noted that the IIP has managed to involve *all* families referred to it in counseling. Thus, the potential drop-out population, frequently used as an inappropriate control group in reports of treatment programs, here contributed to recidivism statistics.

Because of the limited duration of the IIP, it was decided to develop a method to obtain precise descriptive information on program functions and costs. It was also decided that the method permits extension toward programmatic investigation of other issues. The remainder of this paper is devoted to a description of the measures developed for this purpose and the findings associated with their use.

The corresponding crisis intervention *techniques* which are utilized begin with the present problem, but then shift to family interactions in a system, that is, how patterns of interaction maintain the situation that led to the crisis. These techniques include seven components: (1) intellectual understanding of causal relationships between parental and adolescent behaviors; (2) clarification of values and demands of family members regarding critical issues; (3) active involvement of counselors as models, with expression of feelings and thoughts to the family; (4) training family members in expressing themselves clearly and completely; (5) exploration of previous coping methods and their inadequacies; (6) focusing on the present and future to facilitate active, goal-oriented problem solving; and (7) use of behavioral contracts and training in negotiating skills to foster clearly stated rules and consequences for family members' actions and compromises over disagreements.

OTHER AGENCY INVOLVEMENT

Most of the families served by the IIP have reported a history of problems existing back for at least one year. This suggests some agency involvement would be necessary for an extended period to ensure changes are maintained. Yet, it was found that referrals made to community agencies by the court before implementing the IIP were not followed up by the majority of families. Consequently, the IIP routinely offers time-limited intensive services at a time of crisis, and where families require further services to maintain changes, personnel from other agencies are included in counseling sessions before termination. As a result, 90.6% of referrals have been successful.

EFFECTIVENESS

Before the implementation of the IIP, in one study of seventy-seven cases, adolescents charged with PINS offenses had approximately a 70% recidivism rate, as defined by subsequent referrals to the court. An average of 6.7 additional referrals occurred over the course of one year, with virtually all being police referrals. Also, in those cases, thirty-two siblings were known to the family court.

PROGRAM ANALYSIS

Because the IIP is service oriented and accepts all families needing its services, comparisons with a control sample could only be approximated for the IIP program by examining recidivism rates before project implementation. Similarly, isolation of effective treatment components was not possible. However, assuming that reduced recidivism rates are due to project intervention, and assuming further that positive changes observed in the goals of intervention are related to successful diversion, it seemed useful to determine the nature of goals established with families and their relative attainment. Furthermore, indexes of client satisfaction with the program and information on its cost were obtained to provide useful information for other agencies interested in offering a similar program.

A sample of thirty-four successively referred families were selected in the third project year as a source of data for more intensive analysis of program functions, for determining family satisfaction with various program elements, and for making effectiveness/cost statements. Two advanced clinical psychology graduate students who had been serving as counselors and had previous experience with program evaluation volunteered to adapt measures for this project. The program analysis project was supervised by the IIP coordinator.

MEASUREMENT PROCEDURES

In the sample, as in previous follow-up analyses, recidivism was low (14.7%). Also, of the total number of siblings under eighteen in the thirty-four families (66), only one became known to the court during the one-year follow up.

Goal Attainment Measures   In order to document more precisely the goals pursued by counselors and the outcome which immediately resulted from counseling efforts, Goal-Attainment Scaling (GAS), a procedure developed by Kiresuk and Sherman,[6] was adapted for use by counselors. The popularity of GAS has resulted from its applicability to a wide range of service-oriented programs.[7] Indeed, it can be used with diverse presenting problems, for clients widely different in demographic characteristics and expectations for treatment, and by counselors from virtually any therapeutic persuasion.

The typical use of the procedure permits selection of goals with or without the collaboration of clients and may be based on the counselor's theoretical formulations. Each goal is weighted according to its relative importance. The sole restriction in the use of GAS is that outcome criteria be specified in sufficiently objective terms to permit assessment by someone unfamiliar with the case. Outcome criteria are specified according to a common scale at lease at three of five levels (where -2 = the most unfavorable outcome thought likely, -1 = less than expected level of success, 0 = the expected outcome, $+1$ = more than expected, and $+2$ = the most favorable outcome thought likely). Because all goals are thus reduced to a common scale, it is possible to compare outcome across goals. For this purpose, Kiresuk and Sherman developed an equation to derive a total outcome (T) for a given case, with a standardized mean of fifty and a standard deviation of ten.

---

[6]Kiresuk, T.J. and Sherman, R.E., "Goal-attainment scaling: A general method for evaluating comphrehensive community mental health programs," *Community Mental Health Journal*, 1968, *4*, 443–453.

[7]Simons, L.S., Morton, T.L., Wade, T.C., and McSharry, D.M., "Retrospective therapy outcome (GAS) using closed case records." In D.M. McSharry (ed.), *Get the Most Mileage from Program Evaluation: Use GAS (Goal-Attainment Scaling)*, symposium paper presented at the Rocky Mountain Psychological Association in Phoenix, Arizona, 1976. Wade, T.C., and Morton, T.L., "Integrating treatment, training, and evaluation: A goal-oriented systems approach." In D.M. McSharry (Ed.), *Get the Most Mileage from Program Evaluation: Use GAS (Goal-Attainment Scaling)*, symposium paper presented at the Rocky Mountain Psychological Association in Phoenix, Arizona, 1976.

GAS was initially designed for use by an independent intake evaluation team (independent of therapists or counselors). By using GAS in the IIP, supervision centering on decisions of what to target as change goals and subsequently concerning progress on goal attainment, plus accountability to the court, accurate reporting by counselors was ensured.

Treatment Goals and Attainment   Within the first two sessions of counseling, counseling teams established and weighted two to five goals according to their relative importance for each family, and developed outcome scales along with current levels for each scale. At termination, counselors determined the level of goal attainment. Because the IIP deals with a relatively homogeneous set of problems, it was possible to contrast relative attainment of different types of goals using the small sample.

Broadly, the 127 goals established by counselors fell in ten categories which varied substantially in their frequency of occurrence. The more frequently used categories of goals were improved family communication (23.6% of goals), increased school attendance (18.9%) reduced runaways (15.7%), and increased acceptance of responsibility in the family (13.4%). Less frequently used categories were compliance with curfew (7.1%), improved involvement with peers (7.1%), elimination of law violations (4.7%), referral or placement (4.7%), reduction in smoking, drug, and alcohol use (3.1%), and elimination of suicide attempts (.8%).

Overall success of goal attainment, reflected in an aggregate scale outcome score of $T = 56$, indicated more than expected success. Fully eighty-two percent of counselor set goals were attained at or better than the expected level of success, thereby providing validation of the effectiveness of counseling from the counselors' point of view, as well as from recidivism data. Goals focusing on relationships, included both enhancing family communication and new or improved involvement with peers. While attempts to modify family interactions were the single most common goal, the rate of successful attainment was relatively modest (22 of 30 cases, or 73.3%). On the other hand, goals concerning improving relationships with peers were attained in every case.

Goals of a contractual nature, those involving rules within the family and the court authority, comprised seven categories which met with varying degrees of success. Goals dealing with accepting responsibilities within the family were generally successful (14 of 17 goals, or 82.4%). With respect to legally related rules, goals for eliminating runaways and curfew violations were achieved in ninety percent of cases (27), whereas increasing school attendance proved somewhat more difficult (17 of 24 cases, or 70.8%). The more infrequent problems with stealing and shoplifting were typically successfully eliminated. All six cases in which referral or placement with another agency was actually established as a goal were successful.

Family Interviews   Additional data concerning program elements and satisfaction were obtained through structured post-treatment interviews conducted individually with family members by counselors not involved with the family. This provided another perspective on program functions while maintaining low cost. Family members were asked to use a 5-point Likert scale (1 = not useful, 3 = somewhat useful, and 5 = very useful) to rate the value of various features of the IIP program. These included: (1) flexibility in length of sessions; (2) availability of counselors (by phone or in person, and for unscheduled meetings); (3) scheduling meetings after working hours; (4) willingness of counselors to meet in the home; (5) out-reach efforts by counselors; (6) absence of fees; (7) use of counseling teams; (8) possibility of seeing counselors individually as well as in the family; (9) willingness of counselors to deal with other concerns than court business; (10) use of contracts; (11) use of court authority; and (12) use of the detention center.

Family members reported that they found most aspects of the program quite helpful (range of 4–5 for both adolescents and parents). Variability was evident in three areas, however. Parents of adolescents who ultimately were again referred to the court were less satisfied with contracts (mean of 2.2) than were those parents who did not become involved further (4.1). Similarly, the adolescents who were again referred to the court were less satisfied with contracts (2.6) than those who were not (3.5).

With respect to the use of court authority and the detention center, parents of adolescents who became further involved with the court were somewhat less satisfied (3.8 and 4.0, respectively than those parents who did not become further involved (4.4 and 4.2, respectively). Similarly, adolescents who had subsequent court contacts were less satisfied (2.8 and 2.2, respectively) than those who did not (3.2 and 2.8, respectively).

Three additional questions were posed to obtain a rough estimate of satisfaction with services and their outcome. Family members were asked to use three-point scales (1 = no. 2 = yes, a little, and 3 = yes, a lot) to rate: (1) their perception of improvement as a result of IIP services; (2) their satisfaction with the outcome of counseling; and (3) whether or not they would want help in the future if they have further problems. The responses to all three questions were lower for parents of adolescents who had subsequent court contacts (2.0, 2.0, and 2.2, respectively) than for parents who did not (2.5, 2.6, and 2.7, respectively). Similarly, the adolescents who had subsequent court contacts rated the three questions lower (2.0, 2.2, and 2.2, respectively) than those who did not (2.3, 2.5, and 2.5, respectively).

COST

Case Summary Data   Counselors kept records of their activities during the course of treatment and prepared case summaries which were required by the court following termination. The record of time expenditure hence provided one index of program cost. Averages for activities and time per counselor included: (1) direct counseling time (11.7 sessions for 17.7 hours); (2) phone contacts with family members (7.0 contacts for 2.4 hours); (3) in person contacts with schools, agencies, and collaterals (4.9 for 1.2 hours); (4) detention and court hearings (2.1 for 1.8 hours); and (5) paper work (2.8 hours). Thus, the average time per case per counselor was 27.6 hours.

Treatment Adjuncts   In addition, an attempt was made to provide a rough estimate of indirect costs due to consultation and involvement of agency personnel outside the project. This included testing or mental health consultation, and actual involvement by other agencies. Testing and mental health consultation was used in eight cases, while private therapists were involved in three cases. Other personnel involved included other agency staff (9 cases), clergy (2 cases), and youth activity or educational groups (6 cases). It is apparent, therefore, that the diversionary efforts represented a concentrated commitment on the part of the IIP and included involving other agencies with the families served and involvement of the adolescents in alternative activities. In fact, simply documenting counseling sessions provided an incomplete picture of the treatment effort.

SUMMARY AND CONCLUSIONS

The present paper describes a demonstration project, the Intensive Intervention Project or IIP, which was designed to divert first-time adolescent offenders from court involvement, and a measurement system which was used as a first step toward programmatic analysis of treatment functions and outcome. A modified version of Goal Attainment Scaling (GAS) provided a means of measuring the attainment of treatment goals based on the needs of individual families while providing information useful at a program level. Because the IIP served a population with fairly homogeneous problems, GAS could be used to document the goals typically pursued by counselors and to analyze their attainment. Along with GAS, brief structured interviews were conducted with each family member to obtain their opinions concerning the usefulness of program features and their satisfaction with treatment and outcome.

Generally, the IIP has proven highly effective in reducing recidivism, and dramatic decreases in court contacts by siblings suggests added benefits accrue to a family focus in treatment. Among the more important findings associated with the use of GAS was that rule, or contractual goals were more often met than goals directed towards improving communication or relationships within the family. A related finding was that members of families who had no further contacts with the court rated the usefulness of contracts much higher than members of families who did have repeated court contacts. These findings taken together suggest that teaching families to negotiate differences through contracting may be a very important treatment component. Because successful diversion is assumed to be mediated by changes in family interaction, the effectiveness for changing family communication by focusing on acquisition of negotiating skills compared to focusing on communication in a more general sense certainly warrants further research attention.

Another finding relevant to processes mediating diversion was that goals focusing on changes in peer involvements were always successful. Because peer influence can be expected to serve a powerful function in adolescent behavior, often supplanting family influence, a focus on peer involvement may also be a vital program element. Here, again, further research emphasis is warranted.

While many programs have indicated success in diverting adolescent offenders, more detailed reports of program functions are needed. The present paper outlines a methodology of a primarily descriptive sort. The use of GAS in facilitating precise program description represents an innovation in the application of this technique which may serve to further its appeal to agency administrators in a wide variety of settings. Indeed, the first step in a programmatic approach to program evaluation is the acquisition of descriptive data. Also, to provide a basis for replication, a wealth of descriptive data is necessary. GAS provides a convenient technique for gathering such information. By using GAS as a descriptive tool, as well as an outcome measure, information is available concerning program functions and the success that might be expected. However, to extend the programmatic approach to evaluation of the treatment of the juvenile offender, controlled investigations of program elements are necessary. For example, the relationship between successful attainment of frequently used goals and recidivism should be explored.

One major need in the area of juvenile justice is the design of evaluation programs which incorporate sufficient controls to determine which intervention components are actually effective. Determination of the effective components of treatment programs would ensure that adequate attention is devoted to them during treatment, while less effective components could be minimized or deleted. This concern becomes critical when treatment is of limited duration, which is typically the case for programs with limited staff and high demands for services.

Mortillaro and Carmany recently stressed the need to develop models of comprehensive and systematic service in the area of juvenile justice to provide for accurate evaluation of services being rendered.[8] In this regard, GAS appears to hold great promise as a central evaluation measure around which other measures can be devised to meet the idiosyncratic needs of particular

---

[8]Mortillaro, L.F., and Carmany, J.P., "Service accountability model for the juvenile justice system," *Juvenile Justice*, 1975, *26*, 35–39.

programs. In addition to being used as an evaluation tool, GAS can be useful in training and supervision. By relying on counselors to establish goals and scale outcome levels, GAS can provide a framework for case conceptualization. Indeed, the goal orientation provides continuous feedback on case management with respect to court imposed deadlines by demanding that realistic goals are selected and the effects of intervention techniques are monitored. This encourages counselors to pursue responsible contacts with schools and other agency personnel for feedback concerning progress toward treatment goals. Simultaneously, this use of GAS facilitates case supervision with respect to treatment goals and intervention techniques selected to pursue them. Hence, supervisors and administrators may be provided with a precise understanding of what is being attempted by counselors, and allow them to determine what goals are realistic, what scales are appropriate, and what treatment procedures can be expected to be effective.

Although the IPP program itself maintains low direct costs through its reliance on volunteers, records kept by counselors along with case summaries indicated substantial time is devoted to diversion efforts. Also, indirect costs accrue by involving other agencies in referrals. The reliance on other agencies to maintain changes induced by IIP's intensive crisis counseling underscores the importance of successful referrals. The success of IIP referrals can be attributed in large part to the practice of involving personnel from other agencies in counseling sessions before treatment termination. Thus, while adjuncts to treatment available through other agencies entail indirect costs, such ancillary agencies probably contribute greatly to program effectiveness. Future reports of diversion programs should attempt to include information not only concerning their overall costs, including time commitments of adjunct agencies, but details concerning the rate of successful referrals, what is done to ensure success, and what treatment programs are used by referral agencies to maintain changes.

Part IV

Community-Based Programs for Juvenile Offenders

Chapter 9

Editors' Remarks

In Part 3 of this book we presented programs which achieved their success by treating the family of delinquent children and adolescents. Although we stress the value of including the family of the offender in the treatment program, it must be recognized that for many delinquents it is unrealistic to expect that it will be possible to involve the family.

Correctional workers know only too well that there are many families with whom we cannot work either because of major personal shortcomings of some of the members or because of the gross instability of the family relationships or, equally as common, because they adamantly refuse to cooperate with any attempt to involve them in any program effort. Clearly there is a need for an effective program which can be applied in a community setting which does *not* necessitate direct intervention with the delinquent's family.

The program described by O'Donnell, Lydgate and Fo in this chapter clearly meets that need. They train indigenous non-professional adults (''buddies'') to serve as behavior change agents to work directly with the behavior problem youths in their own community. The adult ''buddies'' are supervised by graduate students from the University of Hawaii who are, in turn, directed by a small number of professionals.

The present paper describes the results of the buddy system over a three year period. In a methodologically elegant study using random assignment of subjects to treatment and control groups and a large number of subjects (335 experimental and 218 control subjects) the buddy system has been established as a model for efficient and effective service delivery for the remediation of delinquent behavior which has clear cost-benefits. An earlier paper (Fo & O'Donnell, 1974) may be consulted for more complete program details.

Particularly noteworthy are the results which show that intervention may have salutory effects with some clients but deleterious (iatrogenic) effects with others. Whereas youths with a recent history of offences were likely to benefit from treatment, those who had not previously committed offences did so following treatment. ''The arrest rates ranged from 10.8% to 81% when recent offence history, sex, and experimental condition were considered''!

The matching of the client and his buddy had a strong influence on outcome. This is one of the few research projects which have attended to the very real possibility that treatment programs might have different results for males and females.

The Buddy System: Review and Follow-Up*

Clifford R. O'Donnell, Tony Lydgate and Walter S.O. Fo

Historically, antisocial behavior in children has been an important concern of the helping professions (Levine & Levine, 1970). Within psychology, attempts to prevent and change such behavior date back at least to the work of Witmer (1907). That these efforts are justified has been well documented by Robins (1974) in a 30-year follow-up of 524 children treated in a child guidance clinic. Robins found that youths referred to the clinic for antisocial behaviors had rates of arrest, imprisonment, divorce, alcohol use, and unemployment as adults that were markedly higher than among children not referred.

Many family intervention programs have been developed to reduce children's antisocial behavior and, hopefully, to prevent future problems as these children mature into adults. One type of program has emphasized training parents in behavioral observation and the application of social learning principles (e.g., Patterson, Cobb, & Ray, 1973). The results of these programs have been mixed, however, with parent reports typically favorable, and behavioral data generally showing little evidence of an effect once intervention is terminated (Kent, 1976; O'Donnell, 1977, pp. 81–91).

A second type of family intervention program, which has employed contingency contracting within the families of delinquents, has also shown disappointing results. The few positive results have been limited to juvenile status offenses, and no effect has been reported on criminal offenses (O'Donnell, 1977, pp. 78–79). It also seems likely that even if effective intervention programs were developed, their use would be limited to relatively

*O'Donnell, C.R. et al., "The Buddy System: Review and follow-up," *Child Behavior Therapy*, 1979, *1*(2), 161–169. Copyright © 1979, The Howarth Press, Inc. Reprinted by Permission.

intact, cooperative families. Clearly there is a need for a community-based program that does not depend on the family structure.

The triadic model advanced by Tharp & Wetzel (1969) is a promising framework for the development of such a program. In this model, the necessary intervention expertise is provided by a small number of consultants, supervising a larger number of nonprofessionals, who intervene in turn with a still larger number of youths. In their original program, Tharp & Wetzel found that by six months following the termination of intervention, 35% of the total of 77 youngsters had been arrested for juvenile status or criminal offenses. They also noted that those with offenses prior to intervention were more likely to commit offenses later. Unfortunately, the lack of a control group prevented an assessment of the relative effectiveness of this approach.

A no-treatment control group was used to evaluate a similar program called The Buddy System. In this program, indigenous nonprofessionals were trained in the application of contingency management (see Social Welfare Development and Research Center, 1972, for the training manual) and employed as "buddies" of youngsters referred primarily by public schools for behavior and academic problems. These adult buddies implemented intervention plans in which their relationship and $10 a month was contingently used to improve the behaviors for which their youngsters were referred. These plans were developed during weekly meetings with graduate students who served as supervisors and were, in turn, supervised by professionals.

The behavioral procedures were evaluated in the first project year by comparing contingency management groups with a noncontingent relationship and a no-treatment control group (Fo & O'Donnell, 1974). School attendance of those youths randomly assigned to the contingency groups increased during intervention. Attendance remained virtually unchanged for the other youngsters until contingency procedures were implemented in the relationship group, at which point the attendance of those youngsters also increased. Other problem behaviors, such as fighting, not completing homework assignments, returning home late, and not doing home chores, also improved during intervention, although school grades did not. The degree of improvement was shown to be partly a function of the relative locus of control of buddy-youth pairs: less improvement occurred for pairs in which the youth scored lower in externality than the buddy (O'Donnell & Fo, 1976).

The primary purpose of the Buddy System, however, was the prevention and remediation of delinquent behaviors (prevention referring to those without recent arrests for criminal offenses, remediation to those with such arrests). An assessment of its effectiveness, based only on the first two project years, was reported by Fo and O'Donnell (1975). These data indicated that the program was effective in remediation, but might be counter-effective in prevention. Among youths who had been arrested for a criminal offense in the year before Buddy System participation, only 37.5% were arrested during the project year. This compared favorably with a rate of 64% for those in the control group. The majority of juveniles had not been arrested for a criminal offense in the preceding year; among them, however, 15.7% were arrested during the project year, a rate approximately double that of the control youth (7.2%).

Since that report, additional youngsters have participated in the Buddy System and in the control condition. Furthermore, arrest data have become available for all participants two years after their initial year of participation. This includes the records of all 553 (335 project and 218 control) juveniles who were involved in any of the three years of the project's existence. An evaluation of the effectiveness of the Buddy System, therefore, can now be based on the arrest data of each individual over a three year span. The purpose of this report is to present an analysis of these data and their implications for the prevention and remediation of delinquent behaviors.

METHOD

SUBJECTS

Multi-ethnic youngsters from the Hawaii Model Cities areas, aged 10–17, were referred to the Buddy System for behavior problems primarily by the schools, but also by police, courts, social welfare agencies, and community residents. In each of the three years of the program's operation (1970–1973), youths were randomly assigned to either an experimental group or a no-treatment control group consisting of youngsters who met all criteria of acceptability, but were not invited to participate in that year. Since all youngsters living in the Model Cities areas were eligible to apply each year, many children were referred in two and even three years. Quite frequently, youths who were randomly selected for the control conditions in one year would be referred the next year and be randomly assigned to the Buddy System. In some cases the reverse occurred, i.e., project youth in one year would be randomly distributed to the control group the next year. For the purposes of this study, all youngsters who were in the Buddy System in any of the three years were considered part of the experimental group, and only those who never entered the Buddy System were regarded as members of the control group. For this reason, as well as the fact that the size of the control group each year reflected the excess of referrals over openings, the size of the two groups were not equated. Thus the experimental group consisted of 335 youths (206 boys and 129 girls) and the control group of 218 (151 boys and 67 girls). With the initial year of assignment varying among the three project years, 255 were included in the experimental group for only one year, 73 for two years, and seven for all three years. In the control group 195 were assigned for one year, 23 for two years, and none for three years. Youngsters who dropped out of the Buddy System during the year, for whatever reasons, were nevertheless included in the analyses. This was done to insure that results would not be based on a biased sample of more motivated, cooperative kids.

PROCEDURE

Arrest records from 1969 to 1975 were obtained from the Hawaii Family Court for all youngsters who participated in the Buddy System or in the control group during any of the three project years. These six years of records provided information on arrests for each youth for one year before participation, the year(s) of participation, and two years after the initial year of participation, as well as on the severity of each offense. Offenses were included only if they were on a previously prepared list of what were considered major offenses. This list included murder, manslaughter, rape, robbery, aggravated assault, burglary, larceny, auto theft, other assaults, arson, forgery, counterfeiting, fraud, embezzlement, receiving stolen property, vandalism, weapon offenses, battery, serious drug and sex offenses, and attempts at such offenses. Juvenile status offenses (e.g., runaway, curfew violation, incorrigible, person in need of supervision), as well as traffic violations, technical violations (such as of probation), and minor vice offenses (e.g., paint sniffing, possession of marijuana, gambling, lewd and lascivious behavior) were all specifically excluded. The arrest records of the Hawaii Family Court are based on information provided by the Honolulu Police Department, whose jurisdiction extends throughout the island of Oahu. Therefore the data were not biased by the reporting procedures of different police departments.

The dependent variable in this study was the number of youths arrested for at least one major offense (referred to as the arrest rate) in the three year period which included their initial year of participation plus the next two years. It was thought that data over the three year span would be more reliable than analyses for each year, especially since the Hawaii Family Court records the date they are informed of an arrest, rather than the actual date of arrest.

RESULTS

Inspection of court records on the 553 youngsters showed an overall arrest rate for the three years of 25.7%. This overall rate, however, ranged from 10.8% to 81% when recent offense history, sex, and experimental condition were considered. Comparisons among these rates were made using two-tailed Z tests. Seventy-three of the 553 youths had been arrested for at least one major offense in the year before entering either the experimental or the control condition. The arrest rate of this group, hereafter referred to as the Y's, was

63% for the three-year period. In the year before participation, the remaining 480 juveniles had not been arrested for a major offense; the three year arrest rate for this group, hereafter referred to as the N's, was 20%. Arrest rates for the Y's were significantly higher than for the N's ($Z = 7.82, p < .001$) and as a consequence of this difference, other comparisons were made separately for Y and N individuals.

Sex also influenced the arrest rate: the 58 Y males had a higher rate (69%) than did the 15 Y females (40%), $Z = 2.07, p < .02$. The corresponding figures for N's were 22.7% for the 299 males and 15.5% for the 181 females, $Z = 1.91, p < .03$. Separate figures for both Y and N boys and girls are presented in Table 1 for comparisons between experimental conditions.

TABLE 1

Arrest Rates of Buddy System and Control Youth

Condition	Major offense in previous year	Number	Percent arrested
Males:			
Buddy System	Yes	37	62.2
Control	Yes	21	81.0
Buddy System	No	169	25.4
Control	No	130	19.2
Females:			
Buddy System	Yes	13	38.5
Control	Yes	2	50.0
Buddy System	No	116	18.1
Control	No	65	10.8

The reduced numbers, especially for Y females, precluded meaningful separate statistical analyses by sex. A comparison of Y individuals of both sexes, however, showed a significantly lower arrest rate for Buddy System than for control youth (56.0% to 78.3%), $Z = 1.84, p < .04$.

The corresponding comparison for N individuals revealed that the difference was reversed, i.e., the youngsters in the Buddy System had a significantly higher arrest rate (22.5%) than did those in the control condition (16.4%), $Z = 1.65, p < .05$. This is consistent with the results of the previous report (Fo & O'Donnell, 1975).

ADDITIONAL ANALYSES WITH N YOUTHS

Next an attempt was made to determine whether the source of the higher arrest rate for N youngsters in the Buddy System could be identified. Buddy

System participants were divided into two subgroups: 218 who were members for only one year, and 67 who were members for more than one year. Comparisons were made with the 195 control youth. The percent arrested in each group was 18.8, 34.3, and 16.4 respectively.

Analyses with these groups showed that the arrest rate of those in the Buddy System for more than one year was reliably higher than the rate of both those who participated during only one year ($Z = 2.63$, $p < .01$), and those who were in the control group ($Z = 311$, $p < .01$). No significant difference was found between single year and control group youth.

Interest now focused on why the arrest rate of those who participated in the experimental condition more than one year was higher than that for one year members. One possibility was a selection bias. Perhaps referral sources *continued* referring those youths whose behavior they had more reason to be concerned about each year. Thus a higher proportion of single year youth would necessarily be those who were considered less likely to continue to need special help. To test this possibility a comparison was made between two groups of experimental youngsters. Those who had been referred only once ($N = 186$) were compared with those referred in more than one year, but only accepted once ($N = 32$). This comparison was made in order to determine if, in fact, those in the experimental condition who were referred more often subsequently had higher arrest rates. The arrest rate of those referred more often (21.9%) did not differ significantly from that of once-referred youths (18.3%), $Z = .48$. This suggests that the higher arrest rate for youths who were in the Buddy System for more than one year was not due to a sampling bias, with "the worst kids" more likely to be referred more than once.

This left the possibility that the effect of the experimental condition was more detrimental for those who were exposed to it longer, i.e., for more than one year. To test this, youths who were members of the Buddy System for more than one year ($N = 67$) were compared to youths who were referred more than once, but accepted into the program only during one year ($N = 32$). This comparison showed a trend toward a higher arrest rate for milti-year participants (34.3% to 21.9%, $Z = 1.26$, $p < .10$), lending some support to the view that the higher arrest rate results from spending more years in the Buddy System.

DISCUSSION

As in the previous study (Fo & O'Donnell, 1975), the results presented in this report indicate that the Buddy System is more effective with youngsters who have been arrested for major offenses in the preceding year. The arrest rate among Y individuals across sexes was 22.3% lower for project youth than for control youth. Confidence in this result is increased by the fact that in this study, arrest rates are based on a three year period for each person. It suggests that the Buddy System approach is worth continuing with youngsters *after* they have been arrested for a major criminal offense.

Not so, however, for those who have been arrested for only juvenile status or minor offenses, or who have never been arrested at all. Once again, the arrest rate of these individuals was reliably higher in the experimental condition. This effect occurred largely with those who spent more than one year in the Buddy System. Although a sampling bias cannot be ruled out, evidence for such was evaluated and found lacking. There was some evidence that the higher arrest rate was due to *participating* in the project for more than one year, rather than merely being referred more than once. If this is so, it is consistent with speculation (Fo & O'Donnell, 1975) that during project participation, N youths (those with no arrest for a major offense in the prior year) established friendships with their Y peers (who had been arrested for at least one major offense in the prior year). Opportunities for this were provided by group meetings and shared activities with buddies several times each year. While it was not possible to assess the validity of this speculation, others might wish to give careful consideration to the potential effects of intermixing N and Y youngsters.

Although the arrest rate for Buddy System N youth across sexes was higher by only 6.1% (22.5 − 16.4), it is important to note that the vast majority of youngsters in delinquency prevention programs are those who have never been arrested for a major criminal offense. If these programs increase the arrest rate of this group, a large number of youths are affected. Therefore one should be very cautious about developing a program to prevent major criminal offenses by youngsters with no recent record of such arrests. The need for caution is further underscored by data on the base rate of arrests, provided by youth in the control condition. Using slightly rounded figures, approximately 20% of N males and 10% of N females were arrested for at least one major offense within the three-year period. The effectiveness of preventive intervention with N youngsters is unlikely, given these rather low base rates. They suggest that a program must be more than 80% effective with males and 90% with females to be successful with N individuals.

The opposite, of course, is true for programs designed for Y individuals. Here base rates may be sufficiently high (81% for males in this study) that even moderately effective programs can be successful.

Thus the potential effectiveness of delinquency programs is strongly influenced by base rates, which vary considerably with sex and recent history of major criminal offenses. The effectiveness of a program might be evaluated quite differently depending on the proportion of Y and N youths and whether major criminal offenses are considered separately or lumped together with juvenile status and minor offenses. Therefore it is desirable that the base rates of the target population be considered prior to the implementation of a program and that an evaluation, whenever possible, provide separate data on major criminal offenses.

REFERENCES

Fo, W.S.O., & O'Donnell, C.R., "The Buddy System: Relationship and contingency conditions in a community intervention program for youth with nonprofessionals as behavior change agents," *Journal of Consulting and Clinical Psychology*, 1974, *42*, 163–169.

Fo, W.S.O., & O'Donnell, C.R., "The Buddy System: Effect of community intervention on delinquent offenses," *Behavior Therapy*, 1975, *6*, 522–524.

Kent, R.N., "A methodological critique of interventions for boys with conduct problems," *Journal of Consulting and Clinical Psychology*, 1976, *44*, 297–299.

Levine, M., & Levine, A., *A social history of helping services: Clinic, court, school, and community* (New York: Appleton, 1970).

O'Donnell, C.R., "Behavior modification in community settings." In M. Hersen, R.M. Eisler, & P.M. Miller (eds.), *Progress in Behavior Modification*, Vol. *4* (New York: Academic Press, 1977).

O'Donnell, C.R., & Fo, W.S.O., "The Buddy System: Mediator — target locus of control and behavioral outcome," *American Journal of Community Psychology*, 1976, *4*, 161–166.

Patterson, G.R., Cobb, J.A., & Ray, R.S., "A social engineering technology for retraining the families of aggressive boys." In H.E. Adams & I.P. Unikel (eds.), *Issues and Trends in Behavior Therapy* (Springfield: Thomas, 1973).

Robins, L.N. *Deviant Children Grown Up* (Hungtington, N.Y.: Robert E. Krieger, 1974).

Social Welfare Development and Research Center, *Buddy System Training Manual* (Rep. no. 113) (Honolulu: University of Hawaii, Social Welfare Development and Research Center, August, 1972).

Tharp, R.G., & Wetzel, R.J., *Behavior Modification in the Natural Environment* (New York: Academic Press, 1969).

Witmer, L., "Clinical psychology," *Psychological Clinic*, 1906–1907, *1*, 1–9.

Chapter 10

Editors' Remarks

Lee & Haynes prepared the following article expressly for this book in order to provide a current report on the evaluation of a continuing project in which counseling services are provided to juvenile delinquents in community settings in Gainesville, Florida: Project CREST.

In contrast to many correctional evaluations which base their conclusions as to program efficacy on a single assessment of outcome in a brief post-treatment period, Lee & Haynes have persisted in their evaluation of this program, have continued to improve their experimental design, and have assiduously documented their results. The program serves as a demonstration of the fact that effective programs need not be expensive. The counselors are unpaid graduate students. It also demonstrates the advantages that can accrue through affiliating with a university whose faculty and students can provide treatment and research services to criminal justice agencies (cf. Ross, 1967; Gendreau & Andrews, 1979).

CREST was selected in 1978 as an Exemplary Project by the National Institute of Law Enforcement and Criminal Justice.

REFERENCES

Ross, R.R., "Psychology at the Ontario Training School for Girls at Galt," *Ontario Psychological Quarterly*, 1967, *20*(2), 54–58.

Gendreau, P. & Andrews, D.A., "Psychological consultation in correctional agencies: case studies and general issues." In J.J. Platt & Wicks, A.W. (eds.) *The Psychological Consultant* (New York: Grune & Stratton, 1979).

Project CREST and the Dual-Treatment Approach to Delinquency: Methods and Research Summarized*

Robert Lee and
Nancy McGinnis Haynes

In normal development children have reasonable limits consistently imposed on their behavior, while at the same time they receive attention to their growth as individuals. The lives of seriously misbehaving adolescents often are lacking in one or both of these ingredients, and it would seem that rehabilitation, to be effective, must include structure *and* nurture.

Unfortunately, many programs designed to treat juvenile delinquents overemphasize one ingredient at the expense of the other. Youngsters in the court system typically are placed in an authoritarian program where the main emphasis is on social conformity under the threat of sanctions and confinement. As alternatives to court treatment, liberal reform movements have often generated almost completely non-authoritarian models that feature psychological counseling and other facilitative experiences. In fact, top funding priorities in recent years have been given to those programs designed to divert children from the authoritarian structure of the court system.

To be sure, a number of states have attempted to incorporate humanistic counseling methods into their handling of juvenile cases. Juvenile probation officers, now known in many places as "youth services counselors," are expected to respond to the needs of the child as well as to the needs of society to restrain the child. However, it is extremely difficult for a probation worker to "wear two hats" with some youngsters, especially those who are highly resistant to authority.

---

*This article was prepared especially for inclusion in this book.

Project CREST (Clinical Regional Support Teams) was started with LEAA funds in 1972* to enable the state Youth Services Program (YSP) in the Gainesville area of Florida to wear two hats with children who were failing to respond to probation alone. Teams of university students, most of them enrolled in professional counseling programs, were recruited to provide non-authoritarian outreach services to young "hard core" probationers, who continued to be supervised as usual by their probation counselors. The probation workers have concentrated on adjusting the child to acceptable standards of behavior while CREST counselors deal with the child's private world of thoughts, feelings, values, talents, and aspirations. The mutual goal of this dual approach is that the child develop self-control plus positive self-motivation.

CREST'S METHOD OF TREATMENT

Each CREST team is headed by a paid doctoral student in a university program such as counselor education or counseling psychology. The team leaders usually remain with CREST throughout the entire course of their degree program, which provides the project with considerable stability.

Typically, each team also consists of two or three unpaid practicum or internship students in a graduate counseling program, two or three undergraduate paraprofessional counseling students, and one or more community volunteers. The graduate student counselors provide individual and sometimes group and family counseling for each of the twenty or more clients on the team's caseload. They also offer consultation to the client's family, Youth Services workers, and schools. Members of the team who are not enrolled in the graduate programs are known as "counselor aides." They offer tutoring and "big buddy" services to many of the clients who are also in counseling, and in some cases co-lead groups with the counselors. Non-counseling students are occasionally recruited for specific purposes. For example, a nursing student may conduct a short course in health and hygiene for girls; an intern in occupational therapy may work with a client who has a visual-motor problem; a criminal justice major may discuss with a group of boys the consequences of becoming more deeply involved in the juvenile justice system.

CREST clients are referred to the program by their Youth Services workers. Criteria for referral are minimal: the child must be adjudicated delinquent, show signs of conflict or distress, indicate some willingness to cooperate, and must be a part of a family or home that has a degree of stability. Many cases are considered "hard core" and evaluation studies have shown that at the time

---

*Since 1976 Project CREST has been funded by the Florida Department of Health and Rehabilitative Services. The project is now implemented by CREST Services, Inc., a private non-profit corporation.

of referral, the average CREST client was committing acts of misconduct at a rate higher than that of probationers in general.

Each client is assigned a counselor by the team leader, who also works with a caseload of youngsters. Although the clients may receive more than one kind of service, the basic mode of treatment is one-on-one counseling. The counselors, who have no offices of their own, arrange their sessions once or twice a week where the clients are most comfortable — in homes, schools, playgrounds, cars, or Youth Services offices. Although counseling methods vary with the needs of the client and the expertise of the worker, each CREST counselor is trained to begin "where the client is." This may mean buying a hamburger if the child is hungry, playing a game of pool or basketball, leafing through an automotive magazine, or sitting beside a lake on a sunny afternoon. From that point the counselor attempts to build a facilitative relationship and to nourish the personality growth of the child.

Among the frequently used methods are reality therapy, designed to bring the client to confront the problems of the present rather than dwelling on the past or in prolonged fantasy; rational-emotive therapy, in which the counselor attempts to separate irrational associations in the client's mind, such as the often encountered tendency of delinquent youth to think, "I did something bad, therefore I am bad;" and, client-centered therapy, which focuses on the client's expression of feelings. Techniques of gestalt therapy, such as role playing, are used sometimes to help the client deal more effectively with significant others, e.g., teachers, parents or peers. The positive reinforcement approach of behavior therapy is occasionally employed, but CREST regards behavior modification in general, and particularly the threat or use of sanctions to affect behavior, as the appropriate function of the probation officers.

Underlying the various methods, all of which are well known and established in the counseling profession, there are important common characteristics. CREST counseling is: (a) non-authoritarian, a complement to the authoritative role of probation workers; (b) oriented toward attitudinal and thought processes, particularly important for delinquent youth who tend to be repressed and isolated emotionally; (c) concerned primarily with the perceptions of the client rather than social and institutional norms; and (d) outreach in nature, as opposed to the office-based or medical model.

The goals of counseling are determined by the nature and extent of each client's difficulties, but there are some basic goals. It is expected that all clients will: (a) gain in feelings of self-worth and self-respect, and thereby reverse the patterns of destructive behavior which stem from self-fulfilling prophecy, (b) come to understand themselves better and learn to meet their needs in ways that are not self-defeating, (c) accept more responsibility for their behavior and decisions, thus freeing themselves from over-dependence on such outside forces as negative peer pressure, poor environment, and "fate."

CREST volunteers are equipped to work with the youngsters by means of extensive training and supervision. All personnel attend team meetings and general staff meetings every week. An in-service training curriculum is followed and includes such subjects as counselor self-exploration, developmental needs of adolescents, special techniques for helping youth who are difficult to reach, methods of case management, consultation skills, orientation to the juvenile justice system, role of the counselor in the treatment of delinquents, research on delinquency, and dilemmas in counseling delinquents. Special training is given the counselor aides in basic communication skills, tutoring skills, and the recognition of problems needing attention by the trained counselors.

In addition to their CREST supervision, the graduate counseling students, who must have completed at least two quarters of academic work, receive weekly one hour of individual supervision and one and one-half hours of group supervision at the university. The counselor aides, who are in undergraduate paraprofessional counseling programs, also receive appropriate course work and supervision at their institution.

Project CREST thus provides outreach professional services by well-supervised counselors-in-training as part of a treatment strategy. The clients, however, are not excused from the consequences of their misconduct while they are involved with CREST. The other part of the strategy includes the usual controls and sanctions imposed by the probation officers. Naturally, close cooperation between CREST and YSP is mandatory. CREST volunteers are led to appreciate and respect the role of Youth Services and are required to consult about each case with the referring YSP worker at least bi-weekly. YSP workers, in turn, are asked to respect CREST counselors and the confidentiality that must exist between counselor and client. The philosophy and operation of this dual-treatment approach are more fully discussed elsewhere (Lee and Klopfer, 1978; Lee and Piercy, 1974).

WHAT THE RESEARCH SHOWS

Project CREST emphasizes the need for continuous monitoring of the effects of the program through research. The general procedure has been to compare groups of youths who received CREST treatment in addition to probation with groups of youths who received probation services alone, the main dependent variable being the number and kind of delinquent acts recorded during and after contact with CREST. The designs have varied from year to year depending on conditional factors such as program priorities and research questions of interest. The overwhelming result has been that regardless of differences in counselors, subjects, and mode of measurement, the CREST-treated groups committed at least 50% fewer criminal acts than did the controls.

In this report we will review the results of four separate studies and a two-year follow-up. Table 1 presents the composition and selection methods of the subjects in the first four studies.

TABLE 1

Treatment and Control Groups

Year	N	Experimental (Treatment) Group Selection Procedure	N	Control Group Selection Procedure
1 1972–73	12	Youths on probation with YSP, among 5% of case-load described as "most resistant to help." Participated in a minimum of 10 counseling sessions	15	(Delinquent Control) Youths also considered "hard-core" clients; selected from YSP waiting list
			26	(Normal Control) Random sample of children under 17 yrs of age enrolled in same area
2 1973–74	34	Youths on probation with YSP, referred by YSP for counseling. Participated in a minimum of 10 counseling sessions	31	Non-treated probationers selected by YSP as most similar to counselees
3 1974–75	24	Youths on probation with YSP, referred as experiencing severe adjustment problems. Participated in minimum of 10 counseling sessions	24	Non-treated probationers matched with experimental Ss for age, race, and sex
4 January-June 1976	30	Of 64 referrals by YSP, 30 randomly selected to receive counseling. No minimum number of sessions	34	Of 64 referrals by YSP, 34 randomly selected as controls
Total N	100		130	

As can be seen, there is considerable variation in design among these studies. Study 4 was experimental in nature; that is, subjects were randomly assigned to groups before the observation period began and before treatment began. The other studies had a quasi-experimental design in that referred children were assigned to the treatment group and the controls were selected from the remaining clients on the Youth Services caseloads.

In all these studies, the group receiving CREST treatment was compared to the control groups with regard to selected outcome measures. The variables used in each study are summarized in Table 2.

In the last three studies, we were unable to obtain school data and personality tests. Further, the ultimate goal of the program has been to reduce incidents of juvenile crime and this outcome criterion is a measure of the program's effectiveness. However, we believe that the investigation of personality factors is of prime importance in exploring ways in which we can improve our program — in client selection, referral criteria, treatment, and assessment of the reasons for clients' failure to benefit from the program.

Thus, these four outcome studies have employed a variety of criteria for measuring change in clients' adjustment and also a variety of methods for selection of subjects. However, the designs were consistent in that they included concurrent measures of experimental and control groups.

The most striking finding in these studies was a marked and consistent difference between groups receiving CREST counseling and the non-CREST controls in the number of officially reported acts of misconduct. (See Table 3.)

The levels of statistical significance in these studies vary, as do methods of interpretation. The most important finding is that in all of these comparisons the rate of misconduct for the CREST group is lower than for the controls. Long-term follow-ups show that this effect is stable over time and that a large proportion of CREST clients maintain a clear record for the duration of the observation period.

In the three areas of academic adjustment which we studied (absenteeism, grades, and suspensions), the CREST groups showed consistent improvement. Although some of the findings were not statistically significant, it should be noted that in all the comparisons which were made, the group means showed a greater degree of positive change for the CREST groups than for the control groups. (See Table 4.)

Two personality tests, the Jesness Behavior Check List (JBCL) and the Tennessee Self Concept Scale (TSCS), were used as measures of social adjustment and of self-esteem. The CREST group in the first year showed improved scores on subscales associated with the ability to handle anger and to relate to others in a positive fashion, to see oneself as less deviant, and to feel more positively about oneself. On the JBCL, the CREST group appeared quite similar to the normal controls after treatment. The second year results suggest that, while not statistically significant, the CREST group showed a generalized improvement in self-concept. It should be noted that the significant difference on the Dependence subscale of the JBCL can be interpreted as a lessening of the antisocial, "loner" stance adopted by many delinquent children and as a movement toward relating to others in a way more appropriate to normal adolescence. The CREST experimental group became more similar to the normal controls while diverging from the delinquent controls on these personality measures. (See Table 5.)

TABLE 2

Outcome Measures

Study	Number of Acts of Misconduct	Absences	School Performance Grades	Suspensions	Personality Tests JBCL	TSCS
1. 1972–73	X	X	X	X	X	X
2. 1973–74	X	X	X	X	X	X
3. 1974–75	X	X	X			
4. 1976	X					

"X" indicates measure was included in the particular study.

TABLE 3

Outcome Measure (Acts of Misconduct)

Study	Subjects	Acts of Misconduct	Level of Significance
Piercy and Lee (1976) 1st Year 1972–73	Experimental Delinquent Control Normal Control	Experimental lower than Delinquent Control	$p < .10$
Kemp and Lee (1977) 2nd Year 1973–74	Experimental Control	Experimental lower than Control Percent with no charges during experimental period: Experimental: 76% Control: 56% Experimental reached baseline rate after 4 months; Control reached baseline rate after 10 months	$p < .20$
Kemp and Lee (1975) 3rd Year 1974–75	Experimental Control	Experimental lower than Control Rate of recidivism (% with more than one offense during experimental period): Experimental 29% Control: 50%	$p < .08$
Lee and McGinnis (1976) 4th Year Jan–June 76	Experimental Control	Experimental lower than Control (Number of Acts) Experimental lower than Control (Average monthly rate)	$p < .05$ $p < 0.25$

TABLE 4

Outcome Measure (School Performance)

Study	Subjects	Absences	Grades	Suspensions
First Year (1972–73)	Experimental	Delinquent Control higher than Experimental $p < .05$	Delinquent Control lower than Normal Control $p < .05$	
	Delinquent Control	Delinquent Control higher than Normal Control $p < .01$	Experimental increased slightly but ns	
	Normal Control	Experimental vs. Normal Control ns Normal Control		
Second Year (1973–74)	Experimental Control	Control higher than Experimental $p < .05$	Experimental slightly higher than Control but ns	Control higher than Experimental $p < .01$
Third Year (1974–75)	Experimental Control	Experimental vs. Control	Experimental vs. Control ns Experimental started lower and improved more	

TABLE 5
Outcome Measure (Personality Tests)

Study	Subjects	JBCL	TSCS
First Year (1972–73)	Experimental Delinquent Control	Experimental increased over Delinquent Control on: Social Control $p < .10$ Anger Control $p < .10$ Friendliness $p < .10$	Experimental increased over Delinquent Control on: Number of Deviant Signs $p < 0.5$ Self Satisfaction $p < .10$ Identity $p < .10$
	Normal Control	Experimental vs. Normal Control: ns on all scales post-test	
Second Year (1973–74)	Experimental Control	Experimental higher than Control on: Dependence $p < .05$	ns on any scales Experimental improved more than Control on 15 out of 17 scales but ns

A two-year follow-up of the 1976 experimental evaluation (Study 4) addressed the question of what long-term effects the dual treatment approach may have had on acts of misconduct following the termination of treatment (Lee, Clawson, and L'Abbatte, 1979).

The two groups were first compared on changes in officially reported acts of misconduct over an approximate two year period following CREST treatment.

Although the total acts of misconduct for the CREST group increased from 10 during the treatment period to 23 during the follow-up period, the increase in the number of acts for the control group was from 17 to 65 during the same periods of time. This difference between the groups was significant ($p < .01$). The mean differences are shown in Figure 1.

Average monthly rates of misconduct decreased for both groups from the treatment to the follow-up period. The CREST group fell 37%; the control group fell 16%. This difference between groups was also significant ($p < .05$). The results are presented in Figure 2.

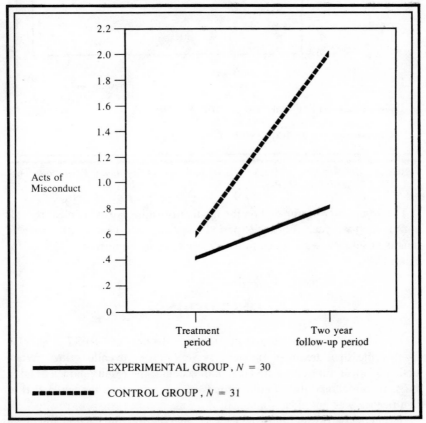

Figure 1   *Mean Acts of Misconduct During Treatment Period and Two Year Follow-up Period.*

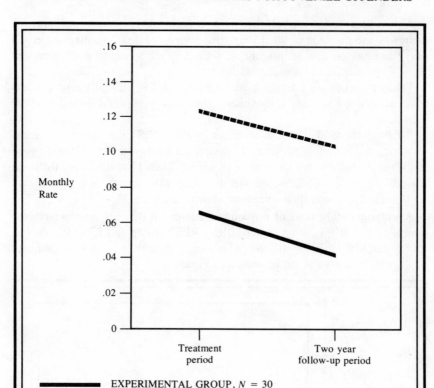

Figure 2 *Monthly Rate of Acts of Misconduct During Treatment Period and Two Year Follow-up Period.*

The groups were compared on the number of subjects having clear records during the two-year follow-up period. Seventy per cent of the CREST treatment subjects were found to have clear records, compared to 48% of the controls.

CONCLUSIONS

Our research findings indicate that the effectiveness of CREST is genuine — that the dual treatment model has impact on juvenile crime. When methodological differences are taken into account, the results show a trend in the same direction with different groups of subjects, even though statistical significance was not always attained.

During the two years following CREST intervention, the CREST treatment group continued to commit acts of misconduct at a level significantly below that of the control group. We must emphasize that our results in no way diminish the effects of probation alone, since about half of the probationers also experienced reductions in criminal acts and lasting clear records. Project CREST as an add-on to probation increases the effectiveness of the juvenile justice system and, we believe, the combined effect of both treatments has a multiplicative, rather than additive, effect.

Whenever one is engaged in treatment and outcome evaluation, it is important to step back and reflect on "What does this all mean?" and "What have we learned?" We have viewed and analyzed great quantities of statistics, test scores, incident reports, and records. The findings give us hope and encouragement that what we are doing is right and helpful to our clients and to society.

We should not forget that behind each subject number and column of figures is a person, a young man or woman who had started on a path which would likely lead to unhappiness, maladjustment, and perhaps incarceration. Each "clear record" in our follow-up studies means that this young person has changed direction and has new opportunities for personal growth and achievement that were not there before.

A CREST case represents a sometimes rocky and sometimes satisfying relationship for both the client and the counselor; the participants will probably never forget each other. This relationship is probably the most crucial and powerful ingredient in CREST's influence on a young person. Regardless of the theoretical orientation, be it gestalt therapy, client-centered therapy, reality therapy, or whatever, the beginning counselor soon learns that he or she has power to change the direction of the client by virtue of coming into a social or emotional vacuum — the child often has no caring, non-judgmental adult available to confide in, to spend time with, to explore feelings with. The counselor takes the child into a new world, lets the child know that the die is not cast permanently into one shape. To be sure, there are some children who do not choose to accept our program or any other guidance. We have developed methods for reaching the reluctant or resistant client, but we must face the fact that some young persons may not be ready to accept our services and that over-zealous persistence may serve to ruin the client for the next counselor when the opportunity arises.

It has been heartening over the years to see young people who believe the CREST program has made an important difference in their lives. We were recently contacted by a young black man who had been a CREST client almost three years ago. He still remembered with great affection the white woman who had been his counselor. He believed that he would be in jail now if he had not had the chance to talk to someone. Instead, he is working, has traveled extensively, seems to be enjoying life, and seems convinced that he will not get into trouble with the law again.

The CREST approach to the treatment of juvenile offenders, with the dual treatment model, is a departure from the traditional rehabilitation models. As has so often been observed in the literature, offender populations are difficult to treat and failures serve to justify a pessimistic outlook on the part of the helping professional. While it is often true that offenders *are* resistant to help, so are most of the other troubled individuals for whom the helping professions offer their services — the alcoholic, the compulsive drug user, the psychotic, the depressed, and other emotionally or socially disturbed persons. The counselor who treats groups of "help-resistant" clients usually remembers some who responded, who changed direction, who are now leading productive and satisfying lives. We believe that clinical pessimism leads to a self-fulfilling prophecy and to an outlook which is unreceptive to innovative, creative thought. In sharing our program, we hope to encourage others to look for alternative approaches which may help those clients who have been labeled as "lost".

REFERENCES*

Kemp, M. and Lee, R., "Professional counseling and the juvenile offender: A field experiment," *L.A.E. Journal*, 1977, *40*, 27–36.

Kemp, M. and Lee, R., "Project CREST: A third year experimental study," Unpublished manuscript, Gainesville, Florida, 1975.

Lee, R., Clawson, L., and L'Abbatte, S., "After CREST, what?: A two-year follow-up study." Unpublished manuscript, Gainesville, Florida, 1979.

Lee, R. and Haynes, N.M., "Counseling juvenile offenders: An experimental evaluation of Project CREST," *Community Mental Health Journal*, 1978, *14*, 267–271.

Lee, R. and Klopfer, C., "Counselors and delinquents: Toward a comprehensive treatment approach," *The Personnel and Guidance Journal*, 1978, *57*, 194–197.

Lee, R. and Piercy, F., "Helping delinquents: A university program," *The Personnel and Guidance Journal*, 1974, *10*, 671–675.

Piercy, F. and Lee, R.M., "Effects of a dual treatment approach on the rehabilitation of habitual juvenile delinquents," *Rehabilitation Counseling Bulletin*, 1976, *19*, 482–492.

*Copies of unpublished manuscripts may be obtained by writing CREST Services, Inc., Box 13776, Gainesville, Florida, 32604.

Chapter 11

Editors' Remarks

The notion that the best way to deal with offenders is to "put them to work" has been popular for many years. The idea has a great deal of merit but like most of the many common-sense approaches to crime prevention it is easier to talk about than to implement. It is by no means a simple matter to "put offenders to work" or having done so, to keep them there. Many offenders lack marketable vocational skills, work experience and motivation to accept work and adjust to the demands of a job. "Putting them to work" may be a singularly unimpressive approach to their rehabilitation. Moreover there is not an abundance of employers who are ready and willing to hire inexperienced and unskilled workers, particularly those who have been in trouble with the law. The "put them to work" exhortation grossly oversimplifies both the needs of employers and the behavior, abilities and motivation of offenders. However, as Timothy Walters and Carolyn Mills show in this chapter, considerable success can be achieved through a program which is not limited to giving offenders jobs but first ensures that jobs are available, employers are motivated and offenders are prepared both in attitude and behavior to accept and perform well in these jobs. They show that such an approach cannot only keep delinquents "on the job" (or in school) but can also significantly reduce their delinquent behavior.

The Walter and Mills program is, in our view, a model for an effective intervention program for adolescent offenders which could and, we hope, will be implemented in many communities. We are grateful to the authors for responding to our request that they expand their previous reports on this valuable project by adding to their description of their program a discussion of *how* they managed to implement such a program and gain the necessary cooperation and support of the community. Description of the nuances of organizing, implementing, and managing effective correctional treatment programs is seldom provided in published reports. The degree of attention which one pays to such extra-program matters can determine both the outcome of the program and, in fact, whether and to what degree the program principles are actually put into practice.

A Behavioral-Employment Intervention Program for Reducing Juvenile Delinquency*

Timothy L. Walter and Carolyn M. Mills

PREFACE

Earlier discussions of the Behavioral-Employment Intervention Program have received enthusiastic responses from members of the professional community in corrections and rehabilitation.** The Behavioral-Employment Intervention Program was successful in terms of significantly increasing delinquent youths' attendance on jobs and in school. Equally important, these youths had significant decreases in their frequency of arrests and institutionalization.

The enthusiasm for the program is often accompanied by two important questions. First, "How did you go about organizing and managing such a program?" Essentially, the concern is, "What did we do to encourage a favorable response from people in the schools, juvenile court workers, prospective employers, and other people in the community who can support or sabotage such a program?" Second, "What guidelines can you offer for those of us interested in running a similar program?"

---

*This study was made possible by a grant from the office of Criminal Justice Training Programs, Grant LEAA No. 01-0492-01 and No. 01-0492-02 through the State of Michigan. The study began December 1, 1971 and ended January 15, 1973.

The authors gratefully acknowledge the assistance of Dr. James V. McConnell and the cooperation of the Washtenaw County Vocational Residential Center.

Walter, T.L. and Mills, C.M., "A behavioral-employment intervention program for reducing juvenile delinquency." In Jerome S. Stumphauzer (Ed.), *Progress in Behavior Therapy with Delinquents* (Springfield, Illinois: Charles C. Thomas, 1979). Copyright © 1979, Charles C. Thomas, Publisher. Reprinted by permission. This is a revised version of the article.

**Behavior Therapy*, 1977, *8* (2).

Although we do not claim to have definitive answers, we do have some suggestions. After describing the program and results, we will offer some guidelines on how to organize and manage a program. We believe these guidelines greatly improve the day to day operation of a Behavioral-Employment Intervention Program.

INTRODUCTION

Behavior intervention studies designed to increase the frequency of pro-social behaviors of juvenile delinquents in non-institutional environments had met with limited success at the time our study was initiated, December 1, 1971 (e.g. Tharp & Wetzel, 1969). These results contrasted with those obtained by investigators working with juvenile delinquents in institutional environments wherein the usual problems of control and assessment were not so great (e.g. Phillips, Phillips, Fixen, and Wolf, 1971). The potential gains associated with developing an effective behavioral intervention program for delinquents residing in their "natural environments" were considerable. The investigation described in this chapter was initiated in order to develop a more effective way of using positive behavior change strategies for delinquents in non-institutional settings.

Four basic considerations guided the design and execution of the Behavioral-Employment Intervention Program. First, as Fleisher's (1966) analysis of sociological data indicates a positive correlation between unemployment and delinquency, job-placement had to be an essential ingredient of the program. Secondly, we wished to increase the likelihood that employers would use positive behavioral strategies for promoting the delinquents' effective task performance. Employers were given basic training in positive reinforcement philosophy. During scheduled sessions between the experimenter and the employer, the experimenter consistently discussed with the employer strategies of praising the employee each time he demonstrated job appropriate behavior. Third, since the culturally deprived backgrounds of many juvenile delinquents (Nye, Short and Olson, 1958) provides them with little in the way of basic job skills and positive job attitudes (e.g. attendance, performance, grooming), the subjects were given considerable training to help correct these deficiencies. Finally, as contingency contracting had proven to be an effective way of insuring subject cooperation (Homme, Csanyi, Gonzales and Rechs, 1969), contracts describing the obligations of the experimenter, subject, and employer were signed by the parties involved.

METHOD

Subjects were adjudicated delinquents referred to the program by the Juvenile Court's probation or intake caseworkers. While arrest records varied, subjects had from one to eight actual convictions with a mean arrest rate of 3.85. Subjects referred were the court's most serious offenders and such felonies as arson, armed robbery, rape and larceny were commonly found in the records of the referrals.

Seventy-six subjects were referred to the program. Out of the seventy-six, twenty-three were in the comparison group and fifty-three were in the experimental group. State and county regulations prohibited random establishment of experimental and control groups. However, if a job was not available within a week of the first interview, the delinquent was assigned to the non-treatment comparison group. Thus, none of the characteristics of the delinquent determined condition assignment. Rather, assignment was left to the vagaries of a highly fluctuating job market. The comparison and experimental groups were similar in age and background. The demographic data is shown in Table 1.

TABLE 1

Demographic Data

Variable	Experimental Group	Comparison Group
Number of subjects	53	23
Age range	14–17	14–17
Mean age	15.7	15.7
Race		
White	34	16
Minority	19	7
Sex		
Male	44	16
Female	9	7
Lived with both parents	22	7
Parents and family members unemployed	19	3
Job history		
1 or more jobs held by subject	48	18
Average tenure on job	– 2 weeks	– 2 weeks
Attending school at time of referral	28	18

PROCEDURES

EMPLOYERS

The forty-five employers who volunteered to hire a delinquent agreed to follow the procedures outlined by the experimenter (second author) in order to maintain consistency in the treatment program. The procedures were:

1. Employers gave the subject's paycheck to the experimenter.
2. Employers filled out weekly feedback sheets describing the subject's performance. The employers gave the feedback sheets to the experimenter. The experimenter then discussed the weekly feedback sheet with the subject. (See Form C.)
3. Starting pay for the subjects was at least $1.60 per hour.
4. Subjects received, as a minimum raise, $.20 per hour at the end of Phase I and Phase II.
5. Each day, employers asked for and initialed the subject's checklist. (See Form A.)
6. Employers met weekly with the experimenter to discuss the subject's progress.
7. Employers terminated a subject who did not meet his or her obligations to the experimenter.
8. Employers signed a contract agreeing to the above.

Employers were reimbursed for 50% of the subject's wages for the first three months the subject worked for the employer. The experimenter scheduled weekly appointments with employers. The main focus of the meeting was to praise the employers for following the guidelines of the program. The employer's positive statements about the subject were consistently responded to positively. The experimenter praised the employer for providing positive feedback to his employee. Negative statements about "delinquents" or about the subject were ignored by the experimenter, unless there was a serious problem affecting the youth's performance on the job.

INTERVIEW

Prior to each subject's interview, the experimenter familiarized herself with the subject via their referral form from the court caseworker. Baseline data were gathered from the referral form, court records and the interview. During the interview conducted with all subjects, the experimenter encouraged subjects to talk about their interests in order to put them at ease and to investigate possible types of job placement. Positive statements subjects made

FORM A

NAME _____
NEXT APPOINTMENT _____
WEEK OF _____

THINGS I WANT TO DO THIS WEEK ON MY JOB MON TUES WED THUR FRI SAT SUN

EMPLOYER'S SIGNATURE

THINGS I NEED TO IMPROVE ON THIS WEEK
1.
2.
3.
4.

GOOD THINGS THAT HAPPENED AT WORK THIS WEEK
1.
2.
3.
4.

THINGS THAT HAPPENED AT WORK THAT I DID NOT LIKE THIS WEEK
1.
2.
3.
4.

FORM C

EMPLOYEE _____
WEEK OF _____

Things did well this week	Things could improve on this week
1.	
2.	
3.	
4.	
5.	
6.	
7.	
8.	

EMPLOYER _____
_____

about their desire for working or how they might get a job were attended to by smiles, head nods or verbal encouragement as it was felt that these statements were a first approximation toward acceptable job performance. If the subjects' appearance promised to eliminate them from the job market, they were asked what they might be willing to do about it. Subjects were praised for any response indicative of positive change. The experimenter told subjects that since only a limited number of jobs were available, it might be months before they could be helped in job placement, hence subjects were offered job finding suggestions in lieu of the possibility that they would not be contacted again. Subjects were praised for any statements they made as to how they would obtain employment. The experimental subjects were contacted from one day to two weeks later about possible placement while comparison subjects were not contacted.

Contingency contracts had to be signed before a youth could be in the program and placed on a job. Major points of the contract were:

1. The subject agreed to see the experimenter weekly during Phase I and biweekly during Phase II.
2. The employer gave the experimenter the subject's paycheck; she in turn presented it to the subject at the completion of the appointment.
3. To receive the paycheck, the subject had to bring in his or her daily checklist report form each week. Failure to do so meant the check was held until the next appointment.

ORIENTATION

In this program, both part-time and full-time jobs were available and subjects preferences were considered whenever possible. When interests, location and availability were matched to a job, the subject was asked to come to the experimenter's office to be taken to the job interview. The experimenter offered advice on grooming and appropriate dress for the interview and the subject was praised for attempts to improve appearance. The experimenter and subject role-played the job interview and, if necessary, role reversal was used. To insure a realistic interview, the experimenter did not participate in the actual job interview.

One to three days before the subjects started work, they were required to attend a counseling session with the experimenter as a prerequisite to entering the job. The focus of the session was to begin praising job appropriate behavior. The subjects were asked to list on a daily checklist report form (see Form A), which was restructured weekly, eight behaviors they felt necessary to maintain their job. First responses were praised even if they were only approximations to the desired behavior. Systematic praising of desired responses helped subjects complete the list of job appropriate behaviors. If the subjects could not produce a list, they were given a list of Employer Expectations with twenty items they could choose from; selections were based on importance to the subject. (See Form B.)

FORM B

EMPLOYER EXPECTATIONS

1. Be on time.
2. Be at work every scheduled day.
3. Do work expected for the job, thoroughly.
4. Dress according to employer guidelines.
5. Follow orders.
6. Cooperativeness.
7. Willingness to learn.
8. Friendliness with co-workers.
9. Friendliness with clients, customers, tenants, etc.
10. Notify employer if going to be late or absent, well before scheduled time.
11. Take only time alloted for breaks, lunch, and only at times specified.
12. Do not use telephone during working hours.
13. Do not have friends, relatives stop in at work.
14. Interest in the organization and your part in it.
15. Get enough sleep to function well on the job.
16. No drugs or alcohol on the job, during breaks or lunch, or before work.
17. Honesty, no stealing or "borrowing" anything belonging to the organization.
18. Little or no smoking on the job.
19. Accepting responsibility, looking for things that need to be done without having to be told, i.e., if work is finished, not sitting around.
20. Transportation to and from work planned for each day, ahead of time.

During the orientation meetings and throughout the Phase I meetings, subjects were required to list, on their report form, behaviors they felt to be important measures of success on the job. Subjects brought the report form to their job each day and earned one point per day for each behavior listed and completed. In addition, subjects earned one point for each behavior listed which their employers indicated the subject had completed. Thus, they could earn a maximum of 2 points a day per behavior. In addition, while in orientation, Phase I, and Phase II, subjects earned two points a week per behavior for listing behaviors on the checklist sheet under the following headings:

"Things I need to improve on this week."
"Good things that happened at work this week."
"Things that happened at work that I did not like this week."

Subjects' points were plotted weekly on individual graphs which hung in the experimenter's office.

The subjects met with the experimenter two to three days after starting work. This final meeting, which ended the orientation phase, was devoted to further praising of job appropriate behaviors. If at any time subjects lost their job due to failure to meet contracted obligations, no further attempt was made to place the subject.

PHASE I

During Phase I, the experimenter attempted to consistently praise the subjects for the job appropriate behavior in which they engaged. These behaviors were recorded on the daily checklist report forms signed by the employer. In conjunction, subjects received points for job appropriate behavior.

Employers verbally praised job appropriate behaviors when signing the checklist report form at the end of each day. Employers also filled out weekly feedback sheets for the subject's positive job behaviors and behaviors needing improvement. (See Form C.) The experimenter collected these feedback sheets once each week. Employers were asked to emphasize positive aspects of subjects's performance. If the employer listed any negative behaviors, the experimenter made use of "sandwiching" procedures in reporting this information to the subject during the weekly counseling sessions. The experimenter first drew attention to a positive point, discussed how well the subject had done on this, then mentioned a negative point and asked the subject what he felt could be done to improve, encouraged his responses, then returned to a positive statement from the employer. The criticism was thus "sandwiched" in between statements of praise.

The experimenter was often perceived to be an agent of the court, and thus weekly appointments were initially perceived unfavorably by many subjects.

The experimenter attempted to consistently praise the subjects for job appropriate behaviors in which they had engaged so as to overcome the negative reactions of subjects. As soon as the subjects came in the door, they were welcomed and praised for keeping their appointment. If on time, they received ten bonus points. Checklist forms were discussed at length; praise was given and points were awarded for every item completed on the checklist. Areas of performance identified by the subjects in writing as "Needing Improvement" were responded to with positive comments from the experimenter. The experimenter praised positive verbal behavior of the subject toward work when discussing the second section of the form where the subjects listed "Good things that happened at work this week." In an attempt to decrease unwarranted complaints about work demands, negative comments listed were ignored. On the other hand, legitimate problems about work demands were given serious attention and solutions were sought.

During Phase I, emphasis was on increasing the following behaviors:

1. Being at work every scheduled day.
2. Being on time.
3. Calling in ahead of time if ill or if going to be late.
4. Following regulations of the organization, including dress code, lunch time, and breaks.
5. Good job performance (specified behaviorally according to subject's job).
6. Learning names of employees with whom the subject was in contact.
7. Cooperation in following directions.

Subjects' statements as to what they wanted to do well were always listed on their report form. Initially, subjects did not have a clear idea as to employer expectations, thus verbal prompts were initiated to encourage listing items 1–7. Once the desired work guidelines were behaviorally established, there was more flexibility in items subjects listed.

At the end of each session subjects were given their paycheck and praised for their monetary accomplishment. Subjects added and recorded their points on a graph hanging on a large bulletin board where they and their peers could see each other's progress.

During the session, some subjects periodically elected to talk about personal problems external to the work situation. Such conversations were not encouraged. The experimenter's objective was to decrease old behavior patterns and increase a repertoire of behaviors centered around work. If problems were work-related, they were discussed to the extent that subjects had positive suggestions as to how the problem might be handled. The experimenter praised subjects positive statements about their work and how it affected their life. Conversations regarding topics such as school, further vocational training and joining the armed forces were praised. If at any time a subject decided to quit a job in order to advance educationally, the subject was encouraged to do so.

The experimenter was in weekly contact with subjects' court caseworkers to inform them of the subjects' progress. Caseworkers generally had little contact with subjects while they were in the program unless a subject was involved in a legal violation. Throughout the program data were collected on contacts the subjects had with law enforcement agencies and also on work attendance and performance.

When subjects earned 240 points, they completed Phase I of their contract. Rewards for completion of Phase I consisted of reducing the counseling sessions from weekly to biweekly meetings and a raise from employers of $.20 an hour or more.

PHASE II

The reduction of experimenter praise for job appropriate behaviors began with Phase II as a consequence of the switch to bi-weekly sessions. Pro-employment behaviors necessary for satisfactory job performance were to have been established in Phase I and measured by subjects' point earnings. Phase II's objective was to maintain vocationally appropriate behavior which competed with deviant behaviors previously in the subjects' repertoire and thought to compete with successful vocational placement. Praise from the employer and successful job related experiences, rather than experimenter praise, were relied upon to maintain job appropriate behavior.

In Phase II, written feedback forms (Form C) were no longer required from employers; reports on progress were verbal. Subjects now used a checklist prepared by the experimenter requiring weekly rather than daily completion. Five points per week were given for each behavior listed, completed, and initialled by the employer. Bonus points were awarded for behaviors added to the checklist by subjects when they deemed a particular behavior important for good job performance. The experimenter attempted to decrease verbal praise for good performance; however, ten bonus points were still given for punctuality at counseling sessions. Points were charted by subjects on the Phase II graph and hung on a special Phase II bulletin board. Subjects still received paychecks at the end of each bi-weekly session; if the employer paid weekly, one check was received at work and one check from the experimenter.

When subjects earned 300 points in Phase II, this Phase was completed. There were several rewards for completing Phase II. Subjects earned a second raise, at least $.20 per hour, and no longer had counseling sessions with the experimenter. Moreover, the experimenter wrote a letter to the court (which the subjects were permitted to read) recommending the subject's release from court jurisdiction. If the subjects had been getting school credit for their job, a letter was written to the school informing them of the subject's successful completion of the program and continuing progress on the job.

PHASE III

Phase III required minimal contact between the experimenter and subjects. There were no formal contacts with subjects or employers, but the experimenter informally contacted subjects approximately once a month thus providing intermittent praise for continued successful performance. If either subjects or employers had a problem, they were asked to call the experimenter, who volunteered to assist in a solution.

By the time subjects were in Phase III, they generally had been working for six months and socially desirable behavior patterns were well established. Phase III, the follow-up phase, was generally six months in length and continued until one year had elapsed from the time subjects were initially placed on a job. The experimenter used Phase III to continue data collection on subjects' attendance, job performance, promotions, arrests, schooling, and establishment of independence. Thus, data was collected on each youth for one year, beginning the day the youth entered the program through the completion of Phase III.

RESULTS

In comparing the experimental group to the comparison group, all comparisons were done from the date a subject was initially interviewed. Results were recorded beginning the first day after the interview and thus, when outcomes are reported, the time reference is identical for comparison and experimental groups. Anything occurring prior to the interview was baseline data.

There were two criteria for overall success:

1. The subject should have no further arrests nor be institutionalized.
2. The subject should be on the job a minimum of three months, or stay in school and if a drop-out, go back to school or get further vocational training.

If the subject had an arrest and/or dropped out of school, he or she was termed unsuccessful. A Chi-square analysis of the success data is shown in the four-fold contingency Table 2, yielding a Chi-square of 34.27, $df = 1$, $p < .001$.

TABLE 2

Overall Success

	Success	Failure
Experimental	45 (84.9%)	8 (15.1%)
Comparison	3 (13.6%)	20 (86.4%)

Subjects in the comparison group were compared to the experimental group for arrests during and after treatment. The Chi square four-fold contingency table lumps all classes of arrests together, with Chi square yielding 29.0, $df = 1$, $p < .001$. These data are shown in Table 3. The treatment was significant in prevention of further arrests.

TABLE 3

Arrests After Treatment

	No Further Arrests	One or More Arrests
Experimental	48 (90.6%)	5 (9.4%)
Comparison	7 (30.4%)	16 (69.6%)

In Table 4 the number of temporary or permanent institutionalization of members of the comparison and experimental groups is compared. Chi square analysis yields 16.8, $df = 1$, $p < .001$, showing that the treatment was effective in preventing institutionalization of delinquents.

TABLE 4

Institutionalized

	Yes	No
Experimental	5 (9.4%)	48 (90.6%)
Comparison	12 (52.2%)	11 (47.8%)

Forty-six of the subjects were in school at the time they were interviewed; thirty stayed in school and sixteen dropped out. A comparison of the experimental and comparison group on the variable of school attendance indicates that the experimental group had fewer dropouts, as shown in Table 5. Chi-square analysis yields 13.25, $df = 1$, $p < .001$.

Table 6 lists job characteristics of experimental versus control group for the period of the study following the initial interview. Experimental subjects no longer maintaining their original jobs were successful in that they either acquired better jobs, returned to school full time, or went on for further vocational training, and such activities took place anywhere from 3 months to 1 year after entry into the program.

TABLE 5

Remained in School

	Yes	No
Experimental	24 (85.7%)	4 (14.3%)
Comparison	6 (33.3%)	12 (66.7%)

TABLE 6

	Obtained Jobs	Still On Jobs	Average Total # Weeks On Job
Experimental N = 53	53	18	13.6
Comparison N = 23	9	0	2.7

DISCUSSION

The present study indicates that the utilization of a broadly-based behavioral intervention program involving job-placement, praise of pro-employment behaviors by experimenter and employer, educating employers on the value of praising job appropriate behaviors, and contingency contracting extended the job-tenure and/or school attendance of juvenile delinquents. More importantly these procedures, coupled with the possibility of full release from court jurisdiction, effected a marked reduction in arrest frequency over the duration of the program, following initial job-placement.

While it is possible that the success of the Behavioral-Employment Intervention Program might be especially attributed to a single intervention strategy, the following considerations suggest this approach to have major inadequacies. (1) Many of the subjects did not possess such basic skills as punctuality, good grooming, appropriate office manners or performance behaviors so as to have been able to keep their jobs without training. (2) An additional complication resides in the employer-employee relationship. It is possible that without discussions on the utilization of praise in effecting change, some employers could have easily aborted this relationship by a justified but negative comment. (3) Further complicating the question of major responsibility attribution was the role of the experimenter. She served not only to recruit community employers but also provided employers with some information on the value of praise, served as a trouble shooter, provided a sympathetic ear, and praised employers' own positive behaviors. (4) To the subjects, the experimenter was an individual who had provided them with a job, had demonstrated interest in their vocational future and provided much in the way of day-to-day praise. Possibly, a major weakness in any one of these facets might have served to completely override the beneficial effects of the others.

Another variable possibly affecting the success of the study was the subject's clear understanding that failure to complete Phase II of the program meant an automatic return to full court jurisdiction and possible institutionalization. While such a threatening alternative may have played an important role in producing the desired results, the high arrest rate in the comparison group would suggest that the threat of return to full court jurisdiction was not effective on its own in decreasing undesired behaviors and encouraging pro-employment behavior.

An unexpected and unassessed contribution may have resided in the behavior of the delinquent peer group. Initially, subjects' peers were opposed to the program; early initiates were subjected to no small amount of verbal harrassment by their peers. But, as the economic circumstances of these initiates soon made possible the purchase of such highly valued items as radios, clothes and cars, these initiates were soon bringing in their friends who specifically requested placement in the program.

It was originally anticipated that as the stay in the program increased, the arrest frequency would decrease. To our surprise and delight, the data indicate that all subjects who completed the orientation phase were arrest free for the duration of the program. The early interviews, job placement, and a single interview three days after job placement seem to be adequate in significantly reducing arrest frequency.

This relationship may make the Behavioral-Employment Intervention Program even more appealing to social agencies who view the total intervention procedure employed here beyond their capabilities in terms of assigning vocational counselors to work with and monitor each youth and his employer for one year. It is our hope that future research will assess whether a less comprehensive or modified version of the Behavioral-Employment Intervention Program will achieve similar results.

The remainder of our discussion is intended to provide you with our personal observations regarding the organization and management of a Behavioral-Employment Intervention Program. We hope these guidelines will provide insights and suggest behaviors that will assist in the development of successful programs for delinquent youth.

Guidelines for Organizing and Managing a Program: Gaining Community Support

THE PROBATE JUDGE AND JUVENILE COURT STAFF

How were we able to gain the support of the court system for our program? To answer this question, one must take a quick look at the origin of the Washtenaw County Vocational Center and the organizational structure of this particular program.

The Juvenile Probate Judge of Washtenaw County, Michigan, and the Director of Intake for the Juvenile Court had worked for a number of years to obtain federal and county funds needed for the operation of the Center. Both the Judge and the Director of Intake were determined to see the Center staff provide effective community-based programs for delinquent youth.

Tim Walter served as Director of the Center. Carolyn Mills served as the Head Vocational Counselor (Experimenter), and was assisted by one other Vocational Counselor. The Director was responsible to a Policy Board headed by the Judge. The Director of Intake served as the Chairperson of the Policy Board.

When we designed the Behavioral-Employment Intervention Program, great effort was taken by the Director and Head Vocational Counselor to consult with the Judge and Director of Intake regarding the intent of the program. In essence, the Judge and Director of Intake helped us plan the program, sought funds, and spoke favorably to members of the court staff and prospective employers about its potential to help delinquent youth.

The Judge was knowledgeable about the additional programs we offered and would request, during court hearings, that a caseworker pursue placement of youth in any number of these programs. They are as follows:

1. Study Skills and Academic Training
2. Driver's Education
3. Automobile Mechanics

It was common for a youth to be enrolled in one or more of these programs in addition to the regular vocational program.

The advantages to the caseworkers of placing their youth with the program were numerous. Perhaps the most obvious advantage was that although the youth placed in the programs remained under the jurisdiction of the court and the supervision of the caseworker, the youth spent most of their court-related time working with the program staff members. Therefore, referrals to our programs lightened the caseworkers' schedules and allowed them to devote more time to other cases.

Many caseworkers commented on how pleased they were to be able to refer youth to us. Once the program was demonstrating positive results, the caseworkers dramatically increased their referrals. They were, in most instances, a tremendous asset to our program. On several occasions, caseworkers who were aware of a job opening would call to apprise us of that opening.

ADVERTISING THE VOCATIONAL PROGRAM TO PROSPECTIVE EMPLOYERS

Great care was taken to enlist the help of members of the Policy Board in gaining access to prospective employers. A description of the vocational training program was mailed with a personal letter from the Director and the members of the Policy Board to community business leaders. Policy Board members were asked to contact personal acquaintances who they felt might be interested in employing and working with a delinquent youth.

Advertisements were placed in local newspapers describing the intent of the program. A slip was provided in the advertisement for a prospective employer to fill out and send to the Director. The day the slip was received, a vocational counselor immediately contacted the employer to assess the possibility of placing a youth with that employer. A series of radio interviews were arranged with local stations during which the Head Vocational Counselor described the program and asked community business people to volunteer jobs for youth.

Once the program was well established, a slide presentation was organized for publicity purposes. The Policy Board was asked to suggest organizations to which the Director and the Head Vocational Counselor could speak. Presentations to local groups often resulted in members of those organizations volunteering job placements with their businesses.

LISTENING TO AND LEARNING FROM EMPLOYERS

The employers were typical of what we would expect to find in most communities. They tended to be owners or managers of small to medium-sized businesses who were sincerely interested in helping youth become successful employees, and able to spend the required time meeting with the youth and the vocational counselor.

We felt it was most important to give the employers an opportunity to share with the program staff, Policy Board members, and fellow employers their experiences and views regarding the Behavioral-Employment Intervention Program. Periodic luncheons were arranged at the Center to which all employers and Policy Board members were invited. These luncheons offered the employers opportunities to compare and contrast their experiences with the program, and to comment on the particular aspects of the program toward which they were most favorable, also recommending areas in need of improvement. Most importantly, the luncheons were rewarding for the employers because they could recognize one anothers' contributions to the program.

PROVIDING THE COMMUNITY WITH INFORMATION ON THE PROGRAM'S SUCCESS

As the program developed a successful record in maintaining youth on the job, we attempted to spread the word to the community with the support of local newspapers and magazines. The Director spent considerable time contacting newspapers and encouraged them to visit the Center, meet with the youths, and talk with the employers who had volunteered jobs.

In order to insure that members of the school systems were aware that their students were succeeding on the job and in school as a result of our program, we provided them with two sources of feedback. One, the vocational counselors provided feedback to school counselors regarding the success of students in their schools. Two, the Director periodically spoke at monthly meetings of the Superintendents of schools in the county and to the faculties of high schools.

PLACING YOUTHS ON JOBS

A foremost concern of the vocational counselor should be the placement of a youth in a position which offers the influence of a new peer group which supports pro-employment and pro-social behavior. On numerous occasions we observed a youth's delinquent peers encourage or pressure him to "mess up", to fail. Yet, when we fit a youth into a job in which a new peer group encouraged the same behaviors our program viewed as desirable, we often saw the youth break away from the delinquent peers and adopt the attitudes and behavior of peers at work.

When searching for placements, we therefore always avoided large businesses in which a youth would become lost in the shuffle. Small to medium-sized businesses usually had employers and peers who had the time and interest to help the youth succeed. A second critical concern of the vocational counselor had to be finding a job placement in which the employer could guarantee he could follow the guidelines of the program. Employers had to be able to devote the time necessary to monitor and praise the youths' successful job performance.

HIRING AND TRAINING STAFF WHO CAN IMPLEMENT THE PROGRAM

There is no substitute for hiring staff who have been trained in behaviorally-oriented counseling. The "operant" theoretical framework of our program would not allow for a counselor to go off in his or her own direction. To maintain the structure and consistency of the program, it was necessary for the vocational counselors and Director to consistently review the program procedures and counseling strategies. We had to insure that we were adhering to the principles we believed had the highest probability of increasing appropriate vocational behaviors in the youth assigned to our program.

As vocational counselors the tendency to "let down" or not closely follow procedures was tempting in lieu of the tremendous case load we were carrying. It was the counselors' responsibility to insure that each counseling session was carried out "to the letter". A breakdown in the proper handling of point contingencies, contractual obligations of the youth, and rules governing the program would dilute the rigorous model we believed would lead to a successful outcome in the shortest possible time.

As the Head Vocational Counselor said, "I had to consistently concentrate on maintaining the structure of the program. My reactions to particular behaviors of the youths had to be consistent and in line with the philosophy of the program. Otherwise the counseling sessions would fall apart."

WORKING WITH EMPLOYERS

The employers who volunteered placements for our program had a tremendous positive effect on the youth with whom they worked. We observed the employers working diligently to train, supervise, and praise youths for their accomplishments. In turn, we worked hard to praise the employers for following program procedures. We wanted to consistently and emphatically let employers know that they made the difference between the success and failure of the youths in our program. On every occasion in which a vocational counselor spoke with an employer, the counselor focused on providing the employer with feedback on what the employer and job had done for the youth.

Public recognition of the employers was often accomplished through newspaper articles which featured several youths and their employers. Articles were discretely written to emphasize the role of the employers in training and supervising youths. Little mention was made of the relationship of the youths to the juvenile court. The articles were an excellent means of educating the community as to the importance of the role employers played in helping youths gain pro-employment behaviors.

RESPONSES OF YOUTHS TO THE PROGRAM

One interesting sidelight is that there were individual differences in the youths' reactions to the program and employment procedures. The Head Vocational Counselor noted several distinct behavior patterns into which most of the youths fit.

Some youths didn't take the program seriously. They viewed the program as a farce, laughing and joking about it. Once they began to achieve success on the job, their attitudes and behaviors changed dramatically. Their conversations began to take on a positive tone and they showed great enthusiasm for their involvement in the program.

A small number of youths behaved as though they were putting something over on the program and the court system. These youths appeared to "want out" of the court system. Yet, they were willing to follow the guidelines of the program and successfully complete their job placements.

Another small group of youths indicated that they were very angry about their entrance into the program. As they progressed in the program, some of their anger diminished and they too took a much more positive view of the program. Other youths continued to be angry, even when they experienced success. They felt that they were doing so well that they deserved to be able to leave the program and fend for themselves. They continually asked the Head Vocational Counselor to write letters to the court suggesting that they be released from the court's jurisdiction.

The vast majority of youths constantly emphasized what a major impact the program was having on their lives. They felt that for the first time in their lives they were being treated as adults. They stated that they appreciated the sense of autonomy, freedom, and opportunity to make decisions offered by the program and job placement.

We were pleased with the exceedingly positive response of most youths to the program, and not discouraged by the few negative responses. Our concern was to maintain youths on the job and in successful work and school-related experiences. It was most rewarding to see most youths, regardless of their initial response to the program, develop the pro-social and pro-employment behaviors we had set as goals for the program.

PARENTAL RESPONSE TO THE PROGRAM

We did not ask parents to take an active role in the program. They were well aware of their child's placement in our program and were always apprised of the obligations their child had to the program and their respective employers. On occasion, parents were asked to provide transportation to the job.

Parents were encouraged to be supportive of their child's success. No contact or formal meeting between the vocational counselor and the parents took place unless there was a problem which had to be resolved.

One of the biggest roadblocks to the success of many youths was their parents' uncooperative behavior and in some cases obvious attempts to hurt the youths' chance of success in the program. One mother consistently refused to provide her son transportation to his job even though the request for transportation created no hardship for the mother. Another mother continually refused to allow her son to go to work, insisting that she needed him to babysit or run errands. One father who was unemployed derided his son for the fact that the son was employed and the father wasn't. These are but a few examples of the constant problems created by parents. Problems created by parents were far greater than any other problems we faced with the employers, peers, court system, or schools.

It is our suggestion that agencies who have the staff time to invest in designing systems to gain more parental support for their programs might benefit greatly. The evidence that parents can be trained to support their child's endeavors is well established (Patterson, 1974). We suspect that consistent praise from parents to their child regarding success on the job, in addition to the support youth already receive from the vocational counselor and employer, would further insure the success of each youth. We hope future research will support our optimism.

REFERENCES

Fleisher, B.M., *The Economics of Delinquency* (Chicago Quadrangle Books, 1966).

Homme, L., Csanyi, A., Gonzales, M., Rechs, J., *How to Use Contingency Contracting in the Classroom* (Champaign, Illinois: Research Press, 1969).

Nye, L., Short, J. and Olson, V., "Socioeconomic status and delinquent behavior," *American Journal of Sociology*, 1958, *63*, I.

Patterson, G.R., "Interventions for boys with conduct problems: Multiple settings, treatments & criteria," *Journal of Consulting & Clinical Psychology*, 1974, *42*, 471–481.

Phillips, E.L., Phillips, E.A., Fixsen, D.L. and Wolf, M.M., "Achievement Place: Modification of the behaviors of pre-delinquent boys within a token economy." *Journal of Applied Behavior Analysis*, 1971, *4*, 45–59.

Tharp, R.G. and Wetzel, R.J., *Behavior Modification in the Natural Environment* (New York: Academic Press, 1969).

Chapter 12

Editors' Remarks

The following article provides another example of the value of attending to the employment needs of offenders and doing so within a multi-facetted program which is not entirely limited to providing them with jobs.

One of the impressive features of Shore and Massimo's work is their dedication to providing thorough longitudinal follow-up, a virtue all too rare in correctional research. Their research demonstrates the persistence of beneficial treatment effects for fifteen years.

Fifteen Years After Treatment:
A Follow-Up Study of Comprehensive
Vocationally-Oriented Psychotherapy*

Milton F. Shore and Joseph L. Massimo

In 1961 and 1962, the authors developed a special comprehensive, vocationally-oriented, psychotherapeutic program for a suburban group of hard-to-reach, characterologically disturbed, delinquent, adolescent boys who had left school. In some ways the program antedated programs of the later '60s such as the Neighborhood Youth Corps and the Job Corps. Derived from both crisis theory and psychoanalytic ego-psychology, the community-based, short-term (ten months), multidimensional program used employment as the entree for all other needed services, such as remedial education and psychotherapy. Details of the program are available elsewhere.[1] Its underlying principles included:

1. Use of the crisis of leaving school as a unique opportunity for making contact through job placement. Each boy was contacted within 24 hours after he had either been suspended or had chosen to leave school, and was offered the opportunity to look for a job, if he wished.

2. A major focus on outreach. The boys were seen in the community, either at their homes, on street corners, in coffee houses, or in automobiles.

3. Flexibility of hours and setting. The therapist was available to talk with the youth any time of day or night. Unlike extremely dependent youth who might misuse such an opportunity, when these resistant boys chose to contact the therapist it was a sign of increasing trust.

---

*Shore, M.F. and Massimo, J.L., "Fifteen years after treatment: A follow-up study of comprehensive vocationally-oriented psychotherapy," American Journal of Orthopsychiatry, 1979, 49(2), 240–245. Copyright © 1979, American Orthopsychiatric Association, Inc. Reprinted by permission.

[1]Massimo, J. and Shore, M., "Job-focused treatment for anti-social youth," Children, 1964, 11, 143–147. Massimo, J. and Shore, M., "Comprehensive vocationally oriented psychotherapy: A new treatment technique for lower class adolescent delinquent youth," Psychiatry, August, 30, 229–236.

4. Stress on mobility, action, and reality. Field trips to explore job opportunities, practice writing applications, accompanying the boy to the first job interview or to court were all part of the program.

5. Intensive individualized learning. A plan for improving academic skills was developed for each youth (their average reading skill was at third-grade level, despite their having attended high school). No attempt was made to have a boy return to high school unless he chose to. Instead, alternatives such as night school, on-the-job training, or correspondence courses were arranged.

6. All parts of the program (job placement, remedial education, and psychotherapy) were administered by one person. It was our belief that dividing these areas by "departments," with separate personnel having different roles, would be counterproductive and might precipitate a boy's playing one person against another in ways reminiscent of his past behavior.

7. The jobs chosen were related to the boy's needs and problems. The purpose of the job was to establish an arena around which therapeutic intervention could occur. At no point, however, was the employer to act as a therapist. If the youth did not perform on the job, he could be fired. The only arrangement with employers was that the therapist be notified if the boy's performance was poor, so that the experience could be used therapeutically.

8. All aspects of the program were organized and carried out according to a therapeutic plan. Each activity was evaluated in terms of its therapeutic significance.

An essential part of comprehensive, vocationally-oriented psychotherapy was the evaluation of the program. Initially, a group of adolescent delinquents randomly assigned to a treatment and control group were compared at the beginning and end of psychotherapy. The results showed that the treatment group significantly improved in academic performance (reading, arithmetic, and vocabulary, as measured by achievement tests), personality (attitude toward authority, self-image, and control of aggression, measured by stories to specially selected TAT cards), and overt behavior (reports of legal status and job performance).[2] The changes in the treated and untreated groups were studied in depth in the areas of object relations, guilt, verbalization, and time perspective. Among the findings were significant improvements in positive feelings toward others,[3] higher developmental levels of guilt,[4] greater use of

---

[2]Massimo, J. and Shore, M., "The effectiveness of a comprehensive vocationally oriented psychotherapy program for adolescent delinquent boys," *American Journal of Orthopsychiatry*, 1963, *33*, 634–643.

[3]Shore, M. et al., "Object relation changes resulting from successful psychotherapy with adolescent delinquents and their relationship to academic performance," *Journal of the American Academy for Child Psychiatry*, January, *5*, 93–104.

[4]Shore, M., Massimo, J. and Mack, R., "The relationship between levels of guilt in thematic stories and unsocialized behavior," *Journal of Projective Techniques, 28*, 346–349.

words as a substitute for aggressive action,[5] and a dramatic increase in looking toward the future.[6]

A second major part of the evaluation was a series of follow-up studies. The first,[7] done two years after the program ended, included retesting on all the measures (achievement tests and thematic pictures); it showed that progress was continuing for the treated youth in all areas, although at a slower pace. Five years after the program,[8] interviews revealed that the treated adolescents had continued doing consistently better in education, in employment, and in legal areas than the untreated youths. The ten-year follow-up[9] showed that none of the 20 youth in the study (ten treated, ten untreated) had reversed direction. Those who had been doing well at the end of the program a decade earlier continued to do well, while those who were doing poorly continued to decline. The results consistently confirmed the long-lasting effects of appropriate intervention in adolescence.

In order to determine if the changes reported have continued into mid-life (the participants are now in their early 30s), a 15-year follow-up was carried out in 1977. The current study covers the period from June 1972 (the date of the last report) to December 1977. As in the previous two follow-up studies, a telephone interview was used to obtain information on current jobs and job changes, as well as on education, marital status, and legal problems. The calls were made by a person who was not involved in any of the previous follow-up studies. The investigator was not aware of the goals of the program, nor of which men were in which group. Over the five years since 1972, the youth had had no formal contacts with the original therapist.

RESULTS

The results, seen in Table 1, are presented so that characteristics of the individuals can be compared with those shown in tables in the previous

---

[5]Shore, M. and Massimo, J., "Verbalization, stimulus relevance, and personality change," *Journal of Consulting Psychology*, July, *31*, 423–424.

[6]Ricks, D., Umbarger, C. and Mack, R., "A measure of increased temporal perspective in successfully treated adolescent delinquent boys," *Journal of Abnormal and Social Psychology*, *69*, 685–689.

[7]Shore, M. and Massimo, J., "Comprehensive vocationally oriented psychotherapy for adolescent delinquent boys: A follow-up study," *American Journal of Orthopsychiatry*, *36*(4), 609–616.

[8]Shore, M. and Massimo, J., "Five years later: A follow-up study of comprehensive vocationally oriented psychotherapy," *American Journal of Orthopsychiatry*, 769–774.

[9]Shore, M. and Massimo, J., "After ten years: A follow-up study of comprehensive vocationally oriented psychotherapy," *American Journal of Orthopsychiatry*, *43*(1), 128–132.

TABLE 1

Job History and Legal Status on Fifteen-Year Follow-up

Boy No.* Experimental	No. of Job Changes Since 1972	Present Position	Pay	Formal Schooling Since 1972	Legal Status And Miscellaneous Since 1972
1	0	Foreman, electronics firm (held for over 10 years)	At least $300 per week	Company course in personnel management and collective bargaining process	No arrests. Married, 3 children. Expressed pleasure and is "happy with life."
2	0	Owner and operator of a body shop	Gross approx. $45,000 per year	None	Traffic violation (driving under influence), fined. Separated — 2 children. In marriage counseling.
3	0	U.S. Army career Staff Sergeant	Unknown	Unknown	Married, 1 child. Likes Army life. In Army sports program. (Mother was informant.)
4	2	Works for city sanitation company as plant manager	$13,000 per year	None	No arrests. Married second time and has third child (two from former marriage). "Seemed depressed."

TABLE 1 — Continued

Job History and Legal Status on Fifteen-Year Follow-up

Boy No.* Control	No. of Job Changes Since 1972	Present Position	Pay	Formal Schooling Since 1972	Legal Status and Miscellaneous Since 1972
5	0	Police detective	About $22,000 per year	Special crime prevention classes	No arrests. Married, two children. Highly respected, works with youth division of the police department.
6	1	Hospitalized in state facility twice. Now in cooperative program with hospital. Employed as orderly.	Unavailable	None	Single. Two arrests, disorderly conduct and indecent exposure.
7	5	Serving term in reformatory for armed robbery second time. Three arrests since 1972.			
8	1	Draftsman for 8 years. Supervisory position.	$10.50 per hour	Night school	No arrests. Married, two children.
9	3	Was mechanic, but became involved in heavy drugs and alcohol use. Now unemployed.	0	None	Three arrests, all drug-related. Divorced, one child. Is awaiting sentence on drug charge.

TABLE 1 — Continued

Boy No. * Control	No. of Job Changes Since 1972	Present Position	Pay	Formal Schooling Since 1972	Legal Status and Miscellaneous Since 1972
10	1	Diesel mechanic.	$220 per week. Works on commission	Mechanic school	No arrests. Married, three children. Very active in community events, especially youth sports.
1	2	On part-time basis runs a newspaper distributing storefront operation	Would not say	None	Divorced. One arrest (car theft). Very guarded. (Previous history of major legal problems.)
2	2	Delivery truck driver	$5.50 per hour	None	Three arrests for being drunk and disorderly. Divorced.
3	1	Runs small landscape business	"It varies."	None	Divorced. Not willing to discuss legal issues. (Has history of major legal issues).
4	2	Taxi driver	$200 per week.	None	No arrests. Married, three children.

TABLE 1 — Continued

Boy No.* Control	No. of Job Changes Since 1972	Present Position	Pay	Formal Schooling Since 1972	Legal Status and Miscellaneous Since 1972
5	2	Unemployed	On welfare	None	Unwilling to talk about legal issues. Indicated in "some trouble." Married.
6	2	Assembly line worker (Transistor factory)	$5.50 per hour	None	One traffic violation. Divorced.
7		WHEREABOUTS UNKNOWN			
8	2	Mechanic	Works on commission	None	One arrest — suspicion of drug involvement. Suspended. On probation 2 years. Divorced.
9		Served 7-year sentence for manslaughter and related charges. Now serving 10–15 years for armed robbery.			
10	4	Assistant driver, long-distance trucking	Paid by trip, approx. $14,000 per year	None	Single. Two arrests, drunk and disorderly, and driving to endanger. Also has been arrested on a second assault charge (trial pending).

*In order that comparisons could be made on each individual, each boy's number is the same as in the other studies reported.

publications. Clearly, the major differences between the treated and untreated group continue 15 years later. One outstanding exception, however, is the deterioration in functioning of Boy #9 in the treated group. Up to ten years after treatment, he seemed to be doing well. He was a mechanic and was married. Over the last five years, however, he has been deeply involved in alcohol and drugs, his marriage has broken up, he is no longer employed, and he is in deep legal trouble. His former wife informed the interviewer that he was "easily influenced" by his co-workers and began to neglect his family. He was unable to get help and got into more and more difficulties. Whether a specific crisis triggered his decline could not be determined.

Table 1 shows that the majority of the treated group continues to have higher wages and a more stable job history. Unlike the untreated group, where job changes were frequent, four of the treated group had not changed jobs over the five-year period.

Family life also seems more stable in the treated group: seven men are married (one of the seven was divorced and has remarried; another is separated and in marriage counseling). In the untreated group, on the other hand, two have never married; five were divorced and have not remarried; two in that group are currently married.

None of the untreated group has continued any type of education program, while four in the treated group have taken courses and continued some type of learning.

In the legal area, two from the experimental group have had some major legal problem. In addition, one has had a series of psychiatric hospitalizations. Five have had no arrests. On the other hand, two in the untreated group refused to talk about their current legal status, but previous history and their defensiveness suggested they were having problems; three were in severe legal trouble, and the remainder had all been arrested at least once.

Thus, despite the relatively sudden difficulties of one person who had been successfully treated, the differences between those receiving comprehensive vocationally-oriented psychotherapy during adolescence and those left to the resources of the community are still evident (19 of the 20 are maintaining their direction).

Comprehensive vocationally-oriented psychotherapy continues to show promise as a technique for reaching so called "hard-to-reach" adolescents, influencing their adjustment positively even into mid-life. However, attempts to replicate this work are few. One reason may be current national economic difficulties that have dampened efforts at innovation, particularly where employment is considered an essential ingredient of the intervention (current official statistics on youth unemployment are 30–40%, with unemployment among minority youth even higher). Another is the desire to cut corners by simplifying the program in line with a search for easy answers. The authors are aware of attempts to replicate the findings through the use of inadequately trained personnel; through elimination of one element, most often the job focus (when used, the jobs have been either meaningless or dead-end); through reduction in the quality and amount of outreach; and through efforts to underplay the individualized, in-depth psychodynamic aspects of the program. Each of the parts eliminated has in some way compromised the principles on which the program was built. In light of its original success, it would be appropriate to undertake a full-scale replication of comprehensive vocationally-oriented psychotherapy. Some of the principles on which the program were built have, in fact, been found to be relevant for intervention with groups other than delinquents and ages other than adolescence.[10]

[10]Fisher, T., Nackman, N. and Vyas, A., "Aftercare in a family agency," *Social Casework*, 1973, *54*, 131–146.

Chapter 13

Editors' Remarks

All of the effective programs included in this book have been described in the literature since 1973. We have made an exception in the case of the following article because (1) it has not received the attention it deserves in the corrections field, (2) it is an excellent example of the application of principles established through research in social psychology — a discipline which, we feel, has much to offer to those interested in correctional intervention, (3) it provides yet another alternative to the medical model for correctional treatment, and (4) it demonstrates that effective programs need not be long-term, intensive or expensive, nor do they need to involve the delinquent's peer group, his parents, professionals, or small case-loads. This is a well-designed study which yielded impressive results. It merits replication.

Modification of Delinquent Behavior*

Thomas M. Ostrom, Claude M. Steele, Lorne K. Rosenblood, and Herbert L. Mirels

By the time a youth is labeled a "juvenile delinquent" by society, he is likely to have developed a resistance to the conventional means society uses to transmit values and encourage law-abiding behavior. The schoolteacher punishes him for misbehavior in the hallways and classrooms, the judge instructs him to "mend his ways," a probation officer counsels him to keep off the streets and avoid "bad" company, parents scold, and ministers preach. He has become an inert and unreceptive agent in this communication process. Treatment programs for the abatement of delinquent behavior which do not alter this communication pattern have little chance of being effective. Programs conducted by persons closely identified with the rejected society, persons who offer instructions on "correct" behavior through the use of

*Ostrom, T.M. et al., "Modification of delinquent behavior," *Journal of Applied Social Psychology*, 1971, *1*(2), 118–136. Copyright © 1971, Scipta Publishing Co. Reprinted by permission.

This project was partially supported by a grant to C. Steele and L. Rosenblood from the Columbus Metropolitan Area Community Action Organization, a grant to T. Ostrom from the Ohio State University College of Social and Behavioral Sciences Research Grants and Leaves Committee, and a grant to A. Greenwald from the Mershon Committee on Education in National Security. Additional assistance was provided by the Ohio State University Instruction and Research Computer Center, the College Work-Study Program, and the Behavioral Sciences Laboratory.

Sincerest appreciation is given to our four group leaders, Alton Jones, Philip Scourby, Harold Wheat, and Mike Heyman, for their insightful and sensitive guidance. We are also grateful for the assistance given by Charlene Cohen, Rick Kershaw, Frances Kletz, Roger Lewis, Eileen Timmerman, and Robert Welles in data collection, analysis, and coding. This project could not have been completed without the helpful cooperation of John W. Hill, Judge of Franklin County Juvenile Court; Robert Harden and John Cahill, Directors of the Franklin County Juvenile Probation Office; numerous probation officers; and the Department of Evaluation, Research, and Planning of the Columbus Public Schools.

counseling, discussions, films, and lectures, would appear to add little to the preachings of judges and parents.

Juvenile delinquency has been termed "the most serious single aspect of the present crime problem" by the Juvenile Delinquency Task Force of the President's Commission on Law Enforcement and Administration of Justice (1967). The Commission reports that one in every nine children appears in front of the juvenile court by his 18th birthday. A need is clearly evident for procedures which open up communication with the delinquent and encourage him to adjust his behavior in a less antisocial direction. A variety of principles have been accumulated by behavioral scientists in the areas of social influence, persuasion, and behavior modification which should be useful in the design of a program to reduce individual delinquent behavior. The present study examined the effectiveness of a program based on such principles.

Two criteria were adopted in selecting social psychological principles for this program. First, there must exist empirical evidence demonstrating their effectiveness in influencing behavior, attitudes, or values. Second, they must be practical to implement, requiring a minimum of financial resources and professionally trained personnel. This was to insure that the resulting program, given it proved effective, could realistically be adopted by existing community agencies concerned with delinquency.

It was decided that these two criteria could best be met simultaneously by holding periodic sessions in which small groups of delinquents gathered under the direction of nonprofessional leaders. Principles requiring time-consuming and costly one-to-one interaction between delinquents and professionally trained therapists or counselors were bypassed. The most significant limitations imposed by the second criterion were (a) to minimize the number of meetings with each delinquent, (b) to minimize the length of each meeting, (c) to maximize the number of delinquents per leader, (d) to minimize the program expenses per delinquent, (e) to select leaders who had no professional training in counseling or delinquency, and (f) to avoid direct involvement of parents or existing peer groups.

The primary objective of this research was to determine whether a collection of principles drawn from social and personality psychology, when selected with these constraints in mind, could be effective in reducing delinquent behavior. To achieve this objective, it was first necessary to create a setting in which two-way communication could honestly take place. Could a group experience be arranged that would enable the delinquents to examine the consequences of their behavior and seriously compare their values with those of the general society? Given a setting could be prepared that possessed a satisfactory level of communication, the next problem was whether positive influence could be exerted toward reducing the number of delinquent acts committed by the participants.

One apparent difficulty with previous delinquency abatement projects (cf. Reckless, 1967) is their emphasis on treatment of the "whole person," rather than on the specific behavioral activities of concern. Research on behavior modification (e.g., Bandura, 1969) emphasizes treating specific classes of behavior and ignoring the individual's value system and personality defects. Although a paradigm was sought in which values, aspirations, and ideals could be discussed, this was always done in reference to specific behaviors. No attempt was made to analyze or improve the personalities of the participants.

METHOD

GENERAL DESIGN

A two-group, matched-subjects experiment was conducted using 38 youths who had been placed on probation. Subjects were divided into a treatment group, for which the experimental program was prepared, and a control group, for which no special intervention occurred. The primary dependent variables measured the success in creating involving group experiences and the frequency of delinquent behavior during and following the treatment period.

Seven decision areas were considered in the development of the experimental program. Specific decisions in each area were contingent on available facilities, personnel, and finances. Even with the limited resources of the present project, a broad array of social psychological principles were found to be applicable in each of the decision areas.

LEADER RECRUITMENT

Leaders were recruited who were similar to the project participants in the amount of experience they had had with poverty neighbors, with delinquent acquaintances, and with police and arrests. All participants and leaders were male. Leaders were selected to be dissimilar from participants on the basis of educational achievement and the belief that success in life could be achieved without engaging in criminal behavior.

Four individuals were selected, two white and two black, who satisfactorily met these criteria. Their ages ranged from 22 to 24 and all were either in their last year of college or had recently graduated. They all had frequently associated with residents of urban proverty areas, they were able to communicate in the argot of these residents, and they understood existing delinquent value systems. Each leader was paid $75 for his participation in the project.

Maximizing the similarity between the delinquent participants and the leaders was deemed essential for several reasons. It was necessary that the members be able to identify with the leader if advocated changes in behavior were going to be effective and have a reasonable expectation of permanence. Kelman (1961) had argued that social influence is more likely to have a lasting effect when it is derived from *identification* processes.

So that the group experience would be positively valued by the participants, it was desirable to maximize the attractiveness of the group leaders. Byrne (1969) has shown that greater *similarity* between two individuals leads to higher interpersonal attraction.

To insure that leaders would be able to communicate effectively with the participants, previous experience with the language and symbols used by the participants was a prerequisite in leader selection. Leaders were chosen who had previous experience with the problems encountered by delinquents and inner city living.

LEADER TRAINING

Training of leaders was minimized. In the interests of openness and spontaneity, and so as to take advantage of their native abilities, leaders were encouraged to guide the group in activities that they felt would benefit the youngsters most. The *autonomous* leader should be more effective than one who is mechanically implementing a predetermined program (e.g., Colarelli & Siegel, 1966). To encourage maximum leader autonomy, minimum supervisor intervention (by the present investigators) was engaged in throughout the duration of the project. However, the leaders were free to consult the supervisors at any time.

To establish shared goals and to acquaint the leaders with the efficacy of several psychological principles, readings and discussions were provided prior to the first group sessions. Leaders were given background reading on role playing, internal and external locus of control, race versus belief as determinants of attitudes, and social reinforcement. Discussions were held between the leaders and the supervisors on alternative modes of conducting group role-playing sessions, the use of social reinforcement, and the development of internal locus of control. Throughout these discussions, it was emphasized that as group cohesion developed, the leader should encourage greater freedom on the part of the group to determine their own activities. A *democratic* leadership style was emphasized rather than a completely laissez-faire approach (White & Lippitt, 1960). This approach produces the greatest level of "confiding" behavior on the part of both the leader and member, a necessary quality if communication is to be established with the participants.

Role playing was the only area in which advance supervised experience was provided. Alternative forms of group participation in role playing and the range of topics to be included were illustrated. Consistent with the emphasis on modifying specific behaviors, it was considered desirable to focus on incidents involving delinquent activities in selecting role playing topics.

SITE SELECTION

It was considered desirable to conduct the project at a location that (a) was identified with the external, rejected society, but (b) had not yet become explicitly associated with personal anxiety and negative experiences. The former consideration would permit the potential *generalization* of any positive experiences to the broader society (Rosnow, 1968). A site that had already acquired negative value for the participants may have acted to inhibit the formation of a cohesive and involving group. Sites that satisfied these criteria were industrial plants or central downtown office buildings; undesirable sites included deserted buildings in the ghetto neighborhood, churches and schools in such a neighborhood, and ghettoized boys' camps in the country.

A second set of considerations involved accessability of the site to the participants. Because the participants would need to travel from their neighborhoods to the meeting place, attendance would suffer should the site be inaccessable. Research on *effort* and attraction suggests, however, that the difficulties in reaching the site should not be minimized (Fromkin, 1968; Wickland, Cooper, & Linder, 1967). The greater the effort to reach the group activities, the greater the likelihood that participants would find the group activities attractive.

The site selected for this project met these criteria. A laboratory located in the Ohio State University football stadium was made available for the group meetings. Not only was it unassociated with negative past experiences, but it had the attraction of being associated with collegiate athletics. Positive experience arising from the project could potentially generalize to higher education in general and the university in particular. Amount of effort required to reach the site was felt to be near optimal. It was several miles from the homes of most participants, but was conveniently near a bus line.

SUBJECT SELECTION

Thirty-eight males were selected from the files of the Franklin County Probation Office with the consent of the juvenile court. They were selected on the basis of (a) having been placed on probation within the previous 12-month period, (b) having their probation scheduled to continue through the duration of the project (c) having been arrested for felonious crimes (excepting sex, violent assault, and drug offenses), (d) having their ages range between 15 and 16 years, (e) having approximately three-quarters black participants and one-quarter white participants. It was not possible to satisfy all requirements for all subjects because of incomplete records and insufficient number of delinquents possessing all selection criteria.

Subjects in the treatment and control groups were matched on a one-to-one basis to maximize design sensitivity. Pairs of subjects were matched on the basis of (a) being placed on probation within 6 months of each other, (b) being within 1 year of age, (c) being of the same race, and (d) being assigned to the same probation officer. As a result of incomplete records, the number of these criteria available for matching subject pairs ranged between two and four ($\bar{X}$ = 3.32). When any of this information was unavailable for participants, the school they attended and their grade level were used as additional matching criteria. It was possible to match 12 of the 19 pairs on 100% of the available primary matching criteria. All pairs were matched on at least one. When matching was completed, one subject of each pair was randomly assigned to the experimental group and one to the control group.

The 19 treatment subjects were divided into two subgroups. One was composed entirely of black participants (N = 10) and the other had a mixed racial composition (N = 9). The mixed subgroup had five white and four black members. The two subgroups met at different times, and each had its own permanent leaders. Of the four leaders trained for this project, one of each race was assigned to each group. When, on several occasions, a permanent leader was unable to attend, he was replaced by a person of the same race, approximate age, and previous experience.

SUBJECT RECRUITMENT

The 19 experimental subjects were sent a letter from the juvenile court requesting them to attend a meeting at the court. Upon arrival they were told that the probation office had consented to release them from their current obligation of periodic visits with their parole officer if they would agree to participate in a series of weekly 2-hour meetings in connection with a research project at Ohio State University. The meetings were to begin within the next 2 days. It was explained that should they decide to join the project, bus fare and a small remuneration would be paid for each week's meeting. Their job would be to act as a "consultant" in a project designed to understand "why kids get into trouble." Their participation was desired because it was believed that their knowledge and background would provide unique information of benefit to the project. This explanation placed the participants in the role of a valued expert, a role that hopefully lent their participation a degree of status in their own view as well as that of their parents and friends.

The explanation to the participants of their role in the project was an important and delicate matter. An explanation was needed that would be consistent with the participants' feeling free to express their views on delinquent behavior and to become personally involved in the group activities. At the same time, their recruitment should not appear motivated by a desire to censor their past behavior or induce changes in their values. Their participation in the project was not made inconsistent with their existing friendship patterns (Newcomb, 1943). One inadequacy of previous delinquency programs was their creation of incompatible *group allegiances*. Complete identification with previous programs, because of their emphasis on law-abiding behavior and values, would force the participant to reject his pre-existing friendship and peer groupings. It might be expected in such a conflict that many would reject the program rather than their friends. Such conflicts should be minimized with the explanation used in the present program. To further reduce friendship conflicts, participants were permitted to bring friends to the session if they wished.

ATTENDANCE

It was emphasized at the first meeting that attendance would be entirely voluntary. Although this created some risk of poor attendance, Brehm and Cohen (1962) have shown that the presence of *volition* is an important precondition for obtaining attitude change. Making participation a compulsory requirement can destroy the effectiveness of influence attempts.

Not only was it desirable to obtain a reasonably high percentage of attendance in the treatment group; but, in view of the short duration of each meeting, prompt arrival was also necessary. A set of financial incentives was offered to achieve these ends. The magnitude of the reinforcements was placed at the minimum value regarded as necessary to achieve reasonably prompt and frequent attendance. The use of *minimum incentives* has been shown (Festinger & Carlsmith, 1959) to maximize change. In addition to bus tokens, participants were paid $2 for arriving, an extra 50 cents if they were on time, and an additional 25 cents if they were at least 5 minutes early. Previous research (Schwitzgebel & Kolb, 1964) has shown the effectiveness of monetary reinforcement in producing prompt attendance among delinquents. In addition to the financial reinforcement, participants were provided a snack of cokes and donuts at the beginning of each meeting. When a participant missed several consecutive meetings, a letter was sent reminding him of the next meeting time.

CONDUCT OF SESSIONS

A total of seven 2-hour sessions extending over a 2-month period were held subsequent to the recruitment meeting. Participants were encouraged to come early, relax, and read in a special room reserved for that purpose. This "consultants lounge" was decorated with posters and supplied with magazines and paperback books.

The leaders focused on encouraging rapport and involvement in group activities, on eliciting free and open expression, and on mutual sharing (themselves included) of life goals and pathways. Most activities and discussions dealt with specific delinquent acts, the consequences of such acts, and alternative activities to achieve the participants' personal goals.

The most extensively employed activity was that of *role playing*, a technique that has shown long term effects on behavior change (Elms, 1967; Mann & Janis, 1968). Group leaders created plots around the theme of delinquent behavior, its impact on all individuals concerned and its consequences for one's future. Participants took the role of parents, arresting officers, victims, law breakers, judges, jailers, schoolteachers and principles, gang leaders, innocent bystanders, militant activists, and obstructive bigots.

A TV camera and videotape recorder were made available for optional use in all sessions. The group decided whether or not to record role-playing sessions and to view them afterwards. Group members who showed an interest were taught how to operate the equipment so that its use was entirely under the group's control. This piece of apparatus was provided to stimulate initial interest in the role playing activities and to increase their sense of *commitment* (Brehm & Cohen, 1962) to the role behavior. Role playing in absence of commitment has little effect on attitude change.

Some role-playing situations were especially created to *innoculate* the participants (McGuire, 1964) against future temptation. These situations posed the kinds of moral dilemmas that participants would encounter in the future should they pursue their present life style. It was believed that future temptation has the same cognitive status as cultural truisms, namely its lack of well-formed supportive or refutative beliefs. Consequently innoculation through role playing should increase resistance to engaging in these behaviors.

Group *cohesion* was enhanced by emphasizing a common group goal that was relevant to the interests and values of the participants (Cartwright, 1968). The group was to provide the investigators with information regarding the nature of the problems surrounding delinquency. To emphasize this group goal, an extra 25 cents was paid each participant if, in the judgment of the group leaders, that particular meeting had been worthwhile. Group decisions were encouraged regarding all activities. The group also was permitted to impose sanctions on deviant group members, even to the extent of financially penalizing him for disruptive behavior.

Group leaders were instructed to respond to the members' behavior with praise and encouragement of self expression. They were especially directed to respond to any incidents of behavior indicating internal, as contrasted to external, *locus of control* (Rotter, 1966). Assuming the delinquent's social and emotional environment supported his delinquent behavior, an internally oriented person should be more successful in changing his behavior than one who has an external locus of control. To augment this within-session emphasis on internal behavior, epistolary reinforcement was employed. Following each session, a letter was written each participant by his group leaders commenting upon his contributions to that session. This letter especially emphasized and praised any internal behavior observed at the meeting.

CONTROL GROUP

The 19 control group subjects continued their previous participation in the program offered by the probation office. For some, this involved periodic meetings with a probation officer. These meetings ranged in frequency from once a week to once every 6 weeks. Also, parole officers occasionally visited the homes of the delinquents to speak with parents. Those who were not assigned to regular probation officers met periodically with adjunct probation officers, most of whom were school teachers and ministers.

DEPENDENT VARIABLES

The primary concern of this study was to reduce delinquent behavior. The arrest record of each participant, and that of his matched control, was obtained from court records and the probation office. Records were searched over a 10-month period beginning with the first month of the project. Because the project overlapped the fall school term (it was conducted in August and September), it was considered reasonable that misbehavior in school could also be considered a form of delinquent behavior. School records were examined for all subjects for the fall term; but since no significant differences between the experimental and control groups were found for attendance, tardiness, or grades, these data will not be discussed further.

Ten months after the inception of this study, all 38 subjects were called into the probation office and interviewed by the project staff. The interview assessed internal-external locus of control, racial attitudes, and assorted other items.

Ratings were made at the end of each session by participants and group leaders. The participants made three ratings reflecting their attitude toward the session. The leaders made four ratings of each participant's behavior and attitudes during the sessions. Difficulty was encountered in insuring that these scales would be completely filled out by each member and leader. The termination of each session was informally conducted with participants and leaders leaving at various times over a half-hour period. Some would leave without having completed all measures.

RESULTS AND DISCUSSION

The success of the experimental program depended on achieving two goals. The first was to demonstrate that the group experience was sufficiently attractive and involving to allow the participants to engage in honest communication regarding their delinquent behaviors. These findings are reported in the sections on attendance and group involvement. Given success in establishing open communication, the second goal was to influence the participants to behave in a less antisocial (and, at the same time, a less self-destructive) manner. The sections on delinquent behavior and locus of control deal with these questions.

ATTENDANCE

Because of the distance most participants had to travel to attend the sessions, the absence of legal coercion to enforce attendance, and the emphasis on voluntary participation, there was no advance guarantee of high attendance. Two features of attendance were of primary interest, the percent who actualy attended meetings and the promptness of arrival.

Over both subgroups, 84% of the 19 participants attended at least one session. Although the typical meeting was attended by only half of its group members ($\bar{x} = 49\%$), 12 of the participants attended three or more of the seven sessions. Table 1 describes the percent attending each meeting. To determine whether attendance significantly decreased toward the later sessions, an index of attendance decline was computed for each subject by subtracting his frequency of attendance over the first sessions from his frequency in the last three sessions. Subjects attended an average of 0.63 fewer sessions in the later period than in the earlier, a difference that was marginally significant ($F = 4.11$; $df = 1,17; p < .06$). The level of attendance was less than desirable, and the effects of the group activities on delinquent behavior should be correspondingly diminished, especially for the infrequent attenders.

TABLE 1

Percent of Members Attending Each Session

	Sessions						
Subgroup	1	2	3	4	5	6	7
Black ($N = 10$)	40	50	60	40	20	30	30
Mixed ($N = 9$)	67	56	89	33	78	33	56
Combined ($N = 19$)	53	53	74	37	47	31	42

Extra monetary incentives were provided to encourage prompt arrival to the sessions. Since the sessions were only 2 hours long, any delays in beginning the activities would seriously shorten the time available for them. Promptness of arrival was quite satisfactory; only 3% of all arrivals were late, and these occurred only in the first three sessions. Ninety percent of all arrivals were early enough to qualify for the 25-cent early arrival bonus.

GROUP INVOLVEMENT

Two sets of data were examined to assess the participants' involvement in the group and their attitudes about the value of the group experience.
Member Ratings   At the end of every session, each participant was asked to evaluate the group's activities on the basis of their (a) liking of the meeting, (b) desire to return to the next meeting, and (c) belief regarding the meetings' potential helpfulness for their everyday lives. A seven-category scale was used for each of the three ratings. Due perhaps to low verbal skills or a social desirability response bias, over 75% of all ratings were placed in the most favorable category. As a consequence, the scales were summed to provide a more discriminating index of attitude toward participation in the group. Even for this index, however, the modal score was the most favorable score possible. The percent of participants who had this modal response increased monotonically from 47% over the first two sessions to 70% for the last two sessions. To determine whether this predicted increase was significant, a sign test was performed on the index by comparing the ratings each participant gave at the first session he attended with those of his last. The significance of the sign test depends on the number of pairs that show some difference, either benefit or decrement. Tied pairs contribute nothing. In reporting tests of significance, the number of pairs showing a difference are given followed by the total number of pairs examined. The one-tailed sign test showed a marginally significant improvement in attitude over the 10 participants for whom complete data were available ($N = 7, 10; p = .062$). A similar trend was observed for each of the three separate scales.
Leader Ratings   After each session, each leader reported his impression of each participants's (a) participation and involvement (b) liking of the meeting, (c) freedom and ease in the group, and (d) amount of constructive behavior. All judgments were made on seven-category scales. For each scale, the average of the two leader ratings given each participant on his first session was compared to that of his last session to determine whether the leaders perceived any improvement in individuals over all the sessions. One-tailed sign tests were calculated for the four scales, and only the rating of freedom and ease was found to be significant ($N = 11, 14; p < .006$). Of the 14 participants who attended at least two sessions, 10 were viewed as showing more freedom and ease during their last session than during their first.

Although individuals were found to improve on only one of the scales, the leaders tended to judge the group as à whole as steadily improving on all four scales. To assess this trend, the median rating for each scale over all participants in all sessions was computed. Table 2 shows that for each scale the percent of members who received favorable (above median) ratings is higher for the later sessions than for the earlier ones. Consistent with the tests of significance, the freedom and ease scale showed the strongest trend.

TABLE 2

Percent of Participants Above the Median For The Leader Ratings

	Sessions		
Rating scale	*1–2*	*3–5*	*6–7*
Participation & involvement	50	45	77
Like the session	30	41	69
Freedom and ease	35	55	85
Constructive behavior	40	45	69
Average of scales	38	47	75
N	20	29	13

Note: N represents the total number of observations for each period.

In aggregate, these data showed that participants, as a function of sessions, felt increasingly positive toward the group's activities and they were perceived by the leaders as behaving with greater freedom and ease. Also, the informal impressions of the leaders and observations of the supervisors supported the conclusion that members valued the group and were open to two-way communication. For example, both subgroups spontaneously recommended that the meetings be continued beyond the seventh and last session, even if no money was available for their weekly wages and transportation.

DELINQUENT BEHAVIOR

The primary concern of this project was with the reduction of delinquent behavior. Court and probation office records of arrests were examined for all 38 individuals over a 10-month period commencing with the first month of the project. From these data, a month-by-month record of the number of arrests of each group was prepared.

It would be expected, in the context of the present matched subjects design, that there should be a predominance of subject pairs in which the experimental member had a lower arrest record than his partner. A supportive pair was one in which the experimental member had no arrests during the time period considered and the control members had at least one arrest. A disconfirmatory pair showed the opposite pattern. If both members of the pair had arrest records, it was considered a tie even if the total number of arrests differed. This was because some arrests lead to confinement thus precluding the possibility of further arrests during that period. An index was constructed to reflect the proportional difference between supportive and disconfirmatory pairs. This index, termed the net percent benefit, was determined by subtracting the percent of pairs (out of 19) which disconfirmed the hypothesis from the percent that supported it. A positive index meant that more pairs showed a benefit to the program than did not; a negative index meant that the experimental subjects had a worse record than their matched controls. An index of zero would indicate there there was no net effect of the experimental program when compared to the control group.

A sign test was used to determine whether this index was significantly different from zero. Because a directional hypothesis was demanded by the study, and since the sample sizes were relatively small, a one-tailed sign test was employed.

The 10-month period was divided into two 5-month blocks. The net percent benefit for the first 5 months (August through December) was found to be 21.0% ($N = 8, 19$; $p = .145$) and for the second 5-month period (January through May) it was $- 5.6\%$ ($N = 7, 18$; $p = .773$). (One subject in the experimental group died during the second 5-month period; therefore, the data for his pair were excluded from this analysis.) Although the net percent benefit for the first 5 months did not reach significance, a sizable reduction in the overall percentage of delinquency was obtained. Of the control group, 47.7% committed at least one delinquent act during this period, whereas only 26.3% of the experimental group did so.

Several considerations led to the expectation that a more sensitive test of the effects of this experimental program could be obtained. First, as noted in the section on attendance, some of the invited delinquents attended no meetings and others attended only once or twice. It was reasonable to assume that the group sessions could have little or no effect on these individuals. Second, since member attraction and freedom of communication was lowest during the first meetings, the training program would have had little influence on delinquent behavior during the first month. Third, because there was no contact with the participants during the follow-up period, any effects of the training program would be expected to dissipate with time. These considerations suggested that additional comparisons be made using just those subject pairs for which the experimental member attended three or more meetings ($N = 12$).

The net percent benefit for those participants who attended three or more sessions over the 4-month period of September through December was 41.6%. The sign test showed this difference to be significant ($N = 5, 12$;

$p = .031$). This level of significance improved to 0.16 ($N = 6, 12$) when the severity of the crimes was used to break tied pairs in which both members committed crimes. Fifty percent of the control group had at least one arrest recorded over this period, whereas only 8.3% of the experimental group had been arrested. Equally significant differences were obtained for the time periods of September through October and September through November. A zero net percent benefit was observed during the second 5-month period ($N = 4, 11; p = .688$).

These findings are illustrated in Figure 1, which gives the cumulative number of arrests for each group at each month. It shows that while the two groups have comparable arrest records for the first month of the project, the experimental group had a much lower rate of arrests over the following several months. The groups tended to converge thereafter.

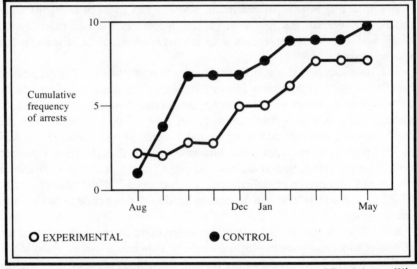

Figure 1   *Cumulative Frequency of Arrests for the Experimental Participants Who Attended Three or More Sessions, Compared with Their Matched Controls.*

In selecting only the relatively frequent attenders for the preceding analyses, it was assumed that frequency of participation in the meetings was related to the net percent benefit index. This premise was examined by dividing the 19 pairs into three subgroups based on the frequency of attendance of their experimental member. For those attending zero to two meetings, the net percent benefit was 0% ($N = 2, 7$); for those attending three to five meetings, the net percent benefit was 28.6% ($N = 4, 7$); and for those attending six to seven meetings, the net percent benefit was 40.0% ($N = 2, 5$). Although the net percent benefit figures show a systematic increase with frequency of attendance, none of the percentages were significantly different from zero. These figures were based on the time period of August through December.

Caution must be exercised when interpreting the results of an experiment in which some subjects have been deleted. Although a sizable net percent benefit was found between the experimental and control groups when all the data were considered over the first 5 months (21%), the group differences reached an acceptable level of statistical significance only when the data for the infrequent attenders was excluded. An alternative possibility exists that these frequent attenders would have shown a low rearrest rate even if they had not participated in the experimental program. Although this explanation cannot be entirely ruled out, the matched-subjects feature of the design argues against it. Subject pairs were matched on the basis of sex, seriousness of the crime that had led to their probationary status (all felonies), race, age, length of time on probation, and assigned probation officer. Assuming one or more of these control variables is related to recidivism, any propensity on the part of the frequent attenders toward a low rearrest record should be shared by their matched controls. Replications that employ larger sample sizes and more effective techniques for encouraging higher voluntary attendance are needed to fully resolve this issue.

INTERNAL-EXTERNAL LOCUS OF CONTROL

One of the objectives of the treatment program was the development of self-supportive attitudes in the participants that would provide them with the kind of independence necessary to resist future temptations toward delinquent behavior. To measure the success of achieving this goal, a revised form of the Rotter internal-external locus of control (1966) scale was orally administered to the control and experimental subjects 9 months after termination of the group sessions. The scale used in this interview consisted of 11 Rotter scale items, most of which had been slightly revised to simplify the phrasing. Items were selected which appeared most relevant to the issue of employment. This version was prepared by the Center for Human Resource Research at Ohio State University for a nationwide survey on the topic of labor market participation. This form correlated .709 with the full Rotter scale over a sample of urban high school students, a correlation that is equivalent to the test-retest reliability of the original Rotter scale.

A total of 13 experimental and 13 control subjects were located for these interviews. As predicted, the experimental subjects gave fewer external responses ($\bar{\chi} = 3.31$) than did the control subjects ($\bar{\chi} = 4.46$). This difference was found to be significant ($t = 1.96$; $df = 24$; $p < .05$, one-tailed). Although the effects of the experimental program on delinquent behavior dissipated by the second 5-month period, it appeared that its effects on locus of control endured 9 months after termination of group meetings. This finding, however, must be interpreted with some caution. Because the interviewers who administered these scales were project personnel, most of the members of the experimental group recognized them as being associated with the project. It is possible that the greater internality of the experimental subjects' responses was due to those subjects recalling the values they had encountered in the project and wanting their answers to please the interviewer.

The other items on this follow-up interview, relating to social attitudes and educational aspirations, showed no significant differences between the experimental and control groups.

PROBLEMS IN APPLICATION

The results of this study indicate that principles drawn from social psychological research, when collectively applied, can have a meaningful impact on fundamental social problems. An involving group experience was produced in which previously unacquainted delinquents openly discussed their illegal behaviors and justifications for them. Further, they appeared to have become receptive to influence from their group leaders, since for those who participated in three or more meetings, the recidivism rate was reduced from 50% to less than 10%. These results were achieved with a maximum of 14 contact hours per participant and at a cost under $600. This total covered the expenses of members, leaders, and refreshments, but it did not include the cost of space, permanent equipment, or salary for the investigators who did the organizing and supervising.

It is clear that psychological principles cannot be mechanically applied to the human situation. This project's success was as much the result of the sensitivity and devotion of the four group leaders as it was to familiarity with social psychological principles. It was they who had the moment-to-moment task of translating the theoretical guidelines into decisions regarding group activities. Although leader selection is important, it is not necessary (or perhaps even desirable) to use professionally trained people. These young people who had an interest in the problem but no professional training, when given freedom of direction, proved quite successful. A large number of such people can be found in any urban community in the United States. Universities are but one of several sources for recruiting such leaders.

It may appear inconsistent to describe this experimental program as based on social psychological principles and yet claim the leaders were untrained and given complete freedom in directing the group activities. However, there were many features of the program external to the group activities, such as the site, recruitment, monetary incentive structure, and group purpose, which were based on such principles. Further, leaders were willing to engage in certain activities suggested by the investigators, but with the understanding that the manner in which such activities were conducted was entirely under their control. Such activities included role playing, praising internal over external behavior, and writing weekly letters to each participant.

It is impossible to base every decision one must make in implementing a training program of this sort solely on social psychological principles and research. The decisions are too many and the principles are too sparse. It is inevitable that a large number of decisions will be based on the intuition and past experiences of the persons responsible for the administration of such a program. It would be futile to search out a principle for every decision.

There was a general orientation adopted by the investigators which influenced decisions regarding the program when no past research was available. A permissive atmosphere was sought in which the participants would feel free to talk about their past behaviors and future intentions without fear of censure or arrest. By the seventh session, participants were relating minute details of crimes for which they had eluded arrest. They were evidently quite confident that these revelations would not jeopardize their freedom. Participants never felt as if group leaders would adopt a moralizing stance toward them or censure them for such free expression. Even the most dishonorable career aspirations were openly discussed.

In addition to encouraging honest communications, the group activities were oriented toward evaluating specific delinquent behaviors. It was believed that focusing on concrete behavioral acts would have greater success in modifying such delinquent behavior than would any approach that was based on reorganizing the whole personality of the participant. Rather than attacking the participants' values and attitudes as a way of producing behavior change, the leaders dealt directly with the kinds of behaviors that had gotten the participants into trouble. A recurrent theme that emerged was that there were better ways to "beat the system" than risking imprisonment. Leaders avoided telling a participant that his interests, values, or goals were wrong, only that a few of his deeds were stupid or "not cool."

The present strategy of putting together a "bundle" of laboratory-derived principles to modify behavior of social consequence has been used by other investigators (e.g., McClelland & Winter, 1969). Although this approach produced a significant overall effect in the present program, the design did not allow determination of which parts of the bundle are expendable and which parts are crucial to retain. The relative importance of the several principles becomes a concern when they compete with one another in the context of a particular decision. For example, the choice of site may be between one that has negative associations but requires optimal effort to reach, and another that has no negative associations but requires no effort to reach. Although laboratory research could not resolve this kind of situation-specific question, it could help resolve problems created when a single variable has competing effects. For example, whereas voluntary attendance may produce positive attraction, it seriously reduces the number who participate. It may be that initial attraction can be safely sacrificed to insure high attendance. If the negative effects of compulsory attendance on attraction disappeared after the first several meetings, it would be advisable to drop the voluntary attendance feature of the present program. Questions such as these could be more easily answered with short term groups in a laboratory experiment.

The effects of this program began to dissipate 2 to 4 months following termination of the sessions. An unanswered question is whether this could have been averted by continuing the program. It would not be plausible for a group to continue its existence beyond 10 or 12 meetings solely on the justification of helping the investigators understand delinquent behavior. For a group to satisfactorily function beyond this time, another group goal might prove more workable. The only way the present research-oriented goal could be retained would be to expand the activities and responsibilities of the group members. Such additional activities might include interviewing other delinquents, judges, and police officers. Formation of a self-perpetuating social structure based on seniority of members would allow continued meaningful participation on the part of older members.

REFERENCES

Bandura, A., *Principles of Behavior Modification* (New York: Holt, Rinehart & Winston, 1969).

Brehm, J.W., & Cohen, A.R., *Explorations in cognitive dissonance* (New York: Wiley, 1962).

Byrne, D., "Attitudes and attraction." In L. Berkowitz (ed.), *Advances in Experimental Social Psychology*, Vol. 4 (New York: Academic Press, 1969).

Cartwright, D., "The nature of group cohesiveness." In D. Cartwright and A. Zander (Eds.), *Group Dynamics: Research and Theory*, 3rd ed (New York: Harper & Row, 1968).

Colarelli, N.J., & Siegel, S.M., *Ward H: An Adventure in Innovation* (Princeton, N.J.: Van Nostrand, 1966).

Elms, A.C., "Role playing, incentive, and dissonance," *Psychological Bulletin*, 1967, *68*, 132–148.

Festinger, L., & Carlsmith, J.M., "Cognitive consequences of forced compliance," *Journal of Abnormal and Social Psychology*, 1959, *58*, 203–210.

Fromkin, H.L., "Reinforcement and effort expenditure: Predictions of 'reinforcement theory' versus predictions of dissonance theory," *Journal of Personality and Social Psychology*, 1968, *9*, 347–352.

Kelman, H.C., "Processes of attitude change," *Public Opinion Quarterly*, 1961, 25, 57–78.

Mann, L., & Janis, I.L., "A follow-up study on the long term effects of emotional role playing," *Journal of Personality and Social Psychology*, 1968, *8*, 339–342.

McClelland, D.C., & Winter, D.G., *Motivating Economic Achievement* (New York: Free Press, 1969).

McGuire, W.J., "Inducing resistance to persuasion." In L. Berkowitz (ed.), *Advances in Experimental Social Psychology*, Vol. 1 (New York: Academic Press, 1964).

Newcomb, T.M., *Personality and Social Change* (New York: Holt, Rinehart & Winston, 1943).

The President's Commission on Law Enforcement and Administration of Justice, Task Force on Juvenile Delinquency, *Juvenile Delinquency and Youth Crime: Report on Juvenile Justice and Consultants Papers* (Washington: U.S. Government Printing Office, 1967).

Reckless, W.C., *The Crime Problem* (New York: Appleton-Century-Crofts, 1967).

Rosnow, R.L., "A 'spread of effect' in attitude formation." In A. Greenwald, T. Brock, and T. Ostrom (eds.), *Psychological Foundations of Attitudes* (New York: Academic Press, 1968).

Rotter, J.A., "Generalized expectances for internal versus external control of reinforcement," *Psychological Monographs*, 1966, *80* (No. 1).

Schwitzgebel, R., & Kolb, D.A., "Inducing behavior change in adolescent delinquents," *Behavior Research and Therapy*, 1964, *1*, 297–304.

White, R.K., & Lippitt, R., *Autocracy and Democracy: An Experimental Inquiry* (New York: Harper & Row, 1960).

Wickland, R.A., Cooper, J., Linder, D.E., "Effects of expected effort on attitude change prior to exposure," *Journal of Experimental and Social Psychology*, 1967, *3*, 416–428.

Chapter 14

Editors' Remarks

The following study by Michael Chandler has to date received very little attention from commentators on correctional treatment. This may, in part, be due to the fact that Chandler's treatment approach and his conceptualization of the underlying dynamics of delinquent behavior are somewhat unorthodox and do not follow the models of any of the traditional therapeutic schools. Chandler focuses on the cognitive rather than the emotional or behavioral shortcomings of his juvenile offender clients, indicates how deficits in cognitive development can interfere with appropriate social behavior, and then describes a treatment program which, by correcting the underlying deficit, effectively reduces the youths' delinquent behavior.

It is all the more surprising that this study has received little attention in corrections in view of the popularity of recent assertions that correctional education and treatment programs, to be effective, must recognize and improve those under-developed or faulty cognitive patterns which are supposed to engender irresponsible behavior and to characterize the "criminal personality" (Yochelson & Samenow, 1976, Ayers, 1979, in press).

REFERENCES

Ayers, J.O., "Education in prisons: A developmental and cultural perspective," *Canadian Journal of Education*, 1979, in press.

Yochelson, S. & Samenow, S.E., *The Criminal Personality, Vol. 1 A Profile For Change* (New York: Jason Arnonson, 1976).

Egocentrism and Antisocial Behavior: The Assessment and Training of Social Perspective-Taking Skills[1]*

Michael J. Chandler[2]

This study was undertaken in an effort to explore the possible role of persistent social egocentrism in the development and maintenance of patterns of chronic antisocial behavior. Egocentric thought, defined here as the relative inability to recognize or take into account the privileged character of one's own private thoughts and feelings, has been shown by Piaget and others (Looft, 1972; Piaget & Inhelder, 1956) to regularly characterize and prejudice the social judgments of young children. In the absence of any real working knowledge of the differences which divide people, young children are typically unable to assess accurately the informational needs of others and have been routinely shown to fail at tasks which require genuine empathy or cooperation (Chandler & Greenspan, 1972). Under normal developmental circumstances, this initial egocentric orientation has been shown to give way gradually to a more relativistic or perspectivistic style of thought which makes possible new levels of social cooperation and competence (Looft, 1972).

Because of the central role assigned to such perspective-taking skills in the normal socialization process, a number of investigators (Anthony, 1959; Chandler, 1972; Feffer, 1970; Gough, 1948; Martin, 1968; Sarbin, 1954; Thompson, 1968) have been prompted to explore the possible relationship between delays in the acquisition of these skills and the development of

---

*Chandler, M.J., "Egocentrism and antisocial behavior: The assessment and training of social perspective-taking skills," *Developmental Psychology*, 1973, *9*, 326–333. Copyright © 1973, American Psychological Association. Reprinted by permission.

[1]This research was supported by grants from the Rochester-Monroe County Youth Board and the Wegman Foundation.

[2]The author wishes to thank the Monroe County Department of Probation for its cooperation in this study. Thanks are also due to Pat Cavanagh, Anne Filer, Beth Kaprove, Carol Markovics and Douglas Stern who served as experimenters.

various forms of social deviation. As a group, these studies have provided considerable support for the view that prosocial behavior is linked to the development of age-appropriate role-taking or perspective-taking skills and have demonstrated that a variety of forms of social deviancy are associated with persistent egocentric thought. Persons demonstrating developmental delays in the acquisition of these skills have been shown to systematically misread societal expectations, to misinterpret the actions and intentions of others, and to act in ways which were judged to be callous and disrespectful of the rights of others.

Drawing upon these findings linking anti-social behavior to developmental delays in the acquisition of role-taking or perspective-taking skills, a relationship was hypothesized between persistent social egocentrism and chronic delinquent behavior, and an attempt was made (a) to compare the developmental course of role-taking or perspective-taking skills in groups of delinquent and nondelinquent youths, (b) to develop and evaluate a program of remedial training in deficient role-taking skills, and (c) to determine the effectiveness of this training on subsequent delinquent behavior.

METHOD

SUBJECTS

The subjects of this comparative study were 45 delinquent and 45 nondelinquent boys between the ages of 11 and 13. Fifteen delinquents and 15 nondelinquents were chosen at each of the three ages studied. The delinquent subjects were located through a search of the files of a metropolitan police registry and were chosen on the basis of their lengthy police and court records. All had multiple contacts with the police, had committed one or more crimes which would have constituted felonies if committed by an adult, and were characterized by court officials as serious and chronic delinquents. Almost all were members of economically marginal families, and all lived in high crime and delinquency areas within a deteriorating center city core. The racial and ethnic background of the group mirrored that of the neighborhoods from which they were drawn. Twenty-four of the 45 subjects were black, 6 were from families recently immigrated from Puerto Rico, and the remainder were distributed among a variety of ethnic groups of largely Western European origin.

The 45 subjects who made up the two nondelinquent comparison groups were drawn from two different populations. Fifteen subjects — 5 from each of the three age groups studied — lived in the same high crime rate areas as did the delinquent subjects, were from families of comparable socio-economic standing, and were of similar racial and ethnic backgrounds. The second of the nondelinquent comparison groups consisted of 30 boys drawn from a predominantly white, middle-class and upper-middle-class suburban school system. None of these subjects had known delinquent histories, and they were all characterized by their teachers as essentially free of any serious antisocial involvements.

ASSESSMENT PROCEDURES

The subjects of this research were seen individually and administered both the Peabody Picture Vocabulary Test (PPVT) and a measure of social egocentrism based on an assessment procedure originally introduced by Flavell, Botkin, Fry, Wright, and Jarvis (1968). In its original form, this procedure consisted of a single cartoon sequence which subjects were asked to describe first from their own point of view and then from the perspective of a coexperimenter who was shown only an abbreviated version of the same stimulus materials. In this way Flavell and his colleagues were able to put their subjects in possession of relevant, but highly privileged, information which was explicitly unavailable to the less well informed bystander whose perspective they ' sought to occupy. Any intrusion of this privileged information into the account intended as descriptive of the perspective of the only partially informed coexperimenter was taken as evidence of an egocentric failure in social role taking.

The assessment procedure employed in this study closely paralleled that of Flavell et al. (1968) and differed only in the identity of the partially informed witness or bystander, whose point of view the subjects were asked to assume. Whereas Flavell and his colleagues had employed a coexperimenter for this purpose, the present study incorporated the witness or bystander as a cartoon character in the stimulus materials themselves.

Ten cartoon sequences following this general format were developed. Each of these depicted a central character caught up in a chain of psychological cause and effect such that his subsequent behavior was shaped by, and fully comprehensible only in terms of, the events which prefixed them. In one of these sequences, for example, a boy, who had been saddened by seeing his father off at the airport, began to cry when he later received as a gift a toy airplane similar to the one which had carried his father away. In a second sequence a boy, who had run home after accidently breaking a window with a baseball, was shown to react with fear when he heard a knock at the door.

Midway into each of these sequences some second character was introduced who, in the role of a late-arriving bystander, witnessed the resultant behaviors of the principal character but was not privy to the antecedent events which brought them about. In the cartoon involving the broken window, for example, the boy's father observed his son's alarm when someone knocked at the door but had no basis for knowing of the earlier events which prompted this reaction. Similarly, in the story dealing with the toy airplane, the gift was delivered by a postman who clearly saw the boy's distress but had no knowledge of the antecedent events which made the receipt of an airplane a legitimate occasion for sadness. Through this process of information engineering, the subject was placed in a privileged position relative to the story character whose role he was later asked to assume. By knowing what information was available to whom, it was possible to specify the degree to which each subject was able to set aside effectively facts known only to himself and adopt a perspective measurably different from his own.

A 5-point scoring system reflecting different levels of potential egocentric intrusion was developed. A score of 4 was assigned to those accounts in which the subjects explicitly attributed to the uninformed witness or bystander knowledge legitimately available only to themselves. A score of 3 was assigned to similar accounts, which were qualified by being couched in conditional or probabilistic terms (e.g., "The father would *probably* think that he broke the window"). A score of 2 was assigned whenever a subject attributed privileged information to the uninformed bystander but embedded this attribution in a series of nonegocentric alternatives (e.g., "The father would think that somebody was chasing him, or that he broke a window, or something"). A score of 1 was employed whenever a subject made an egocentric attribution which he later spontaneously corrected, and zeroes were assigned to accounts which clearly distinguished between privileged information known only to the subjects and facts equally available to the story characters whose role he was asked to assume.

The conduct of this study fell into four distinct subphases. The first of these involved the individual assessment of the 90 delinquent and nondelinquent subjects. The second, or intervention phase, involved only the delinquent subjects and lasted for a period of 10 weeks. This training program was followed by a third, postintervention assessment phase. Finally, 18 months after the completion of the intervention program, a second record search was undertaken in an effort to determine the possible effects of the training on subsequent delinquent behavior. The specific assessment and training procedures employed in each of these program phases are described separately below.

Preintervention Assessment   On the basis of a previous standardization study using 75 normal school children (Chandler, 1971), the original series of 10 cartoon sequences was subdivided into two equivalent subsets of five stories each. The Spearman-Brown split-half reliability coefficient between these alternate forms was .92. The PPVT and one or the other of these alternate egocentrism measures was individually administered to each of the 90 delinquent and nondelinquent subjects. Half of the subjects were tested on each of the alternate egocentrism measures, and the order of presentation of the individual cartoon sequences was randomized in an effort to guard against possible order effects. The subjects were first asked to describe the entire cartoon sequence and were then instructed to retell the story as they thought it would be told by the late-arriving witness or bystander. Subjects were prompted in this second version of the story by the use of a standard probe which consisted of saying, "Now I want you to tell me the story that this person would tell. He (she) would say. . . ." Although many failed to offer stories on the second telling that were substantially different from their own, all of the subjects seemed to appreciate what was being asked of them and most identified spontaneously from whose point of view they were attempting to speak. All probes were carefully worded to insure that it was clear that the witnesses' rather than the subjects' point of view was being inquired into. All subjects were tested by one of three trained graduate assistants, and verbatim recordings were made of the subjects' responses. These transcripts were read and scored by two independent raters who were uninformed as to the social histories of the subjects. Interrater reliabilities computed on a sample of 15 test protocols indicated a high level ($r = .94$) of interrater agreement.

Intervention   Following the initial assessment phase, the 45 delinquent subjects were randomly assigned to one of three treatment conditions. One third of the subjects were placed in a nontreatment control group and, with the exception of the postintervention assessment program to be described below, had no further contact with the research staff. The remaining 30 subjects were invited to participate in a film workshop that was to meet in a neighborhood storefront ½ day a week for a 10-week period. All participants were provided transportation to and from the storefront center and were paid $1 an hour for their participation. All 30 of the subjects agreed to participate and attended regularly throughout this summer period. Absenteeism was extremely low, and the average participant was present for 9.5 of the 10 training sessions.

Fifteen of these subjects were enrolled in an experimental training program which employed drama and the making of video films as vehicles for helping them to see themselves from the perspective of others and for providing remedial training in deficient role-taking skills. It was reasoned that these two training experiences might aid the subjects in stepping outside of their own egocentric vantages and in assuming roles or perspectives different from their own. These subjects met together, in groups of five. During these 3-hour training sessions the subjects were encouraged to develop, portray, and record brief skits dealing with events involving persons of their own age. A staff of three graduate assistants worked with each of the three training groups and attempted to facilitate their dramatic and film-making efforts. While the content and development of these film productions was determined by the program participants, the training staff did attempt to enforce four general ground rules. These included the stipulations that (a) the skits developed by the participants be about persons their own age and depict real-life situations (i.e., not episodes involving TV or movie characters), (b) there be a part for every participant, (c) each skit be rerun until each participant had occupied every role in the plot, and (d) that the video recordings be reviewed at the end of each set or take in an effort to determine ways of improving them. Although every effort was made to maximize the opportunities of these subjects to improve their role-taking and perspective-taking skills, special efforts were made to avoid any procedures which might be directly related to post-test items or procedures.

The remaining 15 experimental subjects were enrolled in a kind of placebo group organized in order to provide a method of disentangling the potential effects of specific training in role-taking skills from the possible impact of other more extraneous and nonspecific treatment influences. Like the members of the experimental training group, these subjects attended the same storefront, interacted with the same research staff, and occupied themselves with the making of films. In contrast to the members of the experimental group, however, these subjects did not make use of closed-circuit TV recording equipment, and consequently were not providing any special opportunities to see themselves from the perspectives of others, and did not receive special training in role-taking skills. Instead, the group was provided with 8-millimeter color film equipment and helped to produce animated cartoons and documentary style films about their neighborhood. The only restriction placed on these activities was that the participants not be the subjects of their own film-making efforts. These activities were intended to mirror, as closely as possible, the program of the experimental training group, with the important distinction that the opportunities for feedback and role-taking practice provided in the film and actors workshop were not present.

Postintervention Assessment   Following the completion of the 10-week summer program, the subjects of the experimental, placebo, and non-treatment control groups were reevaluated using a second series of five cartoon sequences, the equivalency of which had been established in a previous standardization study (Chandler, 1971). The persons administering and scoring these post-program tests did not know the treatment status of the subjects whom they evaluated.

Follow-up   One and a half years after the completion of the intervention phase described above, the police and court records of all the delinquent subjects were reexamined. The total number of recorded delinquent offenses committed during this 18-month period was tallied for each subject and compared with the results of the initial review covering the 18-month period preceding the intervention program.

RESULTS

The results of the preintervention assessment of social egocentrism in delinquent and nondelinquent subjects, the postintervention comparison of the various treatment groups, and the results of the 18-month follow-up study are reported separately below.

PREINTERVENTION ASSESSMENT

Despite the racial, ethnic, and socioeconomic differences which characterized the nondelinquent subjects drawn from high and low crime rate areas, these groups were not measurably different in the level of their social egocentrism. As a consequence, these two groups were combined into a single, nondelinquent sample for the purposes of subsequent analysis.

By contrast, the delinquent and nondelinquent subjects demonstrated marked and statistically significant differences ($F = 80.4$, $df = 1/88$, $p < .001$) in the level of their role-taking skills (see Table 1). The nondelinquent subjects appeared to have little difficulty in adopting the role or perspectives of others, and few marked egocentric intrusions were present in their records.

TABLE 1

Mean Egocentrism Scores for the Age and Delinquency-Status Groups

Age (in years)	Delinquents	Nondelinquents
11	13.8	3.9
12	10.2	3.6
13	10.6	1.7
Combined	11.6	3.1

The delinquent subjects, by contrast, typically demonstrated marked deficits in their ability to differentiate their own point of view from that of others and regularly attributed to others information available only to themselves. There was in fact little overlap between the egocentrism scores of the nondelinquent subjects and their delinquent counterparts, whose scores more closely resembled those of a previously reported sample of nondelinquent children almost half their chronological age (Chandler, 1971).

Although the nondelinquent subjects showed a slight, but regular reduction in egocentric errors with increasing age not apparent in the scores of the delinquent subjects, these age differences were not statistically significant.

The delinquent and nondelinquent subjects were known to have different histories of school attendance and achievement, and it was anticipated that their levels of measured intelligence might also differ. These expectations were substantiated by a comparison of mean PPVT scores for the delinquent and nondelinquent samples, which were 91 and 112, respectively ($t = 1.73$, $df = 88$, $p < .05$). Within each of these groups, level of egocentricity was significantly related to IQ ($r = -.34$ and $-.30$, $p < .05$, for the delinquent and nondelinquent groups, respectively).

Because of these uncontrolled group differences in measured intelligence and because of the observed relationship between IQ and level of egocentricity, an additional test of the differences in social egocentrism between the two groups was required. To this end the variance in observed social egocentrism scores contributed by differences in IQ was controlled by means of co-variance techniques. The delinquent and nondelinquent groups continued to differ sharply in their levels of social egocentrism ($F = 41.4$, $df = 1/87$, $p < .001$).

POSTINTERVENTION ASSESSMENT

Differences between preintervention and postintervention scores on the role-taking tests were taken as an index of change in role-taking ability and are reported in Table 2. Following Hays (1963), a series of planned comparisons were made on these data, the most important of which were (a) whether the subjects of the experimental group changed more than did the members of the placebo and nontreatment control groups and (b) whether the change scores of the subjects of the placebo and control groups were significantly different from one another.

TABLE 2

Mean Preintervention and Postintervention Social Egocentrism Scores

Treatment group	Preintervention	Postintervention
Experimental	12.4	5.5
Placebo	12.2	8.6
Control	10.2	8.0

The first of these analyses demonstrated that as a group the subjects of the experimental training program improved significantly more in their role-taking ability ($F = 9.46$, $df = 1/42$, $p < .01$) than did the subjects of the combined placebo and control groups. Although not statistically independent from this comparison, the differences between the experimental group and either the placebo or the control group taken separately were also statistically significant. The placebo and control groups did not, however, differ significantly from one another ($F = 1.49$, $df = 1/42$, $p < .05$).

FOLLOW-UP

As a result of the high level of mobility which characterized the families of these delinquents, complete data was available on only 33 of the original 45 subjects at the time of the 18-month follow-up. The attrition rate was, however, similar in all three of the treatment groups, and the subjects for whom complete data were not available were not significantly different from the remaining sample on any of the measures of role-taking, IQ, or preintervention delinquency previously collected.

The police and court records of the 33 subjects for whom complete data were available were reviewed and the number of known delinquencies committed during the 18-month period following the intervention program was tallied and compared with the results of a comparable record review for the 18-month period preceding the intervention program (see Table 3). As can

TABLE 3

Mean Number of Delinquent Offenses in Preintervention and Postintervention Periods

Treatment group	Preintervention	Postintervention
Experimental	1.9	1.0
Placebo	2.5	2.1
Control	2.0	1.8

be seen from this table, the subjects of all three treatment groups committed somewhat fewer offenses during the second 18-month period. This difference was, however, most striking for the subjects of the experimental training program who, as a group, committed approximately half as many known delinquencies during the postintervention period. A Kruskal-Wallis one-way analysis of variance by ranks was performed on the difference between the number of preintervention and postintervention delinquencies for the subjects of each of the three treatment groups. These group differences were highly significant ($H = 17.9$, $df = 2$, $p < .001$), indicating a relationship between the type of intervention received and the number of subsequent delinquencies committed. In order to specify further the source of this overall treatment effect, a series of multiple comparisons was carried out between the various treatment conditions utilizing a rank-sum method (Dunn, 1964). Although the differences between the experimental training group and either of the other two treatment groups taken separately did not reach statistical significance, the subjects of the experimental training program in role taking did commit significantly fewer postintervention delinquencies ($Z = 2.4$, $p < .05$) than did subjects of the combined placebo and control group.

DISCUSSION

The results of this study support three general conclusions concerning the role of social egocentrism in antisocial behavior. First, in contrast to their better socialized counterparts, a substantial proportion of the chronically delinquent subjects tested demonstrated a marked developmental lag in their ability to successfully adopt the roles of perspectives of others. These discrepancies persisted despite controls for the differences in socioeconomic and intellectual levels which characterized these groups. Second, intervention efforts focused on specific training in role-taking skills did substantially reduce the high level of social egocentrism which had previously characterized these subjects. The measurable impact of this remedial training program out-weighed changes resulting from other changes ascribable simply to the passage of time. The fact that the subjects of both the experimental and placebo groups met voluntarily on a regular basis and appeared equally involved and committed to their respective projects further strengthens the assumption that the test and behavioral changes observed were directly related to the specific content of the experimental training program. Finally, these observed changes in role-taking skills were associated with a measurable reduction in the amount of reported delinquent behavior among the experimental subjects.

While these findings may provide some new insights into the nature of antisocial behavior, a number of important cautions and qualifications are required. First, it must be stressed that demonstrating a relationship between persistent social egocentrism and antisocial behavior does not, in itself, provide a sufficient basis for inferring a causal relationship between these variables. The fact that experimentally induced improvements in role-taking and perspective-taking skills were associated with reductions in postintervention delinquency does provide somewhat more compelling evidence for such a causal connection. The possibility remains, however, that the experimental training program differed from the training received by the placebo group along dimensions other than the role-taking and perspective-taking training specified and that the observed differences in test performance and delinquent behavior are traceable to these effects. Second, any attempt to generalize these findings to other populations of antisocial youths should reflect an appreciation of the special character of the sample employed in this study. The method of subject selection employed insured that the persons chosen were not only delinquent, but unsuccessfully so. All of the subjects had multiple police and court contacts and are almost necessarily different from other delinquent or antisocial youth who have successfully avoided detection. The possibility exists that the persistent egocentrism which characterized this group was an index of their ineptitude rather than their antisocial orientation. If such were the case, the apparent reduction in delinquent behavior which characterized the subjects of the experimental treatment group might only reflect an improved ability to avoid detection and what looked like a promising intervention technique might prove only to be a "school for scoundrels." Finally, the present research offers no guarantee that the persistent social egocentrism demonstrated by these delinquent subjects is in any way unique to persons whose adaptational failures are of an antisocial sort. To the contrary, the research of Anthony (1956), Looft (1972), and Feffer (1970) would suggest that persistent modes of age-inappropriate egocentric thought frequently characterize persons showing a great variety of adaptational failures ranging from autism to senility.

Despite these qualifications, the results of this study do suggest the utility of attempting to understand delinquent youth in terms of their developmental progress in the acquisition of certain formal, sociocognitive operations necessary for the effective solution of important human interaction problems. This approach not only suggests certain promising diagnostic and intervention strategies but provides a theoretical framework which recognizes the important developmental tasks which confront youthful offenders and permits them to be viewed as other than diminutive adult criminals.

REFERENCES

Anthony, E.J., "An experimental approach to the psychopathology of childhood autism," *British Journal of Medical Psychology*, 1959, *32*, 18–37.

Chandler, M.J., *Egocentrism and Childhood Psychopathology: The Development and Application of Measurement Techniques*. Paper presented at the biennial meeting of the Society for Research in Child Development, Minneapolis, March 1971.

Chandler, M.J., "Egocentrism in normal and pathological child development." In F. Monks, W. Hartup, & J. DeWitt (eds.), *Determinants of behavioral development* (New York: Academic Press, 1972).

Chandler, M.J., & Greenspan, S., "Ersatz egocentrism: A reply to H. Borke," *Developmental Psychology*, 1972, *7*, 104–106.

Dunn, O.J., "Multiple comparisons using rank-sums," *Technometrics*, 1964, *6*, 241–252.

Feffer, M.H., "A developmental analysis of interpersonal behavior," *Psychological Review*, 1970, *77*, 197–214.

Flavell, J.H., Botkin, P.T., Fry, C.L., Wright, J.W., & Jarvis, P.E., *The development of role-taking communication skills in children*, (New York: Wiley, 1968).

Gough, H.G., "A sociological theory of psychopathy," *American Journal of Sociology*, 1948, *53*, 359–366.

Hays, W.L., *Statistics* (New York: Holt, Rinehart & Winston, 1963).

Looft, W.R., "Egocentrism and social interaction across the life span," *Psychological Bulletin*, 1972, *78*, 73–92.

Martin, M., *A Role-taking Theory of Psychopathy* (Doctoral dissertation, University of Oregon, Ann Arbor, Mich.: University Microfilms, 1968, No. 68–11, 957).

Piaget, J., & Inhelder, B., *The child's conception of space* (London: Routledge & Kegan Paul, 1956).

Sarbin, T.R., "Role theory." In G. Lindzey (ed.), *Handbook of Social Psychology* (Cambridge, Mass.: Addison-Wesley, 1954).

Thompson, L.A. *Role playing ability and social adjustment in children*, (Doctoral dissertation, University of Southern California, Ann Arbor, Mich.: University Microfilms, 1968, No. 69–4547).

Chapter 15

Editors' Remarks

No book on correctional treatment would be complete if it did not include a description of the Community Treatment Project directed by Ted Palmer and the California Youth Authority.

This large-scale project provides impressive testimony of a fundamental principle which we have reiterated throughout this book and which has been clearly demonstrated in most of the effective treatment programs we have included: different types of offenders need different kinds of treatment in different settings. There are no panaceas in correctional treatment, but some programs *do* work.

The Youth Authority's Community Treatment Project*

Ted Palmer

From 1961 to the present, the California Youth Authority (CYA) has been conducting a large-scale, two-part experiment known as the Community Treatment Project (CTP). Part 1 was completed in 1969. Its basic goal was to find out if certain kinds of juvenile offenders could be allowed to remain right in their home communities, if given rather intensive supervision and treatment within a small-sized parole caseload. Here, the main question was: Could CYA parole agents work effectively with some of these individuals *without first locking them up for several months* in a large-sized, State institution? The 1961–1969 phase of the Youth Authority's experiment was carried out mainly in Sacramento and Stockton, with San Francisco being added in 1965. Within each of these cities all areas or regions were included. We will now describe part 1 of the experiment. After that, we shall turn to part 2 (1969–1974).

WHO PARTICIPATED?

Eight hundred and two boys and 212 girls participated in the 1961–1969 effort. All economic levels and racial backgrounds were included; and in this respect the CTP "sample" proved to be typical of the Youth Authority's population within the State as a whole. Most of the participants were between 13 and 19 years of age when first sent to the CYA and placed into the experiment. Typically, these individuals had been in trouble with the law on 5.8 occasions at the time they were sent to the Youth Authority by the local juvenile court. Their "troubles" had usually begun several years prior to the

---

*Palmer, T., "The Youth Authority's community treatment project," *Federal Probation*, 1974, March, 3–14. Copyright © 1974, Federal Probation. Reprinted by permission.

burglary, auto theft, etc., which typically preceded their CYA commitment.

Certain youths were not allowed to participate in the experiment. For example, it was necessary to exclude everyone who had been sent to the CYA for offenses such as armed robbery, assault with a deadly weapon, or forcible rape. (These nonparticipants were called "ineligibles"; participants were known as "eligibles.") Despite such restrictions, it was still possible to *include* a total of 65 percent of all boys and 83 percent of all girls who had been sent to the CYA for the first time, from the Sacramento, Stockton, and San Francisco Juvenile Courts. Along this line, it should be kept in mind that the presence of such things as the following did not, in themselves, prevent any youths from participating in the 1961–1969 experiment: Marked drug involvement, homosexuality, chronic or severe neurosis, occasional psychotic episodes, apparent suicidal tendencies.

THE PROGRAM

Part 1 of the CYA experiment was conducted in a careful, scientific manner: A "control" group was set up from the start. This made it possible to compare the performance of (1) youths who were placed directly into the intensive CTP program, without any prior institutionalization, against that of (2) "controls" — i.e., youths who were sent to an institution for several months prior to being returned to their home communities and then being given routine supervision within standard-sized parole caseloads which were operated by a different (non-CTP) group of parole agents.[1] Thus, all eligible youths were randomly assigned to either the *experimental (CTP)* or the *control (traditional)* program — both of which were operated entirely by the Youth Authority. Six hundred and eighty-six experimentals and 328 controls eventually became part of the 1961–1969 experiment, and all research costs were picked up by the National Institute of Mental Health (NIMH).

All CYA youths, or "wards," who were assigned to the *experimental* (CTP) part of the program were placed on a caseload which contained no more than 12 youths for each parole agent. Based upon (1) detailed initial interviews, (2) a careful review of written background material, and (3) a joint conference by responsible CTP staff, a "treatment plan" was developed for each experimental youth shortly after his assignment to the program. This plan tried to take into account each youth's major strengths, weaknesses, and interests, together with his overall "level of maturity," and various

---

[1]It should be mentioned that experimental and control youths both spent an average of 4 to 6 weeks at the Youth Authority's Northern Reception Center and Clinic (NRCC), immediately after having been committed to the Youth Authority. This period of "routine processing" consisted of necessary medical and dental work, standard diagnostic workups and related achievement testing, appearance before the Youth Authority Board, etc. Upon release from NRCC, youths were either sent to a CYA institution for a period which averaged several months or else they were returned directly to their home community, on parole status.

circumstances of his personal, family life, and social situation. Since the resulting plan could vary a great deal from one youth (or type of youth) to the next, the particular approach used in CTP was referred to as "differential treatment." This feature was separate and apart from that of *community-based treatment* per se.

The caseload of each CTP parole officer was limited to only certain "types" of youth or particular "levels of maturity." That is to say, it included only those youths who exhibited a particular *range* of personality characteristics, or who usually displayed certain distinguishing patterns of behavior. In order to make best use of the CTP parole agent's particular skills and interests, each such agent was selected to work primarily with only *certain types* of youth, or "personality patterns." In this sense, they were paired, or "matched," with all youths who were placed on their caseload; and as a result, they were not expected to be all things to *all kinds* of Youth Authority wards.

Certain principles, strategies, and techniques were followed in connection with all youths who were assigned to Community Treatment Project caseloads. Included were: (1) A determination on the parole agent's part to work with individual youths for a number of years if necessary; (2) careful placement planning (e.g., Exactly *where* is this youth going to live, and with *whom?*), especially during early phases of each ward's parole program; (3) parole agent contact on behalf of youths, with any of several community or volunteer agencies (e.g., probation, employment, school); (4) ready access to the parole agent, by the youths, if and when a need or emergency would arise on the youths' part; (5) flexible agent-youth contacts (office or streets; formal or informal), and on a daily basis if necessary; (6) extensive surveillance by the parole agent (e.g., during evenings or weekends) with respect to the youths' community activities, if and as needed.

The following were among the major program elements which could be made available, depending upon the youth's needs and life-situation at the time: (1) Individual and/or group-centered treatment; (2) group homes, individual foster homes, and other out-of-home placements; (3) an accredited school program which was located within the CTP "community center" building, and which included tutoring as well as arts and crafts; (4) recreational opportunities and socializing experiences (e.g., outings and cultural activities) both within and outside the community center.

The next section will contain the main results of the 1961–1969 effort. To help state these findings in a succinct yet meaningful way it will be necesssary to: (1) Focus upon the Sacramento-Stockton area alone;[2] (2) talk about boys

---

[2]In part, this is because the necessary, detailed analyses have not been completed relative to San Francisco youths. Nevertheless, relevant analyses which have been completed suggest that the overall results may be fairly comparable to those which appear in the present report, for the Sacramento-Stockton location alone.

Of the 1,014 eligibles, 72 percent of the boys and 58 percent of the girls were from the Sacramento-Stockton area.

only — although, later on, the main results for girls will be mentioned as well; and (3) refer to three separate groups, or "types," of youth.

A few words must be said about the three groups of youth: *"Passive Conformist," "Power Oriented,"* and *"Neurotic."* These groups have long been recognized by perhaps the majority of practitioners and theorists. They are usually referred to by names which are similar to the ones which are used in this report. Each group is briefly reviewed in Section A of the Appendix. As to quantities, these groups accounted for *14 percent, 21 percent,* and *53 percent* of the 1961–1969 sample of boys, respectively. (Incidentally, the Passive Conformist group seems to account for a considerably larger proportion of the typical California *probation* — i.e., local city and county — population, when compared with that observed within the CYA.[3]) Thus, taken together, the three groups accounted for 7 of every 8 — i.e., 88 percent — of the eligible boys.[4] The remaining 12 percent were made up of four rather rare groups of youth, and will be referred to later on.

> For readers who are familiar with "I-level" theory,[5] it should be mentioned that many practitioners and theorists would refer to the Passive Conformists as "immature conformists" (Cfm's). Similarly, one may think of the Power Oriented group as being made up of "cultural conformists" (Cfc's) and "manipulators" (Mp's), whereas the Neurotic group would be comprised of individuals who are often referred to as "neurotic acting-out" (Na's) and "neurotic anxious" (Nx's).

MAIN RESULTS OF THE 1961–1969 EXPERIMENT

A. — First we will talk about the group which was by far the largest — *Neurotics*. These individuals appeared to perform much better within the intensive CTP program than within the traditional program (i.e., institution plus standard parole). For example, Criminal Identification and Investigation (CI&I) "rap sheets,"[6] which covered each ward's entire Youth Authority

---

[3]For example, an estimated 25 percent of the overall probation population — in contrast to the 14 percent which was observed during the CYA's 1961–1969 effort.

[4]They accounted for 94 percent of the eligible girls.

[5]See: Warren, M.Q. et al., "Interpersonal Maturity Level Classification: Juvenile, Diagnosis and Treatment of Low, Middle, and High Maturity Delinquents." (Sacramento: California Youth Authority, 1966), pp. 1–52, (mimeo.).

[6]These documents are compiled by the State of California, Department of Justice (D.J.). They are based on reports which are routinely, and directly, received by D.J. from police, probation, and sheriffs' departments throughout California. Among other things, the documents may include listings of antisocial activities which had not been mentioned in the (a) formal suspension reports, and (b) "special incident reports," of Youth Authority parole agents who participated in the 1961–1969 effort. (For a variety of reasons, omissions of this nature occurred significantly more often relative to the traditional program, as compared with the CTP program.)

"career,"[7] showed that the controls were arrested 2.7 times more often than experimentals. (Offenses of minor severity were excluded.[8]) More specifically, the rates of arrest in connection with each month "at risk" — i.e., for *each month on parole in the community* — were .080 for controls and .030 for experimentals. This amounted to a difference of about 1.4 arrests per youth, per CYA *career*. In practical terms, this would mean 1,400 fewer arrests per career, for every 1,000 "Neurotic" youths in the CTP program as compared with an equal number of these youths within the traditional program.

> When offenses of minor severity were included, the arrest rates per month-at-risk were .101 for controls (C's) and .044 for experimentals (E's) — a difference of 130 percent in favor of the latter. Statistically speaking, neither of the C vs. E differences which have been mentioned could be explained on the basis of chance alone.

Additional information and findings are given in Section C of the Appendix. The present set of results, which of course apply to the Neurotic group alone, are probably of greater relevance today than they were during much of the 1961–1969 period. This is because the Neurotic group currently appears to make up an even larger proportion (perhaps 70–75 percent) of the Youth Authority's entire population of males, and of females as well. This increase seems to have been an indirect and rather complicated byproduct of the continually increasing average age of CYA first commitments and, of course, recommitments.

B. — *Power Oriented* youths who participated in the intensive CTP program performed substantially *worse* than those within the traditional program, particularly in connection with follow-up periods of relatively long duration. This was in spite of their better showing on a 24-month "recidivism index." See the Appendix, for details.

C. — On balance, *Passive Conformists* who participated in CTP performed somewhat better than those in the traditional program, at least while under Youth Authority jurisdiction. However, the subsample of experimentals who received a *favorable discharge* from the CYA performed somewhat worse than their controls in terms of convictions (but somewhat better in terms of arrests), when one looked at the 4-year period immediately following the termination of that jurisdiction. (See the Appendix.)

D. — *The Relatively Rare Types of Youth:* What about the four groups of youth who, when taken together, accounted for the remaining 12 percent of the sample? Basically, too few cases were present within each of these groups to allow for really firm or definite conclusions. Yet, it makes some sense to

---

[7]The figures which will next be given refer to all youths who received either a favorable or an unfavorable discharge from the CYA by the close of the 1961–1969 experiment, or shortly thereafter.

[8]Arrests of "minor severity" are those which relate to traffic (non-injuries/nonfelonies), runaway, incorrigibility, etc.

briefly state the findings which we do have, on at least a tentative or provisional basis, in contrast to reporting nothing at all about these individuals.

> In the case of one particular group, however, there happened to be a complete absence of cases within the Sacramento-Stockton, experimental sample; as a result, nothing can be said about them. In I-level terms, these youths are referred to as *"asocialized aggressives"* (Aa's). (I-level terminology will also be used in referring to the three remaining personality types: "Ap's, Se's, and Ci's" (see below)). Aa's, Ap's, Se's and Ci's accounted for *1 percent, 4 percent, 2 percent, and 5 percent* of the present sample of E + C boys, respectively.

(1) All things considered, the *"asocialized passive"* group (Ap's) seemed to perform somewhat better within the intensive CTP program than in the traditional Youth Authority program. (2) No substantial E vs. C differences were observed in relation to the *"situational emotional reaction"* group (Se's). Youths of this type appeared to perform consistently well, regardless of which particular program they were in. (3) The *"cultural identifier"* group (Ci's)[9] appeared to perform somewhat better in the traditional program than in CTP.

E. — *The Total Group of Boys (Viewed Collectively).* In this section, the results for *all* Sacramento-Stockton boys are reviewed. This includes the 12 percent which had earlier been set aside.

Based on CI&I rap sheets, the arrest rate was found to be .065 among controls and .040 among experimentals, for each month on parole. This 63 percent difference in favor of the intensive, CTP program cannot be explained in terms of "chance." (A similar nonchance difference was found when offenses of minor severity were included.) In practical terms, this would amount to at least 750 fewer arrests per CYA career, for every 1,000 experimentals as vs. 1,000 controls.

On 24-months-parole follow-up, experimental boys performed significantly better than control boys in terms of recidivism rate: 44 percent vs. 63 percent. (Recidivism is defined in Section C of the Appendix.) Other results are: Fifty percent of the controls, as vs. 69 percent of the experimentals, received a *favorable* discharge from the CYA within 60 months of their first release to the community. Twenty-three percent of the controls, as vs. 16 percent of the experimentals, received an *unfavorable* discharge within 60 months.

It seems clear from the above that boys who participated in the CTP program performed substantially better than those in the traditional program at least during the 2-to-4-year, typical duration of their Youth Authority jurisdiction.

What happened *after* some of these youths left the Youth Authority? If one looks at the subsample of individuals who received a *favorable* discharge from the CYA, control boys were found to have chalked up an average of 1.42

---

[9]More recently referred to as higher maturity "delinquent identifiers" (Di's).

convictions within 48 months after they had left the CYA. The figure for experimentals was 1.67. (Focusing on arrests alone, the figures were 1.72 and 1.94 — a difference of 13 percent. As before, nonsevere offenses were excluded.)[10]

> It should be mentioned that this 18 percent difference, one which favored the traditional program, seemed to largely reflect the comparatively good performance which was chalked up by what amounted to a relatively large number of *Power Oriented* individuals among the "favorable-dischargee control-subsample," when compared with the performance of the relatively smaller number of control *Neurotics* who had also received a favorable discharge. (As seen in Section C of the Appendix, Neurotic *experimental* boys, taken by themselves performed better than their controls, after having left the CYA on the basis of a favorable discharge. Very much the opposite was found in the case of Power Oriented experimentals.) In short, the Power Oriented individuals contributed enough "points" to have tipped the postdischarge balance in favor of the control group — i.e., when all youths were counted at the same time and when the performance of the Power Oriented youths was weighted according to the number of such individuals who were present in this subsample of favorable dischargees.

F. — *Girls*. The following relates to the total sample of girls: On balance, these individuals seemed to perform equally well in the traditional program and in CTP. We say "on balance" because control girls appeared to perform better when one focused on certain measures of effectiveness only, whereas results of an opposite nature were noted when still *other* measures were used. Even when these individuals were analyzed separately with regard to each of the three major personality groupings — Passive Conformist, Power Oriented and Neurotic — no really substantial, overall E vs. C differences were observed.

WHAT ABOUT COSTS?

What was the average cost of sending a youth through the traditional program, as compared with that of CTP? In addressing this question, the first thing we found was that costs for *both* programs rose a great deal from 1961 through 1969. This was mainly due to "normal" increases in salaries and wages, price-of-living, etc. Secondly, costs increased more within the *traditional* program than within CTP; moreover, this trend continued into the 1970's. (See below.)

> This "differential rise in costs" was largely related to the greater relative, and total, amount of time which the control youths were spending within the CYA's increasingly expensive-to-operate institutions, beginning in the middle and later 1960's. In other words, it was mainly a reflection of the amount of institutional

---

[10]As indicated in footnote 31, we have not completed the analysis of post-CYA offense behavior on the part of individuals who had received an *unfavorable* discharge.

time which was being accumulated by controls (particularly those whose parole had been revoked on one or more occasions[11]) as compared with that of experimentals. (Experimentals had been revoked and institutionalized less often than controls, on the average.)

The costs which appear below relate to all Sacramento-Stockton boys who had entered either CTP or the traditional program during 1961–1969, and who received either a favorable or an unfavorable discharge as of March 1, 1973. All reception center (NRCC), institution, camp, and parole costs were included. Separate analyses were made on these 162 C's and 192 E's, depending upon the year in which each individual had first entered the program (i.e., the experiment):

> For youths who entered during the experiment's early years, or "*early period*," 1963 prices were used. For those entering during the "*middle period*," 1966–67 prices were used. For youths who entered during the later years — the "*recent period*" — 1971–72 prices were used.[12]

The average CYA career costs per ward were as follows:

Early period: C — $ 5,734;   E — $ 7,180
Middle period: C —   8,679;   E —   9,911
Recent period: C — 14,327;   E — 14,580

Thus, in earlier years the traditional program was noticeably less expensive than CTP. However, the C vs. E "cost-ratio" underwent a definite change as time went by. This was seen in relation to the early, middle, and more recent cost-ratios, respectively: 0.80 to 1;[13] 0.88 to 1; and 0.98 to 1. As a result, the earlier advantage which was observed for the traditional program had largely faded away by the early 1970s. Stated directly, the actual C vs. E cost difference per youth amounted to *$1,446* during the early period, *$1,232* during the middle period, and *$253* during the more recent period. When one looks at the 1971–72 data in relation to the duration of the average youth's CYA career, the figure of $253 is found to involve a control/experimental difference of $66 per year, or 18 cents a day.

In light of price increases which have been experienced since the early 1970's, it is possible that the cost-balance has by now tipped in "favor" of the CTP program. Aside from this possibility, one which centers around the

---

[11]The periods of incarceration which resulted from these revocations are over and beyond the *initial* period of incarceration which was experienced by the controls, but not by the experimentals, shortly after their original commitment to the Youth Authority.

[12]In connection with the "recent period" the primary question was: What would the program costs look like on the basis of early 1970 prices — yet in relation to the performance of an actual sample of experimentals and controls who had entered the CYA during the later part of the 1961–1969 effort?

[13]Thus, 5,734 divided by 7,180 yields a ratio of 0.80 to 1.

above figures alone, it should be pointed out that the 1971–72 "per ward costs" would be at least a few hundred dollars higher for the traditional program than for CTP if *capital outlay costs* were added to the picture. These costs, which were not included in the figures shown above, would relate to the construction of new institutions. They are estimated as being close to $10,000,000 for each "up-to-date," physically secure, 400-bed facility. Finally, the above figures do not take into account the fairly substantial, *non-CYA correctional costs* which were accounted for by unfavorable discharges who had been sent directly to a State or Federal prison. In this connection, it will be recalled that a greater percentage of controls than experimentals had received a discharge of this type. (Also see footnote 31.)

It appears, then, that current costs for the community program would in no event be substantially greater than those for the traditional program. To all indications they would, in fact, be a little less. This would be highlighted if one focused upon the "Neurotic" youths alone, regardless of whether any post-CYA "career costs" were brought into the picture.

THE PRESENT EXPERIMENT (1969–1974)

Despite the early promise shown by CTP with various groups of youth, it was quite clear by 1965 that there was much room for improvement with regard to still other groups. By 1967–1968, it was the consensus of CTP operations staff, and on-site researchers, that the difficulties and delinquent orientation of 25-to-35 percent of the eligible boys were hardly being influenced by the intensive CTP program. In fact, it had been found that at least one-third of these individuals were again involved in delinquency within a few weeks or months after having entered the program. Much the same was observed with similar types of individuals who had been assigned to the traditional program — i.e., with youths (control subjects) who had spent some 8 or 10 months in a regular CYA institution (or camp) prior to being paroled. These, then, were the type of experiences, findings and impressions which led to the present experiment — part 2 of the Youth Authority's Community Treatment Project.

"Part 2" has several objectives; however, its main thrust relates to the following question: Would many of the above-mentioned youths become less delinquently oriented if they began their CYA career within a certain kind of residential setting (described below), and *not within the community itself?* Thus the title of this 1969–1974 effort: "Settings for the Differential Treatment of Delinquents."[14]

To be sure, the idea of using a residential facility, on a fairly long-term

---

[14]As before, the research costs are picked up by NIMH.

basis if necessary, involved a definite departure from the philosophy which was behind the 1961–1969 effort. Under that philosophy, or set of hypotheses, the treatment-and-control of *all* eligible youths could just as well have begun within the community itself.[15] (Basically, only the research requirement that there be a control group prevented this from actually occurring.) Furthermore, during 1961–1969 the residential setting — in this case NRCC — was to be used (a) only *after* the youths' intensive community program had gotten underway, and (b) on a short-term "temporary detention" basis alone, if at all.

The "Settings" experiment obtains its sample of youths from the greater Sacramento area. This consists entirely of males who (a) may be 13 to 21 years old at intake, and (b) are no longer restricted to being juvenile court commitments. The *key* "ineligibility criteria" — i.e., bases for exclusion — relate to the youths' commitment offense and offense history, as before. However the present set of offense-criteria allow for the inclusion, within the experiment, of a *broader range* of individuals than was possible in 1961–1969. (See below for details.)

PROCEDURES AND OPERATIONS (1969–1974)

The following question is asked by project staff in connection with each newly commited youth who — in accordance with the above criteria — seems likely to later be judged eligible by the Youth Authority Board:[16] "Within which type of setting would it probably be best to initiate the treatment-and-control of this individual"? The choice is between: (1) Initial assignment to an intensive, CTP-staffed-and-operated residential program — later to be followed by release to the intensive CTP community program (staffed-and-operated as in 1961–1969); (2) direct release to the intensive CTP community program (again as per the 1961–1969 pattern).

The project staffing team approaches the above question by first making a careful study of the individual's interests, limitations, immediate pressures and underlying motivations. The main object is to figure out what the most appropriate, yet practical, short-range and long-range goals might be. The resulting "close look" allows staff to next "check the youth out" in terms of written guidelines which are designed to further focus their attention on the

---

[15]At any rate, there seemed to be little if any scientific evidence to suggest that it would be *inappropriate or impractical* to begin the treatment-and-control of eligible wards outside of a traditional institutional setting.

[16]As in 1961–1969, the Youth Authority Board gives the final, legal approval in regard to eligibility. (In the event that the youth is declared eligible, a "random drawing" will alone determine exactly *where* he is to begin his treatment-and-control. See the text.) Prior to the time that a ward is officially declared eligible, he would be referred to as a "pre-eligible."

question of *where* the given treatment-and-control plan might best be started. The guidelines relate to certain categories of youth who, as mentioned earlier, were found to be unusually difficult to "reach" during 1961–1969.

> In these guidelines, a number of distinguishing characteristics are spelled out with regard to five groups of individuals. (According to the hypotheses of this experiment, youths who appear to "fit" any one or more of these descirptions "should" begin their CYA career within the above-mentioned residential setting.) More specifically, the guidelines contain short descriptions of (a) certain patterns of interacting with others, (b) outstanding personality characteristics, (c) underlying motivations, and/or (d) immediate pressures and life-circumstances.[17] The guidelines are outlined in Section D of the Appendix.

Individuals who are seen as needing an initial period of institutionalization are referred to as "Status 1"; those seen as *not* needing this type of initial setting are termed "Status 2." When the staffing team completes its evaluation of an individual and finalizes his "status," a random drawing is then made to determine whether his initial *placement* is to be within the CTP residential component (i.e., program) or else within its community-based component.[18] All CTP parole agents serve both parts of CTP. (Prior to the youth's actual placement into either one or the other of these CTP settings/components, the Youth Authority Board must declare him eligible for CTP per se. It makes this decision without having learned the outcome of the random drawing.)

> This random assignment procedure results in the establishment of four separate youth-groups — two "residential" and two "community-based," with each of the two containing a subgroup of Status 1 and, in addition, Status 2 individuals. The research team later compares each one of these four youth-groups with each of the remaining three, in terms of community adjustment.[19] With certain planned exceptons, parole agents who participate in the experiment can have caseloads which contain individuals from all four youth-groups.

---

[17]Since 1969, these descriptions have been found to be largely, though not entirely, mutually exclusive.

[18]As a result of the random drawing, it not infrequently happens that a Status 1 youth will have to begin his program within the community setting. By the same token, a Status 2 youth may have to begin within the residential facility. (These "less-than-optimal," initial placements serve an essential function in terms of the research design.) When this type of initial placement is called for, the Operations section of the staffing team prepares what is called a "modified treatment-and-control" plan. This differs in several respects from the "optimal . . . plan" which they had prepared just prior to the drawing. The main object of the modified plan is to (a) develop goals which are appropriate to the less-than-optimal setting in which the youth's program is to be initiated, yet which will remain relevant to the individual's needs, and (b) develop strategies which will allow for and at the same time encourage a maximum use of the resources which are available within the particular setting.

[19]The groups which are being compared thus serve as "controls" for one another.

The parole agent who is assigned to work with a given youth, and who has therefore been part of the staffing team, remains assigned to that youth regardless of whether the latter's placement happens to be within the residential or the community section of CTP at any particular point in time. This helps promote continuity within and across settings, with respect to long-term treatment-and-control efforts.[20]

Before presenting the results to date, a few words should be added about the CTP residential unit. This unit ("Dorm 3") is located at NRCC and is a 5- or 10-minute drive from CTP's community center in Sacramento. Dorm 3 normally houses 23 to 25 youths at any one time — CTP youths (males) exclusively — although the number has ranged from 15 to 32. It is staffed by carefully selected "youth counselors" and "group supervisors," and is readily as well as continuously accessible to all remaining CTP personnel. Some parole agents have their office on the dorm. All dorm staff are individually, and officially, paired-up with one or two agents. This makes for better dorm-agent as well as dorm-dorm coordination of efforts with respect to implementing stated goals and strategies for residence-located youths who are on the caseload of the given agents.

Two additional points. (1) *Expanding CTP's Applicability*. Part of the 1969–1974 effort centers around the following question: Can the CTP approach[21] be applied to a *broader range and variety* of offenders than that which was available in connection with the 1961–1969 experiment? This question is dealt with at two levels: First, the "ineligibility criteria" which were used during 1961–1969 have been trimmed back in order to allow for the inclusion of many individuals who would otherwise be *excluded* on the basis of (a) commitment offenses relating to armed robbery, forcible rape, etc., or (b) offense histories of a particularly disturbed or aggressive-appearing nature.[22] However, the Board will declare these particular youths eligible for CTP only with the understanding that their program is to be initiated within Dorm 3. (For research purposes, all such individuals are therefore analyzed as a separate group. They are called "Category B" youths.[23]) Secondly, and aside from the matter of offenses, all first commitments to the CYA from the Sacramento County Superior Court have been made available for inclusion within CTP. This is the first time that adult court commitments have become part of the CTP studies. No restrictions are applied as to *where* these particular individuals may begin their program; etc. (2) *Terminology*. The following should facilitate the presentation of findings:

---

[20]In many cases, individuals whose parole is revoked while they are in the community can be placed into, or returned to, the CTP residential facility. This allows them to remain part of the overall program.

[21]In the present case this includes the "differential treatment" feature in addition to the community-based aspect per se.

[22]That is, regardless of the possible lack of severity of the *commitment* offense itself.

[23]All other youths are referred to as "Category A."

RR = Status 1 youths who were *appropriately placed:* These individuals were diagnosed as needing to begin their program within a residential setting. Their program *did* begin within a residential setting (i.e., Dorm 3).

RC = Status 1 youths who were *inappropriately placed:* Diagnosed as needing to begin in a residential setting; however, their program was initiated within a community setting, as in 1961–1969.

CR = Status 2 youths who were *inappropriately placed:* Diagnosed as being able to begin their program within a community setting; however, their program was initiated within a residential setting (i.e., Dorm 3).

CC = Status 2 youths who were *appropriately placed:* Diagnosed as being able to begin their program within a community setting. Their program *did* begin within a community setting, as in 1961–1969.

MAIN FINDINGS TO DATE (1969–1974 EXPERIMENT)[24]

Status 1 youths who were inappropriately placed are performing considerably worse than those who were appropriately placed: 94 percent of the RC's (inappropriately placed) as vs. 58 percent of the RR's (appropriately placed) have chalked up one or more offenses during their first year-and-a-half on parole.[25] The number of offenses per youth is 1.56 among RC's and 0.96 among RR's. For each month at risk the mean rate of offending is .140 among RC's as vs. .066 among RR's — in other words, one offense for every 7.1 months in the case of RC's, and one per 15.2 months among RR's.[26] This

---

[24](a) These results relate to the first 106 eligible "Category A" males who were paroled as of December 15, 1972. (See footnote 23.) When "Category B" cases are included, the results hardly change. (b) Neurotic, Power Oriented, Passive Conformist, and "rare types" are combined into a single group — 74 percent of which is comprised of the Neurotic category alone. (The findings which are reported — more specifically, the differences between comparison groups — are very largely accounted for by the latter individuals. They receive little if any support in relation to the remaining 26 percent of the sample, when the latter are viewed as a single, separate entity.) This population-distribution probably reflects a broader trend within the CYA as a whole. (c) The present results take into account offenses of all severity levels: however, they are virtually unchanged when those of minor severity are excluded. The latter account for 7 percent of the present, 120 offenses. (d) "Offense" is defined as any delinquent act which results in any one or more of the following, official actions: Revocation of parole; court recommitment; adjudicated court referral to CTP; unfavorable transfer from CTP; suspension of parole. (During the coming year an analysis of CI&I rap sheets will be undertaken for the first time, relative to the 1969–1974 sample.)

[25]As before, "months on parole" is used synonymously with "months in the community" and "months at risk."

[26]By using a closely related yet possibly more refined statistical approach, an even larger difference was obtained between RC's and RR's with respect to the average (mean) monthly rate of offending. When the *median* rather than the *mean* was used in relation to this alternate approach, the monthly rate of offending was .180 for RC's and .060 for RR's.

112 percent difference in rate of offending cannot be explained in terms of "chance."[27]

These findings suggest that the delinquent behavior of the Youth Authority's more troubled, troublesome and/or resistive wards may be substantially reduced — provided that they are first worked with in a setting such as is represented by Dorm 3, as distinct from one which is community-based in the usual sense of the term. The scope, and the potential importance, of any such "reductions" should not be thought of as slight: Status 1 youths represent 46 percent of the total CTP sample.[28] It is likely that they comprise a sizable portion of the Youth Authority's total population, as well.[29]

What about the remaining 54 percent — i.e., the *Status 2* youths? (These youths, it will be recalled, are the less troubled, troublesome and/or resistive individuals.) On balance the present findings suggest that there is little if anything to be gained, with regard to parole performance, by initially placing Status 2 youths into a residential facility,[30] even of the type represented by Dorm 3: The average monthly rates of offending are .086 for CR's (inappropriately placed) and .068 for CC's (appropriately placed) — a difference of 26 percent. On the surface, these rates might suggest that an "inappropriate" (in this case, residential) placement would be slightly *detrimental* to the Status 2 youths, at least when compared with the more appropriate, alternate placement. However, this particular difference in rates of offending may be accounted for by "chance" alone. Together with results from three other measures of performance, the overall picture is one of few substantial and consistent CR vs. CC differences.

Inappropriately placed youths (RC's + CR's) are performing worse than appropriately placed youths (RR's + CC's): For each month spent within the community, the mean rate of offending is .107 among "inappropriates" (INP's) and .067 among "appropriates" (APR's). This amounts to one offense for every 9.3 months on parole in the case of INP's, and one per 14.9 months among APR's. This 60 percent difference cannot be accounted for by "chance." Results from the remaining performance-indicators are consistent with this basic finding, although not as clear-cut.

---

[27]Nor can various background factors account for this difference. These factors include age, IQ, socioeconomic status, race, I-level, "subtype," and level of parole risk ("base expectancy").

[28]With "Category B" youths included, the figure is 49 percent.

[29]In 1968, research staff estimated that 39 percent of all eligible youths would receive a Status 1 diagnosis during the present experiment. Wards who were received by the CYA during the past few years appear to be more involved with delinquency than those received during the 1960's. For example, the present sample of eligible Category A subjects had accumulated an average of 7.1 delinquent contacts by the time of their commitment to the CYA. The figure for 1961–1969 eligibles was 5.8.

[30]This is generally consistent with the main results of the 1961–1969 experiment.

The various findings which have been presented might seem to suggest the obvious: Delinquent behavior can probably be reduced in connection with community and residential programs *alike*, by means of careful diagnosis and subsequent placement of individuals into appropriate rather than inappropriate or less-than-optimal settings and programs. In short, it might be said that it matters *which* youths (or types of youth) are placed into *which* type of setting, and that careful selection may lead to higher rates of success for residential and community-based programs alike. Yet, it is recognized that such a viewpoint or conclusion would by no means be universally accepted as being "obvious," within corrections. For one thing, many people feel that nothing really has much effect on delinquent behavior; others believe that one single approach, and perhaps one particular setting, may well contain "the answer" for all but a tiny portion of the population. At any rate, the present findings will hopefully add new information to a long-standing placement issue which many practitioners do regard as being less than entirely obvious in the majority, if not large majority, of cases: Which youths would best be placed into which types of setting, or program?

Two final points in this connection. (1) The difference in rate of offending which is found *between* the Status 1 groups (RC's *vs.* RR's) is considerably larger than that found between the Status 2 groups (CR's *vs.* CC's). More specifically, Status 1 youths who were inappropriately placed are performing *considerably* worse than those who were appropriately placed; however, in the case of Status 2 youths *no substantial differences* are observed between individuals who were inappropriately placed and those who were appropriately placed. This raises the possibility that initial placement within an inappropriate or less-than-optimal setting might make more of a difference to Status 1 youths than to those diagnosed as Status 2. It may be that the latter, presumably "stronger" individuals are in a better position to compensate for, or otherwise cope with and make the best of, an environment of this nature. (2) The significance, or possible differential significance, of the initial treatment-and-control setting is also suggested by the following: Appropriately placed youths (RR's *and* CC's) are performing about equally well on parole — i.e., regardless of status. However, *inappropriately* placed *Status 1* youths (RC's) are performing substantially worse than inappropriately placed *Status 2* youths (CR's). In other words, appropriate placement may perhaps help to offset or moderate certain pre-existing differences in level of coping ability, on the part of Status 1 vs. Status 2 youths. On the other hand, *inappropriate* or less-than-optimal placement may be more likely to accentuate or activate various differences which relate to their personal or interpersonal liabilities.

Thus far, the CTP approach does seem applicable to categories of offenders other than those which were studied in 1961–1969: Briefly, *Adult Court* commitments have presented few if any special operational problems, or, for that matter, diagnostic problems. Their treatment-and-control requirements differ only slightly from those of Juvenile Court commitments who fall within the 16-and-older age range. In addition, *Category B* youths have presented few unusual or serious operational and diagnostic problems. However, partly because of Board restrictions which are frequently placed upon these individuals with regard to day passes, furloughs or minimum length of residential stay, it has sometimes been difficult to develop treatment-and-control plans which closely resemble those observed in the case of many other residence-located youths. Operations staff nevertheless feel able to engage in productive interactions with most such youths. The parole performance of these individuals has yet to be evaluated in detail.

OVERVIEW AND CONCLUDING REMARKS

Within and outside of corrections, many concerned individuals are currently engaged in an ideological battle over whether to "keep almost all offenders on the streets," or else "lock up nearly all offenders, except for first-timers." This, of course, may be exaggerating the situation to a certain degree; yet at the same time, it may be accurate in its reflection of certain feelings which are often involved. Feelings aside, the facts which have emerged from California's 12-year experiment thus far suggest that both of the above positions may be too extreme, and that a more differentiated or flexible approach may be appropriate. (These considerations would at least apply to the type of individuals who have been studied thus far — youths who have had numerous contacts with the law.) A brief review may illustrate this point:

When an NIMH-funded research team combined several hundred Youth Authority males into a single study group (one which included the full range of CYA "personality types"), it found that (a) "experimentals" who participated in the intensive, 1961–1969 *community-based program (CTP)* had produced substantially less delinquent behavior than (b) "controls" who had participated in the traditional CYA program. (The experimentals and controls had been well-matched on such characteristics as age, IQ, socioeconomic status, race, etc.) However, the researchers also found that much of this difference in favor of the CTP — i.e., noninstitutional — program was accounted for by youths who were referred to as "Neurotics." During the 1960's, these individuals accounted for half of the CYA's population; they currently account for considerably more. By way of contrast, the *traditional CYA program* was found to have a greater influence than CTP in the case of individuals described as "Power Oriented." This particular group now comprises about one-tenth of the CYA population; it previously accounted for twice that amount.

Quite aside from these particular findings and developments, it was observed, prior to 1969, that roughly one-third of the *total* sample were responding somewhat indifferently, and often quite unfavorably, to the community-based and traditional programs alike. Included within this broad, "difficult-to-reach" category were some individuals from nearly all personality groupings. However, it was the difficult-to-reach Neurotics who accounted for the largest total number. (This was possible despite the relatively positive performance by the Neurotic group as a whole.) Since 1969, the distinguishing characteristics of difficult-to-reach "Neurotics" have been largely singled-out. In many cases (perhaps half) operations staff have helped them to engage in less by way of delinquent behavior while in the community. But before this could occur, it was necessary for these individuals to *begin* their Youth Authority program, (a) not within the community per se, (b) not inside a standard CYA institution, but rather (c) within a *medium-sized, CTP-staffed residential facility* — one which was operated in accordance with the 1961–1969 "differential treatment" philosophy. As to the difficult-to-reach "Power Oriented" youths, this same "residence-first" (CTP facility) approach seems to be resulting in relatively little overall improvement in terms of parole performance. Thus, the *traditional* program may still represent the Youth Authority's best alternative for the majority of these particular individuals — especially the subgroup known as "Cfc's." Finally, during 1961–1969 the "Passive Conformists" (now one-tenth of the population) performed somewhat, though not a great deal better in CTP than within the traditional CYA program. Nevertheless, their response to CTP's residential facility (1969-present) has been unfavorable. Thus, in this particular instance the 1961–1969 type of community-based approach would seem to be the treatment of choice.

CTP's originally stated ideal — that of changing delinquents into lifelong nondelinquents — is not being achieved in the large majority of cases. Obviously, the CTP program does not contain a "special potion" which, after having been taken, is capable of eliminating all traces of delinquency, and of fortifying the youths against every form of stress. Nevertheless, the "differential treatments" and "differential settings" which have been utilized in this program do seem capable of *reducing* the total volume of delinquent behavior on the part of many, but by no means all, eligible males. This holds true during the period of their CYA jurisdiction and, to a lesser extent, subsequent to the termination of that jurisdiction. In order to bring about this "reduction," it has very often seemed unnecessary to initially place these individuals within a residential setting (traditional or otherwise); in many other cases, it has seemed quite necessary. As suggested above, it is what goes on *within* the given setting that seems to count, and not just the setting itself. This, of course, may also vary from one type of youth to another.

Nothing in our experience suggests that it is an easy matter to operate a program such as CTP. Implementation and maintenance of a community-based, intensive differential treatment-and-control program involves critical issues, and requires steadfast commitments, with respect to personnel selection, quality of supervision, administrative support, etc. In one form or another, issues of this nature will also be encountered outside the context of large-sized, State agencies such as the CYA. Although challenges of this type have been adequately met in certain instances, it might be well to recognize the fact that any thoroughgoing implementation of CTP — even of the 1961–1969 approach alone — is, at the present time, probably beyond the reach of most probation and parole departments within the USA on anything other than a limited scale. Even so, worthwhile modifications and adaptations of the California program do seem to be well within the realm of possibility; in several instances, they are already in existence.

Whatever the immediate future may hold for programs such as CTP, the research information which has been gathered since 1961 may continue to be of interest to practitioners, administrators and social scientists who still place value upon the concept of actively and directly intervening in the life of personally troubled, developmentally lacking and/or disturbing-aggressive youths and young adults. This should apply in relation to community-based and residential-centered programs alike.

APPENDIX

SECTION A

The three groups of youth which were first mentioned on page 258 may be briefly described as follows:

Passive Conformist   This type of youth usually fears, and responds with strong compliance to, peers and adults who he thinks have the "upper hand" at the moment, or who seem more adequate and assertive than himself. He considers himself to be lacking in social "know-how," and usually expects to be rejected by others in spite of his efforts to please them.

Power Oriented   This group is actually made up of two somewhat different kinds of individuals, who, nevertheless, share several important features with one another. The first likes to think of himself as delinquent and tough. He is often more than willing to "go along" with others, or with a gang, in order to earn a certain degree of status and acceptance, and to later maintain his "reputation." The second type, or "subtype," often attempts to undermine or circumvent the efforts and directions of authority figures. Typically, he does not wish to conform to peers or adults; and not infrequently, he will attempt to assume a leading "power role" for himself.

Passive Conformist and Power Oriented youths are usually thought of as having reached a "middle maturity" level of interpersonal development. The group which is described next is said to have reached a "higher maturity" level. The ''level of interpersonal maturity'' concept is briefly explained in Section B of this Appendix.

Neurotic   Here again, we find two separate personality types which share certain important characteristics with one another. The first type often attempts to deny — to himself and others — his conscious feelings of inadequacy, rejection, or self-condemnation. Not infrequently, he does this by verbally attacking *others* and / or by the use of boisterous distractions plus a variety of ''games.'' The second type often shows various symptoms of emotional disturbance — e.g., chronic or intense depression, or psychosomatic complaints. His tensions and conscious fears usually result from conflicts produced by feelings of failure, inadequacy, or underlying guilt.

SECTION B

The following are brief definitions of the three main levels of interpersonal maturity which are observed within the CYA:

Maturity Level Two (1^2)   An individual whose overall development has reached this level, but has not gone beyond it, views events and objects mainly as sources of short-term pleasure, or else frustration. He distinguishes among individuals largely in terms of their being either ''givers'' or ''withholders,'' and seems to have few ideas of interpersonal refinement beyond this. He has a very low level of frustration-tolerance; moreover, he has a poor capacity for understanding many of the basic reasons for the behavior or attitudes of others toward him.

Maturity Level Three (1^3)   More than the 1^2, an individual at this level recognizes that certain aspects of his own behavior have a good deal to do with whether or not he will get what he wants from others. Such an individual interacts mainly in terms of oversimplified rules and formulas rather than from a set of relatively firm, and generally more complex, internalized standards or ideals. He understands few of the feelings and motives of individuals whose personalities are rather different than his own. More often than the 1^4 (see below), he assumes that peers and adults operate mostly on a rule-oriented or intimidation / manipulation basis.

Maturity Level Four (1^4)   More than the 1^3, an individual at this level has internalized one or more ''sets'' of standards which he frequently uses as a basis for either accepting or rejecting the behavior and attitudes of himself as well as others. (These standards are not always mutually consistent, or consistently applied.) He recognizes interpersonal interactions in which individuals attempt to influence one another by means other than compliance, manipulation, promises of hedonistic or monetary reward, etc. He has a fair ability to understand underlying reasons for behavior, and displays some ability to respond, on a fairly long-term basis, to certain moderately complex expectations on the part of various peers and adults.

SECTION C

For the *Neurotic* group, the additional information and findings are as follows:

(1) Despite its known shortcomings, "rate of recidivism" has long been one of corrections' most widely used measures of parole *failure*. As used in this report, recidivism reflects the occurrence of any one or more of the following events: (a) Revocation of the youth's parole by the Youth Authority Board; (b) recommitment of the youth to the CYA, by either a Juvenile or an Adult Court; (c) unfavorable discharge of the youth by the Youth Authority Board, from the CYA itself. Any one of these events is usually the result of some type of police arrest and subsequent conviction. Events (a) and (b), above, are usually followed by a period of incarceration for several months, within one or another of the Youth Authority's large-sized institutions. (See below, regarding (c).) Thus, the higher the recidivism rate, the greater is the amount of "failure," in one sense of the term. Now then, on 24-months parole follow-up the recidivism rate was 66 percent for controls and 45 percent for experimental.

(2) Within 60 months from the time of their first release to the community (literally, their date of initial parole), 40 percent of the C's as vs. 77 percent of the E's had been officially released by the Youth Authority Board from the CYA's jurisdiction — on the basis of a *favorable discharge*. Also within a period of 60 months, 40 percent of the C's as vs. 17 percent of the E's were released on the basis of an unfavorable discharge. (It should be noted that depending upon an individual's behavior subsequent to one or more prior parole revocations which he may have received, the individual will still be able to eventually obtain *either* a favorable *or* an unfavorable discharge from the CYA.)[31]

(3) What happened *after* the CYA's jurisdiction had ended, in the case of Neurotic youths and young adults who had been given a *favorable discharge* (see (2), above)? At least this much is known: Many of these individuals did not entirely relinquish their delinquent tendencies — despite their experiences within the CYA. Be this as it may, those who had gone through the traditional CYA program seemed, on the average, to have remained somewhat *more* delinquent than those who had completed CTP: Within 48 months after having left the Youth Authority, controls chalked up an average of 1.88 convictions; the figure for experimentals was 1.58. (A somewhat larger C vs. E difference was obtained when one looked at *arrests*, and not simply convictions. As

---

[31]Taking into account all "groups" of boys — i.e., all nine "subtypes" — 50% of the experimentals and 50 percent of the controls who received an unfavorable discharge from the Youth Authority were sent to a State or Federal prison immediately upon receipt of their discharge. Their Court sentence commonly specified a maximum of several years' incarceration. Partly because of this, follow-up (i.e., post-CYA, postprison) analyses have not been completed for the unfavorable dischargee sample.

before, arrests of minor severity were not counted.) In practical terms, this would amount to a difference of about 300 convictions for every 1,000 experimental as well as control "favorable-dischargees," over a 4-year span of time. (The reader may note that this analysis of *post-CYA*, CI&I data has been completed on "arrests" and, also, on the "convictions" which related to those arrests. However, because the earlier-mentioned *parole (CYA-time)* CI&I data were first analyzed during 1973, only the "arrest" information has been looked at thus far, with regard to *parole* time. Judging from the "post-CYA" findings on arrests vs. convictions, the "parole time" results for these same two levels of analysis should be very similar to one another.) Using a 10-point scale, the penalties received for each conviction were somewhat more severe among controls than among experimentals — 5.75 as vs. 4.25, on the average.

The following results relate to *Power Oriented* youths:

(1) CI&I rap sheets showed an arrest rate of .060 for controls and .071 for experimentals, with regard to each month spent within the community. This difference favored the traditional program by 18 percent. (Again, offenses of minor severity were excluded, although the picture hardly changed when they were included.) (2) On 24-months' parole follow-up, the recidivism rate was 66 percent for controls and 40 percent for experimentals. (3) Despite the better showing by experimentals on the 24-month recidivism index, it was found that 53 percent of the controls as vs. 43 percent of the experimentals received a favorable discharge from the Youth Authority within *60* months of their first release to parole. Similarly 15 percent of the C's as vs. 23 percent of the E's received an unfavorable discharge. (4) Within 48 months after being released from the CYA's jurisdiction, the Power Oriented, control *"favorable-discharges"* had chalked up an average of 1.47 convictions; the figure for experimentals was 2.55. (The C vs. E difference was even larger when one focused upon arrests alone, rather than convictions alone.) This was a 73 percent difference in favor of Power Oriented youths who had successfully completed the Youth Authority's traditional program.

The following relates to *Passive Conformist* youths:

(1) CI&I rap sheets showed an arrest rate of .066 for controls and .037 for experimentals, for each month within the community. This difference favored the CTP program by 78 percent. (2) On 24-months' parole follow-up, the recidivism rate was 59 percent for controls and 51 percent for experimentals. (3) 54 percent of the C's as vs. 78 percent of the E's received a favorable discharge from the Youth Authority within 60 months of their first release to the community. Similarly, 14 percent of the C's as vs. 6 percent of the E's received an unfavorable discharge. (4) Within 48 months after termination of their CYA jurisdiction, the Passive Conformist, control "favorable-dischargees" had chalked up an average of 1.44 convictions; the figure for experimentals was 1.80. This was a 25 percent difference in favor of the traditional program.

SECTION D

Basic to the 1969–1974 experiment is the hypothesis that certain youths (five groups in all) would probably derive greater benefit from a course of treatment-and-control which would begin within a residential setting, in contrast to a community setting. Briefly, the groups are:

(1) Youths who are quite disturbed and openly disorganized relative to overall, everyday functioning, and who at times become highly agitated or even delusional when under the pressure of everyday life. (Mostly found among Nx's, Ap's and Aa's.)

(2) Youths who have an intensive drive to prevent other persons from exerting controls upon them, or from substantially influencing the direction of their lives. They are prepared to use virtually "everything" in their power — including runaway, physical resistance, etc. — to avoid the ongoing confrontation of concerned authority figures, and to avoid involvement in nonexploitive relationships with adults in general. (Mostly found among Mp's and Cfc's — the "Power Oriented" group.)

(3) Youths who are unable to recognize, or who vigorously attempt to deny, the existence and influence of the unusually destructive relationships and loyalty-binds in which they are involved, at home and within the community. Were these youths released directly to the community setting, conditions such as these would undermine the youth/parole agent relationship at a time when this relationship would still be in its formative stage, and would operate so as to lead the youth into delinquent acting-out of a frequency or magnitude sufficient to result in an early parole revocation and removal from the community setting. (Mostly found among Na's and Nx's — the "Neurotic" group.)

(4) Youths who are nonneurotic and of a relatively high level of maturity, but who need to actually be shown that their freedom will definitely be withdrawn if they persist in their delinquent patterns. (Mostly found among Ci's.)

(5) Youths who — operating on the basis of underlying motivations of a self-defeating nature — have become increasingly committed to the use of drugs and/or a drug-using subculture, to the point of feeling little interest in coping with long-range social expectations or pressures, or in interacting with others in a nonexploitive manner. (Mostly found among Na's and Nx's.)

Chapter 16

Editors' Remarks

Consistent with our assertion that different types of offenders require different types of treatment are the results of the following program in which the effectiveness of probation was improved by classifying adolescent offenders, matching them with probation officers whose worker style was most appropriate to their needs, and providing them with treatment geared to their particular needs as assessed by the I-level (maturity level) classification system.

We are grateful to Lawrence Barkwell for contributing this original article which provides a 3-year follow-up to his 1976 study.

Differential Probation Treatment of Delinquency*

Lawrence Barkwell

The rationale for development of special juvenile correctional programs is the observed heterogeneity of the delinquent population. Most Probation agencies accept the idea that offenders are different from each other in the reasons for their violations of the law. The widespread use of pre-disposition reports to the courts supports the contention that the goals of probation supervision should relate in a direct manner to the causes of the delinquency. A classification system that reliably discriminates distinct needs in the offender should result in better attempts to meet those needs.

Rudolph Moos (1975) has done considerable research into the contrasting responses different treatment techniques produce with different types of delinquent youngsters. There is also clinical evidence (Kiesler, 1971) to suggest that few if any therapists relate equally well with all types of clients or are equally comfortable with the range of treatment styles required to deal with the wide variety of psychological problems. It was on this premise that the Community Treatment Project (CTP) in California began to match workers whose areas of sensitivity, talents and interests appeared to be right for different types of youths.

Data collected by the Community Treatment Project (Palmer, 1969; Warren, 1966, 1969) indicate that when different types of juvenile offenders are treated by a single approach the treatment effects may be masked. The beneficial effects of the program on some individuals combined with the detrimental effects of that same program on other individuals and tend to cancel each other out (Warren, 1972). The CTP studies resulted in the development of ways of classifying offenders, treatment workers, treatment environments, and treatment methods. The studies then focused on matching these factors to determine which combinations of strategies enhance probation outcome.

---

*This article was prepared especially for inclusion in this book.

Wolfensberger (1975) conceptualizes this sort of matching as "model coherency". He draws the issue by asking whether a number of variables within a program combine harmoniously so as to meet the specific needs of each client at that particular time of his life. That is, "are the right people working with the right clients, who are properly grouped, doing the right thing, using the right methods, and consistently so?"

The Jesness (1970, 1971) and CTP studies have resulted in the Interpersonal Maturity Level Classification System (I-Level) which classifies delinquents by maturity levels and subtypes of response set within the levels. The system suggests a total treatment plan (worker, style, setting, and method) for each level and subtype. By this process one not only applies the best method with the appropriate client, but also capitalizes on the Probation Officer's strengths, sensitivities, and interests in working with certain types of youths.

This approach is based on a concept of personality development which defines a person's characteristic modes of interpersonal relations and his behavior in the community in terms of his diagnosed perceptual abilities. Interpersonal maturity is defined as the ability for perceptual differentiation of the self, others, and the world in general.

The theory describes the individuals' progress through successive integrations of perception of himself and the environment to which he relates. This involves an understanding of what is happening among others, as well as between himself and others. These progressively more complex integrations are seen as necessary conditions for the individual to be able to meet his own needs through increasing involvement with other persons and social institutions.

Should an individual become fixated in one of the early stages of development, he is likely to meet his needs in a socially inappropriate manner or respond to others in a deviant way. An adolescent (or adult) fixated at an early stage of development lacks the capacity to perceive his environment, and the people in it, in sufficiently complex terms to make sound predictions and judgements, or to relate in an age-appropriate manner. Further, lacking strong internal standards, or having standards that are reduced in effectiveness due to emotional problems, the individual in effect takes what he wishes without regard for others and their rights.

CLASSIFICATION

I-Level theory postulates seven successive stages of development and subdivides each level according to the individual's typical behavioral responses. The range of maturity found in the delinquent population is from level two to level five. Individuals diagnosed at level one are usually institutionalized at an early age and not found in natural family settings. Those individuals diagnosed at level five and above usually have sufficient maturity to avoid delinquency since they are able to meet their needs and solve their problems in socially approved ways.

An individual whose behavior and perceptions are integrated at level two are primarily involved with demands that the world take care of them. Level two individuals are unable to see other people in anything but a recipient way; people are evaluated in terms of whether they give or deny, assist or impede, with no graduations between the extremes. Because this individual is cognitively concrete he is not able to organize his experiences in terms of abstract concepts and does not get emotionally involved with objects or people beyond his own needs. In short he behaves impulsively and is apparently unaware of the effects of his behavior upon others.

Adolescents operating at level three are basically power oriented, manipulating the environment to get what they want. They assess others in terms of the power and influence they have and not on the basis of who they are in personal terms. This individual's prediction of events and interpersonal responses in the external world is based on a few concrete rules without understanding the abstract principles which underly relationships. He does not behave on the basis of some inner value system but rather on the basis of whether people can or cannot be useful to him. His manipulations may take the form of either conforming to the rules of whoever seems to have the power at the moment or maneuvering around the power structure. Since problems are viewed as external and due to some aspect of the environment, he is uncomfortable with the suggestion that he should change.

Individuals whose understanding and behavior are integrated at level four make more complex differentiations between people, have strong internal standards and good reasoning ability, but may be emotionally conflicted, situationally upset, or delinquently oriented. To a certain extent he can see his actions and the actions of others as motivated by feelings and past events. He is able to think about the future with personal meaning and plan in relatively realistic ways, although distortion may be present. This youth is aware of the existence of many points of view and of how different roles are assumed in different situations.

It should be noted that the interpersonal development levels described above should be viewed as part of a continuum. The successive steps described within the theory are seen as definable points along the continuum. Individuals are not classified at the level which presents their maximum capabilities under ideal conditions, but rather are categorized at the level which represents their typical functioning or their capacity to function under conditions of stress.

WORKER STYLES

In order to give an idea of the contrasting features which set apart the

Probation Officers who work with each of the subtypes of delinquent youngsters, two contrasting worker styles are described below. These are summarized from Palmer's (1965) descriptions.

The level 3 youngster who has an immature conforming response set, responds with immediate compliance to whoever seems to have power at the moment and, sees himself as rather inferior to most other children his or her age. They do not feel strongly committed to a set of internalized standards.

Individuals who work well with these youths are rather reticent in contrast to being outspoken. Their interactions with others are marked by an atmosphere of calm. They convey mildness as opposed to force and drive. This might be misinterpreted as pacivity since their response to most situations is one of underplaying rather than over-dramatizing the emotional elements. They are usually even tempered and predictable and tend to be non-competitive individuals. In nearly all of their interactions they go out of their way to avoid direct confrontation and open challenge. They feel that those approaches are seldom appropriate and ordinarily humiliating to those who would be on the receiving end of things. Compared with other workers these individuals have usually come from a secure and moderately sheltered upbringing. They are not usually in touch with the jargon and all the latest goings on within the adolescent world. These treaters work towards developing a very strong dependency relationship and usually see this kind of relationship as a necessary prelude to any subsequent expectations. They are able to feel the emotional state of their clients and empathize on non-verbal cues. They tend to have an action orientation.

The youth at maturity level 4 who has a neurotic acting out response set, responds to underlying guilt with attempts to outrun or avoid conscious anxiety and condemnation of self. This type of child prefers to hide personal problems and projects an image of personal adequacy in autonomy.

As a group those who work best with these youngsters are quick thinking, alert and rather forceful individuals. They are internally oriented and comfortable with their identity as therapist. Most often these people are very tuned in to the world of these children and have high credibility in adolescent terms without being adolescents themselves. They tend to have a high degree of firmness of finality about their work. Relative to most adults they are very resourceful and can usually come up with one more place to which to turn. They usually have had an upbringing which is not particularly sheltered and could be said to have had considerable "life experience". They are conscious of hidden or double messages that can be present in verbal communications and are not reticent when it comes to describing and evaluating most of the things they see going on around them. While some adults might find these workers to be opinionated and somewhat hard to get along with, many adolescents look upon them as people who have an interesting story to tell about what adult and late adolescence can be like, along with numerous coping techniques.

CRITIQUES

A number of critiques of the I-Level theory and its research applications have appeared in the literature. Zaidel (1970) questioned the construct validity of I-Level classification. She carried out studies which indicated that the means of assessment, that is, the semi-structured interview, tended to place children with lower intelligence quotients and less verbal facility into the lower levels. However, Zaidel did not make further inferences as to whether the treatment methods designated for the lower levels would be inappropriate for these children. Since differential treatment is not implied on the basis of these factors, the present study did not systemize them as independent variables.

Austin (1975) notes that a youngster's moral orientation makes a significant contribution to the I-Level classification. He suggests that if this factor were given more weight than interpersonal relationships, a more optimal benefit might be realized from differential treatment as applied by the Community Treatment Project.

Gottfredson (1972) questions whether a developmental approach to personality uses a broad enough base of information to be useful for treatment planning. He would give more weight to social and economic factors. He does indicate that I-Level is a step towards increasing integration of psychological and sociological viewpoints in the area of classification.

Robison and Smith (1971) alleged that biases existed across experimental and control groups in the collection of recidivism data in the CTP studies. This criticism was based on the observation that the parole agents collected this data themselves and could exercise individual judgments on technical violations. The same writers also noted that the methodological requirement of random assignment to experimental and alternate treatment groups was not met (in the projects dealing with adults). However, the non-random assignment criticism does not hold for the CTP juvenile studies.

Robison and Smith concluded their review by stating that the most important determinant of treatment outcome was the existence of ideological belief in the effectiveness of the program by program staff. They do not elaborate as to whether this effect was the result of non-random parole officer selection or a result of the demand characteristics of the experiment. In any event, this differentially operating (placebo) effect is not difficult to control. They also object to the fact that most parole failures occurred as a result of parole agent casework decisions, that is, technical violations initiated by the parole agent. They were of the opinion that agents in the experimental group used less rigorous standards than those used by agents in the control group. They also indicate that the control group was not supervised as closely. Whereas smaller caseload sizes were intended in the CTP studies, the observed differences in technical violation rates were not intended, and probably represent the influence of the confounding variable, such as differential criteria across groups.

DIFFERENTIAL TREATMENT APPLIED

At the time this research was done the I-Level approach to classification and treatment had been introduced and implemented in Manitoba with juvenile probationers. This had been done over the previous four years but on a somewhat more limited scale than in California. Since this treatment program had not been fully instituted there was latitude to set up an experimental situation (assignment to different treatments) to examine the effectiveness of I-Level treatment. The study employed an experimental design which attempted to correct for the criticisms noted earlier.

The study used Probation Officers (POs) who had training in I-Level theory and treatment methods as treatment agents for both the control and experimental groups. Caseload size was held constant across the experimental group and one of the control groups. Recidivism data was collected at a different source than was done in the CTP studies, that is, from Court adjudications of delinquency rather than from probation agent reports of recidivism. The CTP studies restricted admission of offenders to those with offences against property. The present study made no such restriction.

The hypothesis for this research is that probation outcome for juveniles is enhanced by the following sequential set of operation: (a) the differential classification of offenders as to the meaning of their crime (in psychogenic terms), (b) the matching of worker styles of probation officers with the classification of the juvenile, and (c) the use of the I-Level treatment program which involves treating the various delinquent subtypes differently.

The study focused on three dependent measures of probation outcome, namely, decrease in recidivism, change in self concept score, and stability measured by school or work attendance. Research by Rose (1966), Palmer (1967), Akman and Normandeau (1975), suggests that the simple comparison of treatment groups as to the number of reinvolvements in delinquency is too gross a measure. Gendreau and Leipeiger (1978) point out that the use of recidivism as an outcome measure based on all or none criteria of success/failure does not fit the reality of criminal histories and has also contributed to the "nothing works" doctrine current in criminal justice. They support the suggestion that recidivism be conceptualized as multi-dimensional with different probabilities associated with different individuals. This study follows Palmer's suggestion that the original delinquency be assigned a severity score which is then compared to the severity score of any subsequent reinvolvement. By this means qualitative differences among offences are taken into account, relative seriousness as well as frequency of the delinquent behavior were included as variables making up the recidivism measure.

One of the personality characteristics considered to be of importance to delinquency prediction and outcome is self-concept (e.g., Gendreau, Grant and Leipciger, 1979.) The self-concept research reviewed extensively by Fitts and Hamner (1969), suggests that the more optimal the individual's self-concept, the more effectively that individual will function. Extensive testing within the delinquent population indicates that actively delinquent children report dissatisfaction with both their behavior and with themselves as persons. Continued delinquent behavior results in further decreases in self-concept scores whereas lower recidivism rates are reported for those whose self-concept improves. Thus there is precedent for the use of self-concept score as an outcome variable.

METHOD

From November 1973 to March 1974 all male juveniles (12–17 years) defined as delinquent under the Juvenile Delinquents Act and who received a Court disposition of "Probation supervision" from the Winnipeg and St. Boniface Juvenile Courts were randomly assigned to three treatment groups.

The research design was a randomized (single factor) three group design with a restriction on the assignment of treatments to subjects in order to ensure an equal number of subjects in each treatment group.

The three levels of treatment were, I-Level treatment, alternate treatment, and surveillance treatment. The last group was meant to control for the effective probation contact as a function of caseload size, as well as any lack of distinction that might have existed between the actual treatment received by the I-Level and alternate treatment groups. Since all Probation Officers had received training in the experimental treatment method, the groups might not have been mutually exclusive as to treatment modality in that the P.O.'s supervising juveniles in the alternate treatment group might intuitively diagnose and treat by I-Level criteria.

The dependent variables were: (a) self concept as measured by the Tennessee Self Concept Scale, (b) recidivism as measured by latency of reinvolvement and change in seriousness of offences over time, (c) stability of functioning as measured by days of school and/or work attendance. The study looked at the effects of six months of probation supervision with regard to variables (a) and (c) and initially measured variable (b) over a 12-month period. This research was originally reported in 1976 when recidivism data was only available for a one year period (Barkwell, 1976). At this time, data on recidivism from the three years following the Court disposition is included.

I-Level classification was made on the basis of a tape recorded interview (semi-structured) in which the youth is questioned about his delinquent involvement, family, friends, school, and future plans. The interview was subsequently rated according to sets of descriptive statements considered characteristic of each level. This interview rating questionnaire (IRQ) has 71 descriptive measures for level, and 54 descriptive measures for subtype. The IRQ is found in Palmer's CTP research series. Reliability coefficients for inter-observer agreement were calculated using Bijou's (1969) method of calculation. The worker style was assessed by use of the guidelines provided in Palmer's (1967), No. 1) CTP Report Series.

PROCEDURE

Subsequent to Court disposition, all juveniles placed on probation were randomly assigned to one of the three treatment groups until each group reached a total of 16. All cases were transferred within one week from the PO doing initial social assessment to the district probation team. District probation units are geographically determined and each one is supervised by a senior probation officer.

Upon assignment to the I-Level treatment group the probationers were given the diagnostic interview by the Co-ordinator of I-Level. Independent IRQ ratings were then completed by the Co-ordinator and the District senior probation officer.

Following the I-Level designation the youths were assigned to the probation officer in the district team whose worker style characteristics best fit the youngster's need as determined by I-Level assessment. Worker styles were determined by having two people at the supervisory level rate each Probation Officer. The youths assigned to this group entered medium intensity caseloads (caseloads comprised of 30–40 clients). I-Level treatment methods were used as outlined by Warren and Palmer with casework supervision provided by the District senior probation officer. There was access to the I-Level Co-Ordinator for consultation. Expectation for contact with the client was a minimum of four times per month.

The youths in the alternate treatment group had their supervision assigned within the district teams without I-Level diagnosis. These probationers were also assigned to medium intensity caseloads. Casework consultation was provided by Forensic Services (a psychiatrist and psychologist). Where I-Level diagnosis is not available the usual criteria for case assignments are: the current caseload compositions of the POs in the district; the presenting problem (delinquency) and; other information outlined in the social history. The senior probation officer weighs all these factors and assigns the juvenile to the PO in his district whom he feels is most appropriate to undertake supervision. Thus criteria for assignment would vary from district to district. Oftentimes assignment is made on a rotation basis in order to keep caseloads within the district at an equal numerical level. This group was considered to be receiving random alternate treatment since the treatment approach could not be described as being the result of a single objectified philosophy of treatment. Contact expectation for the alternate treatment group was a minimum of four times per month.

The surveillance group was assigned to caseloads of sixty or more clients. These caseloads are considered to provide minimal treatment supervision because of reduced contact (and planning) time due to restrictions imposed by the size of the caseload. However, expectation (or demand upon the juvenile) was equalized between this control group and the other two treatment groups.

The juvenile appeared in court, was placed on probation (labelled), expected to report to a probation officer and remain delinquency tree, but was not involved in complex treatment planning. Contact was maintained at four times per month through the use of volunteer involvement or supplemental contact by probation aides.

The subjects of all groups completed the Tennessee Self Concept scale prior to random assignment and were retested six months from the date of the original test (the manual for the scale indicates a test-retest reliability of .92). The tests were administered by the author. Test instruction was standardized by use of the printed instructions which accompany the scale. Following Rosenthal's (1966, 1969) suggestion for reducing evaluation apprehension the experiment was defined for each probationer in such a way that he was led to feel that the experimenter was not so much interested in the results of the individual as he was in the scores obtained by groups.

The data on delinquency at intake (point of referral) and any subsequent recidivism over the following 3 years was taken from the probationer's legal files. Delinquencies were only recorded where a court finding of an offence had been adjudicated. Latency was measured from the date of the occurrence of delinquency resulting in probation, to the date of the reinvolvement, rather than the date of Court disposition.

As noted previously, delinquencies were given a weighted score (cf. Barkwell, 1976). These severity of offence scores were ranked on the basis of level of aggression (physical harm including death inflicted, physical harm threatened but not carried out, no infliction or threat of physical harm) in combination with the type of violation, e.g. indictable offence, non-indictable offence, misdemeanor, or violation of a provincial or municipal statute.

By comparing the relative severity of any subsequent reinvolvement in delinquent acts a more sensitive measure is obtained. For example, the youth placed on probation for housebreaking and reinvolved in a drinking offence would show progress in terms of reduction in severity of offence, whereas simple categorization as recidivist does not reflect the reality of the situation.

The data for days of school and / or work attendance was collected directly from the school or employer in terms of number of days per month over six months.

The study was essentially double blind in that the probationers and their supervising POs were not aware of the hypothesis that was tested or the particular measures that were used (except the self concept measure). A slight ruse was used to achieve this end. The supervising POs were told that the aim of the project was to study changes in self concept in a number of juveniles newly placed on probation. In order to maximize the double blind condition communication of the author's hypothesis through communication from the Senior Probation Officer to supervising Probation Officers was cautioned against.

RESULTS

On each of the dependent measures two planned orthogonal comparisons were of interest: (1) C1 between the I-Level treatment group and the two alternate groups evaluated the specific effects of I-Level procedure, (2) C2 between the alternate and surveillance groups evaluated effects due to caseload size and more than minimal treatment planning.

The results regarding self concept improvement scores are of particular interest since the effects of matching worker style to delinquent subtype would be expected to influence this variable in the I-Level treatment group. In the control groups where random matching took place one would expect the gains from advantageous (random) matches to be cancelled or masked by the negative effects of (random) mismatches with regard to worker style and delinquent subtype. There was no significant differences and among the three groups on pre-test self-concept scores.

The self concept difference scores (positive increase) of the I-Level group were significantly higher than those of the control groups. The effect group was 18.06 while the alternate treatment group had a mean increase of 4.43. The surveillance group had a decrease in self concept of 1.24. The post-test on self concept for the I-Level group was significantly higher than the scores obtained on the pre-test, whereas the alternate treatment group change in this same direction was not significant. The surveillance group change in self concept scores was in terms of a mean decrease which did not reach significance.

The self concept difference scores (positive increase) of the I-Level group were significantly higher than those of the control groups. The effect was significant at the .025 level of probability and the proportion of the effect attributable to the differential manipulation (omega squared) was .09 (see Table 1). The self concept difference scores of the control groups were not significantly different from one another.

TABLE 1

Summary of the Analysis of the Self Concept Difference Scores

	Source	SS	df	MS	F
	Treatment	(3152)*	(2)		
C_1	Between I-Level * Controls	2893	1	2893	5.58
C_2	Between Controls	259	1	259	0.50
	Error Within	233302	45	517.7	
	Total	26454	47		

Constant of 100 added to each difference score to eliminate negative scores.

REDUCTION OF DELINQUENCY

Reduction in severity of delinquent involvement can be regarded as the most important criteria in a corrections program. All other factors can show gains but such gains are easily discounted if accompanied by an increase in delinquent behavior.

As can be seen from Table 2, the severity of delinquent involvement for the I-Level group was lower than that of the two control groups. This trend was consistent over the 36 month follow-up. This effect in favor of the I-Level group was statistically reliable. The data were analysed with a trend analysis of variance and the decrease in delinquency severity over months (Treatment X Trials Interation) was significant ($F = 3.54$, $p < .001$, see Table 3).

TABLE 2

Sum of Severity Scores for Groups in Each Successive 6 Month Block

Months	1–6	7–12	13–18	19–24	25–30	31–36
I-Level	53	50	25	22	16	0
Alternate	110	64	92	110	34	18
Surveillance	56	84	98	23	11	36

TABLE 3

Summary of the Analysis of the Severity of Recidivism Scores

Source	SS	df	MS	F
Treatments	60	2	30	2.25 (ns)
Error a)	598	45	13.3	
Trials (Months)	268	35	7.1	1.24 (ns)
Treatment & Trial	1417	70	20.2	3.54
Error b)	9040	1575	5.7	
Total	11383	1727		

Table 4 shows the percentage of clients reinvolved in delinquency on a group by group basis within each six month period for the three years of follow-up.

The difference in latency of delinquent reinvolvement between the I-Level and control groups did not reach significance ($F = 3.8$, df 1/45, $p < .05$), and the control groups were not significantly different, either.

TABLE 4

Percentage of Recidivist Juveniles in Groups for Each Successive 6 Month Block

Months	1–6	7–12	13–18	19–24	25–30	31–36
I-Level	31%	37%	31%	19%	12%	0%
Alternate	50%	44%	25%	19%	12%	19%
Surveillance	56%	69%	44%	25%	37%	12%

SCHOOL AND/OR WORK ATTENDANCE

The measurement of school and work attendance was of interest since this measure is indicative of the stability and predictability of behavior. Over six months, the mean number of days of attendance of the I-Level group was significantly higher than the means of the control groups. This difference was significant at the .025 level of probability, whereas the means scores of the control groups did not differ significantly on this variable (see Table 5).

TABLE 5

Summary of the Analysis of the School/Work Attendance Scores

	Source	SS	df	MS	F
	Treatments	(292.9)	(2)		
C_1	Between I-Level				
	& Controls	252.85	1	252.85	
C_2	Between Controls	40.05	1	40.05	6.209
	Error Within	1832.42	45	40.72	0.98
	Total	2125.32	47		

The I-Level group had a mean of 17.1 days attendance per month. The alternate group had a mean of 12.1 days per month, and the surveillance group had a mean of 9.88 days attendance per month. Figure 3 depicts the cumulative days of attendance as a function of the number of months on probation. The slopes of the line differ and indicate different rates of attendance both within and between groups.

The reliability coefficients for the interview rating questionnaires were calculated at .92 for level and .84 for subtype.

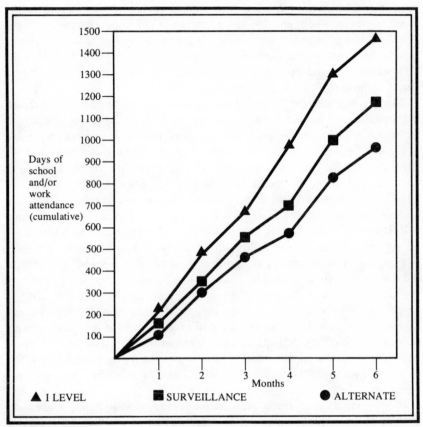

Figure 3

DISCUSSION

The I-Level treatment appears to enhance performance on the three dependent variables. These differences cannot be attributed to caseload size since the same caseload size held for both I-Level and alternate treatment groups. Nor can the differences be attributed to the demand characteristics of the study since it was essentially double blind with regard to the supervising POs and the probationers. The data on PO characteristics indicate that there were no great differences in characteristics such as years of experience or education. It would, therefore, appear that the observed differences resulted from the sequential set of operations subsumed under I-Level treatment.

These findings support the outcomes reported by Palmer (1968, 1971) and Warren (1969). Their findings are extended and given increased external validity since a different (and higher) level of caseload size was used in the comparison. Internal validity problems were corrected by use of a comparison group within caseloads equal in size to these of the I-Level treatment groups. The study has additional import since admission to the three treatment groups was not restricted to offenders against property as done in Phase I and II of the CTP studies. Instead, it included more dangerous offenders, thus encompassing a wider range of offence categories.

The I-Level treatment group did not show significant difference with regard to latency of delinquent reinvolvement. However, the group means do indicate a difference in the predicted direction. The recidivism data presented in Figures 1 and 2 gives credence to the arguments put forward by Fisher and Erickson (1973). They state the recidivism data is only meaningful if trends are analyzed after the point of intervention. The fact that cumulated recidivism rates steadily increase over time does not necessarily reflect a lack of intervention effectiveness. When the percentages of recidivism are calculated in 6 month blocks, these show a downward trend which would not be apparent if the 3 year follow-up period were considered as a whole. Although the I-Level group did significantly better than the other two groups, there were *obvious intervention effects for all groups*. After being placed on probation there was an immediate drop across groups of 64 to 83% in severity of delinquent activity when compared to the prior 6 month period. Likewise, for each six month block significant numbers of probationers were remaining free of any delinquent reinvolvement. In both instances the trends were in a positive direction for all 3 groups over the 3 year period. The effect in the I-Level group was, however; much more immediate, dramatic, and persistent.

In reporting these figures a qualification is necessary. In the area where the study was done, probation supervision is viewed as a residual service and many diversion programs are in operation. Therefore, none of the juveniles placed into the three treatment groups were first offenders, although all of the youths were first time probationers. For this reason the non-recidivist results and proportion of the effects attributable to the differential manipulation can be given more weight than one would attribute to the same results in a study dealing with first offenders.

The graphic representation of school and work attendance shows that the attendance rate is set early in the probation period with a slight reduction in rate occurring through time. Since the days of school attendance makes up the greater part of the mean score on this measure this deterioration effect was not unexpected and appears to be a function of school dropouts. This effect would be expected to become more pronounced as the school year progressed.

The results of the study are consistent with the concept of masked effects. Overall, there may be a relationship between reduced severity, delay in reinvolvement, and enhanced self image. A mixed factorial design and analysis would have the potential for revealing such relations and possible interactions.

The results would suggest that the more intensive the treatment contact, the more essential it becomes to match worker style characteristics with delinquent sub-type. In practical terms the classified matched cases (I-Level) did better than surveillance cases who in turn performed better than medium intensity unclassified cases. In most agencies the last level of treatment is most frequently offered, yet it may be the least effective, and the most expensive related to return in investment. From this study it would seem that cases deemed to require moderate to intensive supervision should all be classified and matched. If a case is not given a full I-Level work-up, a minimum intensity (surveillance) assignment would appear to be most appropriate.

I-Level is a classification system which provides a profile of the offender, prescribes a treatment approach, and advocates the matching of offender sub-type to workers with definable interpersonal style. A similar approach to dealing with the problems of "uniformity assumptions" has been described by Kiesler (1966, 1969) in regard to the practice of psychotherapy. The major implication of both approaches is that worker style must be specified as a variable since it relates to the outcome of the application of a particular treatment method. When a more specific and complex treatment oriented profile is provided the assigned and matched worker can commence treatment more effectively, focusing on the problems and strengths as outlined. I-Level provides a description of the offender's self-image, and prescribes a treatment plan to enhance self-image. Many methods that would be inappropriate for a particular sub-type are identified by I-Level thus helping workers to avoid ineffective or even dangerous methods of treatment.

REFERENCES

Adams, S., "Evaluating correctional treatment", *Criminal Justice & Behavior*, 1977, *4*(4), 323–339.

Austin, R.L., "Construct validity of I-Level classification," *Criminal Justice & Behavior*, 1975, *2*(2), 113–125.

Barkwell, L.J., "Differential treatment of juveniles on probation: an evaluative study," *Canadian Journal of Criminology & Corrections*, 1976, *18*(4), 363–378.

Barkwell, L. and Hammond, A., "A discussion of learning disabilities and their relationship to delinquency," Paper presented at the Canadian Congress of Criminology & Corrections, Calgary, Alberta, July 5, 1977.

Bijou, S. and Peterson, R., "Methodology for experimental studies of young children in natural settings," *Psychological Record*, 1969, *19*, 177–210.

Davis, J. and Cropley, A., "Psychological factors in juvenile delinquency," *Canadian Journal of Behavioural Science*, 1976, 8 (1), 68–77.

Fisher, G. and Ericson, M., "On Assessing the effect of official reactions to juvenile delinquency," *Journal of Research in Crime and Delinquency*, 1973, 177–194.

Fitts, W.H. and Hamner, W.T., "The self concept and delinquency," *Nashville Mental Health Center Monograph*, 1969, *8*.

Gendreau, P., Grant, B.A. and Leipeiger, M., "Self-esteem, incarceration, and recidivism," *Criminal Justice and Behavior*, 1979, *6*, 67–75.

Gendreau, P. and Leipeiger, M. "The development of a recidivism measure and its application in Ontario," *Canadian Journal of Criminology & Corrections*, 1978, *20*, 3–17.

Gottfredson, D.M., "Five challenges," *Journal of Research in Crime and Delinquency*, July 1972, 68–86.

Jesness, C.F. and Wedge, R.F., "Sequential I-Level classification manual," Report made to the Institute for the Study of Crime and Delinquency, August 1970.

Jesness, C.F., "The Preston typology study: an experiment with differential treatment in an institution," *Journal of Research in Crime & Delinquency*, 1971, *2*(1) 38–52.

Kiesler, D.J., "Some myths of psychotherapy research and the search for a paridigm," *Psychological Bulletin*, 1966, *65*(2), 110–136.

Kiesler, D.J., "A grid model for theory and research in the psychotherapies," *Practice in Psychotherapy* (Chicago: Aldine Press, 1969).

Kiesler, D.J., "Experimental designs in psychotherapy research." In A. Bergin & S. Garfield (eds), *Handbook of Psychotherapy and Behavior Change* (New York: John Wiley & Sons, 1971).

Moos, R.H., *Evaluating Correctional and Community Settings* (New York: John Wiley & Sons, 1975).

Palmer, T.B., "Types of treators & types of juvenile offenders," *Youth Authority Quarterly*, 1965, *18*, 14–23.

Palmer, T.B., "Personality characteristics and professional orientations of five groups of community treatment project workers: A preliminary report on differences among treaters," *Community Treatment Report Series*, 1967, *1*.

Palmer, T.B., "Recent research findings and long range developments at the community treatment project." *Community Treatment Project Research Report*, No. 9, Part 2, October 1968.

Palmer, T.B., "A Demonstration Project: An Evaluation of Differential Treatment for Delinquents." California Human Relations Agency, Department of the Youth Authority, State of California, 1969.

Palmer, T.B., "California's community treatment program for delinquent adolescents," *Journal of Research in Crime and Delinquency*, January 1971, 79–92.

Robison, J. and Smith G., "The effectiveness of correctional programs," *Crime and Delinquency*, 1971, *17*(1) 67–80.

Rose, G.N.G., "Concerning the measurement of delinquency," *The British Journal of Criminology*, 1966, *6*, 414–422.

Rosenthal, R., *Experimenter Effects in Behavioral Research* (New York: Appleton-Century-Crofts, 1966).

Rosenthal, R., "Interpersonal expectations: Effects of the experimenters hypothesis," In Rosenthal, R. and Rosnon, R.L. (eds), *Artefact and Behavioral Research* (New York: Academic Press, 1969.

Warren, M.Q., "The Case for Differential Classification of Delinquents," *The Annals of the American Academy of Political and Social Science*, January 1969, 381.

Warren, M.Q., "Action Research as a Change Model for Corrections." Paper presented to the Fourth National Symposium on Law Enforcement Science and Technology, Washington, D.C., May 2, 1972.

Wolfensberger, W., *"Program Analysis of Service Systems"* (Toronto: NIMR, 1975).

Zaidel, S.F., "Intelligence and Affect Awareness in Classifying Delinquents," *Journal of Research in Crime and Delinquency*, January 1973, 47–58.

Chapter 17

Editors' Remarks

The Kentfields program is included because it is a good demonstration of the possibility of treating hard-core chronic delinquents successfully in their own homes. The following article suggests that such youths can be treated through a comprehensive and multi-facetted service: employment, education (with programmed instruction), contingency contracting, and behaviorally oriented group sessions. A major accomplishment of the Kentfields program is that it engenders not only the *acceptance* of the community and the court but their *active* participation and enthusiastic support. In working with such high-risk and high-profile clients the endorsement of the community is absolutely essential not only to the success of the treatment program but to its continuation.

In this chapter Davidson and Robinson describe the program and its outcome during an eighteen month follow-up. That the positive results of intervention are not merely short-term benefits is demonstrated in the following chapter which describes a ten-year follow-up of the Kentfields program.

Community Psychology and Behavior Modification: A Community Based Program for the Prevention of Delinquency*

William S. Davidson II and Michael J. Robinson

Contemporary developments in strategy for the prevention and treatment of juvenile delinquency have found two parallel but relatively independent avenues of promise: community based rather than institutional interventions, and behavior modification. While such avenues each seem prospectively worthwhile, proponents of these two approaches have tended to ignore one another, with the possible exception of Sarason and Ganzer[1] and Tharp and Wetzel[2]. Whether for reasons of polemic or for more scientifically defensible

---

This project was supported by the County of Kent, Michigan. Funds were administered by the Kent County Juvenile Court, Grand Rapids, Michigan. This manuscript was submitted in partial fulfillment of the requirements for the Master of Arts degree to the University of Illinois at Urbana-Champaign. The authors wish to express appreciation for assistance and encouragement to Roger Lewis, Judge John Steketee, Judge Richard Loughrin; to Robert D. O'Connor, of the University of Colorado, for invaluable consultation of the operation of the program; to Julian Rappaport and Edward Seidman, of the University of Illinois, for critical reading of the manuscript; to Lynne A. Davidson for preparation of included figures and support throughout.

[1]Sarason, I.G., and Ganzer, V.J., "Social influence techniques in clinical and community psychology." In C.D. Spielberger (Ed.), *Current Topics in Clinical and Community Psychology* (New York: Academic Press, 1969).

[2]Tharp, R.G., and Wetzel, R.J., *Behavior Modification in the Natural Environment* (New York: Academic Press, 1969).

another. Whether for reasons of polemic or for more scientifically defensible reasons, researchers in the behavior modification camp have tended to ignore the community psychology movement, while community psychologists have frequently failed to make use of the conceptual and technological advances in behavior modification. Interestingly, each of these two independent movements has had its beginnings in a climate of dissatisfaction with the medical model of psychological treatment. The problems with a medical model are well known and need no rehash here. However, what is frequently overlooked is the fact that many who, on the one hand reject the medical model, on the other hand fail to develop a viable alternative to it.

Rappaport and Chinsky[3] have distinguished between two components in any model for delivery of services: the conceptual component and the style of delivery component. Behavior modification oriented psychologists frequently reject the medical conception of psychological treatment while retaining the medical style of service delivery. For example, many behavior modifiers conceptualize psychological disturbance in non-medical terms, but continue to see clients in their private offices, clinics, and hospitals within a doctor-patient relationship. At the same time, while focusing on environmental contingencies in conceptualizing the problem of delinquency, they fail to deal directly with the legal system. Conversely, community psychologists are frequently critical of this doctor-patient, in the office style of delivery, but continue to use traditional medical model conceptions of psychopathology. While ostensibly rejecting the medical model in favor of an environmental contingency conception, few community psychologists have taken advantage of the most fully developed psychological conception of the environment: behavior modification. This paper demonstrates a viable bringing together of the community psychology and behavior modification approaches within one problem area: the prevention and treatment of juvenile delinquency.

To date, most rehabilitation efforts for hard core male delinquent populations, though well intended, have called for large expenditures of money, with less than optimal results.[4] While the principles and techniques of behavior modification have, in general, demonstrated effectiveness in treatment of a wide variety of disorders,[5] specific attempts to apply a behavioral approach to delinquency have been limited. Yates[6] reports that a

---

[3]Rappaport, J., and Chinsky, J.M., *Models for the delivery of service: A Historical and Conceptual Perspective* (Professional Psychology, 1974, in press).

[4]James, H., *Children in Trouble: A National Scandal* (Boston: Christian Science Publishing Society, 1969).

[5]Ullmann, L.P., and Krasner, L., *A Psychological Approach to Abnormal Behavior* (Englewood Cliffs: Prentice Hall, 1969). Franks, C.L., *Behavior Therapy: Appraisal and Status* (New York: McGraw-Hill, 1969). Ulrich, R., Stachnik, T., and Mabry, J., *Control of Human Behavior* (Glenville: Scott, Foresman, 1970).

[6]Yates, A.J., *Behavior Therapy* (New York: John Wiley, 1970).

symposium held in 1965 to discuss the application of behavior therapy to delinquency was restricted exclusively to theoretical issues. Since that time, research has been limited in scope, except for educational interventions generally considered critical to successful rehabilitation.[7] Other interventions reported to date include demonstration of token economy effectiveness,[8] examination of natural reinforcement systems,[9] and enhancement of parole success,[10] all within institutional settings. A number of programs have achieved excellent success with delinquent youth in community based settings.[11] However, they have not conceived their interventions in a behavioral framework.

Nevertheless, a conceptual model for behavioral interventions in the natural environment has been suggested by Tharp and Wetzel.[12] Research utilizing behavioral techniques in community settings include shaping interview attendance and content in a street corner project,[13] increasing self-care and academic performance in a family style residential program for pre-delinquents,[14] and training parents to reduce deviant behavior in their children.[15]

The program to be discussed here had as its focus four problem areas: (1) to

---

[7]Cohen, H.L., "Educational therapy: The design of learning environments," *Research in Psychotherapy*, 1968, *3*, 21–33. Bednar, R.J., Zelhart, P.R., Greathouse, L., and Weinberg, S., "Operant conditioning principles in the treatment of learning and behavioral problems with delinquent boys," *Journal of Counseling Psychology*, 1970, *17*, 492–497. Meichenbaum, D.H., Bowers, K.S., and Ross, R.R., "Modification of classroom behavior of institutionalized female offenders," *Behavior Research and Therapy*, (1968), *6*, 343–353.

[8]Burchard, J.D., "Systematic Socialization: A programmed environment for the habilitation of antisocial retardates," *Psychological Record*, (1967), *17*, 461–476.

[9]Buehler, R.E., Patterson, F.R., and Furness, J.M., "The Reinforcement of Behavior in Institutional Settings," *Behavior Research and Therapy*, 1966, *4*, 157–167.

[10]Petrock, F.A., and Elias, A., "A Summary of the Readjustment Unit Program," (Bordentown, New Jersey: 1969, Mimeographed).

[11]Goldenberg, I., *Build Me a Mountain* (Cambridge: M.I.T. Press, 1971). Klein, W.L., "The training of human service aides." In E.L. Cowen, E.A. Gardner, and M. Zax (Eds.), *Emergent Approaches to Mental Health Problems* (New York: Appleton-Century-Crofts, 1967).

[12]Tharp and Wetzel, *op. cit. supra* note 2.

[13]Schwitzgebel, R.L., "Preliminary socialization for psychotherapy of behavior disordered adolescents," *Journal of Consulting and Clinical Psychology*, 1969, *33*, 71–77.

[14]Phillips, E.L., Phillips, E.A., Fixsen, D., and Wolf, M.M., "Achievement place: Modification of the behaviors of pre-delinquent boys within a token economy," *Journal of Applied Behavior Analysis*, 1971, *4*, 45–59.

[15]Patterson, G.R., Ray, R.S., and Shaw, D.A., "Direct Intervention in Families of Deviant Children," (Eugene, Oregon: Oregon Research Institute, 1969. Mimeographed).

provide a community based, non-residential program as an alternative to institutionalization for hard core male offenders; (2) to increase prosocial behavior in the target population; (4) to reduce the monetary expenditure required for treatment of chronic juvenile offenders. Before turning to an explicit description of the methods utilized, it is important to describe the social setting in which the program was initiated.

SOCIAL CONDITIONS

The Kent County Juvenile Court, in Grand Rapids, Michigan, began administering the Kentfields Rehabilitation Program in 1969. Prior to that time the Court had been institutionalizing large numbers of chronic male offenders. Such a strategy was costing large amounts of money and bringing less than desirable results.

There were many sources of resistance to a non-residential community based program for hard core delinquents. Many of the objections centered around keeping "those kinds of kids" in the community. It is to be remembered that this project was initiated at the high point in the nationwide campaign for "law and order." Primary resistances were centered around the police departments, school administrations, and local governmental officials. The police objected to the Court "mollycoddling" offenders and not forcing them to take full responsibility for their actions. The school had been generally quite satisfied when the subjects with which Kentfields dealt were removed from the community. Now they were being asked to re-enroll and deal with these young men after they had completed Kentfields. The local governmental officials were highly resistant to any further expenditures of tax dollars for new programs which had no guaranteed outcome.

In overcoming such resistances, a number of strategies were implemented. First, a great deal of effort was put into providing the two juvenile court judges with information about the program's potential. Here there was a substantial behavior modification literature to draw upon. Once convinced, the judges were both active in local and state political arenas and utilized their personal influence in convincing community leaders of the need for the Kentfields endeavor. Second, the Director of Court Services, the administrative parallel of the judges, was personally committed to a community-based behavioral approach and to convincing the governmental bodies of its efficiency and effectiveness. He was instrumental in providing local officials with the information and rationale for supporting a community-based behavioral approach. Third, constant efforts were made to provide concerned individuals with monthly, quarterly, and annual reports about the program's progress. In this instance, the local media, T.V., and newspapers were helpful in dissemination of progress data. Their interest was both in the experimental nature of the project and coverage of what had become, at least during the early months, a politically hot issue. Fourth, every effort was made throughout the project to cooperate with other community agencies. This is not to say that at many times our goals were not diametrically opposed to those of other social and educational agencies. However, through consistant contact, both social and professional, cooperative efforts were maintained. The fifth strategy involved one of the program components. The work projects, to be described in detail later, had excellent public relations value. Part of the rationale for initiating the community based approach was that local municipalities and the county would receive partial payback for their investments. Such information was included in program reports and communications.

METHOD

SUBJECTS

From September 1, 1969 through August 31, 1971, 131 males were considered for long term institutional placement by the Kent County Juvenile Court due to chronic delinquency. Of the 131, 125 were referred to the Kentfields Program as an alternative. The remaining six were sent directly to institutions because of serious crimes against persons. All 125 subjects were accepted. Thus, no special criteria for admission were in effect.

An average subject was 16 years of age (range 14 to 17 years), and tended to live in the inner-city area of Grand Rapids, Michigan (80%). Approximately 60% of the target population were non-whites. The subjects had been on probation to the Kent County Juvenile Court a mean of 2.6 years (range two months to seven years).

PROGRAM DESCRIPTION

The Kentfields Program consisted of a contingency point system, utilized in the areas of work performance, academic performance, and appropriate verbalizations in group sessions. The subjects lived in their own homes and were picked up by bus five mornings per week. Each morning, for three hours, the group engaged in various public works projects in the community. These included: tree trimming for local park departments, litter removal for the county highway department, spreading wood chips around playground equipment for the board of education, painting camp buildings for the YMCA and building renovation for the local Community Action Programs. Specific individual and group tasks were established each hour, with specific point payoff for successful performance. The work projects were run by a nonprofessional, who was taking undergraduate courses part time. Lunch was provided by the program. Again, contingencies for various self-care performances were in effect during the lunch period.

The afternoon classroom consisted of individualized (by grade performance level) programmed instruction and performance contracts, which involved contingencies for accurate performance, for three hours per day. At the beginning of the educational session each student was given an outline of the specific tasks, and contingencies, to be completed each hour. Special activities were also provided, including plays and writing newspaper articles. The educational component was conducted by a teacher aide who had completed less than one full year of college. Space for the classroom was provided by a local community center.

Group sessions were held two afternoons per week, following the class, for approximately one hour. They were conducted by one of the upper level subjects, on an alternating basis, who asked each member to respond to a number of questions including: subject's positive accomplishments since the last meeting, personal problems for group solutions, each subject's status in the program, suggested program changes desired by each subject, things subjects would like to earn in the program, and open discussion. Specific contingencies were in effect for topic related responses.

The program included three hierarchial levels through which the subjects were required to move in order to graduate. When a subject entered Kentfields, he was at the "June Bug" level. He was required to perform at an 80% level in all performance areas for two consecutive weeks. After accomplishing the above, the subjects progressed to the "Junior" level where two consecutive weeks of 90% performance were required. The final level, called "Ace" required 100% performance for two weeks. As an "Ace," each subject also chose a goal, i.e., what he was going to do after graduation. Essentially, the options open included return to school or employment. Following this decision, the program director assisted the subjects in accomplishing their chosen goal.

The contingency point system was parallel to programs generally described as token economics[16] except that points were used. Table 1 outlines the contingencies and backup reinforcers used in Kentfields. There were no restrictions on what points could be exchanged for within the system described. In general, the point system can be characterized as an open system.[17] The teacher and work supervisor informed each subject of points earned immediately following each required performance, and current totals were reviewed on an hourly, daily, and weekly basis. Points could be exchanged on a daily and/or weekly basis.

---

[16]Ayllon, T., and Azrin, T., *The Token Economy* (New York: Appleton-Century-Crofts, 1968).

[17]Phillips, Phillips, Fixsen, and Wolf, *Op. cit. supra* note 14.

TABLE 1

Kentfields Point System

Performance	Points earned
A. On time for bus, attend full day	100/day
B. Assigned work task complete	50/hour
C. Entire group assigned work task complete	15/hour (bonus)
D. Extra work tasks complete	0 — 100/day (bonus)
E. Turning in all work tools	20/day
F. Lining up for lunch, washing hands	20/day
C. Cleaning lunch table	40/day
H. 0 — 100% correct on classwork	0 — 100/hour
I. Attending group sessions	25/day
J. Appropriate comments in group sessions	5/response

Privilege	Cost
A. Money	$.01/point
B. Merchandise	$.01/point
C. Recreation Activities (Bowling, roller skating, etc.)	200 points
D. Rock concert tickets	250 points
E. Movie tickets	200 points
F. Cigarettes	40 points
G. Candy, potato chips, etc.	15 points

DESIGN

Two kinds of data were necessary to evaluate the program in the context of both its community and behavior modification perspectives. The operant or behavior modification tradition requires observations of specific performance functionally related to the in-program contingency system. The community psychologist, in addition, must be interested in the follow-up effectiveness and institutional impact of the interventions utilized. Thus, pro and post data on all subjects were recorded.

It must be clearly stated at the outset that no comparison group was available for the outcome portion of this study. The subjects treated were the total population considered. This situation was demanded by the community served, and indeed is one of the "real world" problems the community psychologist-researcher must face. Thus, we have a single group time series analysis.[18] Quasi-control groups from other communities or earlier time

---

[18]Campbell, D.T., and Stanley, J.C., *Experimental and Quasi-Experimental Designs for Research* (Chicago: Rand McNally, 1963).

periods, though considered, failed to provide any legitimate comparison due to differences in court practices, community characteristics, and excessive use of long term institutional placement for similar populations. Thus, concommitant examination of any conjured control group was abandoned.

PRE AND POST MEASURES

Pre-program data were gathered through structured interviews with subjects and their families, examination of juvenile court records, interviews with respective probation officers, and examination of subjects' school records. The information included: (1) a global statement of subject's activity for the year prior to entering Kentfields — enrolled in school, employed, excluded from school, in a correctional institution, (2) length of time on probation, (3) number of police referrals to court (arrests), (4) attendance rate in school (if in school), (5) academic grade level performance measured by the Wide Range Achievement Test.[19]

Follow-up measures were taken an average of 18 months (range 2 to 26 months) after subject had completed Kentfields. The data, collected in a parallel fashion to the pre-program data, was gathered by the program director with the assistance of two Grand Valley State College students. The information was the same as the pre-measures, with the exception of time on probation, which was omitted. At follow-up, arrest rates were gathered from both juvenile court and adult court records since most subjects had reached age 17 and would have come under adult court jurisdiction if apprehended. In addition, a cost comparison of operating Kentfields, as opposed to institutional alternatives was accomplished.

A comparison was also made, at follow-up, of program graduates (96) and non-graduates (27). The reasons for 27 subjects being removed from the program before completion were: (1) being placed in other local educational programs ($N = 11$), (2) subject's family moved from the community ($N = 10$), (3) further law violations ($N = 6$). Generally, the subjects were removed within the first four weeks. Pre-measure comparison of the graduate and non-graduate groups found no significant differences on any of the measures utilized.

IN-PROGRAM MEASURES

Measures of subject's behavior while in the program consisted of the performance rates for each specified response set. These measures included:

---

[19]Jastak, J.F., and Jastak, S.R., "Wide Range Achievement Test," Los Angeles: Western Psychological Services, 1965, Manual).

(1) attendance performance rates of all subjects on Contingency A in Table 1, (2) work behavior — performance rates of all subjects on contingencies through G excluding bonuses, (3) classroom behavior — accuracy rates of all subjects on programmed instruction material, and (4) group sessions behavior — rates of all subjects appropriate verbal responses in group sessions of a criteria ten responses per meeting. The above data was drawn from the records of the contingency point system. In other words, the points earned were based on the observations concerning task completion and accuracy. The hourly point records then were the basis of in-program data. The program offered a senior level seminar with the Psychology Department of Grand Valley State College in Applied Behavioral Science. During ten school days in school year 1970–71, two of the college students independently kept hourly point records for all subjects in the program. Interjudge agreement between the two students and the program staff was 93%. Agreement was based on assignment of exactly the same number of opportunities to assign points. More specific data was collected for a one month period in order to examine the efficacy of the contingency point system utilized in the educational component. Selection of additional target educational behaviors to enable changes in contingencies resulted in examination of: (1) time in seat — percent of time sitting at designated desk, (2) study behavior — percent of time looking at school work, talking to teacher, or writing, (3) percent of accuracy on written classwork, and (4) rate of returning from five minute hourly breaks on time. Nineteen subjects were involved in this subexperiment representing the total program population during the four week period.

Observation techniques involved having two observers (Grand Valley State College psychology students) and the teacher each independently record the above behaviors. The class lasted three hours each day. The 180 minutes were divided into 36 five minute intervals and 12 of the 36 randomly selected each day as observation intervals. Also, an individual student was randomly selected for observation during each time interval. Interjudge agreement (agreements divided by total) was 93%. The observers used an observation sheet with the designated time intervals and subjects' names. Time in seat was recorded by using a hand stop watch. The observers were present in the classroom throughout each educational session included in the study. The experiment included five conditions:

Baseline   Two weeks prior to initiation of the systematic observations, classroom points were put on a non-contingent basis. The third week of non-contingent reinforcement served as baseline.

Manipulation #1   After five days of baseline, the subjects were informed by the teacher that they would receive points each hour on the basis of the percent correct of their classwork. In addition, the subjects earned 50 points for returning from all breaks on time. This condition was in effect four days.

Manipulation #2   The second experimental condition involved changing the contingencies so that an individual subject, by exhibiting study behavior, could earn points for the entire group. The teacher explained that each subject would be observed for some five minute interval. If he was studying for the entire interval he would earn points for everyone. The subjects were not told who would be observed when. The observers signalled the teacher when the group had received points for studying. The returning from break contingency remained in effect. This condition lasted four days.

Manipulation #3   The third manipulation was a return to the baseline condition. This is the A-B-A paradigm prescribed for demonstration of behavior control.[20] This reversal condition lasted two days.

Manipulation #4   The fourth experimental manipulation was parallel to condition two and lasted four days.

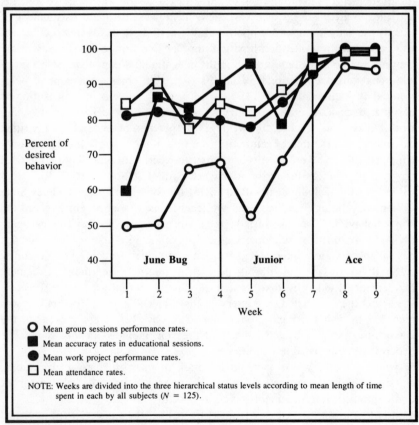

O Mean group sessions performance rates.

■ Mean accuracy rates in educational sessions.

● Mean work project performance rates.

□ Mean attendance rates.

NOTE: Weeks are divided into the three hierarchical status levels according to mean length of time spent in each by all subjects (*N* = 125).

Figure 1   *Mean Percent of Performance in Three Program Components by Mean Number of Weeks to Attain Graduation.*

[20]Sidman, M., *Tactics of Scientific Research* (New York: Basic Books, 1960).

RESULTS

PRE-DATA

The global measures of the subjects' activity for the year prior to Kentfields admission yielded the following: excluded from school — 48%; enrolled in school — 32%; in a correctional institution — 20%; employed — 0%. During the mean of 2.6 years on probation, each subject had committed a mean of 2.95 offenses per year with larceny, breaking and entering, and auto theft the most common. Of those enrolled in school, records indicated they had attended at a 69% rate for the year prior to Kentfields admission. Subjects tested at a mean grade level of 5.3 on the Wide Range Achievement Test.

IN-PROGRAM DATA

Program attendance demonstrated an overall mean of 87%, work behavior a mean of 89%, and group session behavior a mean of 71%.

Figure 1 indicates the pattern of in-program behavior demonstrated by all 125 subjects over the average length of treatment of nine weeks. The graph represents an average pattern and is divided into the three program levels according to the average time spent in each. The performance rates tend to increase with time in the program and progress through the three levels. However, since initial rates were high, it appears that existing behavior was strengthened rather than new performances initiated.

The results of a multiple baseline examination of the classroom contingencies, depicted in Figure 2, demonstrated the efficacy of the techniques utilized. It is interesting to note that experimental conditions one, two, and four produced essentially the same behavior rates even though different behaviors were targeted.

POST-DATA

In examining follow-up measures, separate data are presented for program graduates and non-graduates. At the time of follow-up, 117 of the total subjects were available to provide information other than arrest records. Arrest rates, from court records, were available on all subjects.

Arrest rates for program graduates yield a mean of .46 per year. This represents a significant reduction from 2.95 per year ($t = 13.4$; $df = 96$; $p < .001$). Arrest rates for non-graduates were .64 per year. However, this is a somewhat meaningless measure since more than half of them (55%) were in a correctional institution at the time post-data were gathered.

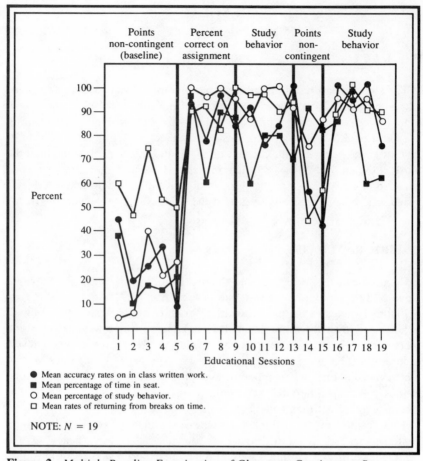

Figure 2 *Multiple Baseline Examination of Classroom Contingency System:*
Performance in Four Classroom Areas by
Educational Sessions (Three Hours Each).

Follow-up global measures demonstrate that graduates, in comparison to non-graduates, tend to return to school, secure employment, if not in school, and stay out of penal institutions. Table 2 demonstrates all graduate versus non-graduate comparisons to be significant in the desired direction using Yates' corrected chi-square method.[21] More specifically, a greater proportion of graduates are employed and in school. Similarly, a smaller proportion are in a correctional institution or unemployed. It should be added that the unemployed category includes only those subjects not in school, not employed, and not in an institution and therefore is not the reciprocal of the employed category.

_____

[21]Hayes, W.L., and Winkler, R.L., *Statistics* (New York: Holt, Rinehart, 1971).

TABLE 2

Outcome Comparison of Graduates vs. Non-graduates

Outcome status	Graduates (95)	Non-graduates (22)	x^2	df
In school	28	0	6.971*	1
Employed	33	2	4.399**	1
In a correctional institution	16	12	8.918***	1
Unemployed	18	10	5.392****	1

*$p < .01$
**$p < .05$
***$p < .005$
****$p < .025$

Post measures of school records indicate a mean attendance rate of 91%. No pre-post statistical comparison is presented, however, since the post subjects enrolled in school were not the same group as the subjects in school prior to the program.

Just prior to completing the program subjects were given the Wide Range Achievement Test a second time. The mean follow-up grade level was 6.3 as compared to a 5.3 level at admission, only nine weeks earlier. This represents a significant increase ($t = 2.18$; $df = 97$; $p < .05$).

The cost of operating Kentfields was $30,000, or $480 per subject treated. This amount is compared to treatment costs of $8,000 (10 month average) for the state training school and $5,000 (12 month average) for private institutions per individual commitment. During the 18 months prior to initiation of the Kentfields Program there were a mean of 82 males in residential institutions from the Kent County Juvenile Court. For the 18 months following initiation of Kentfields the mean was reduced to 56. This represents a significant decrease ($t = 12.2$; $df = 34$; $p < .001$). These data are presented graphically in Figure 3.

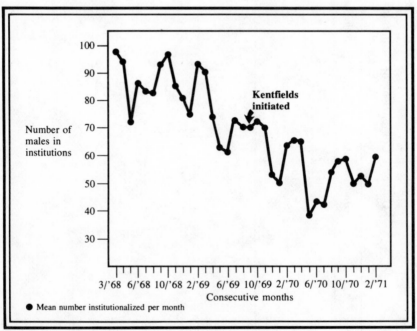

Figure 3 *Number of Males Institutionalized by the Kent County Juvenile Court from March, 1968 to February, 1971.*

DISCUSSION

At the outset, it was stated that the goals of the Kentfields Program included establishment of a community based treatment program as an alternative to institutionalization for hard core juvenile offenders. Within this framework, specific program criteria were to demonstrate the efficacy of behavioral techniques in affecting significant increases in prosocial performances and significant reduction of delinquent behavior in the community. It was similarly proposed that such an approach would require minimal expenditures of funds in comparison to traditional institutional placement.

A high and stable rate of appropriate behavior in all program components was demonstrated. However, since initial rates were high in all areas it is more appropriate to say that existing performances were strengthened rather than new ones initiated. Each program component — work projects, educational sessions, group sessions — involved performance crucial to community adjustment. The only legitimate means to desirable ends[22] for program graduates were return to school and employment. Thus, behavior targeted were directly related to community adjustment.

A common issue raised concerning behavioral approaches to whether or not changes are a function of the contingencies utilized or the mere delivery of rewards. The multiple baseline evaluation of the classroom contingency system, reported in Figure 2, indicates the dependence of the classroom behavior on contingent reinforcement. To a marked extent, generalization is demonstrated between time in seat, study behavior, and performance on written work. Following experimental manipulations one, two, and four, though differential contingencies were in effect, each of the above response sets demonstrated a stable performance pattern.

Of primary interest to those responsible for juvenile corrections planning is the significant reduction in delinquent behavior. Not only is the decrease in reported offenses statistically significant, but the reduction in delinquent activity of 84% has practical significance as well. It is also apparent that completion of the full program sequence is related to socially desirable outcomes (Table 2).

The demonstrated increases in classroom target behavior appear related to academic achievement in general. An increase of one full grade level in an average of nine weeks adds substantial credibility to the approach utilized.

It has been demonstrated that large expenditures of money were not necessary to produce desired changes in delinquent populations. Utilizing a community-based approach, with nonprofessionals serving as treatment agents eliminates the need for large administrative bureaucracy, extensive facilities, and other complex organizational costs. Nearly half of the program's budgeted expenses involved provision of contingent reinforcers.

---

[22]Merton, R.K., *Social Theory and Social Structure* (New York: Glencoe Press, 1957).

Although no hard data are available on the specific effects of the community relations strategy, described earlier, or on the relative potency of its various components, it should be pointed out that the program continued, and continues at this writing, to receive local governmental funding. In many ways this is the essence of what is frequently ignored in psychological descriptions of programs. Such efforts, however, in this program are of equal status with our use of behavioral technology in program success.

Many of the original local governmental officials who were the program's skeptics became its most adamant champions and recommended similar approaches in other areas. Where the initiation of the program had been a political issue, by the end of the time covered in this paper, it was considerably less mass media material, considered a success by local officials, and provided a technical and theoretical base for a half-way house for males and females currently in operation in the same community.

A number of conclusions result from the experimental program examined here. First, although quasi-experimental outcome design was utilized, a viable alternative to long term institutionalization for hard core delinquents has demonstrated promising results. Second, the techniques of behavior modification appear to be effective in increasing prosocial performances with hard core delinquents. It should be kept in mind however, that reported findings, though encouraging, must necessarily be interpreted with some caution, due to possible confounding with subjects' history, maturation, and the interaction of observations and treatment inherent in the design.[23]

Despite the above cautions, the significant reduction in illegal behavior, coupled with the relative inexpensiveness of the described approach enhances its appeal for program planners. While only systematic replication, utilizing control group and factorial research designs will allow causal attribution to the techniques utilized,[24] it appears that a firm basis for more sophisticated approaches to the evaluation of the proposed techniques has been established.

Again, although the results of the educational aspects of the program must be regarded with some caution, since retest reliability statistics for the Wide Range Achievement Test are unavailable for parallel populations over similar time periods, the increase in academic achievement demonstrated is also promising and generally considered central to rehabilitative interventions.[25]

Given the design utilized and the social setting in which this program took place, it is not possible to definitely separate the active program ingredients. Kentfields included the use of a community-based intervention, behavior modification techniques, nonprofessionals, and college volunteers which have

---

[23]Campbell and Stanley, op. cit. supra note 18. Underwood, B.J., *Psychological Research* (New York: Appleton-Century-Crofts, 1957).

[24]Paul, G.L., "Behavior modification research: Design and tactics," In E.M. Franks (Ed.), *Behavior Therapy: Appraisal and Status* (New York: McGraw-Hill, 1969).

[25]Cohen, *op. cit. supra* note 7.

all produced desired outcomes in other situations. Causal attribution to any specific component or examination of the relative potency of each awaits further investigation. Thus, it is concluded that an alternative to institutionalization has established a level of efficacy warranting further investigation in applied settings. In addition, the combination of community psychology and behavior modification conceptions and approaches represents a successful model for the creation of alternative settings for delinquent youth.

Chapter 18

Editors' Remarks

We are grateful to Craig Blakely, William Davidson, Cheryl Saylor of Michigan State University and Michael Robinson of the Kentfields Rehabilitation Program for responding to our request that they provide long-term follow-up data on Kentfields. Their report of a ten-year follow-up demonstrates the persistence of many positive results of the program which was described in the preceding chapter (chapter 17).

Kentfields Rehabilitation Program: Ten Years Later*

Craig H. Blakely, William S. Davidson,
Cheryl A. Saylor and Michael J. Robinson

In 1969, the county of Kent, Michigan began what was then a rather unique program. The purpose of Kentfields was to provide an alternative to committing chronic juvenile offenders to state training schools or private institutions (Davidson & Robinson, 1975). The program was designed to combine the scientifically validated techniques of behavior modification with the emerging trend of community placement. This combination has since provided some encouraging results as evidenced by a vast number of programs and publications in the late sixties and throughout the seventies (Tharp & Wetzel, 1969; Neitzel, Winett, MacDonald, & Davidson, 1977).

The Kentfields program was initially designed to intervene with youth as a final alternative to institutionalization. Youth referred to the program during its initial year had been on probation an average of 2.3 years and the court had accepted an average of 3.2 referrals per youth (Davidson, 1970). Further, the court reported that had this non-residential community placement not been available, three-fourths of the 75 referrals that initial year would have been placed in institutions at the time of referral to Kentfields and the remaining 25% were extremely likely to end up institutionalized within the near future (Davidson & Robinson, 1975).

Since that time, the focus of delinquency prevention had rapidly moved away from institutional placement of repeat offenders. Attention has focused on identification of offenders early in their delinquent careers in order to prevent delinquent activity. This can be evidenced by the great number of diversionary programs (Klein, 1979) and status offender programs (NCCD,

*This research was in part funded through an all university research grant, Michigan State University.

This article was prepared especially for inclusion in this book.

1975). Accompanying this trend has been the tendency for juvenile officers to institutionalize offenders earlier on in their career as well.

Due to these trends, even ten years after its inception, the Kentfields program remains a rather unique attempt to retain the more serious offender in the community setting. The proposed advantages continue to be avoiding the interaction with other offenders in a closed setting (Feldman, Wodarski, Goodman & Flax, 1973); the frequent inability of institutional interventions to impact positively upon the youth's return to the community (Lerman, 1975); the more apparent labeling effects of institutional placement (Empey, 1967); and the overwhelming costs of institutional placement (Palmer, 1974).

Davidson and Robinson (1975) performed an initial evaluation of the Kentfields program for the first two years of its operation (1969–1970). Their results showed a significant reduction in official petitions. Eighteen month follow-up results showed program graduates to have a greater likelihood of being employed or in school following program completion. The present study presents follow-up data on youth referred to the program from January, 1974 through April, 1978.

This research provides several pieces of information not available in the initial eighteen month follow-up. First and perhaps foremost, the data provides a general picture of the impact of a decade's existence upon the philosophy and procedures of a successful court program. In addition, this research provides a replication of the earlier follow-up evaluation, while at the same time allowing for a longer follow-up interval. In short, this study will briefly provide the results of a replication of the initial research nearly a decade later.

METHOD

SUBJECTS

During the above mentioned time interval, 197 youth were referred to the Kentfields program due to repeated contacts (or contacts of sufficient seriousness) with the Kent County Probate Court. At the point of referral to Kentfields the youth averaged 15.1 years. At the point of follow-up interviews, the youth had been out of the Kentfields program for an average period of 34.4 months. Forty-three percent of the youth were nonwhite. Ninety-two percent were male. Each youth averaged 1.92 court petitions on file prior to referral.

MEASURES

Two primary sets were collected, a subset of which are reported here.

Typical archival outcome data was collected from the files at the Kent County Probate Court. Number of petitions, seriousness of petitions, and demographic data was collected. Complete monthly record data was available on all 197 youth. Data was collected for 41 monthly time periods (24 months pre, 5 months during, 12 months follow-up) to allow for the use of interrupted time series analysis (Simonton, 1977).

Due to resource constraints, interview data was collected on only 43 youth. Interviews were of a structured format including items addressing the perceived impact of the program, the degree to which youth had been in school or employed since program termination, and the youth's satisfaction with the program. Interviews were conducted by two court staff trained and supervised by a graduate student from Michigan State University. Youth were paid five dollars for participating.

RESULTS

An interrupted time series analysis of the data available at the forty-one monthly time periods suggested a significant decrease in the frequency of petitions filed following program involvement ($t = 4.03$, $p < .01$). As can be seen in Figure 1, there is a concomitant drop in the curve at the point of program involvement suggesting positive impact.

Sixty percent of the youth interviewed reported having attended school regularly during the year immediately prior to follow-up while fifty-five percent reported part or full-time employment. While seventy-five percent of the youth interviewed felt Kentfields was a good program, ninety-three percent felt they had benefited from the program.

DISCUSSION

The initial goals of the Kentfields program since its inception have been to: (1) increase desired behavior while decreasing undesired behavior, (2) provide a more efficient (less costly) alternative to institutional placement, and (3) assist the youth in becoming more productive members of their communities. Data suggests that these goals continue to be met. Time series results suggested a reduction in the monthly rate of contacts with the authorities. Cost effectiveness figures suggest that the Kentfields program cost is approximately eight percent that of institutional placement in the state training school (Robinson, 1979). In addition, follow-up data suggest that eighty-six percent of the youth interviewed were employed or attended school during a substantial part of the third year following termination from Kentfields.

These rates compare favorably with the initial one year follow-up data on

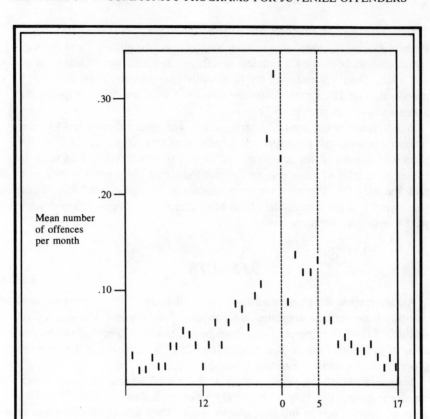

Figure 1 *Average Number of Court Petitions per Month.*

1969–1970 program youth (Davidson & Robinson, 1975). The thirty-six percent recidivism rate found in the present study is virtually identical to the thirty-seven percent rate found in that previously mentioned work. During the year immediately following program involvement, Davidson and Robinson (1975) reported seventy percent of the youth were either employed or back in school. Though a direct comparison is not possible here since the current data was collected during the third year following program involvement, the figures seem comparable. One would expect a slightly higher employment rate merely due to the increased age of the youth.

Though program outcome results appear to be fairly stable throughout Kentfield's ten years of existence, there have been some notable changes. The cost per youth in the program has increased from $480 to $1290. Though this is a substantial increase, inflation and the relative increase in the institutional alternatives can account for better than half the increase in cost. The increase in cost can also be related to the increase in length of involvement. In September of 1977 Kentfields began an aftercare or extension program designed to ease the transition from the structured program community involvement to the youth's independent follow-up community environment. As a result, the average involvement with Kentfields has increased from 42 to 162 days. This figure alone has contributed to the increased cost of the program though it has reduced the per diem cost.

The size of the program has remained fairly stable. During the first year, 75 youth were involved in the program. During 1978, 76 youth were involved in the program, though only 54 were new referrals. Perhaps of most interest is the fact that youth referred are of a less serious nature. During the first year, youth referred to Kentfields averaged 2.95 petitions. Youth involved in the present follow-up averaged only 1.92 petitions prior to program referral. As mentioned earlier, this seems to correspond to the national trend of earlier detection and intervention.

In summary, it appears that the Kentfields program continues to function in an effective and efficient manner. This replication of a previous follow-up evaluation has reached similar conclusions. The community based intervention corresponds with a drop in offense rate. In addition, the program operates at a fraction of the cost of traditional institutional placement. Continued community support strengthens the notion that community placement is a viable alternative to institutionalization of the more serious juvenile offender.

Firmly entrenched in its tenth year as an arm of the Kent County Probate Court, the Kentfields program continues to operate effectively as an alternative to more serious handling of hard core delinquents.

Unfortunately, like the previous work, this study is based upon a within group design lacking comparison groups. In subsequent reviews (Davidson & Seidman, 1974; Braukmann & Fixsen, 1977), the point was made that true experimental designs are virtually nonexistent in the behavioral literature. The authors are currently in the process of making preliminary plans for an experimental outcome comparison of the efficacy of the Kentfields model.

REFERENCES

Braukmann, C.J., & Fixsen, D.L., "Behavior modification with delinquents. In Hersen, M., Eisler, R.M., & Miller, P.M. (eds.), *Progress in Behavior Modification* (New York: Academic Press, 1977).

Davidson, W.S., *Kentfields Rehabilitation Program: The First Annual Report* (Grand Rapids, MI: Ethridge Printing, 1970).

Davidson, W.S., & Robinson, M.J., "Community psychology and behavior modification: A community based program for the prevention of delinquency," *Corrective Psychiatry and Social Psychiatry*, 1975, *21*, 1–12.

Davidson, W.S., & Seidman, E., "Studies of behavior modification and juvenile delinquency: A review, methodological critique, and social perspective," *Psychological Bulletin*, 1974, *81*, 998–1011.

Empey, L.T., *Alternatives to institutionalization* (Washington, D.C.: U.S. Government Printing Office, 1967).

Feldman, R.A., Wodarski, J.S., Goodman, M., & Flax, N., "Prosocial and antisocial boys together," *Journal of Social Work*, 1973, *18*, 26–37.

Klein, M., "Deinstitutionalization and Diversion of Juvenile Offenders: A Litany of Impediments." In Morris, N., & Tonry, M. (Eds.), *Crime and Justice*, 1978 (Chicago, Il: University of Chicago Press, 1979).

Lerman, P., *Community Treatment and Social Control: A Critical Analysis of Juvenile Correctional Policy* (Chicago, Il: University of Chicago Press, 1975).

National Council on Crime and Delinquency, "Jurisdiction over status offenders should be removed from the court," *Crime and Delinquency*, 1975, *21*, 97–99.

Nietzel, M., Winett, R., MacDonald, M., & Davidson, W., *Behavioral Approaches to Community Psychology* (New York: Pergamon, 1977).

Palmer, T.B., "California's community treatment program for delinquent adolescents," *Journal of Research in Crime and Delinquency*, 1971, *8*, 74–92.

Robinson, M.J., *Kentfields Rehabilitation Program: The Ninth Annual Report* (County Juvenile Court mimeo, 1979).

Simonton, D.K., "Cross-sectional time-series experiments: Some suggested statistical analyses," *Psychological Bulletin*, 1977, *84*(3), 489–502.

Tharp, R.G., & Wetzel, R.J., *Behavior Modification in the Natural Environment* (New York: Academic Press, 1969).

Chapter 19

Editors' Remarks

In recent years there has been a remarkable expansion in the use of community-based group homes as alternatives to institutions for the placement of juvenile delinquents who must be removed from their own homes. The quality of the services provided by such homes varies widely and it is clear that merely providing a substitute residence is inadequate for the needs of many delinquents. A model for such homes is presented in this chapter. Through more than ten years of research the staff of Achievement Place in Kansas, have developed a cost efficient community-based family-style-treatment program for pre-delinquent and delinquent youth which has been demonstrated to be effective both in research conducted in the original Kansas setting and in a number of replications in other cities in North America.

Replication of the Achievement Place model has not always been successful, but the disappointing results have been found when the model has been implemented without some of its integral parts or without adequate staff training. The model was developed systematically and carefully over several years and consists of a number of essential components each of which, it appears, are crucial to the treatment program's success. The Achievement Place program is not a simple behavior modification program. Whereas it does include a token economy, contingency contracting and other behavioral methods it also includes an individualized counseling component, a child advocacy service, and a self-government system which mobilizes peer group pressure for prosocial behavior and leads the children to believe that this is *their* program and not merely something which is imposed upon them by adults (cf. Ross & McKay, Chapter 23).

The article which follows provides a good overview of the accomplishments of the Achievement Place research group. There have been many other publications describing the Achievement Place programs and research and some of the major articles are referenced below for the interested reader.

REFERENCES

Bailey, J.S., Wolf, M.M. & Phillips, E.L., "Home-based reinforcement and the modification of pre-delinquents' classroom behavior," *Journal of Applied Behavior Analysis*, 1970, *3*, 223–233.

Fixsen, D.L., Phillips, E.L., & Wolf, M.M., "Achievement Place: experiments in self-government with pre-delinquents," *Journal of Applied Behavior Analysis*, 1973, *6*, 31–57.

Kirigin, K.A., Phillips, E.L., Timbers, G.D., Fixsen, D.L., & Wolf, M.M., "Achievement Place: the modification of academic behavior problems of youths in a group home setting." In B. Etzel, J.M. LeBlanc, and D.M. Baer (Eds.), *New Developments in Behavioral Research: Theory, Method, and Application* (Hillsdale, N.J.: Lawrence Erlbaum Associates, 1977).

Phillips, E.L., "Achievement Place: token reinforcement procedures in a homestyle rehabilitation setting for 'pre-delinquent' boys," *Journal of Applied Behavior Analysis*, 1968, *1*, 213–223.

Phillips, E.L., Fixsen, D.L., Phillips, E.E., & Wolf, M.M., "The teaching-family model: a comprehensive approach to residential treatment of youth." In Cullinan, D. & Epstein, M.H., *Special Education for Adolescents: Issues and Perspectives* (Columbus, Ohio: C.E. Merrill, 1979).

Liberman, R.P., Ferris, C., Salgado, P., & Salgado, J., "Replication of the Achievement Place model in California." *Journal of Applied Behavior Analysis*, 1975, *8*, 287–299.

Achievement Place
Behavior Shaping Works for Delinquents*

Elery L. Phillips, Elaine A. Phillips,
Dean L. Fixsen, and Montrose M. Wolf

Six years ago concerned citizens in Lawrence, Kansas, set up Achievement Place, a community-based, family-style treatment home for delinquent youths. The goal was to teach the youths the basic skills — social, academic, self-help and prevocational — that would help keep them out of trouble with their families, their teachers and the law.

With the approval of the Board of Directors of Achievement Place and the assistance of a research grant from the NIMH Center for Studies of Crime and Delinquency, we began conducting research to develop a model treatment program. We encountered many problems, but after three years of trial and error and careful evaluation we had developed what we considered to be a successful home. We had worked out a behavioral treatment program that produced significant changes in the skills of the six to eight boys who lived in the home with two professional teaching parents. We were convinced, on the basis of several controlled studies, that we had found a usable model for almost any community, one that would help make potential criminals into productive citizens.

We ran into trouble, however, in our first attempt to replicate the model in another community. The program was based on a token-economy system of reinforcement. In this system, the boys receive points each time they complete a task and, at a later time, can exchange the points for desirable objects or for privileges. The token economy had been our chief object of study in the early years, but we came to realize that it was not the heart of the program.

*Phillips, E.L. et al., "Achievement Place: Behavior shaping works for delinquents," *Psychology Today Magazine*, 1973, *6*, 75–79. Copyright © 1973, Ziff-Davis Publishing Co. Reprinted by permission.

The heart of the program was the teaching, social interaction component. It is unfortunately true that a token system by itself doesn't teach the most important, social skills. Teaching involves an active give-and-take process — instruction, demonstration, practice, feedback. This process was the secret behind the success of the first Achievement Place. However, it was only through our original failure to replicate the model that we discovered its importance.

Achievement Place is part of a growing trend to find alternatives to the inhumane and debilitating conditions of traditional institutional treatment programs for children. Institutional life has little relation to the outside world, it usually confines the children's contacts to members of their own sex, teaches them dependency on a hospital-like routine, gives them few work skills they can use outside the institution, and teaches them to live on a "welfare system" rather than to be as responsible as possible for their own needs.

FAILURE OF THE MEDICAL MODEL

We can trace many of the failings of traditional programs to their grounding in the medical model of deviant behavior. If delinquent children were indeed ill, it might be reasonable to place them in large hospital-like institutions and to have their basic needs administered to by attendants. But modern behavior theory, on which we have based our program, suggests a behavior deficiency model; if children have behavior problems it is because they lack essential skills, they have inadequate histories of reinforcement and instruction rather than an illness caused by some hypothetical psychopathology. The goal of behavioral treatment programs like Achievement Place, therefore, is to establish, through instruction, the important behavioral competencies that the child has not learned.

The search for alternatives to institutionalization also includes a world wide move toward community based treatment, which seems to be less expensive, more effective and more humane. In Denmark and Sweden, for example, nearly all deviant and retarded children are treated in their own communities through Government supported programs. In the United States, several states have offered financial incentives for communities to provide local services, and in some instances the reduction in institutionalization of children has been spectacular.

Some programs focus on training the children's natural parents in behavior-shaping and management procedures. Unfortunately, many parents have such severe personal problems that a routine parent-training program may have little effect. In such cases it probably is better to provide special programs in the community to teach severely deviant children all of the complex social, prevocational and self-care skills that they need. If these programs are successful, then the parents may be able to learn to *maintain* the appropriate behavior even though they were not able to *establish* it originally.

We developed Achievement Place to serve as a model for such community-based programs. The youths who come to the home usually are sent by a judge after getting in trouble with the law. They are from 12 to 16 years old, in junior high school, and about three to four years behind academically.

When a boy enters Achievement Place, we introduce him to the other youths and give him a tour of the home, which is located in a quiet residential section of Lawrence. Then we introduce him to the point system (token economy), which we devised to help motivate the youths to learn new, more appropriate behavior. Each youth uses a point card to record his behavior and the number of points he earns and loses.

POINTS FOR PRIVILEGES

At first the new youth exchanges his points for privileges each day, later, after he learns the connection between earning points and earning privileges, he goes on a weekly exchange basis. As soon as possible, we phase out the point system and he goes on a merit system in which no points are given or taken away and all privileges are free. The merit system is the last step each boy must progress through before returning to his own home. When a youth does return home he is on a homeward bound system. If the youth begins to have problems with his parents or teachers, the teaching-parents can intensify their follow-up with the youth and his family or, for more severe problems, they can ask the youth to come back into the program for a few days or weeks to work out the problem.

Privileges come in seven varieties: (1) basics, including use of the telephone, tools, radio, record player, and recreation room, (2) snacks after school and before bedtime, (3) television time, (4) home time, which permits the youths to go home on weekends or to go downtown, (5) allowances of from one to three dollars a week, (6) bonds, which the youths can accumulate to buy clothes or other items they need, and (7) special privileges, which include any other privileges the youths may want. The first four privileges are naturally available in the home and add nothing to the cost of the program.

A typical day begins when the manager — one of the boys who is elected to the job — wakes the other boys up at about 6:30 a.m. The boys then wash their faces, brush their teeth and clean their bathrooms and bedrooms. The manager supervises these chores by assigning specific cleaning tasks to each boy, checking to see whether the tasks are completed, and awarding points for successful performance or taking points away for failure to carry out tasks. While some of the boys do the cleaning, others help the teaching-parent prepare breakfast.

After breakfast the boys check their appearance, pick up their daily report cards and leave for school. Since Achievement Place is a community-based facility, the boys continue to attend the same schools in which they had problems before entering the home. This arrangement permits the teaching-parents to work closely with the school-teachers and administrators to solve the boys' school problems. Teachers provide systematic feedback for each youth by filling out a report card each day. The teacher can quickly answer a series of questions about the youth's behavior (Did he follow the teacher's rules today? Did he make good use of his class time? Did he complete his assignment at an acceptable level of accuracy?) by checking "yes" or "no" on his card. The youth then earns or loses points at Achievement Place depending on the teacher's judgment about his performance.

When the boys return to the home after school they have snacks before starting their homework or other point-earning activities. In the late afternoon, one or two boys usually volunteer to help prepare dinner.

FAMILY CONFERENCE

During or just after dinner the teaching-parents and the youths hold a family conference, which is part of the home's semi-self-government system. The teaching-parents and the youths discuss the day's events, evaluate the manager's performance, establish or modify rules, and decide on consequences for any rule violations that were reported to the teaching-parents. Self-government behaviors are taught specifically to the youths, and they are encouraged to participate in discussions about any aspect of the program.

After the family conference, the boys and the teaching-parents usually engage in family activities such as watching TV, listening to records, or discussing the events of the day. Before going to bed at about 10:30, the boys figure up their point cards for the day.

Although we have evaluated many of the specific procedures developed by the teaching-parents to teach appropriate behaviors, it was not until recently that we began to evaluate the overall effectiveness of Achievement Place. Our data include measures of police and court contacts, recidivism, and grades and attendance at school. We have taken these measures for 16 youths who were committed to Achievement Place, 15 youths who were committed to the Kansas Boys School (an institution for some 250 delinquents), and 13 youths who were placed on formal probation. All 44 youths had been released from treatment for at least a year at the time we collected the data, all had been adjudicated originally by the Douglas County juvenile Court in Lawrence, and all were potential candidates for Achievement Place when they were adjudicated. We should point out that these youths were *not* randomly assigned to each of the three groups, so these data are only preliminary results. However, we have begun randomly selecting youths for Achievement

Place to provide an experimentally valid evaluation of the long-term effects of the program.

Police and Court Contacts

The Achievement Place and the Boys School youths were similar in their contacts with the law before and during treatment, but they were quite different after treatment. The Boys School youths returned to a fairly high number of police and court contacts, while the Achievement Place youths had few contacts. The boys on probation had fewer police or court contacts than the Achievement Place youths before treatment, but after treatment they had more.

It is interesting to note that one argument against community-based group homes is that they expose the community to the continuing law violations of the delinquent youths placed there. However, we found that during treatment the youths placed in the institution 30 miles from Lawrence had as many contacts with the police and court in Lawrence as did the Achievement Place youths. Apparently, Achievement Place offered as much "protection" to the community as the institution did.

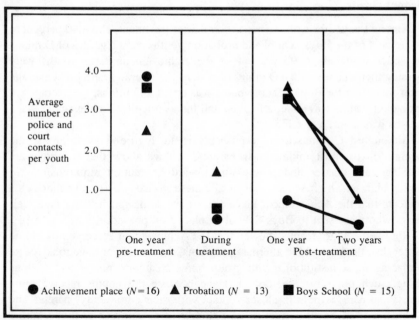

Figure 1 *Police and Court Contacts.*

Postrelease Institutionalization

Two years after treatment, 53 percent of the Boys School youths and 54 percent of the probation youths had committed a delinquent act that resulted in their being readjudicated by the court and placed in a state institution. But only 19 percent of the Achievement Place youths were institutionalized either during or after treatment.

Although these police and court data reveal substantial differences among the groups, they are measures of failure, not of success. It is difficult to argue that lack of failure means success, since there are many things unrelated to a youth's behavior that may influence whether or not he has further trouble with the law. For this reason we also took measures of school behavior.

Dropouts

By the third semester after treatment, 90 percent of the Achievement Place youths were attending public school, while only nine percent of the Boys School youths and 37 percent of the probation youths were still in school. This measure included only those youths who had not been institutionalized after treatment.

School Grades

Among the youths who attended school after treatment, about 40 percent to 50 percent of the Boys School and probation youths earned grades of D minus or better while about 90 percent of the Achievement Place youths were passing their classes with a D minus or better. The overall grade-point average after treatment for Boys School youths was about a D minus; the average for probation youths was about a D plus, and the average for Achievement Place youths was about a C minus.

Although a C minus average probably is not high enough to arouse the admiration of most middle-class parents, it does show that the boys are passing their classes and progressing toward graduation requirements for junior high and high school. All in all, these police, court and school data indicate that the Achievement Place youths are doing much better then their peers who were sent to Boys School or placed on probation.

But even if these results showed that the Achievement Place youths did no better than the boys in the alternate programs, we would continue to advocate replacing most institutions with group home treatment programs. For one thing, such programs are more humane because the youths receive more individual care, remain in closer contact with their community, parents and friends, and learn important social, family, and community-living skills. Second, group homes are less expensive to operate than prison-type institutions. The cost per bed to purchase, renovate and furnish Achievement Place was about one fourth the cost of building an institution in our state.

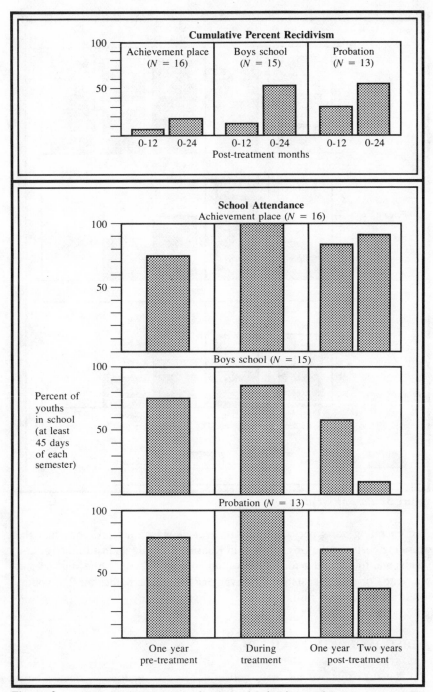

Figure 2   *Cumulative Percent Recidivism and School Attendance.*

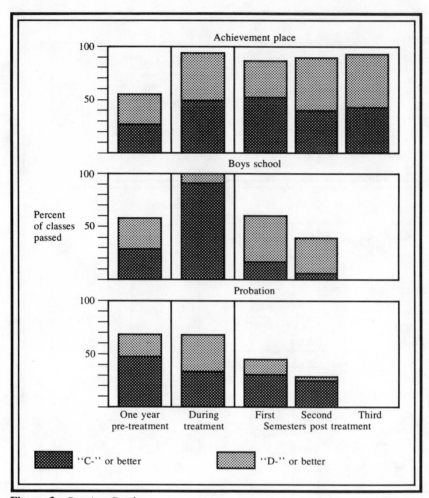

Figure 3   *Passing Grades.*

And operating costs per youth at Achievement Place are less than half the operating costs for the Boys School in Kansas. To build an institution for 250 youths and to operate it for a year would cost $8 million, while start-up and one year's operating costs for Achievement-Place-type homes for 250 youths would be about $2.5 million.

A DISCONCERNING FAILURE

If the data that we are now collecting on the randomly selected boys corroborate our initial findings that systematic group home-treatment programs are also more effective than institutional programs, we can expect a

Comparative Costs	
Achievement Place	*Institution*
Capital Investment per Youth	
$5,000 to $8,000	$20,000 to $30,000
Yearly Operating Cost per Youth	
$4,000 to $5,000	$6,000 to $12,000

major shift away from institutions and toward community-based programs. That is why replication of the Achievement Place model was so important — and why our original failure to replicate it was so disconcerting.

When we began training a new set of teaching-parents to set up a second home in a new community, we were not sure what to teach them other than the token-economy technology. We had the couple observe the social interactions at Achievement Place, but we did not give them specific instructions since we were not certain ourselves which interactions were important. We discovered the critical aspects of the program only after the couple set up a home, when we were able to compare the successful and unsuccessful teaching styles.

Technically, the new home was the same in nearly every way as the older one, and the token-economy system was adequately administered. But the home just did not click. This failure forced us to re-examine our model and to study carefully over the next year the differences between the teaching styles of the successful and the unsuccessful teaching-parents.

We found that many interactions at the second home were quite stern, the kind of interacting that goes on everyday in some families. For example, the teaching-parent would tell a boy, "OK, you clean that table." The boy would begin cleaning it and before long would say, "OK, I'm through now." The teaching-parent would look at it, find a few spots, and say, "That's not every good. You'd better do that again."

When we examined this type of interaction, we realized that the task was not assigned in a positive way, and when the boy said he was finished he was given no encouragement at all, even though he had done at least part of the task. Then too, the teaching-parent failed to point out the youth's specific failures — the spots he had missed, for instance. And when the boy finally completed the task satisfactorily, he got his points but no praise at all.

At Achievement Place, by contrast, the teaching-parents begin giving explicit instructions to a boy as soon as he arrives. At first, the instructions are simple and easy to follow: "Johnny, would you come here, please? I want you to come into the office and look at something with me," or, "Would you come to the back door? I want to show you how to lock it in case you need to," or, "Would you go with Jimmy and sweep the patio?" Gradually the teaching-parents extend the length of time it takes to carry out an instruction, assigning more and more arduous tasks. They give hundreds of low-level instructions, with increasing probes into more difficult ones.

THE PATIO LOOKS GREAT

At the same time, they hand out social as well as token reinforcements. "I sure appreciate your bringing me that," they say, or, "The patio looks great, guys, give yourselves 3,000 points each!"

After a youth has been in the program a few days, they begin introducing negative feedback: "Gee, you didn't do that task when you were supposed to. That's going to cost you 200 points. Now remember, I am going to fine you occasionally. That doesn't mean I am mad at you and you shouldn't be mad at me. After all, these are only points and you can earn them back."

Then they gradually increase the number of times the youth gets negative feedback and fines. But at the same time they instruct him in how to react to criticism: "That was nice. You looked me in the eye. You didn't mumble anything under your breath when I gave you the fine and you said that you would take it off your card and we would discuss it at the family conference tonight. That is perfect. That is exactly the way to do it."

In brief, there were three essential differences between the successful and unsuccessful teaching parents. One was in the social-teaching component — the way they gave instructions and feed-back. Successful teaching-parents teach in a nonconfronting, straightforward, enthusiastic way that gives a positive atmosphere to the whole house.

The second difference was in the social-skill-training component — the teaching of social skills that make the youths more reinforcing and less aversive in interpersonal relationships. The third was the self-government component — teaching the youths how to negotiate and criticize constructively and always including the youths in any decisions about the program.

ACCEPTING CRITICISM

One of the most difficult things for all of us to learn is how to accept criticism and negative feedback. None of us like it, but life is full of it. There will always be a parent, an employer, a teacher, a husband or a wife around to tell us we should have put the cap back on the toothpaste or should have completed some task faster or done it better. Effective social interaction involves learning how to respond to such criticism in a way that doesn't make a relationship deteriorate but instead turns the incident into a learning experience for everyone concerned.

This is particularly true for delinquent youths, since it is their customary belligerent response to criticism that has gotten them expelled from school and labelled as uncontrollable by their parents or incorrigible by the court. This set of defiant, aggressive skills, which may successfully intimidate their peers and an occasional adult, isolates them from opportunities at school, on the job, and in their personal relationships.

In many institutions, when a youth does something wrong, such as calling the psychiatric aide an obscene name, the aide himself has a tantrum and shouts, ''You can't call me that!'' The aide engages in the very behavior he should be teaching the youth to avoid. Many parents and spouses do the same thing.

It seems clear to us now that when token systems have failed in institutional or home settings — and certainly in the first replication of Achievement Place — one reason was because the social-teaching component was missing. When a child does something wrong, he should not be subjected to offensive criticism. Every mistake he makes represents an opportunity to teach him exactly what to do. Given specific instructions, most children, even potential criminals, will learn how to negotiate, how to take criticism, how to respond to negative feedback in ways that are likely to be successful from their own standpoints.

In the self-government component, the teaching-parents instruct the youths in self-government. The teaching-parents are careful to include the youths in all decisions that involve them. Changes in the rules or in the token economy or a potentially large fine for some youth are always brought up in the family conference. The teaching-parents always give a reason, prompt a discussion by the youths about the fairness of the change or fine, have the youths vote on the issue and compromise until a consensus is reached. Since the youths share in the decisionmaking process, they consider the program their own.

CLINICIANS CAN BE RIGHT

Earlier token-economy experiments did not explore the social-teaching, social-skill training, and self-government components, mainly for technical reasons. These all involve social interaction which is a difficult area to study because there are no permanent products: once an interaction occurs, it vanishes. It is not like teaching arithmetic, where a student's answer to the problem of three plus two will remain on the paper for later examination. Transitory interactions can be captured on videotape, however, and we have done this at Achievement Place.

Many clinical colleagues have told us all along that the ''relationship'' is an essential component of any therapy. We are now convinced that they are right. However, we are finding that the "relationship" can be broken into measurable and teachable behavioral terms. As a result, we have been able to show new teaching-parents — about a dozen couples so far — how to interact effectively.

We have found that another important component of our program's success is the establishment of communication between the teaching-parents and their home's board of directors, and with other community agencies, as well as with the boys. It was only after our first new couple ran into trouble that we realized the importance of teaching community-interaction skill. The couple, faced with multiple problems at home, had failed to keep communication going with the agencies they were serving. This situation showed up clearly when we made our first evaluation of the home. The data showed that court, social-welfare and school officials were not satisfied with the couple's performance.

The couple eventually lost the home and had no opportunity to correct the deficiencies. They were determined, however, to be teaching-parents. They came back into our program for retraining, and with what we had learned from our mutual failure we were able to work out ways of teaching community-interaction skills. We have incorporated these techniques, along with the techniques of running a token system and interacting with the boys, into a handbook, and couples in training to become teaching-parents now learn all of these skills.

Unfortunately, most social programs are set up without the preliminary trial-and-error experimentation that was a vital part of the development of the Achievement Place model. An agency puts an untested idea into operation, sometimes on a very large scale, and when it fails in some way the whole program is discredited. Donald Campbell, a social psychologist at Northwestern University, has suggested a far better way to do things. He advocates an "experimenting society," in which new social programs would be considered experimental, with a built-in trial-and-error and evaluation period preceding the adoption of any particular model. The importance of replication and dissemination of prototypic programs is also being acknowledged by some Federal agencies. For example, Saleem Shah, Chief of the Center for Studies of Crime and Delinquency in NIMH, recently pointed out the importance of replication to the development of disseminable treatment programs [see "The Sell Game: New Thinking on Research Use," *Behavior Today*, Volume 3, Number 4].

The trial-and-error period, of course, can be a trying time for everyone concerned. But the final outcome can prove rewarding. Our first couple, with whom we had made so many mistakes, have since learned all the things we neglected to teach them originally and are now running one of the most successful replications of Achievement Place.

Chapter 20

Editors' Remarks

Throughout this book we emphasize the importance of a differential approach to correctional treatment — provide: treatment services which are appropriate to the needs of particular clients. A fundamental requirement for such an approach is an adequate assessment of the client's history, personal strengths and weaknesses, and of the family and environmental resources available to him. The value of such diagnostic services is often assumed but rarely studied. In the following article, Cox, Carmichael and Dightman describe an evaluation of a diagnostic service for juvenile offenders which demonstrates, in a controlled study, that the provision of a community-based diagnostic service can lead to a reduction in institution commitals and decreased recidivism. Moreover, their research shows that an integrated multidisciplinary program can stimulate inter-agency co-operation, identify gaps in available services and, with considerable cost benefits, stimulate the development of alternative community resources for delinquents.

An Evaluation of a Community Based Diagnostic Program for Juvenile Offenders*

Gary B. Cox, Stephen J. Carmichael, and Cameron Dightman

The State of Washington, like many states, has a variety of institutional treatment options for juveniles who must be committed to state resources, rather than treated at the community level. To adequately and most appropriately utilize available state treatment resources, Washington has followed the common practice of developing a centralized diagnostic center to provide evaluations of youngsters committed to the state.

Although many states use this basic model, there are serious deficiencies inherent in the idea of a centralized diagnostic service. These short-comings are as follows:

1. An intensive diagnostic and evaluation procedure occurs after the child is committed to the state, rather than before. If the evaluations were completed before commitment, it might be possible to avoid the commitment to state institutional resources entirely.

2. Diagnosis in an isolated state facility may not provide an accurate picture of the youth or his/her environment. It is very difficult for the centralized diagnostic system to examine such contributing factors to the youngsters' problems as the parents, the school, law enforcement, the court, and the peer group. A careful examination of the causative factors in a youngster's problems should take these environmental influences into consideration.

3. Not only must the environment be considered in the diagnosis but, in a more active sense, if members of the community could be involved in examining and interpreting the case, the diagnosis would benefit. Centralizing diagnosis very nearly precludes this possibility.

*Cox, G.B. et al., "An evaluation of a community based diagnostic program for juvenile offenders," *Juvenile Justice*, 1977, 28(3), 33–41. Copyright © 1977, National Council of Juvenile and Family Judges. Reprinted by permission.

4. If the diagnostic evaluation determines that community treatment is appropriate, continuity between diagnosis and case management will be much harder to establish for a centralized than for community based diagnosis, particularly if the community diagnosis has genuinely involved the community.

5. Institutional diagnosis is expensive, because it requires that all youth be held on a twenty-four-hour security basis even though many of the youngsters could remain out of a confined setting, in their own homes, foster care, or group care while undergoing a diagnostic study.

PROGRAM

In Benton-Franklin counties juvenile justice personnel recognized these problems with a state centralized diagnostic system and developed a program of community based diagnostic studies for the most difficult youngsters coming before the juvenile court. If the program proved to be successful it was felt that it might serve as a model for the entire state by providing a more effective diagnostic evaluation, reducing the number of youngsters sent to state institutions, and providing the service at a reduced cost.

To develop the program, a project supervisor was employed at the juvenile court who was charged with the responsibility of coordinating a diagnostic evaluation for each youngster referred to the project. Youth were referred to the project only if they were considered to be among the most difficult cases to come before the Benton-Franklin counties' juvenile court. Criteria for referral included the extent and seriousness of prior offenses; the nature of the history of delinquent or status offense behavior; the history of responsiveness to prior treatment interventions; the nature of the current offense; and the nature of the current behavioral/living pattern, including such relationships as family, peers, teachers, and employers.

The diagnostic process began after a fact-finding hearing in which the superior court judge determined that the youngster was either delinquent or a status offender. At that time the staff would recommend that the cases identified as most serious be referred for a complete diagnostic study. These were referred on an average of once a week resulting in approximately forty to fifty cases referred for diagnostic study each year.

Once a youngster was selected for diagnostic study and such a study was ordered by the judge, the youngster was seen by the diagnostic coordinator who explained the process to the youth and his/her parents. Parents were asked to share in the cost of the diagnostic evaluation. Costs were negotiated on a case by case basis as a function of family resources, including insurance coverage. Services were never denied because of inability to pay.

The components of each individual diagnostic work-up varied depending on need and opportunity. Generally, the following were included:

Psychological Testing   Psychological tests were conducted by a primate psychologist in the area who administered both projective and intelligence tests.

Education Evaluation   Schools were asked to prepare a full history of the youngster's past performance in school including academic and other behavioral observations.

Ministerial Study   A chaplain assigned to work at the juvenile court conducted an evaluation on each youngster in the project to assess the youngster's religious activities and needs, and to explore potential community resources in the religious area. If the youngster had a family minister, priest, or rabbi, the same type of written report was requested from him.

Detention Evaluation   If the youngster participating in the diagnostic study was housed in detention for the duration of the process, the detention staff observed his/her behavior while in confinement. If the youngster did not need to be detained in secure custody, he/she might be placed in foster care, at a local group home, or with the family. If he/she was in a foster care or group home during the course of the evaluation, supervisors of these resources were asked to write evaluations of his/her stay in the facility.

Family Evaluation   A description of the family dynamics was obtained by evaluative interviews performed by the staff of the local mental health facility. The focus of these interviews was to access family communication and problem-solving patterns.

Psychiatric Evaluation   Both the youngster and each of his/her parents were seen for a psychiatric evaluation.

Medical Evaluation   Basic physical examinations were conducted. If these examinations alerted the diagnostic coordinator to any special additional medical problems, the appropriate additional tests were made (*e.g.*, vision, hearing, neurological).

Other Evaluations   In addition to the above listed evaluation, other agencies who had been involved in work with the family were asked to make written reports of their work.

Arranging for these contracted or voluntary evaluations, conducting them, and preparing the written reports generally consumed a four to six week period. At the conclusion of each of the individual studies, a diagnostic committee was formed for that case, consisting of all of the consultants who had been involved, plus other agency personnel who might have a significant role to play in the future of the case.

This committee read the evaluations and studies that had been completed, conducted an interview with the parents, another interview with the youngster, and still a third interview with two youth whom the youngster had selected as advocates for him/her, and who could relay to the committee information about how this youngster performed on a peer level. Once these interviews were concluded, the diagnostic committee developed a diagnostic statement, identifying the major strengths and weaknesses of the child and family, as well as of community contributing forces. When the diagnostic statement was completed, the committee developed an ideal treatment plan which identified what resources would be necessary to successfully treat this youngster in the community. The purpose of this step was to help identify those services which were missing but needed. Following the development of the ideal treatment plan, a second treatment plan was designed based on available resources. This second treatment plan was then presented to the judge in a dispositional hearing and in almost all cases was accepted by the judge as the appropriate disposition in the case.

From the beginning, there had been an intention to evaluate the program. Initially this consisted of collecting preliminary data on the juveniles in the program. These results were promising, and the need for a better controlled study was apparent. This article is a report on that study, the purpose of which was to compare the efficacy of the community diagnostic program with that of regular court procedures, based on follow-up data collected in ten months after disposition. The object of the study was to compare results only for youths who remained in the community for treatment, in order to examine the premise that increasing the involvement of community resources in diagnosis and treatment would improve outcomes.

METHOD

DESIGN

Random assignment of subjects to Diagnostic (experimental) and control groups was not feasible. This was primarily due to the fact that funding was available to cover the entire anticipated need for diagnostic services. Given this, random assignment to groups would imply that some youths thought to need diagnostic work-ups would not receive them and, conversely, some who did not would receive them anyway. Neither staff nor judicial ethics would permit this. Accordingly, a non-equivalent control group design was adopted, and the control group should be thought of as a Comparison group.

SUBJECTS

During the study, forty youths were referred to the community diagnostic program. Referrals were based on a judgment that the offender was among the most serious cases encountered based on offense data and Case Evaluation Scale ratings. In the absence of the community program, these are the youths who would have been sent to the state diagnostic center. Of the forty, ten were institutionalized, either for a state diagnostic evaluation or subsequent to the community diagnostic evaluation. Their data are not included in the study.

The remaining thirty juveniles comprised the Diagnostic (experimental) group.

On an ongoing basis, staff nominated a pool of cases which they judged to be among the next most complex and difficult. Case Evaluation Scale ratings and offense data were used to select from this pool in a schedule comparable to the selection of Diagnostic cases, the thirty-four next most serious offenders. Of these, three were subsequently institutionalized. The remaining thirty-one juveniles constituted the Comparison group. Except for the collection of the dependent variable data, these control cases were handled according to standard procedures in the system.

MEASURES

Three types of dependent measures were used to assess the impact of the court program on juvenile behavior: the Case Evaluation Scale (also used as part of the selection criteria), offense data (number and types of offenses), and school performance as indicated by Grade Point Average (GPA).

The Case Evaluation Scale is a series of scales intended to assess the youth's adjustment status in a range of social and treatment related areas. Ratings on these scales are made by the court appointed counselor and/or by the research assistant based primarily on interviews with the client and his/her family. The scales are: (1) Community Adjustment/Legal Status; (2) Adjustment to Counseling, Casework, or Probation; (3) Family Progress; (4) Adjustment in Living Situation; (5) Parent-Young Relationships; (6) Peer Relationships; (7) Status in School; and (8) Employment Status.

Each scale consists of eight points, each of which is anchored behaviorally. For example, the eight points on the School Status scale are defined: (1) Expelled or dropped out; (2) Truancy — failing; (3) Truancy — barely passing; (4) Truancy — poor grades, Passive Attitude; (5) Attending — poor grades; (6) Attending — fair grades — Utilizing resources to improve; (7) Attending — fair grades — Improvement evident; and (8) Attending — good grades — Performing at or near capacity.

The number of offenses in the year before inclusion in the study was taken as the premeasure of number of offenses, and the number in the ten months subsequent to inclusion in the study as the post measure. Although these time period are of different lengths, they are the same for both groups and so do not introduce any bias. The Severity-Frequency index was obtained for each period by weighing each offense by its seriousness (status offender = 1, misdemeanor = 2, felony = 3) and summing. Additionally, subjects were classified as Status Offenders, Misdemeanants, or Felons (offense type) according to their most serious (ascending in that order) offense for each time period.

PROCEDURE

The data elements described were collected at the time of referral to the Diagnostic or Comparison groups by a research assistant through interviews with the youth, his/her family, court and community professionals, and from court and school records. Follow-up data was collected at four months, seven months, and ten months. Except for GPA, only the data from time of referral and ten months later will be discussed.

RESULTS

GROUP COMPARABILITY

Group characteristics and initial and final levels on the Clinical Assessment Scale are reported in Tables 1 and 2. The non-random nature of the process for group assignment emphasizes the need for examining the initial stages of the groups to assure that they are reasonably comparable. On the one hand, we would expect the Diagnostic group to have less favorable scores, because it was intentionally selected for severity. On the other, if the two groups are grossly different, the validity of the results are questionable.

Two lines of analysis suggest that a reasonable balance was struck. First, as has been mentioned, of the forty youths initially eligible for or given diagnostic work-ups, ten were institutionalized, as were three of the thirty-four Comparison Ss. Given that the study chose to focus on the impact of community diagnosis on the outcome of community treatment, these Ss were not included in the follow-up. However, the relative rates at which institutionalizations occur reflects on the comparative severity levels. Here we find that the difference in rates does not reach conventional levels of statistical significance (Chi-square $= 3.32$, 1 df, $p = 0.68$).

TABLE 1

Descriptive Data for Diagnostic and Comparison Groups

	Diagnostic Group	Comparison Group
Age		
Mean	15.03	15.41
Standard Deviation	2.24	1.46
Sex		
Male	18	18
Female	12	13
Race/Ethic		
White	26	29
Black	1	1
Chicano	2	1
Native American	1	0

TABLE 2

Means and Standard Deviations of Pre- and Post-Evaluation Scale

| | Diagnostic Group | | | | Comparison Group | | | |
| | Pre | | Post | | Pre | | Post | |
	x	sd	x	sd	x	sd	x	sd
Case Evaluation Scale*								
1. Legal Status	2.40	.77	5.30	1.96	2.33	1.'5	5.25	1.66
2. Adjust. to Counsel.	4.00	1.00	4.80	2.49	4.45	1.15	5.87	1.36
3. Family Progress	3.90	1.05	3.50	1.31	3.18	1.37	4.77	2.01
4. Living Situation	3.37	1.35	5.21	1.62	4.17	1.26	5.52	1.42
5. Parent Youth	3.13	1.36	4.14	1.85	3.31	1.61	4.63	1.93
6. Peer	3.13	1.07	4.65	1.87	2.93	1.08	5.46	1.74
7. School	3.83	1.90	3.79	2.94	3.56	2.06	4.74	2.60
8. Employment	2.50	2.95	4.80	2.74	3.22	2.82	5.67	1.67

*N's vary as a function of applicability of scale.

Second, for the students remaining in the study, there were no statistically significant differences between the two groups as they entered the study on distribution of types of offenses, number of legal problems, Severity-Frequency Index, GPA, or on the set of Case Evaluation Scales. Although the differences in number and severity of offenses were non-significant, they did favor the Comparison group. The presence of pre-existing group differences automatically complicates data analysis by introducing statistical (regression) artifacts. For our data, because the differences were small and statistically non-significant, we assumed there would be relatively little distortion in our results.

OFFENSE DATA

During the ten-month follow-up period, Diagnostic group subjects commit fewer and less serious offenses than Comparison subjects (Figures 1 and 2). Although averages for the ten months favor the Diagnostic group, they do not reach significance for either number of offenses or severity-frequency index. However, if the initially worse condition of the diagnostic group is taken into consideration by finding difference scores, that is, by subtracting the pre-measures from the post-measures, the Diagnostic group does show significantly more improvement, both in the number of offenses ($t = 1.78$, 59 df, $p < .05$, one tailed) and on the severity-frequency index ($t = 2.25$, $p < .025$, one-tailed).

These results included data for one Comparison group S whose scores were at least twice as extreme as the next worst subject in that group. A test applied to this subject shows that he/she is a statistically significant outlier, that is, his/her scores are enough different from the other Ss that he/she may be regarded as being an anomalous subject. As such the youngster's data would

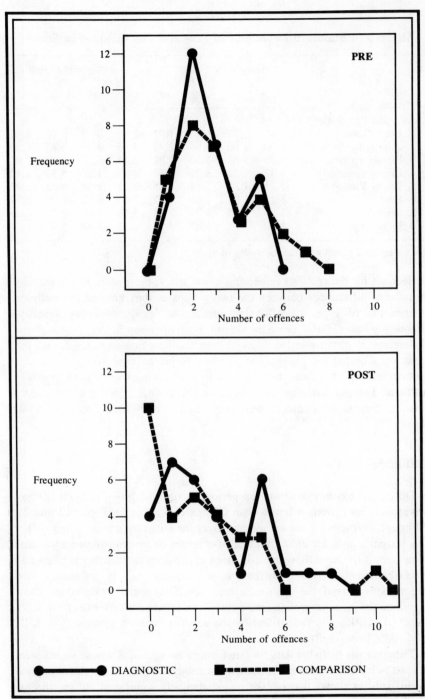

Figure 1 *Pre- and Post-Distributions of Number of Offences.*

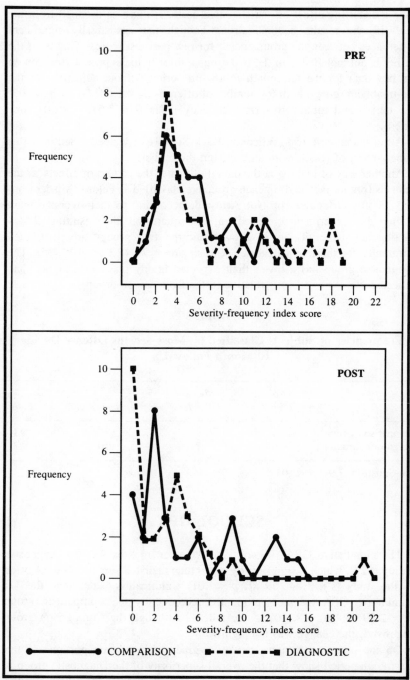

Figure 2 *Pre- and Post-Distributions of Severity-Frequency Index Scores.*

have a distorting effect on the statistical tests. If this S is dropped from the analysis, the results become strong enough that statistically significant differences between the groups occur for raw post-test scores. That is, if the outlier is not included then the two groups differ in the expected direction on the raw data for the ten-month follow-up period without adjusting for the pre-treatment scores, both for number of offenses ($t = 1.84$, 58 df, $p < .05$, one tailed) and for the Severity-frequency index ($t = 2.51$, $p < .01$, one tailed).

A non-parametric test (Wilcoxon Rank Sum Test) yielded essentially this same pattern of results with and without the outlier.

Another way of looking at the data illuminates the pattern of effects. If the subjects (outlier included) in each group are classified as Felons, Misdemeanants, Status Offenders, or Not Arrested, according to their worst offense during the experimental period, a Chi-square on the resulting 2×4 contingency table (Table 3) shows that the two groups are distributed differently for the four categories (Chi-square $= 7.91$, 3 df, $p < .05$). The Diagnostic group has a lower than expected felony rate and a higher than expected Not Arrested rate, relative to the Comparison group.

TABLE 3

Frequencies of Subjects Classified by Most Serious Offense During 10-Month Follow-Up

	No Offense	Status Offender	Misdemeanant	Felon
Comparison Group	4	9	7	11
Diagnostic Group	10	7	10	3

Chi-Square $= 7.91$, $p < .05$

SCHOOL GPA

The cumulative GPA (Figure 3) for the ten months for the Diagnostic Group is 2.2, which is significantly better than their 1.3 cumulative GPA prior to the study ($t = 3.54$, 59 df, $p < .01$) significantly better than the 1.7 cumulative GPA for the ten months recorded by the Comparison group ($t = 2.09$, 59 df, $p < .025$, one tailed). Although the Comparison group improved, the change was not significant.

On the other hand, non-cumulative grades for separate portions of the ten-month period show that the overall superiority of the Diagnostic group is due to an immediate improvement in the early months of the study. For the final three months the two groups obtained equivalent grades. Clearly the

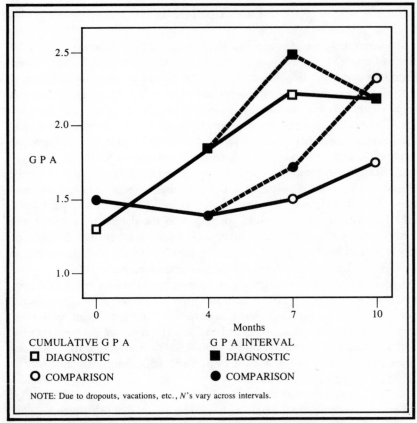

Figure 3   *G P A and Cumulative G P A for Experimental Period.*

higher initial performance is preferable, and it has potential longer range positive effects. However, the Comparison group's improvement is also desirable. Data collection over a longer period would have been helpful in clarifying these trends, particularly as to their long-term stability.

CASE EVALUATION SCALE

In general, both groups showed considerable improvement on all scales: the Comparison group improved significantly on all eight scales, the Diagnostic group improved on all, but missed statistical significance on two scales. The two groups do not differ from each other at the ten-month testing if the set of scales is taken as a whole. Tests for group differences on this battery of measures are by multivariate analysis of variance (MANOVA) which gives a single probability value for the set of dependent measures.

DISCUSSION

The community-based diagnostic program has had significant impact on the Benton-Franklin counties' juvenile court, the local community, and the state diagnostic and institutional system. Some of these outcomes are as follows:

1. There have been reduced commitments to state institutions. Before the development of the community based diagnostic program, the Benton-Franklin counties' juvenile court committed forty to fifty youngsters per year to state institutions. Since the development of the community based diagnostic program these commitments have been reduced to eleven to fifteen youth per year. Because institutional costs for the state are now at approximately $20,000 per committed youth per year, the savings to the state have been quite dramatic.

2. The recidivism rate among youngsters in the diagnostic program has been extremely low, particularly in the area of serious crimes or felonies. Not only is the program successful in reducing the cost of state institutionalization but also in effectively reducing crimes by these juveniles.

3. Diagnostic services conducted at the community level frequently do not require secure custody for the child undergoing diagnostic study. As a result, more of the costs of the diagnostic study at a community level can be directed toward professional consultations and studies. The resulting costs savings for local diagnostic programs is highly significant. Local diagnostic costs are approximately $1000 per diagnostic evaluation, while state costs are closer to $2000 per diagnostic evaluation.

4. The community diagnostic program results in the community agencies and other participants in the process becoming committed to a treatment plan for the youth. The active participation of these members of the community leads to a clearer understanding on their part of the problems of the case and of the rationale and need for community treatment, and of the importance of their role in the treatment process and now the components of the treatment plan need to fit together. All of this facilitates the implementation of a comprehensive, coordinated, community based treatment plan, with the youth the obvious beneficiary.

5. The Diagnostic Committee process develops an ideal treatment plan which is based on the committee's opinion of what is necessary to rehabilitate or treat the client without reference to what resources actually exist. The aggregation of these ideal treatment plans served as a needs assessment for juvenile court services, and the comparison between these needed services and those actually available served as a planning guide by pointing out those resources which were consistently lacking and required for treatment of the most difficult offenders coming before the court. This planning guide assisted in the creation of the most necessary resources. These included thirty specialized intensive treatment foster homes, three small group homes, a day treatment school at the mental health center, and an expanded and

sophisticated juvenile court probation staff. The creation of these additional resources has enabled us to offer community based treatment for almost all the youth coming before this court.

6. In addition, partly because of the experience gained from interacting with community resources in the diagnostic evaluations, court staff have become much more sophisticated users of community resources across the whole range of court cases.

7. Use of the evaluation of the diagnostic program as described in this document has led to the ongoing funding of the diagnostic program, as well as funding for other resources that have been developed. The research was sufficiently convincing to justify continuation funding from both state and county resources. Without the research component of the diagnostic program, it is extremely unlikely that we would have been able to sustain the funding for the diagnostic effort. On the other hand, because the data were used and seen as valuable, research in general has gained credibility and research activity in the court has continued to be supported.

8. Last, but not least, there has been a considerable impact on the state diagnostic and classification system. It is no longer required that youth from this area must go through a state diagnostic process. Instead, the court is able to send each youngster to the institution of its choice when a commitment must take place. This enables a much closer working relationship between the treatment institution and the juvenile court. In addition, two other counties have developed similar diagnostic programs. These three juvenile courts have now entered into a pilot program with the state to determine the feasibility and adequacy of utilizing community based diagnostic services throughout the state as opposed to the centralized diagnostic service provided by the state. The results of this study will be among the factors which will determine the course of the state diagnostic services in the future.

SUMMARY

This paper describes an evaluation of a community based diagnostic program initiated as an alternative to the state operated centralized diagnostic evaluation system. It was felt that the community orientation would provide a broader based, more valid evaluation, and more community involvement in treatment, as well as reducing the number of institutionalizations and being generally less expensive. The evaluation compared ten-month outcome data for thirty-one youths who passed through the Diagnostic group and who were subsequently treated in the community with data for thirty youths in a Comparison group who were also treated in the community but who received no special services or attention except for the collection of dependent variable data. Pre-treatment measures indicate that the two groups were comparable. Follow-up data show that the Diagnostic group committed fewer offenses of a less serious nature and showed a larger gain in cumulative GPA. Both groups show significant improvement on a set of rating scales, but on these there are no group differences. The program did reduce rates of institutionalization, it has reduced costs, and it has increased community involvement in treatment. The evaluation component of the project, results of which are reported in this paper, has been crucial in demonstrating project success and in obtaining on-going funding for the program. Additionally, the data have been important to date in influencing the direction of state diagnostic practice. The value and usefulness of the data has justified the expense of a research component of court activities.

Part V

Programs for Juveniles in Correctional Institutions

Chapter 21

Editors' Remarks

Regardless of the success and popularity of community-based treatment programs, there will undoubtedly continue to be a substantial number of adolescent offenders who will be, for one reason or another, committed to correctional institutions. Accordingly, it is imperative that continuing research be conducted to find effective intervention programs which can be implemented in such settings. The large-scale research project discussed by Carl Jesness in this chapter represents an important step in that direction. The research is remarkable in its design, its scope and in the thoroughness of the analysis. The researchers "took over" two large correctional institutions, thoroughly trained their staff, conducted a large-scale transactional analysis program in one and a behavior modification program in the other, *randomly* assigned delinquents to one or the other institution, then, using multiple measures, compared the effects of the two programs with each other and with other institutions which provided regular programs. In addition, Jesness examined individual differences in response to treatment. *Both* programs were found to lead to approximately 15% lower recidivism rates overall with striking differences in recidivism for different types of offenders. The paper included herein highlights the results of Jesness's research.

Readers who wish to examine this large-scale project in greater detail are advised to review Jesness's article: "Comparative effectiveness of behavior modification and transactional analysis programs for delinquents." *Journal of Consulting & Clinical Psychology*, 1975, *43*(6), 758–779.

Was the Close-Holton Project A "Bummer"?*

Carl F. Jesness

The other day I was startled and dismayed to hear a California Youth Authority administrator ask if the Close-Holton Project had not, in fact, been a "bummer". After assuring him that far from being a bummer the project had been a most emphatic success, I reflected (again) upon our failure as researchers to properly disseminate our findings. If California Youth Authority (CYA) staff perceive our most successful efforts as failures, how awful they must regard our failures. And how do they view our very frequent finding of "no significant differences"? Do they see such studies as a waste of time, or as contributions to our fund of knowledge? Destroying myths is, after all, one of our primary tasks. But the only myth destroyed by the Close-Holton Study (otherwise known as the Youth Center Research Project) was the currently popular notion that "nothing works" — good programs *do* make a difference.

It certainly seems to be an appropriate time to remind ourselves of past successes. The nothing works pessimism that so pervades current thought has seemingly lowered our expectations to the point where programs are now gauged as most successful on the basis that they do the least harm. That is hardly a posture that generates enthusiasm. While one cannot argue against the merits of the current correctional emphasis on fairness, safety, and normalcy, one can vigorously object to the assumption that these goals are sufficient. Although espousing only these objectives conveys the impression of wisdom, mature skepticism, and reality-based thinking, doing so may serve as an excuse for thowing up our hands and doing less in our rehabilitation efforts. The data from the Close-Holton project speak to more ambitious possibilities.

---

*Jesness, C.F., "Was the Close-Holton project a 'bummer'?" *California Youth Authority Quarterly*, 1979, Copyright ©, California Youth Authority Quarterly. Reprinted by permission.

THE PROJECT

Detailed descriptions of the Close-Holton project have been presented elsewhere (Jesness, 1975(a), 1975(b), 1975(c); Jesness, DiRisi, McCormick, & Wedge, 1972; Jesness & DeRisi, 1973). All we will do here is highlight some of its most unique features and the essential results.

The project's research objective was to compare the effectiveness of two widely accepted but theoretically different treatment approaches — behavior modification and transactional analysis. Originally the settings were to have been Preston and Karl Holton. It was former director Allen Breed who encouraged us to go all the way and implement the project in two more closely comparable institutions, O.H. Close and Karl Holton. These institutions had at that time (1968) just begun operation, and in many respects represented an ideal setting for such a comparative research project. They were alike in their organizational structure, staffing patterns, and physical layout. Each was designed to house approximately 400 youths in eight 50-bed living halls. When the project began, boys of nearly the same age were being assigned to the institutions, so that random assignment to either institution was immediately feasible.

Training Of Staff   One of the most remarkable aspects of the study was in the extent of staff involvement in training and later in program implementation. It may be difficult, for example, to imagine how far-out the notion of staff participation in TA marathons was at the time, but believe me, it was heretical. Yet, all but a handful of Close staff voluntarily (with perhaps, a little pressure) attended three-day marathons as part of their training. Paralleling that effort, to recall Holton administrative staff pouring over the Holland & Skinner behavioral textbook hour after hour (for a total of 80!) is equally if not more mind-boggling. Credit is still due all the staff for their efforts, and to the many leaders who made the project go.

Implementation   How successful were staff in developing and using the treatment modalities? Not unexpectedly, some staff were more enthusiastic, committed, and skilled than others, but it is fair to say that most youth in the institutions participated in or were exposed to a much more intensive treatment than they had experienced either before or after. During their stay youth at Close participated in an average of 40 hours of transactional analysis group sessions. In addition to being involved in an institution-wide micro-economy, staff at Holton negotiated an average of 19 written contracts with each ward covering individual critical behavior deficiencies.

RESULTS

Close vs. Holton   There were several important similarities in the outcomes of the two programs — both showed accelerated achievement test gains, reduced evidence of aggressive behavior, reduced use of lock-up ($-$ 60%) and reduced recidivism. But the Close program generated much more positive youth-staff relations and consistently greater gains along attitudinal-psychological dimensions (confidence, withdrawal, etc.). By contrast, youth in the behaviorally oriented programs at Holton not unexpectedly showed greater positive behavior changes. Surprisingly, the I_3 manipulators gained more from the Close TA program (on almost every measure including parole performance). I_2 youth gained more from the behavioral program at Holton. Overall parole performance was about the same for the two programs; parolees from *both* did better than Close and Holton releases from earlier periods and releasees from other comparable CYA institutions.

Parole follow-up   The fact that there were no significant differences between the revocation rates of subjects from the two schools at any parole exposure period probably formed the basis for our administrator friend's impression that the project was unsuccessful. An almost identical 32.2% of Close, and 32.0% of Holton youths had recidivated after 12 months exposure; 47.6% and 48.1% after 24 months. Table 1 shows the parole violation rates of Close and Holton parole release cohorts for the two-year baseline period (1968–69) prior to the full implementation of the experimental programs, and the rates for youths in the project (1970–71). Here a very different picture emerges. The drop in recidivism from baseline to experimental period were statistically significant for both Close and Holton. The parole performance of program participants was clearly superior to that shown by pre-experimental releasees.

TABLE 1

Parole Violation Rates for Holton and Close Release Cohorts 1968[a], 1969[a], 1970[b], and 1971[b] at 12 Months Parole Exposure

	Year of Release	n	Close #V	%V	n	Holton #V	%V
Baseline	1968	253	124	49.0	232	99	42.7
	1969	407	189	46.4	267	109	40.8
Experimental	1970	233	80	34.3	187	58	31.0
	1971	220	69	31.4	211	71	33.6

Note: n refers to the number released; #V refers to the number of violators; %V refers to the percentage of violators.
[a] Includes only wards age 15, 16, or 17 at entry.
[b] Includes project cases only.

Prorated Failure Rates   Further refinements were carried out in order to rule out other explanations. It has been repeatedly shown that age at release is highly correlated with success on parole, with younger subjects being more likely to fail. To make certain that differences in age did not account for these findings, an analysis was run in which age was controlled. The 1968, 1969, 1970, and 1971 release cohorts from each of the two schools were prorated on the basis of the proportion of subjects at each age in the Close-Holton Project sample, and expected violation rates were recalculated for all four years. Analysis of these prorated data again revealed no differences between Close and Holton, but confirmed the differences in rates between baseline and experimental periods of approximately 10 percentage points favoring the experimental period for both schools (42.6% vs. 31.4% violation rate for Close, and 44.9% vs. 35.1% violation rate for Holton).

One further set of data was looked at to see if a general trend toward lower recidivism could account for the results. Recidivism rates were obtained for releases from two other CYA institutions (Nelles and Paso Robles) to which boys of approximately the same age were then being assigned. The violation rates for these release cohorts were also prorated according to the distribution of ages in the project sample. All four schools showed a significant decrease in violation rates over the four years from 1968 to 1972 ($p < .01$). However, the decreases in rates between 1969 (the year prior to the project) and 1970 (the first year of the project) were significant for Close and Holton, but were not for Paso Robles or Nelles.

Table 2 shows a summary of the prorated failure rates for the project period (1970–71) for the combined sample of youths from Close and Holton, and for youths from Nelles and Paso Robles. The 1970–71 prorated failure rate for project parolees released from Close and Holton (33.1%) was significantly lower ($p < .001$) than failure rates for either Nelles (42.5%) or Paso Robles (42.8%). Again nearly a 10 percentage point differential was shown. If we convert this into percentage of recidivism reduced, the figure looks even more

TABLE 2

Prorated Twelve Month Violation Rates Comparing Close-Holton with Nelles and Paso Robles; Combined 1970–71 Release Cohort

Combined 1970–71 Release Cohort	*n*	*#V*	*%V*
Close-Holton	842	279	33.1
Nelles	835	355	42.5
Paso Robles	710	304	42.8

Note: Chi-square for Close-Holton vs. Nelles = 15.42, $p < .001$; Close-Holton vs. Paso Robles = 15.15, $p < .001$.

impressive (i.e., 25%). It does not require a very sharp pencil to translate a 10% recidivism differential into a fairly large amount of dollar savings based on institutional costs alone.

CONCLUSION

We can conclude that the Close-Holton project, far from being a bummer, was an unqualified winner. The implication of the study's findings are unusually favorable. Institution-wide treatment environments and programs of high quality and intensity can be implemented in the CYA. When such programs are introduced they can lead to measurable reduction in management problems; improved behavior; and reduced anxiety, alienation, and hostility. Most important, the programs can effect a reduction in recidivism.

Whether an institution can sustain an intensive or innovative program over a long period of time remains less certain. Although I do not have first-hand knowledge of the status of the Close or Holton programs, I have heard several persons remark that both programs may have gradually become watered down due to a variety of reasons. My own impression (along with data from other studies) suggests that without outside stimulation and reinforcement an organization or institution tends to settle into a state of equilibrium and mutual accommodation that satisfies its own immediate needs, but may lead to a state of stagnation; the program may continue to spin its wheels giving the appearance of activity but without moving forward. Research has as its primary goal the collection of empirical data as the basis for a rational decision and policy making process; but a research project can also serve as a source of stimulation to program development.

There are several "new" treatment modalities in vogue that may deserve a trial, even if one suspects they may be old wine in new bottles. There are obvious advantages in experimenting with such untried methods, particularly in the enthusiasm sometimes generated among staff. More difficult, but probably more rational and effective in the long run are program development efforts that take advantage of and build upon what has already been tried and tested. Over the years, research in the CYA (and elsewhere) has accrued empirical findings that could provide the basis for a model rehabilitation program (or programs).

Data presented here indicate that either the Close or Holton program could provide a sound starting point. Or how about a program integrating the strengths of both behavioral and dynamic theories coupled with an intensive work experience? Behaviorists are increasingly recognizing that behavior is not only a response to external stimuli, but rather an interactive process that includes the individual's expectations, beliefs, self-appraisals, and other cognitive factors. Particularly important in its implications for treatment is the knowledge that persons may show marked individual differences in the extent to which their behavior is controlled by internal rather than external influences.

Other program elements that have been shown to be related to effectiveness include client involvement and responsibility for setting their own goals, and planning their own programs; and opportunity for client choice. Intensive programming in small living units has been shown to be effective, whereas long lengths of stay have not. A trade off of these could be considered when it becomes politically feasible to do so. More immediately feasible would be to take advantage of the knowledge (in part accumulated in the Close-Holton project) that mutual positive regard between staff and youths enhances the impact of intervention efforts regardless of what type. We even know quite a lot about how such mutual regard can be fostered — one of the simplest being the proper matching of client (I-Level) to caseworker style and preference. Implementing these elements in the context of a sound case-management system and continuous feedback to both staff and client could be an exciting challenge.

Most of these elements already exist in bits and pieces within CYA institutions. What would it take to pull them together into a single dynamic program? One immediately thinks of outside funding for supporting the training and enriched staffing that might be needed. But that may not be the most productive long-term way to go. Perhaps we should examine the possibility of designating a single living unit in one (or more) institutions as a demonstration-development unit, and finding means of permanent support within CYA resources? The Close-Holton project could be made to look like a "bummer" in contrast to what such a program might be, but until we succeed in improving upon them the Close-Holton programs remain exemplary.

REFERENCES

Jesness, C.F., "Comparative effectiveness of behavior modification and transactional analysis programs for delinquents," *Journal of Consulting and Clinical Psychology*, 1975(a), *43*, 758–779.

Jesness, C.F. "The impact of behavior modification and transactional analysis on institution social climate." *Journal of Research in Crime and Delinquency*, 1975(b), *12*, 79–91.

Jesness, C.F., "The youth center project: Transactional analysis and behavior modification programs for delinquents," *Behavioral Disorders*, 1975(c), *1*(1).

Jesness, C.F., & DeRisi, W., "Some variations in techniques of contingency management in a school for delinquents." In J.S. Stumphauzer (ed), *Behavioral therapy with delinquents* (Springfield, Ill.: Charles C. Thomas, 1973).

Jesness, C.F., DeRisi, W., McCormick, P.M., & Wedge, R.F., *The Youth Center Research Project* (Sacramento, Calif.: American Justice Institute, July 1972).

Chapter 22

Editors' Remarks

Many reviews of the literature on correctional treatment have described studies which have found no differences in recidivism between an experimental group of offenders provided with "treatment" in an institution and a control group of offenders who did not receive such treatment. Typically it is assumed that the control group is an "untreated" group and that since treatment did not improve on no treatment at all, the treatment was impotent. Researchers and reviewers alike seldom seem to recognize that the control group in correctional evaluation research is unlikely to receive no treatment. In our view it is the rare correctional agency which provides *no* programs for its clients. Accordingly, some treatment evaluation research is really comparing the effectiveness of the experimental treatment with that of some other (usually unspecified) treatment. It is most illogical to conclude, as is usually done, that a failure to find significant differences between what are actually two treatment programs indicates that treatment is ineffective.*

In the program evaluation conducted by Michael Maskin he compares a family oriented counseling program against a type of program which has been very popular in institutional settings for delinquents — a program which seeks to improve the offender's self-concept through work-oriented activities. The study is also a good demonstration of the fact that even in institutional settings there is much to be gained by involving the offender's parents in the treatment of the offender. Maskin's results indicate that it is not only the offender's vocational skills which are important in his rehabilitation, it is also his interpersonal communication skills.

---

*Birkenmayer, A., *Personal Communication*, 1979.

The Differential Impact of Work-oriented vs. Communication-oriented Juvenile Correction Programs Upon Recidivism Rates in Delinquent Males*

Michael B. Maskin

PROBLEM

There is growing public concern over rising juvenile crime rates and delinquency statistics. Recent research by Reckless, et al.[1] suggests the self-concept to be an important variable in delinquent behavior. Generally, delinquents report low self-esteem with little self-respect or sense of worth, and their behavior reflects this poor self-image. Clinical studies by Cohen and Short[2] and Hackler[3] indicate that progressive correctional facilities that emphasize individualized work-oriented treatment afford a clear trend of desirable changes in self-concept structure. Institutional duties such as camp maintenance, food preparation, and work-shop-vocational training are stressed and practiced as part of the therapeutic regimen. In contrast, Maskin

*Maskin, M.B., "The differential impact of work-oriented vs. communication-oriented juvenile correction programs upon recidivism rates in delinquent males," *Journal of Clinical Psychology*, 1976, *32*(2), 432–433. Copyright © 1976, Journal of Clinical Psychology. Reprinted by permission.

[1]Reckless, W.C., Dinitz, S. and Kay, B., "The self component in potential delinquency and potential non-delinquency," *American Sociological Review, 1957, 22*, 566–570. Reckless, W.C., Dinitz, S. and Murray, E., "The good boy in a high delinquency area," *Journal of Criminal Law and Criminology*, 1957, *48*, 18–25.

[2]Cohen, A.K. and Short, J.F. Jr., "Research in delinquent subcultures," *Journal of Social Issues*, 1958, *14*, 20–37.

[3]Hackler, J.C., "Testing of a causal model of delinquency," *Sociology Quarterly*, 1970, *11*, 511–522.

and Brookins[4] have pointed to the importance of family solidarity, involvement, and communication in the overall rehabilitation program for the delinquents.

The present study investigated the differential effects of two distinct correctional programs, one that emphasizes work-oriented intervention and one that emphasizes communication-oriented therapeutic intervention, upon recidivism rates in delinquent males. In addition to providing needed follow-up data to evaluate the efficacy of these strategies, it is the author's contention that the parent-child interaction program wherein family interactions and relationships are facilitated is essential for successful treatment of the offender and positive self-concept change.

METHOD

Subjects and Procedure   Ss were 60 first-time juvenile offenders who never had been admitted to a formal correctional program. All Ss were male and matched for age (15 to 17 years), ethnic origin, educational achievement (9 to 12 grades), and reading score on the Wide Range Achievement Test. Administration of the achievement test is routine to each institution on admission.

Group A, Twin Pines Ranch for Boys, Twin Pines, California, employes a work-oriented program in the rehabilitation of delinquents. The aim of this program is to help the individual to become more self-reliant by developing individual, vocational and personal skills. This training includes various physical and personal duties involved in hygiene, subsistence, ranch maintenance, recreational and sport activity. Group B's program at Verdemont Ranch for Boys, Verdemont, California, emphasizes a "parent-child" interaction through individual and group counseling in order to provide the parents and youth an opportunity to learn better communication skills. A concentrated effort is made to improve family unity.

The total time period of treatment for both programs is 10 months, which is divided into 6 months in residence and 4 months' aftercase. Upon successful completion of the first 6 months the male and his parent(s) continue in aftercare treatment for a period of 4 months while the boy lives at home. Recidivism was defined as (a) two or more detentions by a male in either phase of the program, or (b) institutionalization after completion of residential or aftercare treatment.

---

[4]Maskin, M.B. and Brookins, F., "The effects of parental composition on recidivism rates in delinquent girls," *Journal of Clinical Psychology*, 1974, *30*, 341–342.

RESULTS AND DISCUSSION

For data analysis, two chi squares were computed to compare recidivism rates for both treatment groups. Significant differences were found between groups in both residential and aftercare programs. In the residential program ($x^2 = 6.71$, $df = 1$, $p < .01$), the greatest amount of recidivists were in the work-oriented group. In the aftercare program, which consisted of graduates of the residential program, significant differences ($x^2 = 3.89$, $df = 1$, $p < .05$) were obtained, with the highest frequency of recidivism again in the work-oriented group.

TABLE 1

Recidivism Frequencies in Work-oriented and Communication-oriented Delinquency Correction Programs

Treatment	N	Work-oriented	Communication-oriented	x^2	p
Residential	60	15	4	6.71	< .01
Aftercare	41	8	1	3.89	< .05

It seems possible that this difference could be attributed to the effects of the personnel who were administering the two programs. However, it is the author's opinion that the programs were probably influential. Earlier research[5] has shown that male delinquents in a communication-oriented program that stressed interpersonal competence and family interaction underwent greater positive change in self-concept than did their peers in the work-oriented program. Our evidence suggests that desirable change in self-concept is related directly to eventual recidivism frequency.

Furthermore, this study indicates that a communication-oriented delinquency treatment program has ultimately a greater long-term impact on the juvenile. Improvement of family and social relations appears to influence directly the lower recidivism rates observed in this study. Successful rehabilitation might well involve efforts toward active integration of the delinquent and his family. To isolate the offender in a traditional work-oriented setting seems to neglect interpersonal and familial concerns between the youth and his parents.

[5]Maskin, M.B. and Flescher, B.E., "Change in self-concept in work-oriented versus communication-oriented juvenile correction programs," *Psychological Reports*, 1975; *36*, 460–462.

SUMMARY

This study examined recidivism rates in work-oriented (N = 30) and communication-oriented (N = 30) juvenile delinquency programs for males. Both groups were matched for age, ethnic origin, educational achievement, and reading scores. Chi-square analyses indicated significant differences in recidivism rates between groups in both residential ($x^2 = 6.71$, $df = 1$, $p < .01$) and aftercare ($x^2 = 3.89$, $df = 1$, $p < .05$) programs. In each phase of the treatment program, recidivism was highest in the work-oriented group. The results suggested that (a) facilitation of family interaction and communication is related closely to successful treatment of the delinquent and consequent recidivism; (b) group counseling that provides the youth and parents an opportunity to learn better communication skills appears to improve family cohesion and solidarity; and (c) newer therapeutic approaches in delinquency should concentrate on filial and family-type therapies.

Chapter 23

Editors' Remarks

It seems eminently reasonable to assume that the delinquent, through association with delinquent peers or through a lack of exposure to prosocial models, has failed to acquire adequate information about alternative methods of adapting to his world or has failed to develop attitudes or problem-solving techniques which enable him to function effectively in a prosocial manner. Sarason and Ganzer's work is an impressive example of how a behavioral treatment approach, by focusing on such cognitive processes, can effectively remediate delinquent behavior.

In addition to the results presented in this chapter, Sarason (1978) has reported that the beneficial effects of this program have persisted through a five-year follow-up period: 48% of the control group recidivated within the five year period compared to 23% of the groups which received treatment.

Cognitive behavior modification approaches in the corrections field have not, as yet, been extensively studied but it is interesting to note that impressive improvements were also found in Chandler's study (see Chapter 14) which also focused on cognitive factors (egocentric thought) presumed to be mediating the delinquents' behavior. The results of these studies augur well for the further application of cognitive behavior modification in corrections (e.g., Meichenbaum, 1977).

REFERENCES

Meichenbaum, D., *Cognitive-Behavior Modification* (New York: Plenum, 1977).

Sarason, I.G., "A cognitive social learning approach to juvenile delinquency." In R.D. Hare & D. Schalling (Eds), *Psychopathic Behavior: Approaches to Research* (New York: John Willey, 1978).

Modeling and Group Discussion in the Rehabilitation of Juvenile Delinquents*

Irwin G. Sarason and Victor J. Ganzer

This study represents an experimental exploration of the means by which delinquents' awareness of what constitutes socially acceptable and effective behavior can be heightened. Implicit in the research was the assumption that social behavior, both conventional and deviant, is explainable in terms of the information available to and made salient for individuals. The experimental manipulation consisted of the manner by which information was made available to persons. One third of the subjects were exposed to a sequence of social modeling, a technique used with increasing frequency by counselors and clinicians (Krumboltz & Thoresen, 1969). A second group participated in discussions with an intent similar to that of subjects in the modeling program. The third group of comparable subjects constituted a control condition.

The modeling treatment was derived from social learning theory. For a wide variety of purposes, demonstrations in the form of modeled behavior are effective instructional techniques (Bandura, 1969; LaFleur & Johnson, 1972). Some evidence suggests that institutionalized delinquent boys become more socially adaptive as a function of observational learning opportunities

*Sarason, I.G. and Ganzer, V.J., "Modeling and group discussion in the rehabilitation of juvenile delinquents," *Journal of Counseling Psychology*, 1973, *20*(5), 442–449. Copyright © 1973, American Psychological Association. Reprinted by permission.

This investigation was supported in part by a grant from the Social and Rehabilitation Service, Department of Health, Education, and Welfare. Robert Tropp, William Callahan, and the staff of the Cascadia Juvenile Reception-Diagnostic Center made important contributions, as did Ralph Sherfey, Sarah Sloat, Theodore Sterling, V.M. Tye, J.J. Wahler, Lloyd Bates, and Cameron Dightman. We gratefully acknowledge the contributions of the superintendents and staffs of Washington's juvenile institutions and of these assistants: David Barrett, Peter Carlson, Duane Dahlum, Douglas Denney, Richard Erickson, Robert Howenstine, Robert Kirk, and David Snow.

(Sarason, 1968; Sarason & Ganzer, 1969). Modeling, however, is not the only or necessarily the best way of conveying information. The second experimental approach consisted of providing information about, but not demonstration of, prosocial ways of responding to environmental problems. Delinquent boys under this condition received information about social behavior within a structured discussion or counseling format. In the course of a series of discussions, subjects were given examples of desirable and undesirable ways of coping with social, vocational, and educational situations. Boys in a control group experienced only the normal program offered by a well-staffed institution with a relatively low resident-staff ratio. The control boys received as many contacts with caseworkers and counselors as did experimental group boys.

METHOD

SUBJECTS

The research was conducted at the Cascadia Juvenile Reception-Diagnostic Center in Tacoma, Washington. This institution, which was described in an earlier article (Sarason, 1968), receives all delinquent children committed by Juvenile Court judges to the State's Division of Institutions. The length of stay is approximately six weeks for new commitments. Approximately 12% of the children are paroled directly to their home communities, the majority being transferred to another state facility.

The subjects were 192 male first offenders who at admission were between 15½ and 18 years of age (mean = 16 years, 7 months). The average IQ estimated from the Lorge-Thorndike (Lorge, Thorndike, & Hagen, 1966) Nonverbal Intelligence Scale was 95.3. The three groups were comparable in age, IQ, diagnostic classification made by the Cascadia staff, and type and severity of delinquent behavior prior to institutionalization. There were 64 subjects in each of the modeling, discussion, and control groups. Half of the subjects in the modeling and discussion groups received either audio- or videotaped feedback of their group behavior. Conditions and feedback media were counterbalanced for the two cottages used. Assignment of subjects to conditions was essentially random but was occasionally influenced by weekly admission rates; that is, if too few boys were admitted during a week when a new experimental group was needed, those admissions were all designated as controls.

MODELING CONDITION

Sarason (1968) has described the general procedure used in modeling sessions. In this study modeling was oriented toward a practical approach to the problems of adolescent boys. Each session was attended by four or five subjects and two models. The models were psychology graduate students trained to lead the groups. Each modeling session had a particular theme, such as how to apply for a job, how to resist temptations by peers to engage in antisocial acts, how to take problems to a teacher or a parole counselor, and how to pass up immediate gratification in order to lay the groundwork for achieving more significant goals in the future. Emphasis was placed on the generality of the appropriate behaviors being modeled and on their potential usefulness in different interpersonal situations. Each situation was written to illustrate topics or problem situations that had been nominated frequently by boys in a pilot study as presenting difficulty to them.

One of the models began each session by introducing and describing the scene to be enacted that day. The introduction oriented the subjects to the topic for the day and provided a rationale for the particular scene. After the boys had been briefed concerning points to which they should pay special attention, the models role played the particular situation for the day while the boys observed. Most of the situations were divided into parts. In some cases the first part depicted an undesirable way of coping with a problem and the second a more desirable way. Following the models' enactment of the situation, one boy was called upon to summarize and explain the content and outcome of what had just been modeled. Each meeting was either audio- or videotape recorded.

Recorded segments of the modeled behavior then were played, after which pairs of boys or a boy and a model imitated as closely as possible the behavior that they had just observed. A short break ensued during which soft drinks were served and an audio or video role-playing tape was played. Then the remaining subjects enacted the situation so that each boy participated in each session. The audio- or videotape replay of this enactment was followed by comments and critiques by the boys of their role playing. Each meeting ended with a summary of the session, its most salient aspects, and its generalizability.

Comments and questions by the models were focused on sustaining the group's interest in and attention to the scenes being role played. Remarks made by the models were brief and to the point. Lengthy discussions by group members were not encouraged. The models attempted to get the boys to think about related and similar situations in which the modeled contents of the scene could be applied to their lives. An example is provided by the "Job Interview" scene in which boys observed and imitated appropriate interviewee behaviors and then verbally were given an enumeration of situations in which boys would be required to make a good impression on somebody in authority.

A different topic or situation was modeled for each of the 14 hour-long sessions. Pairs of subjects in the groups formed and enacted their own scenes during the fifteenth session. These scenes subsequently were role played by the other boys. The final session, the sixteenth, served as a review and summary of the work conducted during the previous 15 meetings. This was done through either a video or audio master tape upon which selected aspects of previous scenes had been condensed and recorded.

DISCUSSION CONDITION

Every effort was made to keep the sequence and content of the discussion group meetings as similar as possible to the modeling sessions. The orientation given to the discussion groups presented the same rationale and purposes as that given to the modeling groups, except that all references to role playing were omitted. Each meeting also was either audio- or videotape recorded. An example of how these meetings were conducted is provided by the "Job Interview" discussion. One of the leaders introduced the topic by indicating the importance of jobs as a means of getting money for things that we need. He also emphasized that employment is a way to earn something through one's own effort and to achieve independence. He commented that getting a job isn't easy and that knowledge and skill are relevant to getting jobs. The job interview was described as a key step in this process. One of the two group leaders then asked the boys what interviews they had experienced, what questions had been asked of them, and how they had handled the situations. Interventions of the group leaders were analogous to those used in modeling groups. Audio- and videotape feedback for the discussion group was employed in a manner similar to the modeling situations.

During the fifteenth session the subjects were asked to present topics that they themselves felt should be discussed and to give reasons why these topics were important. The sixteenth meeting was a summary session. While the manner in which the modeling and discussion groups were conducted differed, their content and sequential characteristics were comparable.

DEPENDENT VARIABLES

Three types of dependent variables were premeasures, repeated measures, and postmeasures.

Premeasures   Shortly after admission to Cascadia, subjects were administered a short true-false personality inventory that included Sarason's (Sarason & Ganzer, 1962) Test Anxiety Scale (TAS), the *Pd* scale of the Minnesota Multiphasic Personality Inventory (MMPI) (Dahlstrom & Welsh, 1960), the Gough (1957) Impulsivity Scale, and Navran's (1954) Dependency Scale.

Repeated measures   Additional self-report data and staff behavior ratings were obtained on subjects at the time of the premeasures and again just prior to their release from Cascadia. The interval between pre- and posttesting was approximately five weeks. Self-report measures yielded scores on 10 variables; (a) Wahler's (1969) Self-Description Inventory, which contains descriptions of favorable and unfavorable personal characteristics rated on a scale from "very much like me" to "not at all like me"; (b) the Word Rating Scale, which consists of 12 bipolar semantic differential items designed to measure five aspects of the self-concept (e.g., "Me as I am now," "Me as my parents see me"); (c) a goal scale on which subjects estimated the likelihood that they would achieve various future goals (e.g., "Finish high school"); (d) Lykken's (1957) Activity Preference Questionnaire; and (e) Rotter's (1966) Internalization-Externalization (I-E) Scale.

Cottage counselors completed two kinds of reliability ratings (e.g., interrater rs ranged from .75 to 1.00 on each subject: (a) a Behavior Rating Scale which contained 10 bipolar behavior descriptions (e.g., "Never hits and pushes — Often hits and pushes"), each rated on a 7-point scale, and (b) a Weekly Behavior Summary which included a seven-category behavior checklist dealing with peer and staff relationships, work detail performance, personal habits, and general cottage adjustment.

Postmeasures   Each subjects's case disposition was rank ordered from most favorable (e.g., parole) to least favorable (e.g., transfer to a high security institution). Placement in any given institution was objectively rated by clinical staff as reflecting degrees of maladjustment and need for control. Measures obtained during the postparole follow-up included retesting on several of the previously described measures, interview material, and indices of recidivism. Since the recidivism data were gathered almost three years after administration of the experimental treatments, they were the most significant indices of long-term treatment effects. An initial expectation was that since the treatments were only four weeks in duration, their effects would be more detectable before than after parole.

RESULTS

In spite of some cottage differences, the three treatment groups were comparable across all premeasures. Significant ($p < .05$) positive changes were found from pre to posttesting for 10 of the 12 repeated dependent variables for the pooled groups. Analyses of variance suggested that the subjects tended to show favorable changes in their attitudes, self-concepts, and their rated overt behavior during the five week interval between pre- and postassessment. Comparisons of changes among the three treatment groups revealed two significant differences for the 12 measures. Modeling subjects showed a reduction in emotional reactivity on the Activity Preference Questionnaire that was significantly greater ($p < .05$) than that for the other subjects. Both discussion and modeling subjects showed a greater ($p < .05$) shift toward internalization on the I–E scale than did the control subjects. The difference between modeling and discussion conditions was not significant.

Analyses of variance of the repeated self-reports and staff ratings showed that the televised feedback had different effects on modeling and discussion groups ($p < .01$). The differences were small between the discussion groups that did and did not receive televised feedback. The televised and nontelevised modeling groups differed widely. The latter showed the most and the former the least overall positive change.

One variable, case disposition, was analyzed by nonparametric comparisons because the range and distribution of this measure, suggesting that it did not meet the assumptions required for parametric analyses. Table 1 shows the distribution of case disposition scores for all subjects according to group membership. The eight possible dispositions were combined and reduced to four categories to permit chi-square comparisons. Categories 1–2 represent favorable case dispositions (i.e., 1 = diagnostic parole) and Categories 7–8 represent placement in the more structured, higher security institutions that generally receive more chronically delinquent and maladaptive boys. Approximately three times as many boys in the nontelevised modeling groups received favorable placements as compared with other groups. A chi-square comparison among boys receiving Category 1–2 placements revealed a significant difference ($p < .05$). The number of subjects in the nontelevised modeling group ($n = 14$) was also significantly greater ($p < .01$) than the number of boys in the televised discussion ($n = 5$) or televised modeling ($n = 4$) and nontelevised discussions ($n = 4$). Comparisons across groups within each of the remaining three placement categories did not reveal significant differences. Nontelevised modeling subjects clearly received more favorable case dispositions than did subjects in other groups.

TABLE 1

Comparisons of Placement Ratings for Main Experimental and Control Groups

Group	Combined placement rating			
	1–2 fav- orable	3–4	5–6	7- 8 unfav- orable
Televised modeling	4	9	6	13
Nontelevised modeling	14	7	2	9
Televised discussion	5	8	9	10
Nontelevised discussion	4	11	8	9
Cottage A control	4	12	4	2
Cottage B control	5	7	5	15
Total	36	54	34	68

Note: n = 32 for each group.

Many factors interact to determine the Cascadia Review Board's decision to place a boy in another institution or to return him directly to the community.

Other things being equal, his behavior in the cottage significantly influences his case disposition. It cannot be said with certainty that participation in a modeling group was the major determinant of favorable placement; however, since most boys were comparable across the dimensions measured in this investigation at the time of their admission to Cascadia, the modeling treatment probably did influence boys' attitudes and behaviors for the better, and this difference was to some degree reflected in the favorable decisions made by the Review Board.

The intermediate term data consisted of behavior ratings made by counselors after the subjects had spent approximately four months in the institutions to which they had been sent from Cascadia. Independent and reliable Behavior Rating Scale and Weekly Behavior Summary ratings were obtained from pairs of counselors for each subject. Counselors were not told which boys had been in groups while at Cascadia. Mean behavior rating scores among experimental and control subgroups did not differ significantly. The large differences previously associated with the feedback variable had completely "washed out" by the time the four-month ratings were made.

Further comparisons were made for the behavior rating data of whether subjects showed positive, no further, or negative change from the Cascadia postrating to the subsequent four-month institution rating. The criterion for determining direction of change was based on a one standard deviation of the mean Cascadia postrating. These comparisons are summarized in Table 2.

Between- and within-group comparisons of positive and negative behavior changes were performed by chi-square tests. The proportion of subjects who continued to show positive change did not differ significantly among the three groups. However, a significantly greater proportion of control subjects changed negatively than did either modeling ($p < .01$) or discussion ($p < .07$) subjects. Significantly greater numbers of subjects within both the modeling ($p < .01$) and discussion ($p < .05$) conditions showed positive as opposed to negative behavior changes. This was not the case for the control group.

TABLE 2

Subjects Showing Positive, No Further, or Negative Rated Behavior Change from Cascadia Postraining to Subsequent Institution Rating

		Behavior change				
Subject	%	Positive	No further	Nega-tive	% positive	% negative
Modeling	44	17	23	4	38.6	9.1
Discussion	51	20	23	8	39.2	15.8
Control	57	15	26	16	26.3	28.1

Follow-up interviews and self-report data were obtained for 53 subjects subsequent to their discharge from parole. Of this sample, 20 had been in the modeling, 18 in the discussion, and 15 in the control groups. The sample is biased by (a) early parole discharges given to some boys (the majority of these were in the modeling group), (b) voluntary participation of the interviewees (however, only 7 boys or their parents out of 60 boys who were contacted refused to participate), and (c) urban residence of most subjects.

Three kinds of data were obtained from each follow-up contact: (a) descriptions by subjects of their experiences following release, (b) reports by subjects of their recall, application of, and rated usefulness of their Cascadia experiences, and (c) readministration of several self-report measures including a specially devised checklist on which subjects compared their current adjustment in several areas to that prior to institutionalization.

Blind ratings were made of interview typescripts in order to determine subjects' evaluations of their experiences during institutionalization and parole. Interviews were rated as reflecting positive, neutral, or negative response to these experiences. Only in the case of the modeling group did an absolute majority of the subjects indicate an overall positive response to the state's programs for young offenders ($p < .01$).

Another type of follow-up data was derived from subjects' recollections of their participation in the modeling and discussion groups. Recall of content, procedure, and the group's goals was rated as adequate to good or as poor. A higher percentage of subjects in the modeling group (79%) recalled the content and purpose of the groups than was the case for the discussion group (38%; $p < .05$). Although it was expected that recall of the content would be superior for modeling group boys because of the greater specificity and repetition involved in the imitative procedures, their better recall of the purposes of the groups might not have been anticipated, since approximately the same amount of time was taken by models or leaders in describing this aspect of the group sessions. The subjects also were asked to remember as many of the different topics or scenes as they could without prompting from the interviewer. A subject was considered to have recalled a topic or scene if he was able to describe adequately the concept which had been dealt with and to illustrate that concept (e.g., relating to people in authority — the job problem situation). Fifteen out of 19 boys in the modeling group spontaneously recalled at least two topics ($p < .02$, binomial test). Only 7 of the boys in the discussion group recalled two or more topics.

The interviewer sought to elicit from subjects examples of applications of the concepts and topics to their subsequent lives. This was done to determine if the subjects could make meaningful connections between the topics presented in the group sessions and actual events they had subsequently experienced. They were considered to have applied a topic if they clearly stated that their behavior in the example situation had been a direct function of what had been learned in the group. Sixteen of the 19 subjects in the modeling group applied at least one topic ($p < .01$, binomial test). Seven of these subjects applied three or more. Six of the 13 discussion group subjects applied one topic and 2 made three or more applications. Two subjects in the modeling group stated that they had not understood the concepts and topics and 6 discussion group boys had not understood the material.

Complete records of each subject's movements were obtained, such as leaves, escapes, transfers, discharges, and readmissions. Recidivism was defined as (a) return of a boy to a juvenile institution because of unsatisfactory behavior, (b) conviction in Superior Court resulting in adult status probation, or (c) confinement in an adult correctional institution. A covariate of the recidivism rate is the period at risk, the time elapsed since institutionalization. The cumulative recidivism rate for juvenile offenders in Washington ranges from 22% to over 30%, depending on the period at risk and on yearly fluctuations in the population. The period at risk for the subjects was at least 18 months, which is sufficiently long to warrant confidence in the assumption that the number of recidivists identified closely approximated the maximum number that would eventually occur, because a risk period of this length is estimated to identify over 80% of the maximum expected number.

At a time almost three years after their arrival at Cascadia, 43 of the 192 boys in the sample, or 22.4% had become recidivists. More recidivists were in the control group ($n = 22$) than in the modeling ($n = 12$) and discussion ($n = 9$) groups ($p < .06$, chi-square test). The recidivism rate for the control group (34%) was consistent with the then current cumulative recidivism rate for the male population in the state. Comparisons were made of the proportion of recidivists to nonrecidivists in each of four samples: (a) modeling group, (b) discussion group, (c) control group, and (d) the cumulative Cascadia male population ($n = 1,242$). The Z-score comparisons of differences among proportions indicated that fewer modeling ($p < .06$) and discussion ($p < .009$) subjects became recidivists than did controls. Compared to the base rate of recidivism in the population, these differences are more highly significant (modeling, vs. population, $p < .02$; discussion vs. population, $p < .001$).

An additional set of findings merits reporting because it demonstrates the significant interaction that may take place between the personal characteristics of subjects and the treatments to which they may be subjected. Sarason's (Sarason & Ganzer, 1962) TAS was one of the premeasures obtained on all subjects. Evidence gathered in laboratory studies of college students has suggested that highly anxious subjects scan the environment especially intently for cues and information which might be of assistance in problem solving (Sarason, 1968, 1972; Wine, 1971). High-TAS subjects have been found to show a stronger response to reinforcement than do their lower scoring counterparts (Sarason & Ganzer, 1962). High-TAS scorers have also been found to be more responsive to modeled cues than have low scorers (Sarason, Pederson, & Nyman, 1968). Might test anxiety interact significantly with the conditions of the present investigation?

To answer this question it seemed important to take account of the feedback factor, whether or not a subject viewed videotapes of his own role playing or group discussion behavior. Most of the subjects reported that receiving televised feedback of their own behavior was upsetting because of the contrast between the polished role playing of the models and their own less expert performance. Since highly anxious persons typically do not respond favorably to stress, it was of interest to compare high- and low-TAS groups under televised and nontelevised conditions. For modeling groups in the present study, only 1 out of 15 high-TAS subjects (scores $\leq$ 6) whose role playing was televised and later replayed for them received favorable behavioral ratings (i.e., in a socially desirable direction). Fourteen out of 19 high-TAS subjects who did not receive televised feedback showed positive behavior change ($p < .05$).

Comparison of the relative efficacy of the modeling and discussion techniques for subjects differing in TAS scores yielded one significant result. For nontelevised high-TAS groups, a greater proportion of modeling subjects (14 of the 19) than discussion subjects (6 of the 20) received positive behavior ratings ($p < .02$). Comparisons were also made in which the magnitude as well as the direction of behavior change was taken into account. High- and low-TAS subjects who changed either plus or minus one standard deviation of the sample score mean were compared. For modeling, 6 out of 7 high-TAS subjects who received the televised feedback condition were rated as changing in a negative direction, whereas 7 out of 9 high-TAS boys in the nontelevised condition changed favorably ($p = .05$, Fisher's test). Significant differences did not emerge in other comparisons, and a similar pattern of relationships was not found for televised and nontelevised high-TAS subjects in the discussion groups nor for subjects in the control group.

DISCUSSION

The results of this research suggest that the modeling and the structured discussion approaches had greater concurrent and long-term effects on adolescent delinquents than did the normal program of a high-quality institution. (During the time periods when the modeling and discussion boys were in the experiment, the control boys were participating in a variety of educational, recreational, and vocational activities.) There were no strong, consistent differences between the two experimental groups. Both the modeling and discussion treatments provided personally relevant information to subjects in an interesting and meaningful way, and both treatments were highly structured. They lacked "depth" in that they did not focus on psychodynamic factors. Informal comments by the subjects suggested that they were impressed with and responded favorably to the well-ordered, informational, and no-nonsense approach of both experimental treatments.

As part of the standard routine at Cascadia, most youngsters are diagnosed in accord with a classification system. After completion of our experiment, we examined the diagnosis of boys who had responded differentially to the treatment conditions. Of the boys receiving the modeling sequence and showing improvement on our dependent measures, a disproportionate number bore such diagnoses as "neurosis" and "passive-dependent personality." Case reports tended to describe these types of boys as benign, passive, and markedly deficient in verbal skills. Of the boys who improved while receiving the discussion treatment, a disproportionate number bore such diagnoses as "passive-aggressive personality" and "sociopathic personality." Case reports tended to describe these types of boys as socially active, hostile, and verbally aggressive. These differences suggest the possibility that social modeling and group discussion regimes have different effects on identifiable, relatively homogeneous groups. Future research aimed at systematically evaluating this differential responsiveness would be helpful both from a practical treatment and a theoretical standpoint.

Another issue arising from the present investigation which merits further study concerns the similarities and differences between the modeling and discussion formats and their psychological impacts on the subjects. The treatments were similar in that they were highly structured, but they differed in their amounts of physical and social activity. Recently, several attempts have been made to increase adaptive behavior through highly structured informational and counseling programs similar to our modeling and discussion conditions. These attempts have been directed toward behavior in a variety of educational and vocational settings: reclaiming high school dropouts, strengthening work-related behaviors in unemployed persons, and providing therapeutic avenues for disturbed individuals (Krumboltz & Thoresen, 1969; Sarason & Ganzer, 1969; Vriend, 1969). Further inquiry into these types of questions will advance both theory and practice. What are the desirable personal qualities of an effective model? How similar should a model or discussion leader be to the persons with whom he works (e.g., with regard to age, socioeconomic status, and level of adjustment)? To what degree are modeling and discussion effects separable?

A question arises from the fact that both experimental groups showed greater increases in adaptive behavior than did the control group. Could this have happened because these groups received more attention at Cascadia than did the control group? While a positive answer to this question cannot be completely ruled out, it seems unlikely that extra attention is a sufficient explanation of the results presented here. Of several reasons for this conclusion, the most obvious is the long-term effects. It is difficult to imagine that simply giving attention to boys for a few hours a week over a period of 1 month would bring about significant differences in recidivism almost three years after treatment. Furthermore, as was mentioned earlier, the Cascadia environment is not the impoverished one in which one would expect attention effects to flourish. Finally, the relative recidivism rates for the modeling, discussion, and control groups have remained relatively stable over the entire follow-up period. If anything, the differences in recidivism between the experimental and the control groups have been somewhat greater for the last 12 than for the first 12 follow-up months.

The findings related to subjects' TAS scores suggested the hypothesis that high-anxiety persons are more sensitive to cues provided by the behavior of others (models) than are low-anxiety persons. However, the salutary effects of this sensitivity were found only when a stressful element (television) was omitted from the situation. It would thus seem important to minimize and control stressful elements in situations designed to be therapeutic for high-anxiety individuals but which do not focus on the reduction of anxiety per se. Modeling appeared to be superior to discussion as a means of effecting behavior change among high-anxiety persons. Research is needed to clarify the interactions among treatments and personal characteristics for the gamut of psychological therapies.

REFERENCES

Bandura, A., *Principles of Behavior Modification* (New York: Holt, Rinehart & Winston, 1969).

Dahlstrom, W.G., & Welsh, G.S. (eds.), *An MMPI Handbook*. Minneapolis: University of Minnesota Press 1960.

Gough, H.G., *California Psychological Inventory Manual* (Palo Alto, Calif.: Consulting Psychologists Press, 1957).

Krumboltz, J.D., & Thoresen, C.E. (eds.), *Behavioral Counseling: Cases and Techniques* (New York: Holt, Rinehart & Winston, 1969).

LaFleur, N.K., & Johnson, R.G., "Separate effects of social modeling and reinforcement in counseling adolescents," *Journal of Counseling Psychology*, 1972, *19*, 292–295.

Lorge, I., Thorndike, R.L., & Hagen, E., *Technical Manual: Lorge-Thorndike Intelligence Test* (Boston: Houghton-Mifflin, 1966).

Lykken, D.T., "A study of anxiety in the sociopathic personality," *Journal of Abnormal and Social Psychology*, 1957, *55*, 6–10.

Nayran, L.A., "A rationally derived MMPI scale to measure dependence," *Journal of Consulting Psychology*, 1954, *18*, 192.

Rotter, J.B., "Generalized expectancies for internal versus external control of reinforcement," *Psychological Monographs*, 1966, *80* (1, Whole No. 609).

Sarason, I.G., "Verbal learning, modeling, and juvenile delinquency," *American Psychologist*, 1968, *23*, 254–266.

Sarason, I.G., "Experimental approaches to test anxiety: Attention and the uses of information." In C.D. Spielberger (ed.), *Anxiety: Current Trends in Research and Theory*, Vol. 2, (New York: Academic Press, 1972).

Sarason, I.G., & Ganzer, V.J., "Anxiety, reinforcement, and experimental instructions in a free verbalization situation," *Journal of Abnormal and Social Psychology*, 1962, *65*, 300–307.

Sarason, I.G., & Ganzer, V.J., "Social influence techniques in clinical and community psychology." In C.D. Spielberger (ed.), *Current topics in Clinical and Community Psychology*, Vol. 1, (New York: Academic Press, 1969).

Sarason, I.G., Pederson, A.M., & Nyman B. "Test anxiety and the observation of models," *Journal of Personality*, 1968, *36*, 493–511.

Vriend, T.J., "High performing inner-city adolescents assist low-performing peers in counseling groups," *Personnel and Guidance Journal*, 1969, *47*, 897–904.

Wahler, H.J., *Wahler Self-Description Inventory* (Los Angeles, Calif.: Western Psychological Services, 1969).

Wine, J., "Test anxiety and direction of attention," *Psychological Bulletin*, 1971, *76*, 92–104.

Chapter 24

Editors' Remarks

There has been an unfortunate tendency in corrections to react to programs that fail with summary dismissal and to view failure as a total loss. The Ross & McKay study suggests that there is much to be gained by carefully examining our failures because they might suggest to us not only what we should *not* do but also provide hints about what we *should* do. This study also confirms our view that treatment approaches which have been effective in some settings with some types of offenders may be ineffective or even have deleterious effects when employed in other settings with other types of offenders.

The study found that a behavior modification program lead to a substantial *increase* in the recidivism of institutionalized female adolescent offenders with severe and chronic behavior problems relative to that of their matched controls.

By close inspection of the possible reasons for the failure of their programs Ross & McKay developed an unorthodox program which was found to be highly effective with their atypical correctional clients and might have value for other correctional populations. Their successful program has been described in detail in a recent book (Ross & McKay, 1979).

REFERENCE

Ross, R.R. & McKay, H.B., *Self-Mutilation* (Lexington, Massachusetts: Lexington Books/D.C. Heath, 1979).

A Study of Institutional Treatment Programs*

Robert R. Ross and Bryan McKay

INTRODUCTION

Several years ago the Psychology Department of the University of Waterloo (Canada), in collaboration with the Ministry of Correctional Services of the Province of Ontario, engaged upon a long-term treatment-research project which aimed to assess the efficacy of behavior modification strategies in the treatment of female adolescent offenders who were housed in a special unit of a correctional institution in Ontario. Throughout the course of the project we were faced with results which perplexed us at the time and which we now feel will generate considerable controversy regarding behavioral programs with offenders. Our attempts to understand the paradoxical results which we obtained led us to the development of a highly promising treatment strategy for correctional populations.

Our subjects were 13 to 17 year old "unmanageable" delinquent girls with chronic and severe behavior problems. Prior to institutionalization many forms of therapy had been provided for them with little success. They had presented serious management problems in institutional settings (community treatment centres, other training schools or psychiatric hospitals); abscondance, vandalism, suicide gestures, assault, self-mutilation, theft.

*Research reported herein was supported by a grant (No. 200) from the Ontario Mental Health Foundation.

Ross, R.R. and McKay, B., "A study of institutional treatment programs," *International Journal of Offender Therapy and Comparative Criminology*, 1976, *20*(2), 167–173. Copyright © 1976, International Journal of Offender Therapy and Comparative Criminology. Reprinted by permission.

EARLY INDICATIONS OF SUCCESS

One of the first cases presented to us in this institution was that of a 13-year-old grossly obese, mildly retarded, epileptic girl who had presented major management problems throughout the several months since her admission and who seemed to be beyond the control of the staff. We established a behavioral program for her (an individualised token economy) and quickly obtained control over every one of her major behavior problems: feigned seizures, vandalism, disruption of classroom activities, temper tantrums, gross insolence, flagrant disobedience and assault.

Following the apparent success with this girl, behavior modification was extended to include nine other girls in one of the institution's treatment units. These girls had not responded to four or five months of individual and group psychotherapy in a "therapeutic milieu". (This rather traditional treatment program seemed unable to prevent the deterioration in their behavior and may, we suspect, have been fostering it.) Many major behavior problems (assault, property damage, self-inflicted injuries, suicide gestures and abscondance) were eliminated after only a few weeks from the inception of the new program. This improvement was maintained throughout the remainder of the program (five months) when most of the girls were released. In contrast to similar girls who had not been involved in the pilot program, the adjustment of the behaviorally-treated girls, during the first nine months of their supervised placement in the community, was remarkable, persistent and impressive. Only one girl evidenced behavior problems that necessitated her return to institutional care; for the others, after-care officers' reports were exceptionally favourable.

Obviously these pilot studies provided only crude and largely anecdotal evidence of the effectiveness of a behavioral strategy, but they justified the expansion of operant conditioning programs into a long-term treatment-research project involving both units of a 50-bed treatment facility in the institutional complex.*

The sequential nature of our project prevented us from using random assignment of subjects to the various treatment and control groups. However, we were able to select from the population of offenders treated (approximately 200) comparison groups of subjects matched on a variety of factors deemed important, viz. age, length of institutionalization and IQ. There were no pre-treatment differences in the institutional behavior of participants in different treatment or control groups.

The program was monitored on a continuing basis by obtaining data on each girl's institutional and post-institutional adjustment. These data led us to

---

*The total institutional complex provided bed-space for up to 150 residents. The facility served other distinct functions, that is a reception and diagnostic centre as well as an educational and vocational training school.

introduce major changes in our program from time to time in an attempt to improve treatment outcome.

The outcome of our programs was assessed in terms of institutional adjustment (offences committed throughout the girl's stay in the institution) and post-institutionalized adjustment over a nine-month follow-up period: (a) percent of those returned to institutional care because of behavior problems, (b) behavioral incidents reported by after-care officers. In each comparison, data were obtained for groups of matched subjects.

Four treatment programs were run in the following order:

1. Phase 1 behavior modification
2. Phase 2 behavior modification
3. Phase 2 behavior modification plus peer therapist program
4. Peer therapist program alone

PHASE 1 BEHAVIOR MODIFICATION

In the first part of our project we established an elaborate and sophisticated token economy program which incorporated sequential stages or levels through which each girl progressed as she earned her return to community living. As she was promoted she enjoyed gradually increasing freedom, material comforts and privileges with the accompanying increase of responsibility for her own behavior. Her progress through the stages was entirely contingent on her behavior. A girl, by earning promotion, could greatly improve her environment, increase accessibility to a variety of reinforcers as well as reduce the duration of her incarceration. In addition to the token economy, individualized behavior contracts were utilized within each stage whereby the girl, through performing specified behaviors, could earn certain privileges of commodities not ordinarily provided in that stage. The amount of surveillance and the number of explicit contingencies varied from stage to stage such that there was a gradual transition from external control to self-control both in terms of freedom from supervision and in terms of the relationship between privileges and behavior. The fading out of behavior modification procedures was arranged during the final stage in order to provide a gradual transition from the token economy to community life.

The results of this program were clear cut. Compared with a matched group of non-treatment control subjects, the girls in the behavior modification program evidenced *more* behavior problems during their institutionalization, and were considerably *less* successful in adjustment in the community during a nine-month period following their release from the institution. 53.3 percent of the behaviorally-treated girls recidivated compared to only 33.3 percent of the non-treatment controls.

These findings led us to considerable speculation as to the cause of the difference between the success of the pilot program and the apparent failure of our more sophisticated behavior modification program.

The pilot program had been a very simplified token economy. Privileges were earned contingent on the girls' daily performance as assessed on a crude rating scale of their acceptable social behavior. However, in the Phase I program, we used a sophisticated behavior checking system in which behavior credits were earned if the girls performed specified positive social behaviors and *did not evidence antisocial behaviors*. By requiring the supervisors to note the occurrence of such antisocial acts, we may have created the expectancy that such acts would indeed occur. We felt that we had heightened the sensitivity of staff and girls to antisocial behavior, and increased the perceived importance of such behavior. The staff, we thought, were being inadvertently and subtly obliged to become hypervigilant in seeking out negative behavior and expecting the worst of the girls. We began to wonder whether behavior modification programs might generate "self-fulfilling prophecies" for antisocial behavior (Rosenthal & Jacobson, 1968).

PHASE 2 BEHAVIOR MODIFICATION

Our interpretation of the discrepancy between the failure of the Phase 1 program and the success of the pilot program led us to the development of an improved behavior modification program which was strictly positive in emphasis. The Phase 2 program was identical to the Phase 1 program except that in Phase 2 rewards were contingent *only* upon performance of specified positive social acts. Behavior credits were earned for prosocial behavior regardless of whether the girls emitted antisocial or inappropriate behaviors.

The results of the Phase 2 program appear much more reassuring for the behavior modification enthusiasts at first glance. The girls in this program committed significantly fewer offences during their incarceration than did the matched control subjects who had been involved in the standard training school program. However, we now encounter an interesting paradox. In terms of post-institutional adjustment the Phase 2 girls do much *worse* than either the Phase 1 behaviorally-treated girls or the training school control subjects. Sixty-six percent recidivated during the nine-month follow-up. This is twice as bad as the recidivism rate (33.3 percent) for the non-treatment controls. Moreover, significantly more antisocial behavior is reported for them by after-care officers.

The inordinately high recidivism rate for the behaviorally-treated offenders raised questions for us as to an explanation of the extraordinary success of our pilot subjects who had also been treated in a behavioral program. Re-examination of our pilot studies revealed that factors other than behavior modification may have been involved in our program. We noted that while we were conducting the token economy, some of the girls were becoming very familiar with reinforcement therapy techniques and were, in fact, actually using these techniques to influence their peers. They had developed and were conducting a behavior modification program of their own! We hypothesized that the success of our pilot program was attributable to the combination of this peer "program" and the token economy. We reasoned that improving the behavioral program used in the pilot study and maintaining the peer aspects might maximize the efficacy of our treatment even beyond the extraordinary success of our pilot program.

PHASE 2 BEHAVIOR MODIFICATION PLUS PEER THERAPIST PROGRAM

Consequently, in the next stage of our study the Phase 2 token economy was maintained, but a new factor was added to the treatment approach: peer training. Girls in the token economy were provided with specific training in reinforcement therapy principles and encouraged to utilize these principles in attempting to modify the behavior of their peers.

In terms of institutional management the results of this program are impressive. These subjects show a significant decrease in the frequency of offences committed while they are in the institution. However, when these girls are returned to the community their adjustment is no better than that of the Phase 2 Behavior Modification Group. In effect, they recidivate far more frequently (60.6 percent recidivism rate) and engage in many more antisocial acts following treatment than do matched subjects who are involved in the traditional training school program (33.3 percent recidivism rate).

At this point in our program we were about to accept the notion that these were completely intractable clients and give up. However, the fact that our pilot cases were still adjusting well in the community (some three years after treatment) motivated us to continue to try to replicate the pilot findings.

Clearly the extraordinary success of our highly simplified behavior modification pilot program could not be repeated with a more exacting behavioral program. This led us to an unorthodox hypothesis. We wondered whether a token economy program might have a deleterious effect on the success of an otherwise valuable intervention strategy.

PEER THERAPIST PROGRAM ALONE

In the final experimental treatment program, the subjects were trained in reinforcement therapy principles and persuaded to act as therapists for each other. As each girl progressed through the program she was exposed to these procedures not only by us but more importantly through the application of the techniques now being applied by her previously trained peers. Thus, each girl eventually functions as a "therapist". However, for this group *no other aspects of the behavior modification programs were employed.* In short, the token economy program was dropped and only the peer therapist program was maintained. It required a considerable amount of skillful and subtle persuasion to convince the girls that they had the requisite interpersonal skills, motivation and intelligence to function as "therapists" for each other. Throughout the program the girls' confidence and motivation was maintained through the judicious application of social reinforcement in the form of recognition, status enhancement and praise.

The results of this program are impressive. In the peer program major institutional adjustment problems were very quickly eliminated. In fact, in many cases, the number of offences (assault, vandalism, self-inflicted injuries, suicide gestures and abscondance) they committed became zero within a few weeks and most did not recur during the remainder of their confinement (three months).*

In terms of post-institutional adjustment, the girls in this program are much more successful than their matched controls in any other program including the traditional training school program.

Table 1 presents the rehabilitation data for each group in terms of the number of girls whose behavior necessitated their return to the institution.

TABLE 1

Treatment Outcome

Girls returned to Training School following unacceptable behavior in community. Nine month follow-up

	N	Number Returned	Percent
Pilot program	10	1	10.0%
Training school control	15	5	33.3%
Behavior modification (1)	15	8	53.3%
Behavior modification (2)	15	10	66.6%
Behavior mod. (2) + peer	15	9	60.0%
Peer therapist program	15	1	6.6%
Total	85		

Note: Each group is matched with every other group (except pilot program) on age, length of institutionalization and IQ.

*Throughout the project the institutional staff who supervised the girls wrote daily logs on the problems they encountered each day for each girl. These logs were coded and independent raters recorded for each S the number of offences committed by each girl throughout her stay in the institution.

Support for the outcome data is provided by a second measure of post-institutional adjustment. Table 2 presents, for each group, the incidence of behavior problems reported by after-care officers during the girls' first nine months in the community. The after-care officers did not know which girl was in which program nor, indeed, if she were a research subject.

TABLE 2

Treatment Outcome

Total number of behavior incidents reported by after-care officers during nine-month follow-up

	N	Pro-Social behavior incidents	Anti-Social behavior incidents
Training school control	15	65	85
Behavior modification (1)	15	65	85
Behavior modification (2)	15	51	124
Behavior mod. (2) + peer	15	33	120
Peer therapist program	15	107	26

Note: Each group is matched with every other group (except pilot program) on age, length of institutionalization and IQ.

At least two conclusions seem warranted by these data:

1. Behavior modification is by no means a panacea for the offender. In fact, rather than ameliorating the offender's antisocial behavior problems behavior modification *may* have a deleterious effect on both institutional adaptation and post-institutional adjustment.
2. Post-treatment persistence of appropriate social behavior does not follow naturally from effective control over institutional behavior. The meaningfulness or predictive value of institutional adaptation is questionable.

The peer intervention strategy which we developed in this project seems to have considerable potential as a therapeutic regimen for adolescent offenders. It has many qualities which recommend it: first, it recognizes that the most important influence on the adolescent offender in a correctional institution (perhaps adolescents in general) is his/her peers. It provides an effective means of manipulating the peer group interaction so that it provides pressure towards prosocial behavior rather than, as is usually the case, towards antisocial behavior. This program treats the offender with considerable respect by focusing on the offender's strengths rather than on her personal shortcomings, her pathology, or her problems as is typically the case with correctional treatment programs. In fact our subjects were treated as therapists rather than patients, as colleagues rather than clients. This re-labelling process is an important ingredient in our program. It is designed not only to motivate the offenders toward responsible behavior with each other but also to improve their self-concept and to persuade them that they are prosocial individuals. Such attribution of positive characteristics through labelling techniques has been shown in experimental studies to be effective in eliciting and maintaining prosocial behavior (e.g. Miller et al., 1975).

Training of the offenders in the principles of reinforcement therapy may indeed provide them with a social skill through which they can have successful commerce with their post institutional environment in a positive way.

Bem (1967) has argued that a person can become committed to a position through advocating it. Bem points out that if we wish to change someone's attitude we should first subtly manipulate her into changing her behavior to a form which is consistent with the attitude we wish to foster. By making our manipulation subtle enough so that the new behavior cannot be attributed to some external force the individual then begins to view herself as the kind of person who would naturally behave in that way. By re-labelling our offenders as gregarious, altruistic helpers, by treating them as advocates of prosocial behavior and by subtly persuading them to encourage and reinforce such behavior in their peers we succeeded in having these girls come to view themselves as individuals who valued these attitudes and behavior, i.e., we succeeded in making them committed to positive social behavior themselves.

Finally, the offenders in our peer therapist program see it as their own program and not, as in the case of a token economy, as a program externally imposed on them by authority figures. In this respect our findings provide important confirmation in a field setting of laboratory studies of the attributional process (Lepper, Greene and Nisbett, 1973; Shaver, 1975). It has been demonstrated that intrinsic motivation, enjoyment of learning and the persistence of behavior change is most likely to occur under conditions where the person cannot readily identify the external factors which are directing his behavior (Bowers & Ross, 1973). In our token economy the girls saw their behavior as dependent on external rewards and contingencies. Thus there was no reason for their behavior to persist once they left the institution and the environmental contingencies changed (Davison & Valins, 1969). However, in the peer therapist program without a superimposed external behavioral program, the girls saw themselves as responsible for any changes that occurred to them. *It is, after all, difficult when acting as a therapist to continue to act as a patient.* In retrospect, we may have created the optimal conditions for self-attribution of behavior change and the resultant development of intrinsic motivation and behavioral persistence so often lacking in correctional programs and in treatment programs for adolescents.

REFERENCES

Bem, D.J., "Self-perception Theory." In L. Berkowitz (Ed.), *Advances in Experimental Social Psychology*, Vol. 6 (New York, Academic Press, 1972).

Bowers, K.S. and Ross, M., *Intrinsic Motivation in the Classroom: An Attributional Model of Education*. Unpublished manuscript, Waterloo University, 1973.

Davidson, W.S. and Seidman, E., "Studies in behavior modification and juvenile delinquency: A review, methodological critique and social perspective," *Psychological Bulletin*, 1974, *81*, 998–1011.

Davidson, G. and Valins, S., "Maintenance of self-attributed and drug-attributed behavior change," *Journal of Personality and Social Psychology*, 1969, *11*, 25–33.

Lepper, M.R., Greene, D. and Nisbett, R.E., "Undermining Children's intrinsic interest with extrinsic reward: A test of the 'overjustification' hypothesis," *Journal of Personality and Social Psychology*, 1973, *28*, 129–137.

Miller, R.L., Brickman, P. and Boien, D., "Attribution versus persuasion as a means for modifying behavior." *Journal of Personality and Social Psychology*, 1975, *31*, 430–441.

O'Leary, D.D. and Drabman, R., "Token reinforcement programs in the classroom: A review," *Psychological Bulletin*, 1971, *75*, 379–398.

Rosenthal, R. and Jacobson, L., *Pygmalion in the Classroom* (USA: Holt, Rinehart & Winston, 1968).

Ross, R.R. and McKay, H.B., *Rewards for Offenders: Modifying the Correctional Environment*. Unpublished Manuscript, Waterloo University, 1974.

Ross, R.R. and Price, M.J., "Behavior Modification in Corrections: Autopsy before Mortification," *International Journal of Criminology and Penology*, 1976, *4*, 305–315.

Shaver, K.G., *An Introduction to Attribution Processes* (USA: Winthrop, 1975).

Strickland, L.H., "Surveillance and Trust." *Journal of Personality*, *26*, 1958.

Stuart, R.B., *Trick or Treatment: How and When Psychotherapy Fails* (U.S.A.: Research Press, 1970).

Part VI

Programs for Adult Offenders

Chapter 25

Editors' Remarks

Some of the most difficult offenders with whom correctional practitioners must deal are those with long histories of both criminal behavior and mental health problems. Such individuals present a complexity of problems. They are often reluctant to participate in programs provided either by correctional or mental health agencies, and correctional and mental health agencies are often reluctant to provide services to them. In this chapter James Kloss describes a comprehensive community treatment program in which a multidisciplinary team provided intensive services to such high-risk offenders in a community-based treatment-research program.

The treatment program was intensive and provided high frequency client-staff contacts. It consisted of a wide variety of individualized approaches appropriate to the complexity of the offender's problems. In general, the program principles were based on social learning theory and emphasis was placed on skill-building (including employment-seeking skills) and contingency contracting.

Dr. Kloss kindly prepared the present description of the Complex Offender Project specifically for this book. We are particularly grateful to him for conducting the detailed analysis of the results of his program in sufficient detail to do justice to the complexity of the problem of evaluating treatment program effectiveness.

Success and Failure in the Evaluation of Behavioral Community Treatment*

James D. Kloss

Developing out of its successful experience in providing community treatment to the chronic mentally ill, Mendota Mental Health Institute sought a similar model to meet the needs of people whose involvement with the criminal justice system seemed to be part of a larger picture of social maladjustment and whose needs for services far exceeded the capability of existing programs. The resulting Complex Offender Project (COP) was not based on any assumptions about the relationship between mental illness and criminal behavior; rather it assumed that criminal behavior was a part of an individual's adjustment to the needs of community living and that a reduction in illegal activities could not be expected until different, more successful means of coping with life's problems were available. This working assumption was translated into a program which was intensive, demanding, and responsive to the individual needs of its clients. Because of a strong commitment to evaluation, the effectiveness of the Project in working with difficult, resistant clients, in improving their social adjustment, and in reducing their involvement with the criminal justice system has been assessed, and these findings may provide some guides to others seeking more effective correctional programs.

A "complex offender" was operationally defined as a person between age 18 and 30 who was currently on probation, who had at least one prior

---

*The Complex Offender Project was supported by grants 74-03-02-01, 75-03-02-01 and 76-11B-SC-2618-6 from the Wisconsin Council on Criminal Justice and by Mendota Mental Health Institute, Division of Community Services, Department of Health and Social Services, State of Wisconsin and this paper is based in part on the final report of that Project. Opinions expressed herein are those of the author and not the policy of the sponsoring agencies. The assistance of Dennis Sherry and Gerry Burns in computer analysis of data is gratefully acknowledged.
This article was prepared especially for inclusion in this book.

conviction and who had some previous involvement with the mental health system. The demographic and background characteristics of the 119 people referred to the Project clearly demonstrated that these were troubled individuals who posed severe problems for society. The typical complex offender was a young white male who had been involved with the juvenile courts and gone on to be convicted of several adult offenses resulting in sentences of jail or probation. The average client had served 21 months on probation, and 53% of the clients had served jail terms. Those jailed had served a mean of 2.1 terms, each averaging 16 weeks. The complex offender was chronically unemployed (14 of the past 24 months) and had a poor record of vocational adjustment to those jobs he had obtained, usually keeping jobs for less than three months. He typically came from a broken home and had had an unstable childhood including nine moves in four different towns and living 21 months outside the parental home. If he had been in the military, he was unable to obtain an honorable discharge, and if he had married, that too had failed. This picture of severe social maladjustment was complicated by mental disorders that had led 40% of these clients to be hospitalized, usually more than once, and 58% had received outpatient counseling. Forty-four percent of the clients reported problems with abuse of alcohol, and 53% reported using hard drugs at some time. Only about 10% of the clients in the treatment group were diagnosed as psychotic and another 10% had basic difficulties with routine aspects of community life due to developmental disabilities or inadequate personalities. It was those two groups which had originally come to the attention of the community and for whom the need of an alternative system seemed most obvious. Another 10% of the clients were characterized by problems relating to drug or alcohol abuse, and the rest, approximately 70% of the total, were less obviously "mentally ill" or in need of special treatment. A number of labels could be attached to this group — character and behavior disorders, sociopathic personalities, culturally maladjusted — but no attempt was made to systematically classify clients since it was felt that special labels often contribute more to clients' problems than to treatment efforts.

It is important to identify this largest element of the client group, however, because these clients share many of the attributes most troubling in any correctional population and are exactly the clients which the mental health system has been unwilling or unable to serve effectively. It may be easier to exclude these people from rehabilitational opportunities than it is to develop opportunities at which they can succeed, but it is because their personal problems extend into virtually every social problem area that the complex offenders place such a heavy burden on the community and require special programs like the Complex Offender Project.

Many aspects of the COP's treatment approach have been described elsewhere (Kloss, 1978; Crozat & Kloss, 1979; Kloss & Karan, in press) but several features should be emphasized. COP operated as a multidisciplinary team consisting of a psychologist, social workers, counselors, nurses, and paraprofessionals. Responsibility for working with each client remained with the entire team, and COP resisted pressures to assign ''case loads'' to its staff. Although this increased the complexity of internal and external communication, it brought the full resources of many people with different perspectives to bear on each client's problems.

The overwhelming advantage of the team approach was that it made possible the intensity and comprehensiveness of services that were so essential. Banks, Siler, and Rardin (1977) have criticized previous studies of intensive probationary supervision by noting that intensity was often defined by a low caseload rather than by the quantity (or quality) of interaction with clients. This was not the case with COP. Client involvement ranged from less than a dozen contacts (for a few clients who withdrew their voluntary participation soon after services began) to one client who was seen 17 times per week over 9 months of treatment. Client contacts were usually face-to-face interactions in the community, but office visits, phone calls and coordinating contact with other agencies also contributed to the high level of involvement. Altogether COP dealt with the average client 5.7 times per week over 12 months of treatment, and this does not include time spent in planning, record keeping, or for missed appointments.

Certainly COP achieved its objective of providing intensive treatment, and this intensity allowed comprehensive consideration of a client's overall social adjustment. Staff at one time boasted that virtually any client service could be provided by COP either directly or through referral to another agency. This comprehensiveness greatly facilitated individualized treatment planning and allowed COP to do whatever necessary to achieve any goals the client might set. This element of self-determination in turn facilitated client participation; as participation proved to be beneficial from the client's perspective, goals could be gradually shifted into areas the client might have originally denied or resisted.

The diversity of the individualized treatment plan was increased by COP's use of different treatment approaches dependent upon clients' needs, even when addressing a common goal. A general precept was to do whatever necessary to help a client while still intervening in the minimally effective manner. The purpose of this strategem was to increase the clients' responsibility for themselves and to avoid counterproductive dependency on the Project. Thus a treatment plan might have facilitated change through provision of direct services, through referral and agency coordination, or through the gradual shaping of small behavioral changes that result in a major change in adjustment. A client's need for a stable residence, for example, could be met by directly providing a room at the YMCA, by coordinating welfare eligibility and referring the client to a housing agency, or by teaching the client how to budget, use public transportation, and hunt for an apartment on a day-by-day basis until an independent living arrangement was found.

Of course relationships with other agencies were important with this approach. COP attempted to avoid duplicating the services of other social service or manpower programs; instead COP's services were tailored to compliment other agencies and to enhance their effectiveness. COP provided virtually no direct educational services, for example, although treated clients had higher rates of enrollment and graduation than did offenders in the comparison group. This was accomplished by working closely with existing programs, notably the Omega Night School and the Madison Area Technical College. COP encouraged its clients to explore the options available, supported participation by providing transportation assistance, monitored performance and arranged for payment of tuition and fees, and even offered financial incentives for educational accomplishments. Similarly with employment and training programs, COP would assist its clients through the bureaucratic intake system, arrange for funding — including direct subsidization in some cases — and work as closely as possible with the manpower programs to resolve employment hindering problems.

As these examples suggest, COP's program was behavioral in the sense that treatment goals were real-world accomplishments rather than intrapsychic changes. Clear expectations for client behavior were set through negotiated treatment ''contracts;'' these contracts often contained specific contingencies for rewards and were usually reviewed and revised each week. Schwitzgebel's (1964) work with juveniles is probably the closest precursor to COP's use of incentives, and the contractual model proved useful in clarifying goals and evaluating client progress even when specific contingencies were not involved.

PROGRAM EVALUATION

COP was evaluated through structured interviews conducted at the time of referral and at four-month intervals thereafter. Since half of the referrals who voluntarily agreed to participate were randomly assigned to a control group, comparisons between offenders receiving COP's intensive treatment and similar people receiving traditional probationary supervision were possible over time.

In a previous report (Kloss, 1978) differences between the 2 groups of complex offenders after 4 months and after 16 months were described. Those analyses indicated that the treated group was hospitalized less, had lower unemployment, more participation in educational programs, spent more time living independently in the community, received less subsidized income and were more socially active than the control group. Although downward trends in arrests, convictions and incarcerations were observed in the treated group, both groups continued to be frequently involved with the criminal justice system.

In reviewing these data, questions arose concerning the relative contribution to the overall results of clients active in treatment and those who had been discharged. The impact of those clients who had "failed," i.e., those whose probation had been revoked or who had spent more than 60 days in inpatient treatment, was especially problematic, and so additional analyses were conducted.

Analysis 1   In the first analysis, all subjects who had been interviewed 20 months after referral were classified as (1) still active in treatment, (2) discharged as a success, i.e., completion of the term of probation, or (3) discharged as a failure as defined above. 20 months — 6 interview periods — was the longest follow-up period for which sufficient data to allow reliable statistical comparisons were available as well as being the longest length of time permitted in active treatment. Thus data from 52 subjects on 21 summary measures of employment, independent living, psychiatric and legal involvement were analyzed using a $2 \times 3 \times 6$ (group by termination status by interview period) repeated measures analysis of variance.

RESULTS

The classification by termination status was a meaningful one, as shown by significant differences between groups on ten of the measures. Not surprisingly the greatest differences were between the groups classified as successful and unsuccessful; clients who terminated successfully performed best on all but one measure of recidivism — they had a significantly higher rate of unofficial police contacts. Clients who remained in treatment (or on probation) for the entire 20 months were intermediate in performance, but more closely resembled the successfully discharged group. There were also differing trends over time for the three categories of discharge status.

Although there were relatively few differences between the three groups of clients prior to treatment (at baseline), the group eventually classified as failures showed little or no decline in arrests during the first four months after referral. At baseline the successful group had been arrested more often but spent less time incarcerated than the other two groups; this group continued to be arrested about as frequently as the others but spent very little time incarcerated. The group discharged as successes also had the highest rate of unofficial police contacts, especially during the 16- to 20-month follow-up period. More positively, the group discharged as successes also had the highest rate of employment, highest earned income and highest level of independent living over time. The percentage of time this group was competitively employed declined toward the end of the 20 months while employment of the group still active in treatment continued to increase. Employment of the group classified as treatment failures remained low, perhaps due in part to the high level of institutional placement.

TABLE 1

Significant differences between groups classified by treatment status 20 months after referral

	Still Active	Discharged as Success	Discharged as Failure	p
	n = 33	n = 13	n = 17	
Mean number of incarcerations*	0.61	0.54	0.91	.10
% time incarcerated*	7.9	1.6	34.7	.001
Mean number of unofficial police contacts	0.15	0.32	0.07	.10
% time hospitalized	1.2	0.0	10.9	.001
% time living independently	66.0	70.7	22.7	.001
Mean number of jobs held	1.25	1.49	.66	.001
% time competitively employed	47.4	70.5	20.6	.001
% time semicompetitively employed	11.6	20.4	3.8	.01
Mean wages ($)	802.	1326	317	.001
% of work missed (absenteeism)	3.9	3.3	1.8	.10

*Means and percentages are for a four-month interview period.

While these findings help clarify the results of treatment by differentiating three groups of clients who would be expected to differ in social adjustment, evaluation of the Complex Offender Project itself must be based on the difference between the treatment and comparison groups and on differences between groups within categories of termination status. This analysis also extended the results presented earlier (Kloss, 1978) for an additional four months after referral.

Treated clients spent less time in psychiatric hospitals (1% vs 6%, $p < .10$) and were committed to psychiatric facilities less than comparison clients (0.0 vs 0.5 commitments/client, $p < .10$) across all time periods. They also received less public subsidy ($7 vs $125, $p < .10$) but their absenteeism was also greater (3.7% vs 2.8%, $p < .10$). Enrollment in educational programs was greater among the treatment group (37% vs 16%, $p < .005$) as was participation in semi-competitive employment and training programs (16% of the time vs 7%, $p < .005$).

Downward trends in legal involvement (arrests, convictions and incarcerations) were observed for both groups, ($p < .001$) but the pattern of legal involvement differed between groups. As can be seen in Figure 1, legal involvement of the control group declined more in the first four months after referral but then remained relatively stable over time. Treated clients on the other hand showed a steady decline in legal involvement over time; linear regression analysis indicated that arrests, convictions and incarcerations in the treatment group could be described by straight downward sloping lines despite the increase in convictions and incarcerations at the 8-month interview.

Although the impact of COP on recidivism would certainly be clearer if these downward trends had resulted in a lower overall rate of recidivism, neither should the significance of the steady reduction in legal involvement be underestimated. Other data indicate that the reduction occurred in the number of *persons* offending, not just in the number of offenses, and there was some tendency for members of the control group to increase their legal involvement in the later follow-up periods.

There were also significant differences between successes and failures in the treatment and control groups. Comparison subjects who were discharged from probation were incarcerated more often than "successes" in the treatment group, and they also had a large increase in unofficial police contacts and psychiatric hospitalizations at the 20-month follow-up period ($p < .05$). Failures in the treatment group were incarcerated more than controls who were so classified, but this last group had the highest level of psychiatric hospitalization (21% of the time overall). It is also important to note that the performance of clients classified as successes deteriorated on some critical measures over time while the performance of those clients still active in treatment continued to improve. Such was the case with employment, psychiatric hospitalization, arrests and convictions.

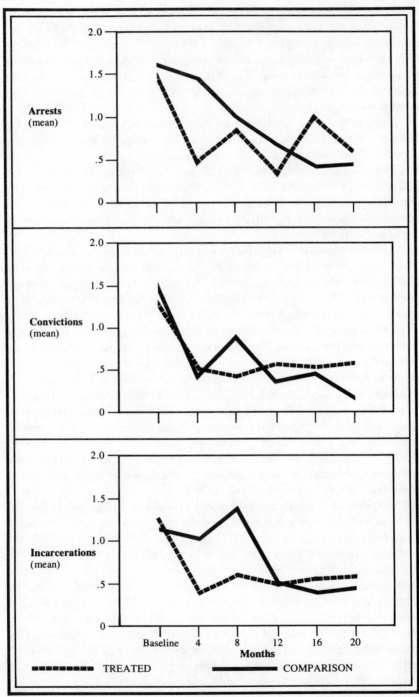

Figure 1   *Measures of Legal Involvement of Subjects After Referral to COP*

Analysis 2   The use of a factorial analysis clarified and extended the results presented earlier for an additional 4 months after referral, but this analysis did not differentiate between behavior during treatment and behavior after termination of services. Post-treatment follow-up studies of community corrections are relatively rare, but they commonly fail to show the maintenance of treatment effects regardless of the nature of treatment or the magnitude of effect during treatment. There is some debate as to whether this is attributable to the programs, to recalcitrance of client problems or to the post-treatment environment, but such follow-up certainly provides an additional basis for program evaluation. To evaluate whether or not the effects of participation in the Complex Offender Project would persist after termination of services, data were available from 32 clients who had completed at least two interviews spanning 8 months after discharge. Since the nature of discharge — successful or unsuccessful as defined above — seemed to be a powerful discriminator, these subjects were so classified. Data on 21 summary variables were then analyzed using $2 \times 2 \times 2$ (group by termination status by time period) analysis of variance. Please note that this analysis is not independent of the previous analysis since some observations were used in both.

RESULTS

As expected, successfully discharged clients spent much less time incarcerated (1% vs 47%, $p < .001$), and were employed more often (80% vs 15%, $p < .001$), and had higher earned income than did clients discharged as failures. Somewhat surprisingly, they also had higher rates of absenteeism (3% vs 0, $p < .001$) and more frequent unofficial police contacts ($\bar{X} = .5$ vs 0.0, $p < .10$). These differences increased as time progressed ($p < .10$ and $p < .20$, respectively).

Clients who were unsuccessful had a decrease in psychiatric commitments and a decrease in the amount of time spent in psychiatric hospitals over time, perhaps reflecting the cyclical nature of these problems. A significant regression toward the mean was observed in the number of convictions, in employment and in earned income, but the successful group continued to be better adjusted than the unsuccessful group.

Clients treated by the Complex Offender Project continued to be committed less often than did comparison clients ($p < .20$) and this difference was especially apparent between the successfully discharged clients in each group. Treated clients were also convicted of fewer offenses post-treatment ($X = .2$ vs $.6$, $p < .10$) and continued to participate more in semi-competitive employment and training opportunities (16% vs 1%, $p < .05$) than did clients in the comparison groups.

In many ways the performance of clients in the comparison group who were discharged as successes was anomalous. This subgroup of clients was arrested more often post-treatment than any other group ($\bar{x} = 1.1$ vs $.5$, $p < .10$) and convicted of more offenses post-treatment than any other subgroup ($\bar{x} = 0.6$ vs 0.3). This difference appeared most strongly in the second period post-treatment ($p < .005$) at which point this group also had higher incidences of psychiatric hospitalization ($p < .20$) and of unofficial police contact ($p < .20$). These unexpected differences between clients who "successfully" complete a period of probationary supervision and those who successfully complete the COP treatment program are shown in Figures 2 and 3.

These results must of course be interpreted with caution due to the small sample size. Especially considering the sample size, it is not surprising that some treatment effects were not maintained and that some regression toward the mean was observed. Still the basic goal of COP seems to have been achieved: treated clients had fewer psychiatric hospitalizations and less involvement with the criminal justice system even after the termination of services.

DISCUSSION

There are two reasonable responses to the "nothing works" assessment of correctional treatment programs; one is to abandon rehabilitation as a goal and to develop a criminal justice system based solely on theories of deterrence or incapacitation. The other response is to increase efforts to develop and evaluate innovative programs. As the various contributions to this volume indicate, there are many promising lines of development for more effective correctional programs, and perhaps the greatest need is for systematic replication of previously effective treatment programs. In anticipation of this process, three things can be learned from the Complex Offender Project.

The first point is that even the most difficult clients can be helped given the proper intervention, but the nature of the target group needs to be considered when evaluating success. When working with severe problems, even small improvements need to be recognized as progress. Thus the downward trend in criminal involvement of clients treated by COP is noteworthy even though their offense rate was actually higher than comparison subjects' at some points in time. Similarly, COP's program to facilitate employment did not solve the client problems leading to rapid job turnover, but the 11% reduction in unemployment which was maintained for over two years is a promising indicator of effectiveness that should lead to further program development.

Second, it is apparent that the relationship between measures of social adjustment and criminal behavior is not a simple one, and programs should not be evaluated by a single criterion. Successful completion of probation was an intuitively attractive criterion for evaluating COP, but results described

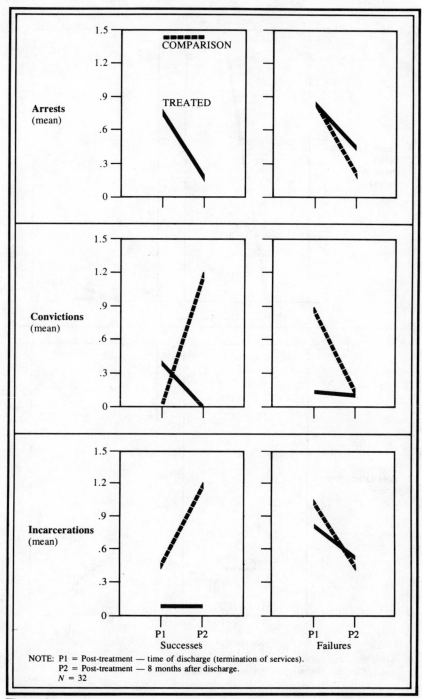

Figure 2 *Measures of Legal Involvement of Subjects Classified by Type of Discharge.*

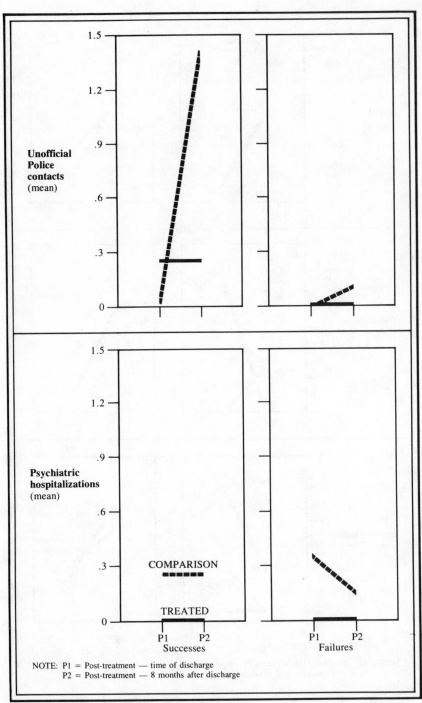

Figure 3 *Post-treatment Contacts with Police and Psychiatric Hospitalizations for Subjects Classified as "Successes" or "Failures".*

above raise serious questions about its validity and the poor performance of clients in the comparison group who were discharged as "successes" requires some comment.

COP was designed as an intensive treatment program whereas probationary supervision is sometimes only minimal supervision indeed. It could be that successful participation in COP was a tougher test, that clients could not coast through without making some changes in their daily lives. It is also possible that some clients in the comparison group were discharged from probation (a successful termination) regardless of their social adjustment difficulties just to "clear the books."

Finally, and most importantly, COP did succeed in achieving its goals: it worked intensively for long periods of time with the clients most social agencies would try to avoid as "burn-out artists." Treated clients achieved a more satisfactory adjustment to community living as measured by several variables, and the need for psychiatric hospitalization was virtually eliminated. Legal involvement declined, and this decline persisted for at least 8 months after the termination of services. For all of those reasons, we hope that people interested in developing more effective correctional programs can benefit from COP's experience, and that will be its real success.

REFERENCES

Banks, J., Siler, T., & Rardin, R., "Past and present findings in intensive adult probation," *Federal Probation*, 1977, *41*, 10–25.

Crozat, P., & Kloss, J., "Intensive community treatment: An approach to facilitating the employment of offenders," *Criminal Justice and Behavior*, 1979, *6*, 133–143.

Kloss, J., "The impact of comprehensive community treatment: An assessment of the Complex Offender Project," *Offender Rehabilitation*, 1978, *3*, 81–108.

Kloss, J. & Karan, J., "Community interventions for reluctant clients," *Federal Probation*, in press.

Schwitzgebel, R., "Street Corner Research: An Experimental Approach to the Juvenile Delinquent (Cambridge: Harvard, 1964).

Chapter 26

Editor's Remarks

The following chapter describes a treatment program for adult male heroin addicts which demonstrates that such offenders can be effectively treated in a correctional setting through a multi-facetted treatment approach. We are grateful to the authors of this chapter for providing a comprehensive description of their complex and innovative intervention approach and its results.

The Evaluation of a Heroin Addiction Treatment Program within a Correctional Environment

Jerome J. Platt, Gerald M. Perry,
and David S. Metzger*

SECTION I

INTRODUCTION

The Wharton Tract Narcotics Treatment Program was located in a satellite unit some distance from its parent institution, the Youth Reception and Correction Center at Yardville, New Jersey. Situated in the Wharton State forest, at the site of a former state forestry camp, the open-door building had a capacity of 45 residents. The Program began operations in 1970 in response to the growing incidence of drug addiction problems among those youths committed to the Youth Correctional Institutional Complex. Funded by the State Law Enforcement Planning Agency under a Criminal Justice Improvement Grant, the Program had built into it a strong research and evaluation component which yielded a significant amount of data on 1600 subjects over a seven year period.

ADMISSIONS

New admissions to the Youth Correctional Institutional Complex were initially assessed at the Youth Reception and Correctional Center at Yardville,

*The senior author designed and conducted the evaluation. The two junior authors were involved with the data analysis.
This article was prepared especially for inclusion in this book.

New Jersey. Following the completion of medical, educational, and psychological profiles, offenders were assigned to the Annandale, Bordentown, or Yardville Correctional Center. The Wharton Tract Narcotics Treatment Program was one of four satellite units of the Yardville Center.

Admission was open to all males, age 19 or above, who had expressed an interest in a narcotics treatment program while at the Youth Reception Center, and had met the following additional criteria:

(a) An expected period of 8 to 20 months of incarceration.
(b) A history of heroin dependency of at least 6 months but not more than 5 years duration.
(c) No gross psychopathology.
(d) No recent escape history.
(e) No serious offenses pending.

PROGRAM PHILOSOPHY

The Wharton Tract Narcotics Treatment Program employed a therapeutic community approach to treatment. All daily activities and communications were expected to be consciously conducted in a therapeutic manner. Free and open communication was encouraged in order to bridge the gap between staff and inmates which is typically found in correctional institutions. The responsibility for the overall functioning of the program was shared by staff and inmates alike. Decisions which affected all were discussed and voted upon by the community in a weekly town meeting.

Inmates also were expected to take an active part in their own therapy, as well as in the other inmates' treatment process. The self-help concept was focused upon not only in group therapy, but also in the day-to-day activities of living. By placing increased amounts of responsibility on the inmates, and by encouraging open communication and confrontation, program participants were expected to "model and adjust their behaviors through learning, testing, and fixating newer and more effective modes of perceiving and relating to others" (Reimer 1967).

GUIDED GROUP INTERACTION (GGI)

An integral part of the therapeutic regime at the Wharton Tract Program was Guided Group Interaction (GGI), a group therapy technique which is especially tailored for use in correctional rehabilitation. GGI was first used with youthful offenders on an experimental basis in what was known as the *Highfields Project* in New Jersey shortly after World War II (McCorkle, et al., 1958). It has since been implemented in various other correctional environments with generally positive results (Wicks 1974). Major features of Guided Group Interaction include the following:

1. The therapist plays an *active* role in group discussions, especially in the early phases of the group.
2. The major emphasis is on the group and its development, rather than on the treatment of individuals within the group.
3. The atmosphere of the group is one of support, structure, caring, and freedom of expression.
4. Each group member is seen as a potential agent for creating changes in the other individuals.
5. Overt behavior, and not unconscious processes, is the prime target for discussion and change.
6. By learning appropriate communication and problem-solving skills via feedback from other group members, the inmate begins to deal more effectively with interpersonal conflicts, and becomes increasingly aware of how his behavior affects himself and others.

As Wicks (1974) has pointed out:

> The object of GGI sessions is to provide members with enough information, understanding, and motivation to adapt to society.

TRAINING PROGRAM IN INTERPERSONAL PROBLEM-SOLVING SKILLS

Platt, Spivack, and Swift (1974) originally designed, and Platt and Spivack (1976) further developed, a highly structured program for adolescents and adults entitled Interpersonal Problem-solving Group Therapy, which was incorporated into the GGI structure at the Wharton Tract Program. The program was divided into nineteen consecutive units and concentrated on teaching the following skills:

1. Knowing when a problem exists.
2. Defining the problem by putting it into words.
3. Identifying the feeling associated with the problem.
4. Separating facts from opinions.
5. Getting all of the necessary information.
6. Generating alternative solutions.
7. Considering all of the consequences.
8. Deciding and acting on the best choice.

In carrying out the program, major emphasis was placed on encouraging the group members themselves to generate as many of the elements of the problem-solving process as possible. As the focus of the group was on actual current problems, group members were encouraged to bring their own interpersonal problems to the entire group for the purpose of solving them.

DESCRIPTION OF PROGRAM

The design and philosophy of the Wharton Tract Program especially emphasized: (1) a consecutive-step approach, whereby a resident "graduated" from one phase into the next, (2) the acquisition of an increased amount of responsibility for one's own actions; (3) periodic self-evaluations and peer review, and (4) a gradual transition from the institution into the community by earning work release status.

Phase one was an evaluation period lasting approximately 30 days, during which time it was determined if the "resident trainee" would remain in the program. The inmate began group therapy, individual counseling, and work assignments within the unit. Orientation was provided by the Program Supervisor, the Custody Supervisor, and members of the work-release group, who represented the senior residents in the program. Particular attention was paid to the inmate's adjustment to the program in terms of motivation, ability to work with others, and commitment to the program. At the end of this period the inmate was rated by his work supervisor, therapy group, and other staff members. He also performed a self-evaluation at this time. The final decision on a trainee's promotion to phase two was made by the Program Supervisor after he had carefully reviewed all evaluation reports. If the trainee's evaluations were not satisfactory, he either continued in phase one for a longer period, or returned to the Yardville Correctional Center. If the latter decision was made, the inmate was not penalized for failing the program. If the inmate was promoted to phase two, however, his status changed from "resident trainee" to "resident".

During phase two, the inmate continued to participate in group and individual therapies, and began an educational program if he so desired. He also was given the opportunity to develop good work habits by participating in a work program made possible with the cooperation of the State Department of Environmental Protection. Particular job tasks included the construction of firebreakers and the maintenance of public campsites. During this period, however, personal responsibility for one's actions and job performance were stressed, rather than the learning of specific job skills. Phase two lasted a minimum of 60 days, during which time periodic evaluations of the inmate's performance were conducted by program staff, other residents, and the inmate himself. These periodic evaluations enabled the resident to recognize and change inappropriate behaviors prior to promotion to phase three.

Phase three was the beginning of a transition process designed to ease the resident back into society. While he continued to participate in his regular therapy group and educational program, he now was eligible for trips to the community where he could go shopping, bowling, attend concerts, or go to the movies. In addition to trips, those residents who were ninety days short of parole were eligible for weekend furloughs to return home for the weekend.

Besides the added personal responsibility of maintaining himself in the community, the resident also was eligible to earn a more responsible job. He might have become a teaching assistant, resident clerk, or laundryman. However, since only a limited number of such jobs were available, most residents remained on one of the two forest details listed in phase two. Now, however, he was eligible to earn a promotion from Detail #2 to Detail #1. Residents in Detail #1 were engaged in more desirable jobs, had more contact with the general public, and, in general, were expected to represent the more responsible residents on the details.

Because there was no time limit for phase three, the resident had to request advancement to phase four when he believed he was eligible. Once he received satisfactory evaluations from his work supervisor, therapy group, and other staff, he was eligible to begin phase four.

The fourth, and final, phase of the program allowed the resident to spend more time in the community. Having obtained work release status, he now was eligible to work in a community-based job, which allowed him to further develop successful work habits and to expand and sharpen his job skills. He also could keep his earnings in preparation for his eventual release from the institution. Some of the jobs available to him were with local contractors, a car dealership, a diner, and a nursery.

As soon as the resident began work release, he became involved in the work release therapy group. This group focused on the problems which the resident would face in making a reentry back into society. Using a problem-solving approach, he was encouraged to make realistic plans for his future. He examined how he had changed, what he had gained from the program, and how he could apply these gains to his new life in the community. He was made to focus on his feelings about himself, his use of drugs, and his previous confinement. Did he feel he was ready to be paroled?

Residents on work release were expected to set an example for others in the program to follow. They were expected to continue being involved with program activities while they were in the unit, and in so doing act as role-models for the other inmates.

RESIDENT EVALUATIONS AND PAROLE REVIEW

Each resident was rated once a month for his progress within the program in the following areas: work, treatment, and group living. His work rating which reflected his progress within his particular job, was done by his work supervisor, and represented 40% of his total monthly evaluation. His treatment rating, also 40% of total evaluation, reflected his progress within his GGI group, and was done by the group itself. The final 20% of the monthly evaluation, his group living progress, was completed by the entire Wharton Tract staff. Each resident received a detailed written evaluation in each area so that he had an opportunity to better his ratings before the next evaluation period.

A classification committee composed of all Wharton Tract staff was held each month for the purpose of reviewing the progress of those residents who had reached the anticipated midpoint of their stay in the institution. Based on his average monthly ratings, the resident was eligible to earn a certain amount of time off his sentence. He also was eligible at this time for a parole review, which allowed him to earn as much as an additional thirty days off his sentence. Based on the classification committee's evaluation, a parole date was then set for the resident.

ADDITIONAL PROGRAM SERVICES

Couple Therapy Group was a voluntary group of residents and their wives who met every Sunday for one and one-half hours before visiting time. The resident became eligible to join the group as soon as he had entered phase two. Before being accepted into the group, however, each couple was interviewed by the Program Supervisor to determine if their motivations, goals, and expectations were congruent with those of the group. Led by the Program Supervisor, the group focused on the marital relationship, issues of drug abuse, and the ramifications of institutional confinement.

Family Counseling was provided by the Program Supervisor each Sunday during visiting hours for families who wished to see him. Typical discussions centered around drug abuse, family communication styles, values clarification, and post-release planning. It was hoped that a better relationship would be developed between the inmate and his family which would continue as the resident progressed through his treatment in the program.

Individual Counseling was available to the resident by each and every staff member. Residents were encouraged to speak freely to staff about any problem which might have arisen. If a resident was having problems with a particular staff member, the Program Supervisor arranged to meet with both on an ongoing basis until the difficulty was resolved. In certain cases, residents were assigned to individual counseling on a mandatory basis when it appeared that such sessions were necessary.

Town Meetings were held each Sunday after visiting hours. The entire resident population along with the Program Supervisor and all available staff met as a unit to discuss matters that affected the entire community.

The purposes of the Town Meeting included the following:

1. Minimize inter-group conflict by providing a total group (community) feeling.
2. Disseminate information that pertains to the entire community.
3. Use as a forum for decision-making regarding matters that affect all.
4. Allow the entire resident group to evaluate particular program elements.

Recreational Activities were available to residents and trainees throughout all phases of the program. Facilities were available for such activities as basketball, softball, ping-pong, pool, weight training, and football. Two television rooms were available in addition to a very good resident library of books, magazines, periodicals, and newspapers.

SECTION II

EVALUATION APPROACH

There are many vantage points from which to view models of intervention, such as the program described in the preceeding sections. Clinicians will obviously focus their concerns upon the underlying theories and strategies of the treatment approach. Program administrators will, out of necessity, be most concerned with issues of economics, logistics, and the feasibility of implementation. Line staff may well be focused upon the impact the intervention will have upon the current routine, workload, and structure of the program.

While it is obvious that the particular role one fills within the organization of change will generate questions, concerns and issues relevant to that role, there is a class of issues and concerns common to all who interact with the intervention strategy. This class of issues and concerns is evaluative in nature and its understanding crystallizes with the question, "Does the program work?" Clearly, the answer to this question will have a direct impact upon all of those involved in the administration and delivery of the intervention strategy. Through the comprehensive and accurate assessment of program outcomes, many issues of service delivery (process issues) can be clarified and resolved.

It is with these concerns in mind that the evaluation of the Wharton Tract Narcotics Treatment Program began.

The evaluator selected for the project was an outside consultant, a research psychologist already working within the New Jersey correctional system. He contracted to visit the institution at least twice weekly, during which time he supervised the activities of the research staff which consisted of one BA statistician and a statistical clerk. These two staff members carried out the data gathering and analysis tasks during the normal work week.

The program coordinator, who was responsible for all satellite units, including the Wharton Tract, was available for consultation with the research consultant during the time that the latter was in the institution, and a close liaison was maintained. In an initial series of meetings arranged and chaired by the program coordinator, the consultant met with the program director and staff at the Wharton Tract unit and explained that he would be working closely with them to determine the effectiveness of the program. It was expressly stated that he was not going to be concerned with evaluation of individual staff members, but rather with the rehabilitation aspects of the program.

Thereafter, the consultant visited the unit every third week to informally answer questions posed by the staff members (as well as by the program participants).

In addition, every 6 months the research consultant attended a staff meeting and provided feedback on the results of the evaluation. During these meetings, feedback was solicited from staff as to concerns they had regarding evaluation-related issues, such as scheduling data collection sessions so as to minimally interfere with other program activities.

Every 3 to 6 months, the consultant met with the superintendent of the institution to review progress up to that point and to discuss the evaluator's plans for the next several months. This was done so that the necessary institutional personnel could be contacted in order to facilitate the evaluation. It is perhaps significant to note that the evaluation continued under three consecutive superintendents and under as many program directors. This fact, in part, reflected the ongoing institutional commitment to program evaluation.

The evaluation plan was developed over the initial months during which the consultant was assigned to the program. A broad outline of the plan was first prepared by the consultant, who then met some four times with a committee appointed by the superintendent. This committee consisted of the institutional drug treatment program directors, the director of professional services, the chief psychologist, and staff psychologist. During these meetings the consultant solicited the views of committee members regarding the kinds of changes which participation in the program might effect in participants. Appropriate measurement devices were selected by the consultant to measure these variables, then presented to the committee for approval. The committee was very cooperative, due perhaps to the fact that the consultant worked directly for the superintendent's office. Surprisingly, the committee members expressed no real interest in participating in the conduct of the evaluation themselves. The reasons for this were always difficult to define, but included the following: (1) they perceived that evaluation was not an area of expertise for them, and thus they should not attempt it, and (2) they were concerned about adding to their present workloads.

As developed, the plan for initiating a research and evaluation procedure had several general objectives:

1. To institute a system for monitoring the incidence of substance abuse among new admissions to the institution. This system would provide administration with necessary information for programming.
2. To determine the program's effectiveness in meeting its goal of changing participants along important dimensions of personality, cognition, and attitudes so as to reduce the likelihood of future drug use and related criminal behavior. Such determination would include systematic testing of program participants, to establish if change had taken place, as well as monitoring of parole performance.

3. The determination of those factors related to parole success of heroin-addicted offenders at Yardville, as well as the development of a systematic, statistically based method for predicting outcome both in the program and upon release from the institution.

All procedures developed to implement objectives 1 and 2 were piloted in one of the other institutional drug programs before being implemented at the Wharton Tract. These three areas were seen as important elements of the evaluation so that in addition to overall effectiveness of the program: (1) a clear understanding of the level of need for narcotics treatment programming within the correctional system could be delineated, and, (2) an exploration of the potentials for predicting parole success could be developed. Due to the limited scope of this article, only the method and results of the assessment of program effectiveness will be detailed.

EVALUATION METHOD

The transfer of classical experimental methodology to the active program setting is rarely an option for the evaluator attempting to assess program effectiveness. The random assignment of subjects into experimental and control groups, the complete control of extraneous variables, and the number of individuals able to be involved in the study are all difficult methodological issues for the evaluator to resolve. Obviously these difficulties are intensified in the correctional setting where alternative programming is limited, and flexibility in admissions, program assignment, and discharge decisions strictly controlled.

These realities of the program environment mandated creativity (and much energy) on the part of the evaluator who had to hold true to the principles of experimentation while working within the program's structure and processes.

Control groups were able to be utilized for both of the evaluation phases described in the following sections. Members of the control group were selected using the following criteria:

(a) Being the next consecutive admission to the correction center after an inmate had completed the program.
(b) Meeting all criteria for admission into the Wharton Tract Program, including those for age, drug use, escape history, time goal set by classification committee, absence of psychiatric disturbance, and no pending detainers.

Using these criteria it was possible to identify 148 control subjects, all of whom were utilized in the follow-up (parole performance) phase of the evaluation. There were no significant differences between these control group members and those inmates who participated in the Wharton Tract Program.

The evaluation proceeded in two critical areas: (1) the assessment of cognitive, personality, and motivational changes in program participants and controls, and, (2) the assessment of the parole performance of program graduates and controls.

PSYCHOLOGICAL CHANGES

The first phase of program assessment focused upon the determination of changes in internal psychological variables among the program participants and their matched controls. A basic pre-post design was utilized within which existed a battery of tests specifically suited to measure those internal variables targeted for change by the program. The test battery included:

Self-Evaluation Questionnaire (Cutick 1962; Farnham-Diggory 1964). This psychological variable reflects the extent to which an individual believes that he is, and can be, successful in certain situations. This dimension of personality has been shown to be related to overt behavior in many situations. An example here would be resistance to group pressures to conform (Diggory 1966), an attitude of very great importance in the former addict who is trying to stay off drugs. The importance of the self-evaluation dimension as measured by the Self-Evaluation Questionnaire is that this aspect of personality is seen as being a part of the self-system that regulates the extent to which this system is maintained under conditions of stress. For example, during the processing of new information concerning the self, new evaluations of either a positive or negative nature do not evoke immediate, corresponding action by the individual with high self-esteem. On the other hand, for the individual with low self-esteem, new information (of a threatening nature) concerning the self may evoke immediate escape (e.g., drug use) or other behavior aimed at bolstering faltering self-esteem.

Anomie   This term was first introduced by Emile Durkheim (1951) who used it to refer to the breakdown of norms or standards that guide the aspirations and behavior of individuals. Other writers have defined anomie as having no control over one's life or surroundings, as having feelings of isolation and alienation (Hunter 1964), or as the "breakdown of an individual's sense of attachment to society" (McIver 1950, p. 18).

Locus of Control   This variable is a general expectancy operating across a large variety of situations, and it relates to whether the individual believes that he possesses or lacks the power to affect what happens to him. The role of such expectancies has implications regarding the efforts expended in affecting the events in one's life. Among the behavioral dimensions which are correlates of these generalized expectancies for reinforcement, one is particularly relevant to the present evaluation in that it is concerned with an individual's setting and attaining goals for the future. Seeman (1963) found a significant relationship for a sample of reformatory inmates between locus of control and the recall of facts which might affect ''chances'' for success after being released.

Sensation Seeking   The Sensation Seeking Scale (Zuckerman et al. 1964) represents, according to its authors, an attempt to quantify the construct of ''optimal level of stimulation''. This scale represents preferences for extremes of sensation, the new and unfamiliar, irregularity as opposed to regularity and routine, enjoyment of danger and thrills, social stimulation, adventure, and general excitement, all factors which have been described as being characteristic of the drug user. The four subscales and the dimensions they measure are as follows:

1. *Thrill and adventure seeking*. A high score reflects a desire to engage in activities involving elements of speed or danger.
2. *Experience seeking*. This factor can be defined as ''experience for its own sake''. And it reflects, among other things, wanderlust, exhibitionism, the use of marijuana and hallucinatory drugs, associating with unusual and unconventional persons, and the flouting of authority.
3. *Disinhibition*. This factor reflects a hedonistic outlook in life, including heavy drinking, wild parties, and gambling.
4. *Boredom susceptibility*. This scale contains items reflecting a dislike of routine work; predictable, dull, or boring people; a preference for exciting people; and a restlessness when things are unchanging.

Death Concern   This dimension reflects concern over conscious awareness of one's own mortality (Dickstein and Blatt 1966). It may be important in the personality structure of the addict in that the addict who shows little concern with the risks involved in his drug use will be more likely to fail on parole.

Pretest batteries were administered to program participants within the first week of their involvement in the Wharton Tract program. The control group members who were dispersed throughout the general institutional population, were administered the pretest package within several days of the completion of the test battery by the Wharton Tract program participants.

Post-testing was conducted at two weeks prior to the inmates' scheduled release date. Retesting of the matched control group subjects followed procedures identical to those used in retesting the program participants. The post-testing of the controls, however, presented many difficulties as their ongoing programs, release dates, and locations were extremely variable. In all, complete pre-post test batteries were collected on 48 Wharton Tract program participants and 18 heroin addict controls.

RESULTS OF PRE AND POST-TEST BATTERIES

The analysis of the pre and post-tests revealed that the Wharton Tract program participants changed, in statistically significant ways on three of the scales: (1) the Diggory Self Evaluation measure, suggesting possession of greater resistence to conformity pressures; (2) Locus of Control scale, suggesting that program participants had increased their belief in personal fate control, and, (3) the Sensation Seeking Scale, suggesting a decreased preference for high levels of stimulation and excitement.

These results increase in their importance when one considers that the control group showed no significant differences on any of the scales between pre and post measurement. While both the program participants and their control counterparts began their respective programs essentially equivalent, they ended their incarceration with very different profiles. This suggests very clearly that the different program experiences had in fact produced differences between the two groups on the variables targeted for change by the Wharton Tract programs.

The importance of pre and post-test differences is, in many ways, limited. While such data is critical in understanding how participants have changed, it cannot address the more significant questions relating to the consequences of that change. In order to effectively deal with these important questions of long-term impact, it was necessary to perform a follow-up study comparing the parole performance of program participants and their controls.

PAROLE PERFORMANCE OF WHARTON TRACT PROGRAM GRADUATES AND CONTROLS

The assessment of behavior while on parole was accomplished through the close examination of parole reports which were submitted by parole officers every six months. These detailed reports were reviewed after they had been sent to the institution and placed in the parolee's file. At no time was contact ever made with the parole officers regarding these reports. Consequently, the Wharton Tract program participants, as well as the controls, were singled out as being of special interest. At the same time, independent verification of arrests was obtained from state police records, in order to verify the accuracy of the parole data. This verification revealed almost 100 percent agreement between the two sources of arrest data.

Although data on parole status were tabulated and reported to the institutional administration at six month intervals, only the results pertaining to the final status of all program graduates at the end of the 2 year follow-up period will be discussed here. The parole follow-up date collected on program graduates and addict controls represent information on a wide range of parole outcomes, including recommitment status, mortality, adjustment on parole, and drug use. The following is a descriptive summary of the most significant differences which emerged between the two groups.

Recommitment   Wharton Tract graduates had a significantly lower ($p < 0.05$) recommitment rate (18%) than controls (30%). Both groups had a very low rate of recommitment for drug offenses (3%), and program graduates were thus much lower in recommitment for nondrug offenses (15%) than controls (27%). This difference was statistically significant at the .01 level. *Good Adjustment; Assigned Good*   At the end of the 2-year follow-up period, there were a significantly higher number of Wharton Tract graduates than controls in both the good adjustment while on parole category (33 versus 19, $p < 0.05$) and in the "assigned good" category (27 versus 13, $p < 0.05$). The "assigned good" category represents those men for whom detailed parole reports had not been filed for the fourth 6-month follow-up, but on whom no arrests, parole violations, or recommitments had been reported.

Used Heroin on Parole   While the differences are not large, it was found that fewer program graduates (37, or 23%) than controls (45, or 28%) were reported using heroin on parole. Of all outcome categories, this is probably the least reliable one, since it would be difficult for a parole officer to determine use with a high degree of certainty unless it were blatant. Also, these data were not reported for some of the recommitments. For both reasons, it may represent an underestimate of drug use behavior.

Participation in Drug Program   Another small difference occurred on this rating. More controls (22%) than graduates (18%) were participating in drug programs while on parole, perhaps indicating a greater need for supervision in this area.

Other Measures from Parole Report   On other measures derived from the parole report (awaiting trial status, missing, deceased, discharged, maximum terminated, and poor adjustment) the differences between the two groups were not significant.

FIRST ARREST STATUS

One of the most important differences to emerge was the fact that significantly more Wharton Tract graduates remained arrest-free (51% versus 34%), and that if and when they were arrested, this event occurred later during parole (at 238 days versus 168 days). Finally, it is of interest to note that there were significantly fewer arrests in the experimental group for nonindictable, nondrug offenses than in the control group. Of even more interest, perhaps, is the finding that the two groups did not differ with respect to the number of both indictable and nonindictable drug offenses.

RELATIONSHIP BETWEEN PROGRAM COMPLETION AND PAROLE SUCCESS

During the course of the program there were a number of inmates admitted who did not successfully complete all phases of the program. Most of these "dropouts" were due to administrative transfer for early release, attendance at special educational, medical, or other treatment programs at the parent institution. During the course of the evaluation, 29% of the entrants did not complete the program. Arrest rates were also examined, and 30.4% were found to be arrest free after 2 years of parole. This figure differs significantly from the 51% arrest free rate for men completing the program ($p < .001$), but not from the 34% rate for control subjects.

IMPLICATIONS

The results of these two phases of the evaluation of the Wharton Tract program strongly suggest a powerful and effective approach to the treatment of the incarcerated heroin addict. More definitive statements regarding the effectiveness of the program cannot be made due to the absence of random assignment of subjects to the treatment and control categories. The data, however, do clearly indicate that: (1) program participants changed significantly on target variables between program entry and discharge and their control counterpart did not; (2) over a two year follow-up period program participants had significantly better parole performance than controls; and (3) program graduates were significantly more successful on parole than those program participants who did not successfully complete the program.

These findings provide a strong foundation for belief in the ability of the Wharton Tract Narcotics Treatment Program and others like it, to promote constructive rehabilitative change.

REFERENCES

Cutick, R.A., "Self-evaluation of capacities as a function of self-esteem and the characteristics of a model." Unpublished doctoral dissertation, University of Pennsylvania, 1962.

Dickstein, L.A., and Blatt, S.J., "Death concern, futurity, and anticipation," *Journal of Consulting Psychology*, 1966, *30*, 11–17.

Diggory, J.C., *Self-evaluation: Concepts and Studies* (New York: Wiley, 1966).

Elias, A., "Group Treatment program for juvenile delinquents," *Child Welfare*, 1968, *47*, 281–290.

Farnham — Diggory, S., "Self-evaluation and subjective life expectancy among suicidal and nonsuicidal psychotic males," *Journal of Abnormal and Social Psychology*, 1964, *69*, 628–634.

Hunter, D.A., *The Slums; Challenge and Response* (New York: Free Press, 1964).

McCorkle, L.W., Elias, A., and Bixby, F.L., *The Highfields Story* (Henry Holt and Company, Inc., 1958).

McIver, R., *The rampants we guard* (New York: Macmillan, 1950).

Pilnick, S. and Associates, *Collegefields: From delinquency to freedom* (Newark, N.J.: Newark State College, 1967).

Platt, J.J. et al., "Adolescent problem-solving thinking," *Journal of Consulting and Clinical Psychology*, 1974, *42*, 787–793.

Platt, J.J. and Duome, M.J., *TIPS: Training in Interpersonal Problem-Solving Skills*, Department of Mental Health Sciences, Hahnemann Medical College & Hospital, Revised Ed., October, 1979.

Platt, J.J., Hoffman, A.R., and Elbert, R.K., "Recent trends in the demography of heroin addiction among youthful offenders," *International Journal of Addictions*, 1976, *11*, 221–236.

Platt, J.J., and Labate, C., *Heroin Addiction: Theory, Research, and Treatment* (New York: Wiley-Interscience, 1976).

Platt, J.J., Labate, C., and Wicks, R.J., *Evaluative Research in Correctional Drug Abuse Treatment* (Lexington: D.C. Heath and Company, 1977).

Platt, J.J., and Scura, W.C., "Peer judgments of parole success in institutionalized heroin addicts: Personality correlates and validity," *Journal of Counseling Psychology*, 1974, *21*, 511–515.

Platt, J.J., Scura, W.C., and Hannon, J.R., "Problem-solving thinking of youthful incarcerated heroin addicts," *Journal of Community Psychology*, 1973, 408–411.

Platt, J.J., Spivack, G., and Swift, M., "Interpersonal problem-solving group therapy," *Research and Evaluation Report #31*, Hahnemann Medical College & Hospital, 1974.

Platt, J.J., and Spivack, G., "Measures of interpersonal cognitive problem-solving for adults and adolescents," Department of Mental Health Sciences, Hahnemann Medical College & Hospital, July, 1977.

President's Commission on Law Enforcement and the Administration of Justice, *Task Force Report: Corrections* (Washington: U.S. Government Printing Office, 1967).

Reimer, E.G., "Introducing the correctional community program into the correctional institution." In, Fenton, N., Reimer, E.G., and Wilmer, H.A., (eds.), *The Correctional Community* (Los Angeles: University of California Press, 1967).

Seeman, M., "Alienation and social learning in a reformatory," *American Journal of Sociology*, 1963, *69*, 270–284.

Seidl, R.A., Hoffman, A.R., and Turner, A.C., *Wharton Tract Narcotic Treatment Unit: A Program Synopsis*, Youth Reception and Correction Center, Yardville, New Jersey, September, 1973.

Spivack, G., Platt, J.J., and Shure, M.B., *The Problem-Solving Approach to Adjustment* (San Francisco: Jossey-Bass, 1976).

Wicks, R.J., *Correctional Psychology: Themes and Problems in Correcting the Offender* (Harper & Row, New York, 1974).

Yalom, I.D., *The Theory and Practice of Group Psychotherapy*, Second Edition (New York: Basic Books, Inc., 1975).

Zuckerman, M. et al., "Development of a sensation-seeking Scale," *Journal of Consulting Psychology*, 1964, *28*, 477–482.

SUPPLEMENTARY REFERENCES

Ausubel, D.P., *Drug Addiction: Physiological, Psychological, and Sociological Aspects* (New York: Random House, 1958; 1964).

Baer, D.J., and Corrado, J., "Heroin addict relationships with parents during childhood and early adolescent years," *Journal of Genetic Psychology*, 1974, *124*, 99–103.

Baganz, P., and Jarvis, J., "Work and study release in the rehabilitation of the narcotic addict," *Rehabilitation Literature*, 1971, *32*, 354–359.

Ball, J.C., Chambers, C.D. (eds.), *The Epidemiology of Opiate Addiction in the United States* (Springfield, Ill., Charles C. Thomas, 1970).

Bejerot, N., *Addiction: An Artifically Induced Drive* (Springfield, Ill: Charles C. Thomas, 1972).

Bloch, H.A., and Geis, H., *Man, Crime, and Society* (New York: Random House, 1965).

Bowden, C.L., and Langenauer, B.J., "Success and failure in the NARA addiction program," *American Journal of Psychiatry*, 1972, *128*, 853–856.

Braceland, F., Freeman, D., and Rickels, K., *Drug Abuse: Medical and Criminal Aspects* (New York: MSS Information Corporation, 1972).

Bratter, T.E., "Group therapy of affluent, alienated, adolescent drug abusers: A reality therapy and confrontational approach," *Psychotherapy: Theory, Research, and Practice*, 1972, *9*, 308–313.

Bratter, T.E., "Treating alienated, unmotivated drug abusing adolescents," *American Journal of Psychotherapy*, 1973, *27*, 585–598.

Cockett, R., *Drug Abuse and Personality in Young Offenders* (London: Butterworth, 1971).

Cushman, P., "Narcotic addiction and crime," *Rhode Island Medical Journal*, 1974a, *57*, 197–204.

Dole, V.P., "Detoxification of sick addicts in prison," *Journal of the American Medical Association*, 1972, *220*, 366–369.

Edmundson, W.F., Davies, J.E., Acker, J.D., and Myer, B., "Patterns of drug epidemiology in prisoners," *Industrial Medicine and Surgery*, 1972, *41*, 15–19.

Fracchia, J., Shepherd, C., and Merlis, S., "Some comments about the personality comparison of incarcerated and street heroin addicts," *Psychological Reports*, 1973a, *33*, 413–414.

Frankel, K.A., "Heroin and crime." *New England Journal of Medicine*, 1973, *289*, 430–431.

Geis, G., "A halfway house is not a home: Notes on the failure of a narcotic rehabilitation project," *Drug Forum*, 1974, *4*, 7–14.

Harms, E. (Ed.), *Drug Addiction in Youth* (New York: Pergamon, 1965).

Helms, D.J., Scura, W.C., and Fisher, C.C., "Treatment of the addict in correctional institutions." In Richter, R.W. (Ed.), *Medical Aspects of Drug Abuse* (Hagerstown, Md.: Harper and Row, 1975).

Huberty, D.J., "Civil commitmnet of the narcotic addict: Evaluation of a treatment model," *Crime and Delinquency*, 1972, *18*, 99–109.

Ketai, R., "Peer-observed psychotherapy with institutionalized narcotic addicts," *Archives of General Psychiatry*, 1973, *29*, 51–53.

Kozel, N.J., DuPont, R.L., and Brown, B.S., "Narcotics and crime: A study of narcotic involvement in an offender population," *International Journal of the Addictions*, 1972, *7*, 443–450.

Lindesmith, A.R., *The Addict and the Law* (New York: Vintage Books, 1967).

McKee, M.R., "Addicts and rehabilitation. Whom to send where?" *Psychological Reports*, 1972, *30*, 731–755.

Nash, G., *The Impact of Drug Abuse Treatment Upon Criminality: A Look At 19 Programs* (Montclair State College, New Jersey: 1973).

Nurco, D.N., and Lerner, M., "Characteristics of drug abusers in a correctional system," *Journal of Drug Issues*, 1972, *2*, 49–56.

Obitz, F.W., Oziel, L.J., and Unmacht, J.J., "General and specific perceived locus of control in delinquent drug users," *International Journal of the Addictions*, 1973, *8*, 723–727.

Panton, J.H., and Behre, C., "Characteristics associated with drug addiction in a state prison population, *Journal of Community Psychology*, 1973, *1*, 411–416.

Peck, M.L., and Klugman, D.J., "Rehabilitation of drug dependent offenders: An alternative approach," *Federal Probation*, 1973, *37*, 18–23.

Raynes, A.E., Climent, C., Patch, V.D., and Ervine, F., "Factors related to imprisonment in female heroin addicts," *International Journal of the Addictions*, 1974, *9*, 145–150.

Reasons, C.E., "The addict as a criminal — Perpetration of a legend," *Crime and Delinquency*, 1975, *21*, 19–27.

Singh, J.M., Miller, L., and Lah, H. (eds.), *Drug addiction: Clinical and Socio-legal Aspects*, (Vol. 2) (Mount Kisco, New York: Futura, 1972).

Sutker, P.B., "Personality differences and sociopathy in heroin addicts and non-addict prisoners," *Journal of Abnormal Psychology*, 1971, *78*, 247–251.

Sutker, P.B., and Moan, C.E., "A psychosocial description of penitentiary inmates," *Archives of General Psychiatry*, 1973, *29*, 663–667.

Vorenberg, J., and Lukoff, I.F., "Addiction, crime, and the criminal justice system," *Federal Probation*, 1973, *37*, 3–7.

Zimmering, P., Toolan, J., Sofrin, R., and Wortis, S.B., "Drug addiction in relation to problems of adolescence," *American Journal of Psychiatry*, 1952, *109*, 272–278.

Chapter 27

Editors' Remarks

The final chapter in this volume describes Andrews's and Kiessling's three year treatment/research project which has examined the effectiveness of probation officers and volunteers in counseling adult probationers.

It is fitting that we should end with the contribution by Andrews and Kiessling. The oft-repeated theme of this book has been that although there are no cure-alls, *some* correctional treatment programs do "work". In weighing the evidence we must take into consideration not only the nature of the intervention but also the characteristics of the practitioners, the type of clients and the appropriateness of our measures of change. In support of that theme Andrews and Kiessling have contributed not mere rhetoric but convincing evidence derived from well-conceptualized and carefully designed research.

Program Structure and Effective Correctional Practices: A Summary of the CaVIC Research*

D.A. Andrews and Jerry J. Kiessling

Canadian Volunteers in Corrections (CaVIC) was a three year project which generated some 30 manuals and reports concerning a variety of management, operational, and research issues (Andrews & Kiessling, 1979a). The present paper is a summary of the research component of CaVIC. This research involved a comprehensive comparison of citizen volunteer and professional supervision of adult probationers in a one-to-one program (Andrews, Kiessling, et al., 1979). In this paper we summarize the major findings and provide a glimpse of the data on which our conclusions were based, but we would encourage the reader with technical interests in the area to consult the original report for details. For example, we will not be

*The CaVIC project was funded by the Law Reform Commission of Canada (1974–75), the Ontario Ministry of Correctional Services (1974–77), the Correctional Consultation Centre (1974–77) and the Research Division (1975–77) of the Ministry of the Solicitor General of Canada. A Canada Council leave fellowship (1976–77) to D.A. Andrews helped make the literature reviews possible as well as the development of the conceptual elements of the project. Opinions expressed in this summary paper are those of the authors and are not to be interpreted as reflections of the policy of the funding agencies.

Thanks to the many people who made the project possible and assisted in its development and operation; within the Ontario Ministry: Leah Lambert, Andy Birkenmayer, Bob Fox, Ruth Pitman, Elmer Toffelmire, Bill Jackson, Morgan Newton, and the professionals of the Ottawa office; within the Federal system: Michel Vallée, Jody Gomber, Sheila Arthurs; within the community: T. Swaby, R. Marin, Kathleen Harris, Linda Barkley, Mary Fereday, Jan and Chuck Miller, Mauren Paleczny, Alixe Lillico; on the research team: R.J. Russell, B. Grant, C. Kennedy, K. Conley, D. Collard, H. Tully, L. Kennedy, D. Hayes, C. Lo, B. Anderson, G. Zimmer, S. Colleta, S. Mickus.

This article was prepared especially for inclusion in this book.

discussing the specifics of scale and test construction in this summary but such information is available in the original report.

The CaVIC findings have already had an impact on the design and management of volunteer services in the Ottawa office in which the study was conducted (Andrews & Kiessling, 1978) and we sense that its findings are of importance for the design of programs in other areas. The strength of the practical implications of CaVIC may be traced in part to the conceptualization of program evaluation research and correctional operations which was at the base of the research.

This summary of the CaVIC research begins with a look at that conceptual base and then reviews the findings under the following headings: the nature and quality of volunteer supervision of probationers, the differential effectiveness of volunteer and professional supervision with different types of clients, officer characteristics and the matching of officer and client, the measurement of supervision practices and their relation to outcome, the differential effectiveness of different supervision practices with different types of clients, and the selection of intermediate targets.

THE CONCEPTUAL AND METHODOLOGICAL BASE

When social scientists enter an area of high political, economic and human interest such as that of corrections, they are given to finding and reporting on "gaps". Nearly always there is a reference to the wide "gap" between social science theory and social service and very often "gaps" are detected between theory and research, between the concerns of managers and the concerns of workers, and between the concerns of clients and the concerns of everyone else in the service system. There are also the inter-disciplinary squabbles for which corrections is infamous. The assumption is that a narrowing of the gaps would be beneficial to social services and social theory. While the truth value of that assumption is open to empirical examination, a necessary first step is to begin to become specific about the links which exist or might exist among the concerns of policy and management persons, practitioners, theoreticians, researchers and clients.

Figure I provides the outlines of a perspective on program operations and evaluation which suggests some specific links. The various components of the criminal justice system serve a multitude of functions and corrections too may be seen as multi-functional. The specific function of concern in Figure I is the public expectation that correctional efforts serve to reduce the probability of criminal activity on the part of adjudicated offenders, certainly during the period of supervision and perhaps even after the expiration of sentence. This major function does not exist in a political-ethical vacuum and hence there is also the concern that this function be served in a cost-efficient manner and in a manner which is not offensive to the sentiments of the public, or to those of

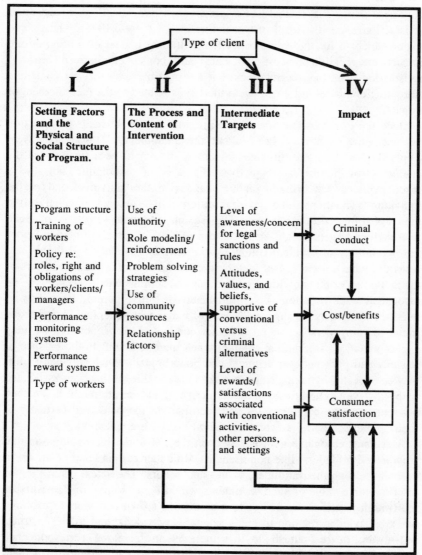

Figure 1   *The Major Components of Program Operation and Evaluation.*

the more direct participants in the system. The policy and management person who wished to survive would pay attention to the satisfaction of workers and offenders with a given program since positive impact on objective indices of criminal behavior would not itself guarantee program acceptance and maintenance. The lore of correctional managers, practitioners and clients includes many examples of the ability of either of the three groups to sabotage an apparently sound program because of the program's insensitivity to their concerns. Even the radical behaviorists now pay attention to consumer satisfaction under the label of "social validity" (Wolf, 1978). Thus, three major elements for the assessment of the ultimate impact of a program are impact on recidivism, cost efficiency and consumer (defined broadly) satisfaction. The inter-correlations that are possible with that set constitute intriguing empirical questions as do the issues related to the measurement of impact.

Once the ultimate objectives for a program are established, the question becomes that of how to bring about the attainment of those objectives. Typically, reaching the ultimate objectives is seen to be a function of the attainment of intermediate objectives. There is the assumption, not always made explicit, that bringing about changes in the individual and/or the individual's situations and behavioral settings will be associated with a shift in the probability of recidivism. The search for and selection of such intermediate targets should bring the correctional effort deep into studies of the psychology of criminal conduct: according to psychological theory and research, what are the *causal* factors in criminal conduct? What attributes of the individual or the individual's situations and settings would, *if changed*, be associated with variations in criminal activity? In Figure I, three sets of intermediate targets are suggested, each of which was generated from a broad social learning perspective on criminal conduct. Most generally, we may expect variations in criminal conduct when there is a shift in the balance of rewards and punishers for criminal and noncriminal behaviors. Such a shift may be expected by taking steps to make the formal legal sanctions associated with law violations function as effective punishers through heightened awareness of the contingencies and increases in the perceived certainty of their application and the perceived validity of their application.

A second reasonable goal is based on the not untenable assumption that adjudicated offenders, like nonoffenders, do under certain conditions, act in accordance with their attitudes, values and beliefs. The actual controlling or discriminative value of such sentiments would depend upon one's ability or motivation to self-manage, i.e. to monitor one's own behavior, to examine one's behavior in relation to one's standards or values, and to self-instruct, self-reward or self-punish so that there is an increased correspondence between one's standards and one's behavior. Thus, the second intermediate objective is to bring about changes in the sentiments of offenders such that conventional alternatives to crime are perceived as positive and worthy, and to encourage self-management with reference to those prosocial attitudes, values and beliefs.

The third intermediate target is a broad one and would encompass a variety of specific objectives depending upon the type of client and resources available to an agency. Generally, if the frequency, variety and quality of satisfactions and rewards associated with conventional pursuits with conventional others in conventional settings such as home, school and work can be enhanced, then a reduction in the probability of recidivism may be expected. The successful attainment of the third objective would have that positive impact on recidivism in at least two ways. First, the motivational base for some forms of crime would be reduced in that money, property, interpersonal satisfactions, etc. are now accruing from noncriminal behavior. Secondly, an increase in the density of rewards for noncriminal behavior simultaneously increases the potential costs associated with crime in that there is more to lose should criminal activity be detected and sanctions imposed.

Given that any correctional program has made choices regarding its intermediate and ultimate targets, the next question is how to bring about the desired changes on those intermediate factors. Here again, the practitioner and the manager are brought into contact with psychology, specifically the psychology of counseling and behavioral influence. What specific counseling or behavioral influence practices are likely to bring about the desired changes in the offender's situations and behavioral settings? A multitude of influence systems and associated technologies have been generated in the medical, psychological and social sciences and practices range from some rather major alterations in the biological state of the human organism through the variety of psycho- and socio-therapies of Freud, Adler, Glaser, Rogers, TA, TM, GGI, etc.

Figure 1 lists five major approaches to correctional counseling and supervision which we have found cut across the more formal attempts to systematize behavioral influence practices. We have found that our classification of practices has several distinct advantages. First, the classification of intervention practices retains close ties with past efforts at correctional programming. Second, its use brings some degree of order to what have been confusing and inconsistent findings in past evaluations of correctional programs. Third, it is translated readily into the language and practices of the social learning approaches. Fourth, it is readily operationalized for purposes of monitoring the ongoing correctional process. Fifth, it has direct implications for the selection and training of correctional workers. Sixth, it is linked to the three sets of intermediate targets. Finally, we believe it is sufficiently flexible that it would not have the effect of blocking innovative programming.

The five major approaches are as follows:

A. *Authority*   With this approach the correctional officer makes explicit use of the formal rules associated with correctional settings such that the formal legal sanctions are made more vivid, understandable and certain in their application. This dimension of correctional practice relates to the first intermediate objective (Andrews, 1979: Chapter 2).

B. *Anticriminal Modeling and Reinforcement*   The correctional worker acting as a model and a source of social reinforcement may promote the acquisition of prosocial and anticriminal attitudinal, cognitive and behavioral patterns. Anticriminal expressions and behaviors are those which are positive and supportive regarding conventional alternatives to crime in terms of activities, other persons and behavioral settings. Procriminal expressions are those which support criminal activities, associates and settings. This dimension relates to the second intermediate objective (Andrews, 1979: Chapter 3).

C. *Problem-solving*   As a knowledgeable and skilled individual, the correctional worker may engage the client in the process of resolving those personal, interpersonal or community-based difficulties which are resulting in reduced levels of satisfaction and reward for noncriminal pursuits. For analytic purposes, problem-solving efforts may be further classified according to whether the focus is on concrete community and interpersonal problems (in areas such as work, family, education, peers, finances and housing), or whether the focus is on recreational or personal/emotional problems. The latter two foci are separated because the recreational focus has been typical of volunteer programs while the personal/emotional focus is typical of the insight and relationship oriented counseling schools. This dimension relates to the third intermediate objective (Andrews, 1979: Chapter 4).

D. *Use of Community Resources*   This set, often called environmental facilitation or the advocate/broker role, is another special subset of problem-solving. It is worthy of separate attention because of the emphasis placed on advocacy/brokerage models today. Its value of course, would depend upon how well the resource to which a client is referred is in fact able to provide service (Andrews, 1979: Chapter 4).

E. *Quality of interpersonal relationships*   This set includes practices of the socio-emotional type such as the expression of warmth, concern and active listening or empathy, and the creation of conditions of trust and open communication. Within this classification of supervision practices, it is assumed that high quality interpersonal relationships strengthen the force of messages which are given by way of the four more directive elements of supervision and counseling (Andrews, 1979: Chapter 1).

With decisions made regarding the practices likely to be most effective with reference to the selected intermediate targets, the next level of concern is that of designing a program, which by the nature of its physical and social structure, will encourage the actual use of the intervention practices judged most appropriate. This is the policy and management level of programming and here the most relevant body of theory and research is likely to be found in the organizational studies of social psychologists, sociologists and the management and policy analysts. When considering the social structure of a program, the three major concepts employed by sociologists are those of membership composition (the characterization of an organization in terms of the personal characteristics of its members), roles (the sets of behaviors which anyone in a given position within the organization would enact), and statuses (the rights and obligations associated with any given position in the organization). In brief, a task of the manager is to create a structure which, on the basis of its role, status and membership composition, generates effective practices and appropriate intermediate gains for ultimately positive outcome. For example, some obvious management level functions have profound implications for the social structure of a program: the selection of workers on practice-relevant dimensions (membership composition), the preservice and inservice training of workers or the creation of new positions (roles), the development of explicit policy and procedures (status), and the structural mix approaches such as the matching of clients and workers or the differential assignment of clients to officers in different roles. The management level of operations is discussed in some detail by Kiessling and Andrews (1979).

The characteristics of the clients are an element of the social structure of correctional programs which appears so potentially important that it has been pulled out of the social structure box and given special attention within Figure 1. It is the case that different intermediate targets may be differentially important for different types of clients and that different types of clients may be differentially responsive to different types of practices. Moreover, factors such as client age, criminal history or sex are likely to set certain limits upon the extent to which any given program is able to produce variations in recidivism rates. For example, even a small impact upon a ''psychopathic'' or ''undersocialized'' sample may be of more theoretical and practical significance than an apparently larger impact upon a ''nonpsychopathic'' or ''socialized'' sample.

When program operations and their evaluation are reviewed for the perspective of Figure 1, it becomes clear why there has been so much controversy surrounding the question of the efficacy of correctional treatment and supervision. Most reviewers of the evaluation literature and most evaluators of specific programs have looked for relationships between Set I (the structural level of programs) and Set IV (ultimate impact) without considering what services are actually being delivered (Set II), and whether the program achieved its intermediate objectives (Set III). The potential for confusion is great when one considers the possibilities: a given program may have selected intermediate targets which were appropriate or inappropriate for their clients, may or may not have successfully influenced the target conditions, and may or may not have arranged for the delivery of the appropriate services. Such a range of possibilities renders any attempt to reach conclusions on ''what works'' simply silly when the major categories of treatment are as grossly defined as they typically are. We refer to categorizations of treatment such as ''probation'' or ''group counseling'' or ''individual counseling'' or ''vocational programs''. The variety and mix of structural factors, actual practices, and intermediate gains (or losses) which might be represented within any set of ''probation'' or ''group'' programs simply makes a reasonable and useful summary statement of the efficacy impossible.

With that conceptual and methodological base, the overall research objective of CaVIC was to explore some of the theoretical and empirical links among and within the components of program operations represented in

Figure I. The three major controlled or experimental manipulations of CaVIC research were at the structural or management level: one, the addition of a new role, volunteer probation officer, which could be compared with the more traditional role of professional probation officer; two, the assessment of membership composition effects by assigning probationers to officers, volunteer or professional, who differed in their predispositions to establish high levels of the relationship and anticriminal modeling dimensions of correctional practice; three, an examination of how role (volunteer versus professional) and membership composition (type of client) factors may interact and produce differential treatment effects.

The impact of each of these three management level manipulations were examined with reference to their impact on the content and process of intervention (Set II in Figure 1), intermediate gains (Set III in Figure 1) and ultimate impact on recidivism (Set IV). In order to assess impact on actual practices, a number of measures had to be developed. Most importantly, objective behavioral measures of each of the five dimensions of correctional practice were developed for use with audio-taped samples of actual supervision sessions involving the officers and their clients. In addition, we asked the managers of the volunteer program, the screening interviewer and the trainer of volunteers, to evaluate the volunteers on the dimensions. We also asked the volunteers and professionals to report via standardized questionnaires on their preferred approaches to supervision. Finally, we asked the officers and the probationers to evaluate, again via standardized questionnaires, the quality of supervision which was being offered and received. While the measures derived from the content analyses of audio-taped supervision sessions were, by definition, the more objective indicators of supervision process, the reports of program managers and of officers and probationers have the special feature of also being indices of the consumer satisfaction type. The more traditional records of frequency and location of contacts were also kept. Kiessling (1979) has reported on cost-efficiency elsewhere.

Intermediate gains were assessed by way of self-report attitude and personality changes (post-minus-prescores) observed over the first six months of supervision. The ultimate impact was assessed through analyses of inprogram recidivism of convictions for new offenses occurring during the supervision period. A three year post-probation follow-up is currently underway.

The study involved 96 probationers randomly assigned to a professional officer pool of 14, and 94 probationers assigned to a citizen volunteer pool of 60. Assignment of clients to officers within the pool was on the basis of availability and not tied to officer or client characteristics. The integrity of the random assignment was maintained for purposes of evaluating attitude change and recidivism data but many of the measures of supervision process and practice were based on reduced samples. Table 1 presents a comparison of the professional, volunteer and probationer samples on basic demographic and personal history factors.

TABLE 1

Some Bio-Social Information on the Officers and the Probationers

	Professional Officers (n = 14)		Volunteer Officers (n = 60)		Probationers (n = 184)*	
	f	%	f	%	f	%
Age						
16–19	0	0.0	3	5.0	103	56.0
20–29	3	21.4	29	48.3	60	32.6
30–39	4	28.6	13	21.7	17	9.2
40–49	7	50.0	9	15.0	3	1.6
50 plus	0	0.0	6	10.0	1	.1
Sex						
Male	9	64.3	25	41.7	144	78.3
Female	5	35.7	35	58.3	40	21.7
Education						
Grade 10 or less	0	0.0	3	5.0	107	66.0
11–13	0	0.0	11	18.3	48	29.6
Any Postsecondary	13	100.0	46	76.7	17	10.4
Marital Status						
Unattached	2	14.2	29	48.4	144	80.0
Attached	12	85.8	31	51.6	36	20.0
Occupation						
Student	0	0.0	7	11.9	36	23.8
Labourer	0	0.0	4	6.8	69	45.7
Houseperson	0	0.0	8	13.5	6	4.0
White Collar	0	0.0	14	23.7	33	21.9
Supervisor/Manager Professional	14	100.0	26	44.1	7	4.6

*Probationers represented are those who completed the A&P battery at pretest. Conclusions did not vary when the additional six probationers were added.

THE NATURE AND QUALITY OF VOLUNTEER SUPERVISION

Finding 1

Volunteer and professional supervision differed greatly in terms of the frequency, duration and types of contacts which were made with probationers. Relative to the clients of the professionals, the clients of the volunteers were seen in person twice as often; contacted by telephone some four times as often and the contacts were six times longer on average. The volunteers also had more frequent contacts with the families, friends and other associates of their probationers than did the professionals. Finally, there were four times as many client initiated contacts within the volunteer sample and more of the volunteer contacts occurred outside of the probation office.

Comment   In terms of the traditional criteria of case-load size and frequency of contact, volunteer supervision over the first 3 months was more intensive than professional supervision. Low case-load volunteer supervision also appeared to better match an ideal of community-based supervision, i.e. one that is client responsive, that is wide ranging in terms of the setting within which it occurs, and one that involves not only the client but the client's social network.

TABLE 2

Frequency, Duration and Type of Client Contacts During the First Three Months of Volunteer and Professional Supervision

	Professionals ($n = 65$)		Volunteers ($n = 62$)		
	Mean	SD	Mean	SD	F
Contacts With Clients					
In Person	4.49	2.09	10.28	5.42	64.92**
Telephone	2.41	2.63	10.68	10.67	36.79**
Other	.00	.00	.31	1.55	2.59
Officer Initiated	5.29	3.17	11.82	6.95	47.92**
Probationer Initiated	1.51	1.90	6.32	7.90	22.82**
Office	4.25	1.90	3.60	4.78	1.02
Probationer's Home	.25	.85	4.00	3.82	60.02**
Other Places	.11	.56	2.94	3.16	50.80**
Hours	3.06	2.33	19.85	15.69	72.92**
Contacts With Significant Others					
Family	.72	1.91	2.41	2.11	23.36*
Employer	.18	.52	.18	.52	< 1.0
School Officials	.03	.17	.16	.68	2.25
Police	.06	.24	.01	.12	2.01
Others	.71	1.35	1.59	3.36	3.86
Hours	.75	.81	3.71	4.36	28.76**

*$p < .05$; **$p < .01$

Finding 2

When provided with a set of items describing preferred roles and activities, the professional officers strongly endorsed the authority and active counseling orientations toward their roles while volunteers opted for items which stressed a friendship or socio-emotional orientation (Table 3).

Comment   These findings are in no way surprising in that they reflect exactly the roles and training of volunteers and professionals in the program studied.

TABLE 3

A Comparison of Volunteer and Professional Supervision According to Officers' Role Preferences and Probationer and Officer Evaluations of Supervision

| | Professionals | | Volunteers | | |
	Mean	SD	Mean	SD	F
Officer Role Preferences					
	(n − 12)		(n = 38)		
Authority	16.08	2.75	13.32	2.22	12.65**
Active Intervention	9.75	2.26	7.63	2.49	19.99**
Relationship	4.00	2.33	7.63	2.15	25.01**
Probationers' Evaluations					
	(n = 32)		(n = 78)		
Relationship	32.52	6.05	34.51	4.19	3.90*
Help	13.53	3.43	14.76	1.99	5.49**
Direction	3.87	1.68	3.76	1.96	< 1.0
Officers' Evaluations					
Relationship	30.50	3.84	32.67	4.94	4.92*
Help	12.59	2.80	13.33	2.53	1.82
Direction	6.66	1.39	6.34	1.51	1.05

*$p < .05$; **$p < .01$

Finding 3

Both sets of participants, the probationers and the officers, were asked to report on their perceptions of the quality of supervision being offered and received. The volunteers and their clients reported more open and warm relationships with each other than did the professionals and their clients. The clients of the volunteers also reported receiving more real assistance and help from probation than did the clients of the professionals (Table 3). Surprisingly, although the validity of the scale was suspect, the volunteer and professional samples did not differ on a measure of perceived direction by the officer (the officer's use of authority).

Comment The findings with participant reports replicate and extend previous studies in the area. When participant reports are employed as consumer satisfaction indices, it appears that the volunteer program had the advantage over the professional program. Consumer satisfaction indices, however, do not necessarily relate to more objective measures of impact as additional findings confirmed.

Finding 4

Supervision sessions between officers and their clients were audio-taped on two separate occasions. During these sessions, the professionals made more and higher level references to the probation order (i.e. use of authority) than did the volunteers; were more prosocial in their verbal approval of the probationers' prosocial expressions and disapproval of the probationers' criminal expressions (differential reinforcement); and engaged in less problem-solving with a recreational focus. On relationship indices, the professionals tended to self-disclose less, and emitted fewer friendly statements. The sessions involving volunteer officers were significantly longer than those involving professional officers and, when controls for length of interview were introduced, the above-noted effects on the authority, anticriminal, recreational problem-solving and self-disclosure indices remained. With controls for length of interview introduced, it also became clear that the professionals were tending to engage in more and higher level problem-solving with a community focus than were the volunteers. The professionals were also asking for and offering concrete factual information more often than were the volunteers. There were no differences between the volunteer and professional samples on problem-solving with a personal-emotional focus or on an index of use of community resources. All of these findings are summarized in Table 4 and, as noted in the introduction, the operational definitions for the behavioral indices are provided in Andrews, Kiessling et al. (1979).

TABLE 4

Professional and Volunteer Officer Behavior During Audio-Taped Sessions

| | Professionals (n = 24) | | Volunteers (n = 24) | | |
	Mean	SD	Mean	SD	F
Authority	.75	.45	.21	.20	29.13**
Anticriminal					
Reinforcement	.97	.12	.79	.34	4.19*
Problem Solving					
Community	3.05	1.40	2.48	.79	3.07
Recreational	.25	.38	.54	.46	5.62*
Personal/Emotional	.42	.51	.21	.48	2.14
Use of Community Resources	.26	.42	.14	.26	1.39
Relationship					
Active Listening	.30	.25	.30	.24	< 1.0
Self Disclosure	.25	.24	.40	.31	3.38
Friendly Expressions†	3.58	2.64	5.67	4.17	4.28*
Information	.84	.23	.71	.20	4.19*
Duration of Interviews (# of 2 minute segments)	17.08	10.08	25.33	7.83	10.02**

†Uncorrected for duration of interviews.
*$p < .05$; **$p < .01$

Comment   The above set of findings represents the most comprehensive and *objective* description of what goes on in probation supervision ever completed. Again, as was noted with reference to the other findings on the nature and quality of supervision, the implications for impact is a separate question discussed below. It does appear that the time-limits imposed upon the high case-load professionals resulted in more efficient intervention.

Finding 5

The vast majority of the probationers, nearly 90% of the total sample, completed their sentences under supervision in the community without incarceration and 76.3% completed their probation period without a reconviction or absconding. There were no differences between the volunteer and professional supervised samples in terms of number of new offenses overall, number of new offenses excluding the technical violations of failing to keep the conditions of the probation order, severity of new offenses, or disposition of the new offenses.

Comment   The overall success rates correspond to available data on Ontario probation samples and the failure to discover any differences between the volunteer and professional samples is consistent with the published reports of other well-controlled studies in which Type of Client was not considered in relation to Type of Program or in which clients were not initially assigned to officers or programs on the basis of their apparent needs.

Finding 6

The relative effectiveness of volunteer and professional supervision depended upon the type of probationer assigned to the officers. Two sets of attributes of the probationers were important: one, their pretested risk level and two, their pretested interpersonal skills or empathy levels. Among low risk probationers, those who were older (20 years of age or older in our sample) and/or who scored above the median on Gough (1969) Socialization, the professional status of officers was unrelated to recidivism. Among the higher risk probationers, the young and the unsocialized, volunteer supervision was significantly more effective than professional supervision (31.00% recidivists *versus* 58.52%, $F(1/54) = 4.92$, $p < .03$) and, as inspection of Table 5 reveals, particularly so among those young unsocialized probationers who scored above the median on Hogan (1969) Empathy.

Comment   The findings are consistent with a number of investigations of differential treatment, particularly as those investigations are reviewed by Glaser (1974). Intensive intervention programs which place an emphasis on the quality of interpersonal relationships between worker and client are most effective with moderate-to-high risk clients who are relatively verbal and communicative. Objective criteria are suggested for assignment of clients to intensive volunteer supervision.

TABLE 5

Percent Recidivists By Professional Status of Officer and Type of Client

	Professional (n)		Volunteer (n)		P
Low Risk Clients [a]	10.48	(62)	16.58	(58)	ns
High Risk Clients [b]					
High Empathy	80.00	(10)	00.00	(11)	.01
Low Empathy	48.31	(13)	42.25	(23)	ns

[a] Probationers 20 years of age and over and/or scoring above the median on Socialization.
[b] Young Probationers scoring below the median on Socialization.
Note: The *p* values are based on an analysis of simple effects using sex as a covariate; see text.

OFFICER CHARACTERISTICS AND THE MATCHING OF OFFICER AND PROBATIONER

Finding 7

Probation officers, volunteers or professional, who were interpersonally sensitive (above average on the Empathy scale) *in addition to* being sensitive to conventional rules of conduct (above average on the Socialization Scale) were the most effective one-to-one supervisors according to the reports of the program managers, the reports of the officers themselves, the reports of the probationers, the officers' actual behavior during audio-taped sessions with probationers, the attitudinal gains exhibited by probationers, and recidivism rates.

A. The professional coordinator of the volunteer program, who screened potential volunteers, as well as the officers who offered preservice training to the volunteers gave the most positive ratings on overall suitability to those volunteers who scored relatively high on interpersonal skills; the correlations between volunteers' empathy and the ratings of the coordinator and the trainers were .37 ($p < .01$) and .33 ($p < .01$) respectively.

B. The inservice supervisors gave the high socialization volunteers relatively high ratings for their problem-solving abilities with clients (.29, $p < .05$).

C. The clients of those officers who scored high on interpersonal skills and socialization, as well as those officers themselves, reported the highest levels of satisfaction with supervision in terms of the quality of their interpersonal relationships and the amount of real help and assistance being offered and received; the correlation between officer empathy and officer ratings on the quality of the relationship established with clients was .27 ($p < .05$) and it was .29 ($p < .05$) with the probationer ratings; officer socialization scores yielded a correlation of .33 ($p < .01$) with officers ratings of help offered and .32 ($p < .01$) with probationers ratings of help received.

D. During audio-taped sections of actual supervision sessions, the high socialization officers were the most prosocial in their verbal expressions (anticriminal modeling) $r = .36, p < .05$), were the most likely to approve of their clients' prosocial expressions and to disapprove of their clients' antisocial expressions (anticriminal differential reinforcement, $r = .45, p < .01$), and directed fewer noncontingent or gratuitous friendly expressions toward their probationers ($r = -.40, p < .01$).

E. Probationers assigned to officers who presented the preferred pattern of personality traits showed the greatest gains on attitudinal indices of respect for the law, courts and police, the greatest reductions in acceptance of rationalizations for law violations and the lowest recidivism rates: the important finding with reference to recidivism was that the interpersonal skills of officers interacted with officer socialization levels — neither empathy nor socialization signalled reduced recidivism unless both were present at relatively high levels.

Comment   (a) The above set of findings confirm and extend the results of several previous investigations of roles for volunteers in prison-based group counseling (for a review see Andrews, 1979). The findings are the most consistent yet reported in the literature and resolve what were heretofore some conflicting and confusing trends in that literature. Specifically, for workers in correctional settings, interpersonal skills and a conventional orientation must be considered *in combination*. To select on the basis of a single dimension is to invite negative impact for clients.

(b) The implications for screening and selection programs are clear. By paying attention to both the interpersonal skills and the socialization level of applicants, the program manager is in a position to create a program which is not only more positively evaluated by all (the managers and trainers, the workers themselves, the probationers), but one which also has more positive impact on the more objective indices of outcome (attitude change and recidivism).

Finding 8

The importance of matching officer and client on biosocial factors such as age, sex, education, marital status, occupational status and social class origins depended upon the personality of the officer. Bio-social matching was positively associated with attitudinal gains when the officers were of the high empathy/high socialization type but unrelated or negatively related to attitude gains when the officers presented other than that preferred personality pattern (Table 6).

Comment   This finding suggests two things. One, the importance of the indigenous worker principle may have been over-stated since no effects were evident on recidivism. Two, the indigenous workers principle only applies when the indigenous workers possess the preferred personality dispositions.

TABLE 6

The Correlations Between The Bio-Social Matching of Officers and Probationers and Probationer Attitude Change By Type of Officer

	High Empathy High Sociali- zation Officers (n = 60)	Officers With Other Combinations of Empathy and Socialization (n = 106)	Z
Law, Courts, Police	.31**	− .10	2.48*
Tolerance For Law Violations	− .08	− .05	ns
Identification With Criminal Others	− .16	.21*	2.20*
Socialization	.28**	− .11	2.31*

*p < .05; **p < .01

Note: The Matching index was the simple sum of six component scores reflecting officer-probationer similarity on age, sex, education, marital status, occupational status, and socio-economic status based on father's occupation. The matching index was correlated with change (post — minus — prescores) scores on the attitude and personality battery with probationer sex, prescores, change on "faking good" and professional status of officer partialled out.

MEASURES OF SUPERVISION PRACTICE IN RELATION TO IMPACT

Finding 9

A number of the measures of the quality of supervision were of the type that are routinely used by managers and officers in their day-to-day assessments of how supervision is proceeding. Ratings of volunteers by program managers (the screening officer, the pre-service trainers and the in-service supervisors of volunteers) were employed as were statements by officers on their preferred styles of supervision, and of course, frequency of supervision contacts. None of these measures related in any consistent or direct way to recidivism and, in fact, one measure, positive reports by clients on amount of real help being received, was mildly associated with an increased chance of recidivism (.26, p < .02).

Comment   While we would not want to rule out the possibility that reliable and valid indicators of the types noted above can be developed, the results suggest the extreme caution that must be exercised when such indices are employed in evaluating the performance of individual workers or clients or of a whole program.

Finding 10

The objective ratings of the officers' behavior during audio-taped sessions with probationers were predictive of recidivism (Table 7). Officer behaviors which were associated with a reduced chance of recidivism include discussions of the probation order (authority), problem solving with a concrete community focus, differential reinforcement of the probationer's prosocial and antisocial expressions and the explicit verbal expression of prosocial sentiments. Officer behaviors which were associated with an increased chance of recidivism were the paraphrasing of the substance of the client's statements and reflection of the client's feelings, i.e. the active listening strategy of the non-directive, client-centered schools of counseling. Problem-solving with either a recreational or personal-emotional focus was unrelated to recidivism. Similarly, referral to community resources and self-disclosure or friendly expressions by the officers were unrelated to recidivism.

Comment   Some care was taken in the full research report to place the appropriate methodological limitations upon the above findings. In spite of the fact that the basic relationship remained when various controls were introduced for officer and client characteristics, the findings in section ten were based upon correlational rather than experimental data. However, the results are generally consistent with the theoretical rationale underlying the project and with experimental investigations of the various approaches in isolation (Andrews, 1979). The above description of how the audio-tape measures related to outcome is the most comprehensive assessment of objective measures of ongoing correctional practice in relation to impact ever completed.

Finding 11

Based on the audio-taped measures of supervision practices, officer efforts on the authority, anticriminal reinforcement and concrete-based problem solving dimensions were associated with reduced levels of recidivism regardless of the officer's practices on the relationship dimension.

Comment   This finding suggests that the effective directive components of supervision may be practiced without the officer being too concerned about relationship factors such as engaging in active listening as it is typically operationalized by the non-directive school. However, it should be underscored that the anticriminal differential reinforcement measure employed in the study was itself a special type of relationship measure — a measure of how the officer used his/her relationship with the client in a contingent as opposed to noncontingent manner. That is, high level functioning on the anticriminal differential reinforcement dimension represented expressions of positive concern and attention by the officer whenever the probationer expressed prosocial sentiments. It also reflected explicit

TABLE 7

The Correlations Between Officer Behavior During Audio-Taped Sessions and Recidivism, Overall and By Type of Client

	Overall (n = 48)	Low Empathy Probationers (n = 28)	High Empathy Probationers (n = 20)	Z
Authority	− .40**	− .44**	− .37	ns
Anticriminal				
Modeling	− .42**			ns
Differential Reinforcement	− .35**	− .24	− .59**	ns
Problem Solving				
Community	− .32**	− .46**	− .23	ns
Recreational	.08	.23	− .17	ns
Personal/Emotional	.02	.14	− .23	ns
Use of Community Resources	− .15	− .14	.22	ns
Relationship				
Active Listening	.26*	.66**	.46*	3.95**
Self-Disclosure	.12	.29	.08	ns
Friendly	− .15	.17	− .60**	2.65**
Information (Ask for/Officer)	− .21	− .08	.43	ns
Multiple R (F)	.60(6.31**)	.70(7.59**)	.78(7.07**)	

*p .05; **p .01
Note: Because of missing values, Modeling was not allowed to enter the MR.

expressions of disapproval when the probationer expressed antisocial sentiments.

Finding 12

Based on the audio-taped measures of supervision practices, the relationship strategy of engaging in active listening, i.e. paraphrasing the client's statements and reflection of the client's feelings, was not always associated with increased recidivism but only when the officer was not during the same interview also engaging in directive supervision, specifically authority practices ($r = .45$, $p < .01$ for low authority conditions; $r = - .17$, *ns*, for high authority conditions, $z = 2.27$, $p < .01$).

Comment   Consistent with a number of findings outlined in the CaVIC reviews of the literature, it appears that the client-centered practices are most destructive when the officer does not take explicit steps to make his/her own position on the rules and conventions clear to the client. In supplementary analyses of the Ottawa data, the strong suggestion was that high levels of active listening and a low level emphasis on authority practices were particularly negative in their impact when offered during interviews of short duration.

DIFFERENTIAL TREATMENT: THE RELATIVE EFFECTIVENESS OF DIFFERENT SUPERVISION PRACTICES WITH DIFFERENT TYPES OF CLIENTS

Finding 13

Based on the audio-tape measures of officer supervision practices and the pretest scores of probationers on the Empathy scale, officer efforts at active listening and friendly expressions were associated with increased recidivism among the less interpersonally skilled probationers but with decreased recidivism with the more interpersonally skilled probationers (Table 7). The differential effectiveness of the relationship practices was particularly evident when the probationers also scored relatively low on the Gough Socialization measure ($r = .71$, $p < .01$, for low empathy probationers and $r = - .83$, $p < .05$ for high empathy probationers).

Comment   These findings recall the differential effectiveness of volunteer and professional supervisors when assigned probationers who varied on interpersonal skills and socialization (finding 6 above). The findings are also the cleanest and strongest yet in a series of investigations from other settings which suggest the same conclusion: intensive, relationship-oriented supervision or counseling is inappropriate for correctional clients who are not themselves relatively interpersonally sensitive and communicative.

Finding 14

Based on the audio-taped measures of supervision practice, there was no strong or consistent evidence that use of authority, anticriminal modeling and reinforcement, or problem-solving with a community focus were associated with increased recidivism with any type of probationer and in fact they were reliably associated with decreased recidivism for most sub-types of probationers.

Comment   The authority, anticriminal and community-oriented problem-solving approaches appear to be the most basic elements of effective supervisory practice. One or more of them will apply to most cases without fear of producing negative impact and their use, we expect, will neutralize any tendency for relationship practices to induce negative impact for some types of clients.

Finding 15

With one exception, the above series of findings regarding the degree of association between supervision practice and recidivism were found within both the volunteer and professional samples. The one exception was that the anticriminal modeling and reinforcement indices were associated with reduced recidivism only among those probationers supervised by volunteers.

Comment   Two points are evident. One, the process which governs behavioral influence is the same regardless of whether we are talking about treatment by volunteers or professionals. Secondly, influence by modeling and reinforcement would presumably require considerable exposure to the officer and, of course, this is exactly what intensive supervision by volunteers provides.

THE SELECTION OF APPROPRIATE INTERMEDIATE TARGETS

Finding 16

While probationer recidivism was positively associated with *prescores* on attitude and personality scales measuring factors such as low self-esteem, anxiety, neuroticism and awareness of limited opportunity, *changes* on such measures were not associated reliably with variations in recidivism. That is, probationers who were the most alienated and who reported the highest levels of subjective discomfort and the least satisfaction with themselves, were among the more likely to recidivate. However, increases or decreases in sense of personal and social adequacy during the supervision period were not related to recidivism.

Comment   There is an important distinction in the selection of appropriate intermediate targets between individual differences measures with *predictive validity* and measures with *dynamic validity*. The identification of attributes of the individual and/or the individual's situation which forecast future criminal activity may be useful in establishing the *a priori* probability of a program influencing such individuals but such attributes do not automatically translate into the most appropriate intermediate targets for change. More appropriate guides for the selection of intermediate targets are measures which have documented dynamic validity i.e. measures of attributes or situations which, if changed, are associated with increases or decreases in the probability of recidivism. Neither CaVIC, nor to our knowledge other empirical studies (Andrews, 1979), have produced evidence that factors such as self-esteem or subjective distress are, by themselves, the most appropriate intermediate targets when a program wishes to influence recidivism. This is certainly not to argue that the correctional workers be insensitive to the distress of their clients but to suggest that such sensitivity should not be thought to necessarily influence recidivism.

Finding 17

Three sets of attitude and personality measures did show dynamic validity in that changes in the measures were associated with reduced recidivism. First, increases on an attitudinal measure of respect for the criminal justice system were associated with reduced recidivism. This measure of attitudes toward the law, courts and police was the closest we had to a measure of the first intermediate targets suggested in the review of the conceptual roots of the project i.e. of increasing the effective control properties of the formal legal system. Secondly, decreases on a measure of tolerance for law violations and on a measure of identification with offenders were associated with reduced recidivism. This finding relates to the second intermediate objective referred to earlier i.e. reducing endorsement of criminal sentiments and increasing the endorsement of more conventional sentiments. Thirdly, increased socialization scores were associated with reduced recidivism. If socialization is accepted as a measure of the nature of one's ties to conventional settings and others, then the dynamic significance of the third set of suggested intermediate targets was supported.

Comment   (a) With reference to findings 16 and 17, the suggestion is that correctional researchers and programmers must forge a strong alliance with theorists in criminology if the causal factors in criminality are to be understood. Theorists seek to identify and cast in general terms the necessary and sufficient conditions for criminal conduct. Researchers and practitioners seek to document and influence the factors associated with variations in criminal behavior. As argued elsewhere (Andrews, 1979b) and as outlined in Figure 1, systematic program evaluations provide a particularly valuable base for the alliance since there is the opportunity to examine variations in how theoretically important factors may be produced and how such variations relate to criminal conduct.

(b) The search for factors of dynamic significance in criminal conduct should be expanded to include approaches which are less dependent upon self-report than were the CaVIC attitude and personality measures. For example, direct observation of settings and behavioral ratings are obvious choices for future efforts. Equally important is the notion that measures, or changes on measures, of individuals and their situations may be differentially predictive depending upon other characteristics of the individuals or their situations. For example, Andrews, Kiessling et al. (1979: Appendix D) have shown that the endorsement of criminal sentiments was most predictive of recidivism among those probationers who were already relatively free of conventional controls.

CONCLUSIONS AND FUTURE EFFORTS

The findings reviewed deserve and require replication and extension. They were judged sufficiently strong to warrant a new, full scale investigation within a project in which the intensive nature of supervision, the personality characteristics of workers and the training to which workers are exposed are each being brought under experimental control (Andrews & Kiessling, 1978). In this way, currently we are examining the extent to which training may influence supervision practice and how such controlled variations in correctional practice may influence intermediate and ultimate targets. Training may also serve to improve the success rates of volunteers working with those probationers who appeared insensitive to intensive relationship oriented supervision. Training may also enhance the performance of volunteers who enter the program with poorer than average interpersonal skills and/or lower than average socialization scores. With random assignment of probationers to intensive versus nonintensive supervision we also hope to generate additional objective criteria by which to assign clients to the most appropriate program.

As the length of the list of recommendations included in the full research report indicates we are not hesitant to suggest that CaVIC, in conjunction with the findings of other studies (Andrews, 1979a), has direct and immediate implications for service. Specifically, as long as the community supervision of adjudicated offenders remains a responsibility of probation and parole agencies, there are means of reducing the chances of additional criminal activity. Basically, the officer exposes and makes attractive concrete alternatives to crime. This will not be accomplished by simply creating an open, warm, empathic relationship with the probationer, nor by hoping that the client may self-discover the alternatives; but rather, by vividly demonstrating conventional alternatives through words and action, by encouraging the exploration of alternatives through reinforcement of such explorations, and by providing concrete guidance and advice as to how to determine which alternatives are most feasible and attractive. The results suggest that the authority position of the officer may itself have positive impact when the use of authority involves specific attention to the formal rules and sanctions as opposed to interpersonal domination.

An image of the effective correctional counselor and the practices he engages in, has emerged from CaVIC and other systematic empirical efforts. That person is relatively sensitive to rules and conventions yet warm, tolerant, flexible and sensitive in interpersonal style. When such a person makes use of the authority inherent in his position, demonstrates in vivid ways his own prosocial attitudes, values, beliefs, and enthusiastically engages the client in the process of increasing rewards for noncriminal activity, then a reduction in the probability of recidivism may be expected.

In conclusion, we expect that there is the opportunity for a renewed intellectual and practical enthusiasm in both criminology and corrections if the disciplinary and political rhetoric of the last decade is allowed to dissipate and the theoretical and practical significance of ongoing and projected correctional efforts are examined systematically through controlled program evaluations. Particularly interesting will be attempts to move beyond the current rhetoric of a political economy of crime and to begin to examine how broad political economic factors shape and possibly interact with the elements of the conceptual system employed in this paper.

REFERENCES

Andrews, D.A., *The Dimensions of Correctional Counseling and of Supervisory Process in Probation and Parole* (Toronto: Ontario Ministry of Correctional Services, 1979(a)).

Andrews, D.A., "Some experimental investigations of the principles of differential association through deliberate manipulation of the structure of service systems." A manuscript submitted for publication 1979(b).

Andrews, D.A. & Kiessling, J.J., *An Introduction to Reports in the CaVIC Series* (Toronto: Ontario Ministry of Correctional Services, 1979).

Andrews, D.A. & Kiessling, J.J., "The selection and training of citizen volunteers for intensive probation supervision." An ongoing project, 1978.

Andrews, D.A., Kiessling, J.J., Russell, R.J. & Grant, B.A., *Volunteers and the One-to-One Supervision of Adult Probationers* (Toronto: Ontario Ministry of Correctional Services, 1979).

Glaser, D., Remedies for the key deficiency in criminal justice evaluation research," *Journal of Research in Crime and Delinquency*, 1974, *10*, 144–154.

Gough, H.H., *Manual for the CPI* (Palo Alto: Consulting Psychologist, 1969).

Hogan, R., "Development of an empathy scale," *Journal of Consulting and Clinical Psychology*, 1969, *33*, 307–16.

Kiessling, J.J., *A Cost-Effectiveness Analysis of the Ottawa Volunteer Program* (Ottawa: A CaVIC module, 1976).

Kiessling, J.J. & Andrews, D.A., "Behavioural analysis systems in corrections (BASIC)." A manuscript submitted for publication, 1979.

Wolf, M.H., "Social Validity: The case for subjective measurement or how applied behavior analysis is finding its heart," *Journal of Applied Behavior Analysis*, 1978, *11*, 203–214.

ABOUT THE EDITORS

Bob Ross is Professor of Criminology, University of Ottawa. He received the Ph.D. in Psychology from the University of Toronto. Dr. Ross has been Research Associate, Human Justice Program, University of Regina; Lecturer, Wilfred Laurier University; and Associate Professor of Psychology, University of Waterloo. His experience in criminal justice is extensive and includes more than ten years as a clinical psychologist in a wide variety of correctional institutions for juveniles and adults and twelve years as Chief Psychologist for the Ontario Government's Ministry of Correctional Services. He has also been a faculty member for the Ontario Department of Education's programs for special education teachers, and Consultant to the Department of Educational Television. He is the recipient of the Atkinson Foundation Fellowship and the Centennial Medal of Canada. Dr. Ross's publications include articles in professional journals in psychology, criminology and corrections, and chapters in several books on behavior modification, corrections, and criminology. His other books are: *Self-Multilation* (with H.B. McKay), *Illiteracy and Crime* (with F. Blum & D. Blum), and *The Correctional Officer* (Butterworths, in press).

Paul Gendreau is Regional Coordinating Psychologist of the Ontario Ministry of Correctional Services. He is also an Adjunct Professor with the Department of Psychology, University of Ottawa. He received his Ph.D. in Psychology from Queen's University at Kingston. Previously, he was Assistant Professor of Psychology, Trent University and Adjunct Professor of Psychology at Carleton University. He also worked as a consultant psychologist with the Canadian Penitentiary Service of Canada, the Ontario Ministry of Correctional Services and the Ministry of National Security and Justice of Jamaica. Dr. Gendreau has published widely in the areas of solitary confinement, psychodiagnostics, prediction of recidivism and correctional programming.